Pat Keel-Diffey was born in Edgbaston, Birmingham in 1926. In 1930 she moved to Harborne with her family, living there until she married a veterinary surgeon who, after seven years as an assistant in St Albans, opened a practice in Henley on Thames, where they lived for 30 years.

After raising a family and helping her husband in his developing veterinary practice, Pat Keel-Diffey became teacher of Senior Art at the local Secondary School.

She then became heavily involved in environmental work until, feeling she had fulfilled her debt to society, she returned to the Art she loved, becoming, for 20 years, a widely exhibited painter/printmaker with works in collections word-wide, until she became disabled by Post-Polio Syndrome. She lives with her husband in Devon.

SYLLABLES OF TIME

War Diaries and Letters 1939-1946

Pat Keel-Diffey

Gabriel

Published by Gabriel Books
Frogmore
Vicarage Road
Stoke Gabriel
Devon TQ9 6QP

Pat Keel-Diffey asserts her moral right under the Copyright, Designs and Patents Act 1988 to be identified as the author of this work

British Library Cataloguing-in-Publication Data
A catalogue record for this book is available from the British Library

ISBN 0-9549296-0-8

All rights reserved. No part of this publication may be reproduced, stored in a retrieval system, rebound or transmitted in any form or by any means, electronic, mechanical, photocopying, recording or otherwise, without the prior permission of the publisher

Printed in Great Britain by
Antony Rowe Ltd.
Chippenham
Wiltshire

To absent friends.

CONTENTS

Page

1	Prologue
57	1939, August to December
131	1940 Aged 13 ½
132	*Illustrations*
273	1941 Aged 14 ½
274	*Illustrations*
317	1942 Aged 15 ½
318	*Illustrations*
361	1943 Aged 16 ½
362	*Illustrations*
463	1944 Aged 17 ½
464	*Illustrations*
499	1945 Aged 18 ½
500	*Illustrations*
555	1946 Aged 19 ½
556	*Illustrations*
571	Malta Epilogue I & II & *Illustrations*

LIST OF ILLUSTRATIONS

Prologue

Page

1	Grey Cottage before the extension
2	Building the extension – with Pat
4	The back of Grey Cottage before the extension – with Pat
8	'Pierrot', Pat, Mother and the trout
10	'Gran' (Grandma Knight)
11	Mother with 'Mac'
12	Mother and Dad at the Croft, Wishaw, in 1915
13	Gran with Uncle Den at the Croft
23	Aunt Belle's house, Manor Farm, Austrey – with Pat
23	Pat with Cecil's little daughter, Jill, at Austrey
27	Grandpa Dawes
30	Grandma Dawes with her dog, 'Boots'
44	Philip, Dennis, Brian and Bill
52	Dennis, Bill, Brian and Vivian
54	'Officers of the Quintuple Alliance in solemn conclave' -- Vivian, Dennis and Bill
55	Pat and Kelvin at Sidmouth

1939 August to December

Page

57	Pat, Dennis and friends 'surfing'
58	Pat 'in wonderful pose' on classroom steps waiting for evacuation
66	Dennis in his new sergeant's uniform
67	Dennis with Dorothy and Olwen in Newquay
72	Mrs Thatcher
79	Esme and 'Ginger'
99	Sherry glass sketch
110	Alexandra hotel
112	Civilians—RAFVR Sergeants
116	Polyphoto of Dennis
119	Signed photograph of Sergeants on St Leonard's seafront
122	Diagram of jump
133	Plan of racecourse 1
135	Plan of racecourse 2

ACKNOWLEDGEMENTS

My thanks are due to many people, especially for their help with certain details in the prologue. In particular I should like to thank Maria Twist, Senior Librarian of the department of Local Studies and History, Birmingham, for her readiness to search records regarding the founding of Adie Bros., silversmiths of Birmingham, by my great grandfather. Also, in this context I should like to thank Phyllis Benedikz, Librarian and Curator at the Birmingham Assay Office for the information she provided me with.

My thanks are due also to Patrick Maclure, Secretary of the Wykehamist Society of Winchester College, for providing me with additional information regarding my mother's cousin, 'Tom' Gaunt (the Rev Howard Charles Adie Gaunt).

My thanks, also, to my cousins, Margaret Johnson, Kathleen Batterby, and Howard Dawes, and my brother's great friend and mine, Vivian Morgan, who helped to fill in odd gaps in the prologue to this book.

Last, but not least, I must thank my husband, Stuart, for his encouragement and support, and endless proof reading and constructive comments as I edited the material down to half it's original size.

The entire collection of original letters and diaries was purchased by the Imperial War Museum in 2003.

*Tomorrow, and tomorrow, and tomorrow,
Creeps in this petty pace from day to day,
To the last syllable of recorded time;*

William Shakespeare; Macbeth.

In September 1939, in the early days of the war, the seeds of intent to write this book were sown.

I was a 13 year-old evacuee when I began writing notes on torn-out diary pages and then in school notebooks, recording my life in the new environment of war.

Letters began to flow between my mother, father, brother and me like a conversation, and, later, letters from others joined in.

These diaries and letters form a continuous narrative from September 1939 to June 1946, manifesting the years of war and the difficult adjustment to peace afterwards.

This, then, is my war story.

But first I must tell you a little about the people and places you will meet in the book.

Prologue

People and Places

My father was a quiet, intelligent, sensitive man with a mischievous sense of humour. He was a man of great integrity, and he adored my mother. She was the warm, understanding, loving pivot of the family, and she adored my father, who was five years her senior. Five years younger than my brother, Dennis, I was born on May 19th 1926, a week after the end of the General Strike, during which time, feeling a sense of duty and responsibility, my father had volunteered to work as a stevedore in the Birmingham goods yards, unloading girders and other industrial building materials and returning home with his thin shoulders lacerated and bleeding from the unaccustomed harsh weight bearing.

He was, in fact, Chief Works Chemist at Albright & Wilsons chemical works at Oldbury, to which he commuted, at first by motorbike, and later by car, from our house in Harborne, which had been built for Percy Edgar, a director of the B.B.C., who had aptly named it 'Grey Cottage'. It was a grey stucco-covered house with leaded casement windows and a tiled, gabled roof.

In 1933 we added a fourth bedroom, as the third one was occupied by the maid, and Dennis and I were getting too old to share, and under the new bedroom which became Dennis's was added a large garage in place of the earlier wooden one.

The wide, shallow front garden was fronted by a scalloped privet hedge, cut to the shape of the oak picket fence enclosing a smallish lawn with two dark red flowering plum trees with leaves so dark that they appeared almost black. A crazy paving path led from the slightly sloping crazy paved drive and the front gate up to the front door, and along the front of the house to the back gate where a narrow covered yard joined front to back gardens.

The wide, studded front door was set back in a porch, up a deep brick step.

Inside was a large, square, quarry-tiled hall which contained a 'monk's bench', where we kept car rugs etc., and an enormous antique oak chest which contained spare blankets, a Samurai sword, a Gurkha kukri, my father's medals and .45 revolver from the 1914 War, and various articles of silver not in frequent use.

An archway led into an inner hall where the stairs angled round an open stair well, completing a 360° turn to reach the open landing. For many years we enjoyed the inherited wallpaper, a riot of parrots and foliage on a midnight blue background.

In the wall at the bottom of the stairs, beside a row of hooks where hung hats, coats and macs, a door led into the kitchen where I would help Mother make cakes and pastry, and, when I was old enough, we would take it in turns to make the large fruit cake and small iced cakes that we made every week.

Here there was a black-leaded range in which, in winter, burned a glowing coke fire, and in the oven of which at times would simmer such winter warmers as Irish stew or Lancashire hot-pot in a fat-bellied brown crock casserole. Heavy iron saucepans of vegetables sometimes simmered on the hot-plate.

Besides the hall door, three further doors led off the kitchen; one to the larder, under the stairs, at the front of the house, one to the pantry, and beside that one into the scullery. This was tiny, and contained a large stone sink with a long very narrow draining board, and, behind the door into the kitchen was squeezed a New World Regulo gas cooker. I am not sure, but I think this was a concession to modernity added by my parents.

(In the evening the kitchen became the maid's sitting room and the last one we had, probably about 1936/37 was an Irish maid called Margaret. My brother's friend Billy always maintained that she was a member of the I.R.A. as it seemed that every time she had a day off a bomb exploded in a letter box. However, we all thought she was mad as a hatter. From time to time she would do the strangest things.

On one occasion after dinner Mother told her to save what was left of the joint, and also the custard, and put them in the larder. (We had no fridge in those days.) Later, when I went into the larder to fetch the milk for tea, I found that she had, indeed, put them both in the larder, but she had poured the custard over the joint!

One evening Mother went into the kitchen and found Margaret had pulled a chair over in front of the range, and was kneeling on the chair saying her rosary. She stopped when Mother went in, so Mother asked her why she had moved the chair and was kneeling there. Margaret replied that, by kneeling on the chair she was higher up and therefore nearer to God, and the heat from the range would send the prayers upwards!)

Two other doors led off the hall, one into the dining room, where a deep bay, with leaded windows and door, opened onto the garden. The other door led to the lounge, also with a bay with a door into the garden.

We eventually opened a wide archway between the two rooms, turning them into one large sunny room. On cold winter evenings thick velvet curtains were drawn across the archway and a fire burned in the open hearth of the lounge, but in the warm days of summer, the garden doors would be open to a crazy-paved area where, at one side, stood a large black and white painted summerhouse.

Beyond the lawn small rock steps led up through a rock garden to a small raised area of garden backed by a hawthorn hedge, and it was here that we were to build our air-raid shelter as war loomed.

The builders of Grey Cottage and Garth, where our elderly, very pleasant neighbours, Mr and Mrs Ensell lived, had divided the interjacent plot between the two properties. (They were number 1 and we were number 5; there was therefore no number 3 Crosbie road, although, when in his 'teens, Dennis adopted '3 & 5 Crosbie Road' as the address of the Quintuple Alliance - a group he formed with four close friends.)

The gardens were divided by a long, tall privet hedge which, when I was old enough, I would volunteer to cut from time to time for sixpence or a shilling; but while I was still a little girl I would ride my fairy cycle round the crazy paving paths that traversed the ornamental rose-borders that had been laid out on this area.

It was Dennis, of course, who had taught me to ride a bike, as he, a little later, was to teach me to swim, and then to dive and, later still, to skate. He was a wonderful teacher. He made everything seem so easy to do; even my maths homework. He also showed me how to walk backwards on the garden roller - and, after crashing into a standard rose in the lawn, how to repair it with sticking-plaster!

One Christmas I was given a doll's house; it was a white, flat-roofed modernistic house with a curved end wall and a hand-operated lift up to the roof. Dennis rigged it up with little electric lights in every room, and made me furniture and tiny books for the bookcase, some of which could be opened to read such older brotherly maxims as, "Be good, sweet maid, and let who will be clever".

When I was ready to graduate from my fairy cycle Den bought himself a racing bike and sold me his old bike for sixpence. I consequently learned to get on and off bikes by cocking my leg up over the saddle, because of the cross-bar. It proved a hard habit to break when, much later, I had a girl's bike with no cross-bar.

One of my great friends in those early days was Valerie, the younger sister of one of Den's friends. We would cycle round Harborne together, sometimes going down War Lane to a place we had named 'The Ripples'. This was an old field that ancient cultivation had transformed into an undulating expanse covered in short grass. We would tear around on our bikes, wheels leaping off the ground as we sped from crest to crest. Once, the rusting front mudguard detached itself and caught in the spokes of my front wheel, and I went straight over the handlebars, but it was all great fun.

There was a hazard that we sometimes had to negotiate as we made our way down the lane and over the culvert and into the field. This was an old 'witch' who lived rough, sometimes sitting under the hedge at the side of the lane, shouting and screaming and throwing old clothes and rags at us as we ran the gauntlet of her abuse.

I was also friendly with a group of, mostly, small boys, with whom I was often to be found climbing the May trees that grew in two decorative semi-circular plantations either side of Carless Avenue, nearby. I loved climbing trees.

I had been christened 'Helen Patricia', and as a baby had been called Helen. However, as I started into my tomboy lifestyle, I decided that 'Pat' was more suitable, and so for the rest of my life I was Pat - apart from the odd occasion when (besides other epithets!) boyfriends would decide to address me as Helen.

In those days Harborne was still a village, fairly large with, besides butchers, grocers, fishmongers, chemists, cake-shops etc., a police station, cinema (The Royalty) and swimming baths. There was also the Harborne Picture House, commonly known as the 'flea pit'; a small, moth-eaten little cinema that, somehow, not only managed to keep running, but to often obtain the best films. Pattisons, the cake shop, was most conveniently opposite the swimming baths, so that when I came out, somewhat cold and hungry, I could cross the road and buy myself not one, but two Nottingham buns, delicious, light, citrusy buns with a thick but delicate lemon icing. Ooh! What bliss!

Next door to the cake shop was Baughans, who sold sweets, cigarettes and tobacco and also possessed an extremely good circulating library. Further up the road, towards the village centre, past the Duke of York, and by the bus stop into town, was Sadlers, a small paper shop where Dad bought his papers, Den and I our comics and, on early November's dark afternoons, we would sort through exciting boxes containing rockets and Roman Candles, Vesuvius, Golden Rain, matches that burned red or green and, of course, sparklers.

Actually, I started life as a very delicate child and was unable to take any form of fats, and even collapsed into a coma to later awaken from delirious dreams in the Birmingham Children's Hospital. I continued to be ill with varying degrees of severity, and it became necessary for me to return to the hospital again when I was about three years old.

When I was five or six, I was then diagnosed as having rickets, due to my constrained diet.

In spite of the care taken, I was constantly ill and I remember many, many summer evenings lying in bed, feeling quite ill, listening to the whirr of a neighbour's lawn mower, the click of bat on ball and voices from neighbouring gardens, but especially the chattering of sparrows on the guttering outside my window. In the winter there would be the hiss of the gas fire, the early dusk, and the smell of baking from downstairs.

I was a great hand at amusing myself. I would draw and paint and read and, later, I grew expert at making beautiful and extremely life-like crepe paper roses.

Sometimes, of course, I would get bored, and Mother would come and discuss things I might like to do. She would suggest a puzzle, a magic painting book, a book of paper dolls to dress, and would 'magic' my choice (bought specially for such occasions, unknown to me) from a high cupboard above my built-in wardrobe.

Den would come home from school and have me in fits of laughter as he impersonated a crabby old doctor with a battered attaché case, intoning, "I am the doctor, don't you know my voice?" Or sometimes he would be a demented gorilla, scratching at its armpits. And Dad would bring me home armfuls of American 'Funnies', with the request, "Can I borrow them after you've finished?"

And, during this time, Mother was suffering from medical problems even more serious than mine.

Following an appendectomy in a private nursing home she was allowed to fall out of her bed while still under the effects of the anaesthetic. She suffered a heart attack, and was in heart failure and delirious when my grandmother insisted on bringing in a first rate heart specialist she knew. Her life was saved, but she was very ill for a while.

Then, in her early thirties, she was diagnosed as having cancer of the uterus and ovaries. I can't have been very old, but I clearly remember trying to comfort my silently weeping father as we waited outside her ward shortly after her operation. However, she did recover after what must have been pretty primitive radiotherapy. She described afterwards how she was put into a "sort of cage" for the treatment.

One summer, when I was 5 or 6 and Dennis 10 or 11, we stayed at a guest house in Tal-y-bont in North Wales. He and I went exploring behind the house, along beside a swirling stream overhung by wild fuchsia wet with spray. We ran the gauntlet of an exceedingly bad tempered old man who lived in a hovel beside the stream and went on into the woods. At this point Den decided that we were lost - whether in fact, or to tease me, I don't know - at which point I became frightened of everything I could or could not see, or which moved or did not move.

So he told me to link arms with him, back to back, and while I walked forward he walked backwards, to see that nothing nasty jumped out behind us, while we both called out "Mu-u-um, Da-a-ad" at the tops of our voices.

We probably weren't lost at all, because in no time we were once again avoiding the unpleasant old man and scrambling down past the rushing water and dripping fuchsias back to the house.

Most summer Sundays we would all pile into the car and drive off into the countryside; sometimes to Henley-in-Arden, where we would join the cars parked all down either side of the main street and sit eating the incomparable ice creams that were made and sold in a shop there. On other occasions we would fetch the black rexine-covered picnic case, with its fitted black and white china, silver plated cutlery and boxes and thermoses, all strapped neatly into place with little leather straps; and we would fill the boxes with sandwiches and hard boiled eggs, tomatoes and lettuce, cakes and chocolate, and the thermoses with tea and milk, and finding room

somewhere for a bottle of Corona we would set off for the Shropshire borders; to the Valley of the Ravens, with its high moorland, its branching valleys, and its sparkling, rushing mountain streams.

On one occasion we took my Uncle Ted, when still a young batchelor, and he caught a trout for his supper by throwing a well aimed stone at it.

I have a photograph of Mother holding the trout, with me in an enormous straw hat, and my dog Pierrot looking on in admiration. I was then, I suppose, about seven years old.

Pierrot was an amazing dog. We had gone to kennels at Shirley to buy me a dog. I didn't mind what breed it was so long as I had a dog. But my father had set his heart on a smooth haired fox terrier and it transpired that the kennels did not have one for sale. Dad said we would have to go elsewhere, and I was filled with disappointment, when the kennel-owner, seeing they were about to lose a sale, announced that they had a two year old ex-show dog which they might consider selling at the right price. His whole life had been spent at stud and showing, and it must have seemed something of a remote hope for my parents.

However it was decided that my parents would have a look at him to see if his temperament would be possible for a pet. I was to wait outside for safety. The moment the enclosure gate was opened he rushed out past the three alarmed adults straight to me, and greeted me with a wagging tail and obvious friendly delight. Needless to say I was thrilled, and a deal was concluded. When I opened the car door I didn't need to encourage him in for he jumped straight in and sat happily waiting for me to join him.

He adopted me as his own from the start. He considered it his duty to guard and protect me, and I had to 'introduce' him to family and friends before he would allow them near me. Once introduced, they were then permanently accepted, although for some reason he would never accept my Uncle Ted, who had to behave impeccably, barely moving a muscle when Pierrot was around. And yet I could do anything with Pierrot. My favourite game was to dress him up in a doll's nightie and bonnet, tuck him up in my doll's bed and feed him water from a baby's bottle. He would join in the game whole-heartedly, but Mother told me that when I left the room, having told him to "stay", (which he did as long as I was there) he would lift his head off the pillow and, if he thought the coast was clear or the game over, jump out of bed trailing his long nightgown!

Sadly, only a few years later, when I was in hospital recovering from an appendectomy, he ate a marrow bone and the splinter pierced his gut and he was 'put down', though for years I believed he had been sent to a sort of dog's care home, an idea my parents fostered to help ease my heartache. And when one of the most popular patients in my ward, a desperately ill little boy of about four, suddenly was removed in the middle of the night they encouraged me in the belief that he had been taken on holiday to the seaside. Again, only later did they tell me that he had died.

They were such a gentle and loving couple, and between them they brought together the two disparate sides of the large families.

*

My father was the second of the three sons of Thomas Henry Knight, gentleman farmer of Wishaw, near Birmingham. My grandfather was a man of high principles and iron will who on one occasion, shotgun in hand, ordered a transgressing hunt off his land
.   My grandmother was, judging from early photographs, a strikingly beautiful woman, who in old age, with her snow-white hair, perfect skin and chiselled features was what I can only describe as a very handsome woman.   She was a strange mixture; didactic, loyally loving yet emotionally detached, generous, and with a great sense of fun.

Tom, the eldest son, was the only child of my grandfather and his first wife, Ada, who died of puerperal fever, leaving the tiny baby to be cared for by my grandfather's sister Helen who, for some reason, called him Tim. After a short time, my grandfather married Ada's friend Helen, my grandmother, and subsequently my father, Fred, and then his brother, Den, were born.

Den was the fun-loving clown of the family; the farming son, due to inherit Bricklyn Farm, and for this eventuality my grandparents built a large house nearby, The Croft, which they moved into, installing a farm manager at Bricklyn Farm.

They also owned two further houses nearby, Poole Hall and The Grove, a lovely old timbered house. I don't know if he had intended that the other boys should inherit these properties, but eventually they were sold, perhaps when it became clear that Tom intended becoming a solicitor, and my father an industrial chemist. One of my grandfather's brothers, Fred, had married a cousin of my maternal grandmother's, Mary (Popsy), and they had a daughter, Freda. They owned a farm not far from my grandfather, and in the holidays my mother and her sisters would go and stay with Uncle Fred and Aunt Popsy.

It was inevitable that the boys and girls would meet and visit. They would go on shooting parties together, and the boys would take the girls for drives in my grandmother's dog cart drawn by Mac, my grandmother's gentle old horse.

Unfortunately, he suffered from a flatulence problem, and to the amusement of the young people, their progress along the country lanes was noisily accompanied by Mac's musical trumpeting.

Thus it was that my mother and father met.

(By the time that I first remember Uncle Fred's farm, it was no longer a working farm, the old farmyard which was now a large garden with sweeping gravel drive and huge lawn, was separated from the surrounding fields by large trees and shrubs.

The old courtyard remained with its pump, for all the water locally was drawn up from artesian wells.

It was approached by a long gravel drive, which led up from the road through the long grass of an orchard, in springtime foaming with blossom and carpeted with great swathes of fluttering golden daffodils - I believe it probably didn't look so different from those carefree days before the 1914 War.)

But a dark shadow fell across their bright lives.

My father was about nineteen years old when, as he and his father were being driven near the farm, their car hit some obstruction and my grandfather was thrown out, his head striking a tree, and he was killed.

That was in 1912. Two years later came the War.

At the start of the 1914 war my father was at Toronto University studying for his M.A. in chemistry, having taken his B.Sc. at Birmingham University. He joined up with the Canadian Expeditionary Force (Machine Gun Corps), and thus returned to England with Canada flashes on his uniform, apparently ensuring him instant hospitality wherever he went!

Mother & Dad at the Croft in 1915

His brothers Tom and Den joined up, as did their three cousins, sons of my grandfather's brother Arthur, but the war treated the Knights terribly cruelly. Arthur's three boys were all killed.

My father was wounded in the thigh and groin by a shell exploding near him in the trenches. Tom was gassed, temporarily blinded, his lungs permanently wrecked.

Gran with Uncle Den at the Croft

And the letters from France from the young clown Den, in 1917, tell the terrible tale of what happened to him.

B' Battery France

242 (SM) Brigade
(Army) F.A.
April 21st

Dear Mother

Just a few lines to let you know I am still going strong, although we are having a hotter time than we have ever had. I have not received a parcel this week, I am looking forward to it hoping I shall find a currant loaf. For my 21st birthday will you please send me a bought birthday cake instead of buying me anything else, because nothing else would be any good to me out here, also send me a nice parcel you know, plenty of good things. You waste too much of the parcel in packing, I do not think it is

necessary for half so much. It is up to you to spread the news that I am twenty one, I shall receive all the more parcels then. Also I want you to send me the remainder of my money for my birthday. I do not think there will be over 30/-. I shall try and send some more home in about a month. I do not think I have any news for you. I have been having very little post from anyone lately but I am hoping it will all come with a rush. I expect Tom is in training by now. He went home just at the right time, we have been through something just lately.
    With love
    Yours E. Dennis Knight

April 23rd

Dear Mother
    You will be sorry to hear that I was wounded on the 21st, a shell dropped on a dug out. There were seven of us in, five were wounded and the other two were killed. They sent me to the casualty clearing station, I expect I shall be going down to the base soon and then I hope I shall not be long before I cross over. The worst of it is my legs have to be in splints and I cannot sleep at nights for them. I have had chloroform twice and gas once, I am afraid you will not be able to write to me as I do not know where I shall be two days together.
    Your loving son
    Den

25/4/17 France

Dear Mrs Knight

You have probably already received official information that your son (Gunner E. D. Knight) is wounded, and as I am sure you are anxiously waiting for further news of him I am writing to you. He is in No. 6 Casualty Clearing Station, wounded in both legs and the right arm. I deeply regret to tell you that his wounds are of a serious nature and his condition is causing a good deal of anxiety. It is my last wish to alarm you unnecessarily, but this letter will be both valueless and unfair unless I am quite frank about him and therefore I have endeavoured to be so. He asks me to send you his love and to say he hopes you will not worry about him. He is in good spirits, and though he does not suffer much pain, he finds it difficult to sleep.

I am afraid this news about him will be terribly upsetting to you, but it may be some consolation to know that he is in a comfortable bed, and that yesterday we were able to move his bed out into the sun for some hours. He is in very good hands here, and everything that can possibly be done for him is being done. You may rest assured that he will not lack for care and attention, and I trust that for your sake he may be spared.

    Yours very truly
    A. Jarvis
    Church of England Chaplain.

B.E.F.

27/4/17

Dear Mrs Knight

I am just sending you word to say that your son is improving and is getting on as well as can be expected.

He is being sent to the Base tomorrow and I have no doubt he will be able to get somebody to write for him from there to let you know how he is getting on.

    Yours very truly
    A. Jarvis
    Church of England Chaplain

No.7. Stationary Hospital
B.E.F., France

28-4-17

Dear Madam,
     Your son, Gunner E. D. Knight, 836307, 242. S. M. Brigade A.F.A. wishes me to write a few lines to tell you he had arrived at this Base and is making very good progress. He is hoping it will not now be long before the doctors will be able to send him over to England. So he hopes you will not worry. He is longing to hear from you. His address here is, No. 13 General Hospital, Boulogne S/Mer, France.
     He hopes you have good news of Fred and Tom.
     Yours sincerely
     H. Morbey   'A'.S. Reader

POST OFFICE TELEGRAPHS

Via Woolwich
OHMS
Royal Dockyard
Read from Sutton Coldfield
2 May, 17
Knight Custom Stn. Hotel Ldn

Regret to inform you that 836307 Gunner E. D. Knight 252 Bde R.F.A. is dangerously ill at 13 General Hospital Boulogne France suffering from gun shot wounds leg knee shoulder permission to visit cannot be granted Artillery Records

May 8, 1917

Dear Mrs Knight
    Before this reaches you in answer to your note of the 4th you will have had the sad news of your son's death.
    As I write to you, his wounds were very severe and the shock was too great in spite of his youth and natural strength.
    With renewed sympathy
    I am
    Yours truly
    A. F. Gerald Lister

13 General Hosp:
B.E.F.
France

May 19 - 17

Dear Mrs Knight
    I quite well understand how distressed you are at your son's death. Yes, he received a letter from you. His belongings, that is, which he brought in with him, for much is lost on the field, will be forwarded to you in due time. His leg was so badly injured that it was found necessary to take it off in order to attempt to save his life but unfortunately the poison had spread too far and he died, from the effects of general infection.
I fear that this is all very meagre information but unfortunately it is all I can write in answer to your letter.

    Believe me
    Yours truly
    A. F. Gerald Lister

13 General Hospital
B.S.E.
France

Then, like a terrible tease, a letter arrived from the Record Office, its message so cruelly redundant –

H&RFA Record Office *Woolwich*
Station *May 24, 1917*

Army Form B. 104-80

No 115/3667h
(If replying, please quote above No.)

Sir/*Madam*
    I regret to have to inform that a report has this day been received from the War Office to the effect that (No.) *836307* (Rank) *Gunner* (Name) *E. D. Knight* (Regiment) *Royal Field Artillery* is at *13 General Hospital Boulogne, France*, suffering from *Gun Shot Wounds in Legs (severe)*.
    I am at the same time to express the sympathy and regret of the Army council.
    Any further information received in this office as to his condition or progress will be notified to you at once.
    Sir/*Madam*
    Your obedient Servant,
    i/e R. H. & R.F.A. RECORDS
    A. Chase for Colonel

Officer in charge of Records.

*

    The two surviving boys were shipped back to 'Blighty', where Tom was nursed back to a semblance of health by Edith, a V.A.D., whose nickname was 'Sunny' due to her lovely smile and sunny disposition, and whom he subsequently married.

My father was also nursed back to health in the Canadian hospital, although some of the shrapnel remained in his groin for the rest of his life. He married my mother, which he had declared as his intention when he was nineteen and she was fourteen.

At first my grandmother, 'Gran', sold The Croft and moved into a cottage with a companion but she later, inexpediently, moved in with Tom and Edith and their baby Kathleen, where she remained for the rest of Uncle Tom's life. This was a foolish and potentially disastrous move, for the powerfully didactic side of her personality was at times very hard to take.

Once, I can't remember when, she tearfully accused me of not loving her. I must have been fairly young, perhaps ten or eleven. I replied, "I love you, but I don't like you!" And I did love her. She was kind, generous, warm-hearted, fair-minded and funny. She just couldn't avoid interfering in domestic matters. She should, of course, have remained running her own home.

Uncle Tom, Aunty Edith, Kathleen and Gran lived at Sutton Coldfield. It was a somewhat strangely shaped house, very long from front to back. Behind the hall and sitting-room was the dining room, which led into the garden, and beside the dining room was a long, panelled corridor, smelling faintly and intriguingly of a mixture of oranges and lemons and polish, which led to the kitchen area at the back.

At the end of the long garden, which housed a creosote scented shed and a swing among the lawns and borders, was a gate into the tennis courts, and a path behind, through an area used by the park gardeners. There were great, rotting heaps of sweet-smelling grass mowings and creosoted sheds containing enormous mowers, paint-machines for marking the tennis courts and, outside, a huge grass-roller.

The smell of creosote and rotting grass almost become tangible as I recall that exciting area between the high wire mesh surrounding the tennis courts and the hedges and fences of the gardens that backed on to the park.

However, eventually we would return for tea in the sitting room and poor Uncle Tom inevitably suffering one of his terrible fits of coughing. I would fear for his life as I watched him wracked with seemingly endless coughing which rendered him unable to draw breath, his face turning dark with strain and lack of air. He must have suffered terribly, but I never heard him complain.

Wishaw lay just a few miles further out from Sutton Coldfield, and Grandpa Knight's few surviving sisters and brother still lived there. He had, in fact, been one of ten children. Aunt Sarah had been killed in a train crash in which her sister, Aunt Helen, was also involved. Besides Aunt Helen, his only brother and sister that I remember are Uncle Fred and Aunt Millie.

Uncle Fred was somewhat deaf, and spoke in a rather high-pitched, wavering voice. He wore heavy tweed suits and boots, even though his farming days were long over when I knew him.

His wife, Grandma's cousin Aunt Popsy, was a warm, plump and welcoming person, but she had an alarming mole on her chin that sprouted several stiff hairs which I struggled to avoid when being folded to her ample bosom in enthusiastic greeting.

Their daughter, Freda, who worked for the local council, by this time had grown into a plump, rather plain, intelligent woman with pebble glasses, but warm and friendly like her mother.

Aunt Helen was so deaf that she had to resort to an ear-trumpet, which I found somewhat daunting, as however loudly or clearly I tried to speak, she had the utmost difficulty understanding me; Mother, on the other hand, she understood perfectly.

She was very softly-spoken - perhaps because of her deafness - with a little bun on top of her head, a fine, rosy, transparent skin, completely innocent of make-up, and dressed in ankle-length, long-sleeved dresses with little ruffles at neck and cuff; as did her sister Millicent (Millie).

Aunt Helen lived alone in a small brick house, adjacent to her brother Fred's much larger farmhouse. She spent most of her time in the kitchen, with its shining, black-leaded range, gleaming brass and comfortable Victorian chaise-longue and chairs. Through windows overflowing with an abundance of pots of geraniums, one looked out onto her garden, trim with neat gravel paths and tiny box hedges enclosing flower borders.

There was also a vast yew hedge enclosing 'The Pit'. It seemed that most of the Knights' properties possessed a Pit. This was a large, dark, deep pond, whose origin and purpose I didn't understand. However, my grandmother used to relate the tale of how, at their farm, Bricklyn Farm, when my father was about ten years old, one of the servants had come rushing in, very distressed, saying "Master Fred has fallen in the Pit, and we can't find him anywhere!" Since my father was unable to swim, this was terrible news to my grandmother, but after the initial horror it emerged that my father had, indeed, fallen in, but had scrambled out and run off to hide, fearful of the wrath to come!

From Aunt Helen's other kitchen window, through the geraniums and snowy lace curtains, one could see what must have originally been a farm yard, brick paved, with yellow musk springing up through every crevice, and perfuming the yard with it's heavy scent.

Across the yard was a barn, cavernous and dark, illuminated by the occasional shaft of sunlight. One end was filled with bales of sweet-smelling hay stacked high up into the roof and where, having exhausted the possibilities of the meandering gravel paths with their miniature hedges, Den and I would go to leap from ever increasing heights. The resulting red itchy rashes were as nothing compared with the sheer delight of the flying acrobatics among the dappled, springing bales.

And, for a change, sometimes we would clamber down to where the shafts of dust-filled sunlight picked out a strange looking sort of outsize mincer, which we would feed with the odd roots left lying on the earth floor and, turning the handle, produce an interesting chopped-up mush which fell onto the dusty floor.

Around the back of Aunt Helen's house, against the back wall, well hidden among flowers and foliage, was a small but roomy, outbuilding. This was her earth-closet, and like everything to do with Aunt Helen, it was spotless and sweet-smelling. Neat bundles of torn-up newspapers were threaded through with string and hung from a hook. The closet itself was a large, rectangular wooden box with not one, but two holes in the top, so, if one so desired, one could have company! After use, a lever was pulled, and earth would fall down into the cavity.

Aunt Helen's house held one other secret treasure, so rare that only once was I allowed to touch it, but for ever after the knowledge of its magic became a tantalizing, but unattainable dream

And what was this wondrous thing? A harmonium!

It dwelled in her parlour, a room but rarely used, spotless, spick and span and ever-ready for a visit from the vicar, or the doctor, but never, ever, family!

On this solitary, enchanted occasion somehow Mother managed to persuade Aunt Helen of my burning fascination with this exotic instrument, and I was allowed into the parlour to sit at the keyboard.

I was totally unmusical and could not play a note, but I worked the pedals with my feet and moved my fingers over the keys, and there issued forth this wonderful cacophony of sound. Oh, what joy! What transports of delight!

All too soon my 'musical interlude' was declared over, and never again was I invited to 'play', nor indeed, was I ever again invited into the parlour.

Aunt Helen's sister, Aunt Millie, also lived in Wishaw and as I have said, dressed very much like her in long, concealing dresses. But Aunt Millie completed the effect of a vision from the past by also wearing a little mob-cap. She, too, was very soft-spoken, but she was not a spinster. She had, indeed, been married twice. Her second husband, Uncle Frank Foden, was twelve years her junior, and had fallen in love with her when still a very young man, and her first husband still living. When he died, Uncle Frank leaped into the void and married her.

Now, if this makes him sound dynamic and masculine, I must add that Aunt Millie had a nickname for him - Tiger!!

However, a less dynamic-seeming personality would be hard to imagine. He was extremely quiet and gentle in his manner, and spoke softly like his wife. He dressed in a dark suit with, I seem to remember, a shirt with a stiff collar, even on hot summer days, when we would be offered tea in the garden beneath a weeping ash tree. A table would be brought out and laid with a hand-crocheted lace table-cloth, and cucumber sandwiches and seed-cake would be handed round by this softly spoken, gentle couple.

He was very proud of his garden and our visits would always include an escorted tour round lawns and herbaceous borders, serried rows of vegetables, and productive cold frames. In fact I have absolutely no recollection of the house at all, other than a faint impression of a porch leading from hot, bright sunshine into a cool, dark hall.

My father's mother Helen (Gran) had two sisters, and I later learned that there were also three brothers who had gone to Canada; but they were never discussed and I never knew their names or why they went to Canada. It all seemed very mysterious.

The sisters, Isobel and Charlotte, 'Belle' and 'Lot' were as different as it would be possible to imagine. Aunt Lot had married a clergyman and lived at Tankerton on the coast of Kent. She was quite a severe lady, dressed in plain black, whom we rarely visited.

Aunt Belle, like Gran, had married a farmer, but their farm was at Austrey, near Tamworth. In those days it was utterly rural. Manor Farm was a beautiful black and white timbered house with an enormous ingle-nook in the kitchen in which one could sit and look upwards to the sky. Upstairs the huge, ancient floorboards sloped at an alarming angle towards the windows at the front of the house so that, when one opened a bedroom door, one felt in imminent danger of sliding rapidly across the large room and out of the window! The ancient house was large and dark, and Aunt Belle's sight was not especially good, so that when she came out to greet us, an extraordinary apparition would emerge. Her hair was dyed a flaming red, her face powdered a deathly white, and great dabs of deep pink rouge adorned her cheeks.

Her two daughters, Marjorie and Sybil, who later married, would usually be at home, and they had long, blonde hair wound into plaited 'earphones', and soft honeyed voices. Her son, Cecil, already married, lived across the road at 'Home Farm' with his family and, as Aunt Belle was by this time widowed, he ran the farm. Once again, Dennis and I enjoyed the excitement and freedom of exploring and playing in a farm - this time a working one, so we had to act somewhat more circumspectly - but also with added pleasures such as rides on tractors and hay-wagons, and visits to see the ferrets Cecil kept for rabbiting.

Pat with Cecil's little daughter, Jill

23

When I was ten or thereabouts, I desperately wanted another pet so, after enquiries, it was discovered that Cecil had a farm kitten to spare. We duly drove to Austrey and after tea drove home with a nervous little bundle of black, brown and gold with, I swear, <u>pink</u> fur on her tummy! The first thing she did, when we had got into the house and I put her down, was to fly across the room to the fireplace and up the chimney. I also dashed across the room, and putting my arm up the chimney was just able to grab the tip of her tail and pull her down. Unsurprisingly I then and there named her Sooty.

As she was a farm kitten it was decided to settle her in by letting her sleep in the summerhouse. It was quite a large summerhouse, and besides garden tools, deck chairs etc, had a large wooden workbench with a tool drawer under.

I put Sooty in her new basket and made her cosy in her blankets, said "Goodnight", and went out, shutting the door behind me.

Next morning I rushed down excitedly to the summerhouse to greet my new friend and, oh horror! there was no sign of her.

I rushed into the house and told Mother and Dad and we all went back to the summerhouse. We couldn't see how she could have got out, and then, in desperation, as there was nowhere else to look, I opened the tool drawer. There, curled up sleepily amid the hammers and screwdrivers, was Sooty!

My mother's grandfather, Grandma Dawes's father, James Adie, in partnership with an Alfred Lovekin, had begun trading as a silversmith in Snape Street, Hockley, Birmingham, registering with the Assay office in Birmingham in 1879, becoming incorporated as a limited company in 1889.

They soon became one of the most prosperous in the industry, my great-grandfather subsequently becoming one of the founders of the Jewellers' and Silversmiths' Association.

He retired from business in 1892, and in May of that year was elected a member of the City Council as a Liberal Unionist representative for the All Saints' Ward.

He devoted the remainder of his life to Civic duties and died in April 1913, having seen his sons, Percy and Hubert register with the Assay Office as Adie Bros., silversmiths of 45 Frederick Street, in 1907.

They, also, went from strength to strength, opening further premises in Birmingham and in London, regularly exhibiting their work, producing many famous and beautiful items, which included a gold tea set for King Farouk of Egypt. Their chief designer for twenty years, Fernand Piret, was made a freeman of the Goldsmiths Company in 1933.

In May 1914 Uncle Percy, his wife Aunt Marie, and niece, Doris Gaunt, were returning to England after a visit to New York, Boston and Montreal, when their ship The Empress of Ireland, was rammed in thick fog on the St. Lawrence river by the Norwegian steamer, Storstad. Their ship began to sink immediately. Their companion, Gordon Maginnis of Mappin and Webb was drowned, but although Doris went deep into the water and began to drown, she was pulled into a lifeboat and, with her uncle and aunt, was among the 463 survivors. They were exceedingly lucky; 1014 were drowned.

Besides his sons, Percy and Hubert, great grandpa Adie had another son, Ernest and four daughters:- Mardie, whom I never knew, Winifred (Winnie), Gertrude (Gertie) and my grandmother Emily (Lily).

Winnie married the very handsome Charles Gaunt, and they had five equally good-looking children: Howard (known as Tom), Nancibel (Nancie), Doris, Jeanne and Meryl.
Tom, after Assistant and Headmasterships at King Edward's Birmingham, Rugby and Malvern, took Holy Orders and became Chaplain at Winchester College. His wife Mabel (Bel) apparently had an interest in both spiritualism and fine wines, and consequently was known around the school as "Wines and Spirits"! In 1963 Tom left the College to become Sacrist at Winchester Cathedral, subsequently becoming Honorary Canon there until his retirement. According to Aunt Winnie, when she stayed with them she would be miserably cold most of the time as Tom would not allow the fires to be lighted before 4 pm!

Nancie, the sweetest of the sisters, married Frank Halliday, also a schoolmaster, and they had a son, Sebastian. They subsequently became the close and supportive friends of Barbara Hepworth at St. Ives.

Doris married Edmund Flower, and they had three sons, Raymond, Neville and Derek.

Jeanne married Ronnie Ravel, and they became theatrical exhibition ballroom dancers, performing at The Windmill theatre during the war.

The youngest sister Meryl also became a dancer but, tragically, she broke her ankle, developed pneumonia and died while still young.

There is a story, which may be apocryphal, that Meryl and Jeanne were independently walking down The Strand when each of them saw, approaching, a woman with strange coloured hair - blue or green or whatever. As they drew nearer, it became apparent that each had spotted the other!

Grandma's other brother, Uncle Ernest, although I don't remember him, was alive when I was a very little girl. He was my godfather, and gave me a wooden sailing barge, which I named Helen, and sailed in my bath for many years. Mother remembered Uncle Ernest as a gentle, loving person like my grandmother. He suffered from epilepsy, and one night had a fit and suffocated with his face in the pillow.

I think this must have frightened me. For many years after, I would go through a night-time ritual when Mother said "Goodnight." I would repeat the mantra "God bless Mummy, Daddy, Dennis and Maude" (our current maid), then "Shall I die tonight?" I did, of course, feel pretty ill a lot of the time, so I suppose it seemed a logical question. But it was also a sort of talisman. If Mother said "No", which of course she did, I would happily settle down; but sometimes I would forget to repeat the whole mantra and I would call downstairs, "Shall I die tonight?" To which, sometimes, Dad and Den would call up "Yes!" and Mother would have to cancel it by calling up, "No darling".

Auntie Gertie married John Kerr and they had two children, Hilda and Douglas. Hilda married but Douglas was dominated by his relentless father, and suffered appallingly from asthma and the most terrible eczema, to the extent that he had to keep his peeling skin covered, as it fell off in great flakes. He always wore gloves, and had to undress standing on a sheet or towel.

I think Uncle John must have had a pretty awful temper. My mother used to relate how her brother George, I imagine then a young teenager, was chased round the billiard table by an irate Uncle John, and shouted over his shoulder, rather bravely, under the circumstances, "Kerr by name, and cur by nature!"

Grandma married George Walter Dawes, who was a well-known and well-thought of figure in Birmingham, with his twinkling eyes, snowy hair and moustache and silver-topped cane. He was a manufacturer, an inventive entrepreneur; and invented the 'Roman rim' bicycle wheel, which became very popular, being, I believe, constructed of light weight aluminium.

They had nine children:- Reggie, Kathleen, Marjorie, Gladys (my mother), Jim, Freda, George, Dorothy and Ted. Reggie died young, aged about fourteen. His illness was never diagnosed, but from my mother's description of his deteriorating condition it seems to have been a muscle-wasting disease similar to muscular dystrophy.

Grandpa and Grandma lived with their large family on the Hagley road at Rolandseck, which had originally belonged to Great Grandpa and Grandma Adie. I was too young to remember it but from what my mother told me, it must have been very large, with a billiard room, a coach-house - where my mother kept her bull mastiffs - and stables where horses were kept.

(Once, some of the children, including my mother, were returning from town when they saw fire engines racing toward a fire. They hurried to see what was happening and were horrified to see that the coach-house and stables were ablaze. The horses were saved, but Mother's bull mastiffs perished as they were in the coach-house where the fire had started. It was thought that it had inadvertently been caused by a tramp.)

The financial situation of the family would oscillate wildly. At times my Mother would mention that she wanted a goldfish, or a budgerigar, and a large aquarium of tropical fish, or a huge aviary of exotic birds would appear in the conservatory. There would be tennis parties and in the winter, when it was cold enough, they would flood the court and use it to skate on.

On warm summer afternoons a large oriental brass table top would be rolled down the garden like a hoop, while another of the children carried the elaborately turned folding legs, and the table would be set up and laid with lace cloth and tea would be served from Grandma's enormous silver tea pot.

But at times, I have been told, there would not be enough money to repair their shoes, which they would line with paper, and stew would replace the incredible assortment of meat and game that they normally enjoyed. Grandpa lost a considerable amount of his money when, at the outbreak of the 1914 War, his factory was commandeered for making munitions.

When, after the war, most of the children married and moved away, Grandma and Grandpa moved to a smaller, but still quite large, Victorian house at the top end of Park Road in Moseley. It was a rambling three-storey house with a large - but empty! - wine cellar, and extraordinary changes in floor levels.

In the large, light porch or vestibule, stood an ornate painted iron umbrella stand and on the wall hung a barometer with long tubes of coloured liquids which showed the maximum and minimum temperatures.

Inside the door into the mosaic-tiled hall was a walking-stick stand where Grandpa kept his silver-topped canes. Across the hall the stairs led up to a half-landing where a stained glass window strewed splinters of coloured light across the stairs. To the right the hall continued towards the back of the house, past the dining room and the telephone room on the right and down steep stone steps to the kitchen and breakfast room, to the opposite of which was the cellar door, and facing the steps was a seldom-used stained glass door into the garden.

Mother told me that when I was very small, and on my way from the hall to the kitchen, I found the steps too much of an obstacle, but as Grandpa appeared I turned to him and, to his great amusement said, "Will you please lift me down these damn steps, Mr Dawes?!" To the left of the front door was the sitting room, which had a deep bay window facing the front garden and huge bowed French windows opening onto steps which led down into the large back garden.

In winter a huge fire burned in the stone hearth, and the room seemed to me as fascinating as an Aladdin's Cave. On the floor were deep Indian carpets and the settees and chairs were covered in thick patterned cut moquette and backed in deep, rich red.

There were many pieces of antique and oriental furniture, and the walls were hung with pictures; one, an oil by Grandma, of a boy playing a flute, painted when she was nineteen. Mother told me they once owned a Turner, but when or how that disappeared, I don't know.

There were delicate ivory carvings, of elaborate intricacy, of elephants, birds, Chinamen walking over an arched bridge, a ceramic Chinaman sitting astride a tiger. There was a carved wooden box with a small drawer which, when opened, triggered a little wooden snake to spring out of the top and 'bite' you on the back of your hand with a fine metal spike.

In cupboards and drawers were relics of Grandpa's inventiveness. I especially enjoyed playing with a sort of metal calculator which, by turning knobs, would reveal the distances between different towns in the British Isles.

Beside Grandpa's chair, which was to the left of the fire, with its back to the front bay window, was a darkly varnished octagonal table where was displayed a beautiful chased silver cigar box which, upon opening, released heady aromas of sandalwood and Corona Coronas.

There was also Grandpa's silver snuff box and, of course, a cut glass decanter and tumbler for his beloved whiskey. And to complete the picture, there would be Grandpa, sitting in his chair, in his black velvet smoking jacket and sometimes his tasselled velvet smoking cap, his snowy moustache heavily tinted with the snuff he frequently tipped onto the back of his hand and sniffed, with the resultant resounding sneeze!

Grandma, like Gran, dressed in black with a little white lace or broiderie anglaise 'dicky' at the neck. There the similarity ended. She was a diminutive person, heavily lined, her little hands encrusted with beautiful diamond rings, and a black ribbon round her throat with a magnificent diamond crescent brooch fastened at the front.

Like the 'Dear Octopus' of Barrie's play, her caring tentacles would lovingly enfold every member of her large family.

When her youngest son, Ted, married Nita, an American dancer, even tinier and daintier than Grandma, she treated her as her own young daughter, and Nita loved her as if she were her own mother. (As far as I know, Nita's only family were a grandfather, whom she adored, and an ambitious mother. Both, of course, lived in the USA).

In order to sit down anywhere, one usually had to move an assortment of half-finished arms, legs, heads, dresses etc. of the dolls that Grandma spent so much of her time making for her many grandchildren.

For her grandchildren she had also made a wonderful playhouse in the garden. It was, in fact, once some kind of outbuilding, but she had had it converted so that in front it had a little garden, surrounded by a low wall, where there was a see-saw and little stools to sit on. A choice of two separate entrances led to the brick 'up and down' house. Steps led down into a slightly damp-smelling room full of sand, with spades and buckets ready for use; the walls transformed by Grandma's paint brush into a sea-side landscape.

Wooden balustraded steps also led up from the garden to the upper floor, with its own front door and windows, and there one would find little chairs and tables where one could play 'house'. All was painted by Grandma in gay sea-side colours of blue and yellow and pink.

Between the playhouse and the front drive another large old outbuilding had been turned into a garage, thick with oil and dust, and above it, reached by a vertical ladder through a trap door was a large loft, even thicker in dust. It was here that, after a frightening - to me, anyway – climb up through the trap door, Dennis and I found a toy steam engine which we brought down and asked Grandma if we could keep. Of course she said "Yes", and we took it home, and Dennis managed to get it working. It was the sort that made real steam from its boiler, using a little pellet which burned as fuel.

When Grandma's youngest son, Ted, was still living at home, going into the garage could present some exciting surprises. He was always keen on cars, motorbikes and things mechanical, and one never quite knew what one would find there. Sometimes a motorbike, frequently a racing car, and on one surprising occasion, a hydroplane!

Between this area and the scullery, a large covered yard housed a mixture of laundry appliances; a mangle, tin baths, a 'dolly' and 'dolly peg' and so on. The scullery was large and somewhat ill-lit by its small casement windows.

This was Maude's domain, with quarry-tiled floor, large stone sink and wooden draining boards, ancient gas cooker and big iron saucepans. Maude was Grandma's faithful maid, ancient, lisping and none too bright, but she adored Grandma and worked diligently for her for many years.

The scullery led to the huge kitchen with large black leaded range flanked from ceiling to floor by cupboards, one of which Grandma had stocked with enormous bottles of sweets, gobstoppers, dolly mixture, barley sugar, all for her beloved grandchildren. In the middle of the room was a large scrubbed wooden table, and at Christmas the whole area would be a hive of activity with Grandma and a host of her daughters and grandchildren all working away at their allotted tasks. (In those days the men, of course, were enjoying their whiskey, exchanging risqué jokes and waiting happily for the females to reappear, followed subsequently by Christmas dinner!)

My cousin Margaret (three years older than me) and I would always volunteer to prepare the sausage meat for the turkey. This was because not only did we enjoy squeezing the meat out of the bulging sausage skins but, all unknowing of any health risks in those days, we would surreptitiously eat small mouthfuls of the delicious raw sausage meat as we worked.

Christmas dinners were traditional and memorable. In the dining room the big sideboard with its bronzes of near-naked men struggling to hold rearing stallions, and the huge dining table, both practically groaned under the weight of the plentiful food, and always some exciting creation of Grandma's; perhaps a little house, covered in cotton-wool snow, containing presents for all, or wonderful home-made crackers.

After the turkey, with all its accompaniments, the Christmas puddings with their 3d bits, mince pies, custard, fruit and nuts et al had been consumed, indoor fireworks would be produced and, as writhing 'snakes' and mini 'Vesuviuses' erupted on the plates, the room filled with a thick mixture of firework and cigar smoke. When the fireworks were finished the children were allowed to 'get down' from the table and wave sparklers around.

One memorable Christmas, for the children Grandma had turned an entire room upstairs into an enormous snow scene, with little houses and bridges, trees, animals, people and sleds in a wonderland of cotton wool snow while, from the ceiling, were suspended on long strands of pale cotton, 'snowflakes' of cotton wool. It was a magical wonderland, and the children loved it. We were given severe warnings not to take our sparklers into the 'snowroom'. However, my young cousin Michael, believing his sparkler to be out, went into the room and put it down, still hot, onto the cotton wool snow and set the whole thing on fire.

An advantage of a large family, most with spouses, was that there were many willing hands to pass buckets of water to throw onto the blaze. It was put out eventually but, alas, the snow scene was no more and the room was a scorched, soggy mess.

It was on the first floor of the house that the floor levels, for some reason, became somewhat eccentric. The two large rooms over the sitting room and dining room only were on the same level as the 'snowroom', which was at the front of the house, between them.

At the beginning of the war Grandma's sister, Winnie, lived for a while at Park Road, and used the room over the downstairs sitting room as her sitting room, where she also installed her Bechstein. She had trained as a pianist with Myra Hess (presumably as fellow students) but married and raised a family and never played for the public; officially, that is, for the sounds of her wonderful playing, especially of Liszt, would float out through the big front window and entrance passers-by.

The 'snowroom', which also had a connecting door to her sitting room, became her bedroom. Grandpa and Grandma's bedroom was over the dining room, and I remember it mostly for its whiteness. Walls, bedspreads and furniture were all white, while on the fireplace wall was a solid phalanx of photographs of her beloved family.

And here one encountered one of the strange changes in floor levels, for in this wall was an opening which led up steps to the door of their bathroom. Another door led out of the bathroom to a little landing, where another door led to an ancient throne-like lavatory. The throne-like impression was made even stronger when, from the main landing, one approached along a corridor at the end of which a flight of steps led up to the large imposing mahogany lavatory door.

Down a few stairs from the landing, a door led off the stained-glass illuminated half landing. Behind this lay a suite of rooms that in my memory are always fragrant with perfume and powder, pastel swansdown floats from powder puffs and female voices fill the air. These were the rooms allocated to the relatives from afar; Aunty Marjorie and her daughter Margaret, and Aunty Freda and Uncle Roy. The rooms were also used by the females of the family to 'freshen up', re-apply make-up and tidy their hair.

I can't remember clearly what the suite of rooms comprised, but memory tells me that it was two bedrooms and a bathroom.

A flight of narrow stairs with close walls led up between Grandma and Grandpa's bedroom and the 'snowroom' to the top floor attic bedrooms where Maude and Aunty Dorothy slept.

Aunty Dorothy, nicknamed 'Dimpy' when she was a girl, was Grandma and Grandpa's youngest daughter. She had been born with German Measles, and this had left her very slightly simple and child-like. She loved children and, in turn, was loved by them. When she was nineteen she then had the terrible misfortune to be knocked down by a double-decker bus, which then ran right over her body. Incredibly, she survived, but besides a broken arm, her pelvis was shattered, as were any possibilities of child-bearing. Most fortunately, many years later she met and married an ex-merchant seaman, a widower with a small son, so her desperate desire for motherhood was fulfilled to a certain extent.

Right along the back of the house, leading off both bedrooms, was a long narrow room where there were shelves of books that had been discarded by the family. I spent many happy hours up here, rummaging amongst them, sometimes unearthing some long-hidden treasure that I would carry down to Grandma and ask if I could keep it. She invariably said "Yes". I thus accumulated a miscellaneous collection of ageing books; Grandma's prayer book, a beautifully illustrated volume of Norse Legends and many others which have become relegated and lost once more.

Aunty Kathleen was the oldest of the surviving children. She married a dashing officer returned from war, Uncle Eustace. He was a doctor, and practised from a large house they lived in at Handsworth.

It was a strange house to visit, somewhat gloomy, with a strong antiseptic smell as you entered the hall, for on the left, at the front of the house, were his consulting rooms. You would approach the front door from the gravel drive, where Dobbins, the chauffeur, in smart grey uniform and shiny leather gaiters would greet you as he waited by the equally gleaming car, ready to take my uncle on his house calls.

Pulling the old-fashioned bell knob you wondered if it was working, for the distance from the front door to the back kitchen, where the bells rang, was immense. After an uncertain wait, suddenly the door would be opened by a tall, angular, sour-faced woman who had been nanny to the two boys, John and Paul, and was now housekeeper, and dispenser for the practice. She idolised my uncle, always referring to him as 'the doctor', and she despised my aunt. She would invite you inside, and leave you to wait just inside the door, whereupon two hateful sealyhams, Tim and Sam, would come yapping and snapping down the hall. Tim was evil, growling and snarling, and waiting to pounce and bite if you dared to move a muscle.

Nan would disappear to inform 'madam' that she had visitors. What seemed an eternity later, while one remained frozen in desperate immobility, Aunty Kathleen would make her impressive entrance down the magnificent iron-balustraded, curved staircase at the further end of the hall. At this point came relief from one's canine tormentors, who rushed excitedly down the hall to their mistress.

Aunty Kathleen, an elegant, cultivated woman, was the most exotic of the Dawes girls. As children they had had a German governess, 'Fraulein', and Aunty Kathleen had spent some time abroad, improving her languages. Unfortunately, with the advent of the 1914 war, the other girls were unable to travel, and 'Fraulein' returned to Germany, leaving a lingering suspicion that she might have been a spy all along. As a result, although they were left with an assortment of German collocations, it was only Aunty Kathleen that was a fluent linguist, especially in French, in which she was occasionally liable to address you, which was somewhat disconcerting.

She had other advantages which peacetime and money had allowed her. She was a competent horsewoman and pianist and, naturally, possessed a Bechstein in the beautiful drawing room, with it's great mahogany Adam doorways and William Morris wallpaper, where we would have polite tea and conversation. Or perhaps we would be sent past the dispensary smelling of medicines for nursery tea in the kitchen with Nan and the boys.

Mother used to tell me how Aunty Kathleen, presumably when a young woman, would write her name underneath those possessions of my grandparents that she fancied.

Her worst offence was almost unbelievable. When my mother became engaged, Grandma gave her a beautiful cloisonné bowl that she possessed, as an engagement present. Grandma's daughters were, of course, still living at home at that time. Somehow Aunty Kathleen, fully aware, purloined it, and it subsequently became part of her considerable acquisition at Handsworth.

Mother naturally wanted it back, but it was not until they were both widows in their late 70s, that Aunty Kathleen suddenly presented the bowl to Mother, declaring that she believed it was hers.

Upstairs at Handsworth, elegant bedrooms and suites led off the galleried landing, but one of the front bedrooms presented something of a surprise, for it was devoid of carpet or furniture, and instead contained an immense waist-high layout of railway lines, signals, tunnels and scenic landscape peopled with passengers and train staff, and round which charged magnificent engines, pulling a variety of trucks, Pullman carriages and so on.

What lucky boys my cousins were, you might think. But you would be wrong. This was not for them. This was Uncle Eustace's domain.

Besides the beautiful sweeping staircase, there were also back stairs that led down to the considerable kitchen quarters, and at memorable large family parties, we would play 'Murder in the Dark', with most of the 'murders' taking place on the dark and winding back stairs. One would creep up the stairs with a delightful frisson of fear, expecting at any moment to be 'murdered'.

Later, parlour tricks would be performed and my uncles, of course, would tell risqué jokes. I once came upon my youngest Uncle, Ted, leaning on one hand against the closed door to the dining room, out in the hall, patiently explaining, over and over, to a mystified Aunty Kathleen, the subtle point of the naughty joke he had just told to the highly appreciative assembled family.

Aunty Marjorie was the artist of the Dawes family. She studied at the Byam Shaw School of Art and, at the end of the 1914 war, Grandma and Grandpa bought her a cottage at Shottery, near Anne Hathaway's cottage. Here she lived and painted for the next six or seven years.

In about 1920, in the days before Egyptian Independence, Aunty Marjorie visited Cairo with her cousin, Doris Gaunt, and went with her to a Government party. There she was introduced to 'Tommy' (Ernest Seymour Thomas).

He was an Archaeologist/Egyptologist who, as Assistant Oriental Secretary in Cairo and Government Representative, had been present at the opening of the tomb of Tutenkhamun. Aunty Marjorie asked him to write something for her in Arabic, when she learned that he was fluent in both speaking and writing the language. He wouldn't say what he had written, and only later did she learn that it read: "Beautiful lady, shining like the sun, beloved of Isis"! Needless to say he intrigued her. He was twenty years her senior.

Sometime later he returned to England on leave and they met up again, and he asked her to marry him. After the wedding they went to live in Egypt, but after my cousin Margaret was conceived, Aunty Marjorie came back to Birmingham for the birth, returning to Egypt when her baby was a few weeks old.

However, the trouble leading up to Egyptian Independence began soon after, and Egypt was considered too dangerous for women with young children, so Aunty Marjorie and Margaret returned to England, leaving Uncle Tommy behind to advise the new Egyptian Government; and, in that capacity, he wore the official fez.

He subsequently returned to England, becoming Assistant Curator at the Pitt Rivers Museum in Oxford. His work was cataloguing the entire African and ancient Eygptian collections. (Fortunately, he had completed this task when he died suddenly, like all those who were present at the opening of the tomb of Tutankhamun - the famous curse!)

They lived at 'Sundown', Bickerton Road in Headington and, to me, it was the most exotic house of the family. Uncle Tommy had his own study, full of Egyptian relics and mementos, and through that, at the back, was Aunty Majorie's studio. Uncle Tommy had made a small stained glass window of a reaper in a cornfield, which had been inserted high up in the large window. Besides his profession he was also a very competent painter, and painted lovely pre-Raphaelite style watercolours. Aunty Marjorie was a professional miniature painter, and painted exquisite tiny portraits on ivory. The finest she ever did was of Uncle Tommy at his desk but, alas, years later it was destroyed in a fire along with two oil paintings she had done of Margaret, one at her homework, and the other, getting out of her four-poster bed. Many other of her beautiful works perished in that blaze.

The sitting room, also, was full of character, with an attractive flooring resembling dark quarry tiles, on which were beautiful oriental rugs; there were comfortable chairs, and dressers and cupboards with more Egyptian relics and a large open range fire and, of course, the walls were hung with many of their paintings.

The garden was enormous with, down at the bottom, a tennis court surrounded by a tall wire mesh fence, where they held tennis parties, and during the war, chickens were kept. There was also a wild area, where I once managed to fall full length into a bed of nettles, and was duly taken indoors and swabbed down with quantities of Milton.

When Margaret was thirteen Uncle Tommy died. The doctors had diagnosed typhoid, but he had, in fact, undiagnosed peritonitis. Aunty Marjorie was forced to take in lodgers to make ends meet, then she herself became very ill, and having had an operation on her throat, when she nearly died, she took Margaret to Egypt to recuperate and rest. I think the change did them both good, but it was unfortunate that Margaret was bitten by a rabid dog and had to undergo the gruesome injections necessary as a consequence.

Fortunately, all went well and when staying at Grandma's at Christmas, Margaret was able to relate the tale to me, also explaining the rainbow of tinkling glass bracelets on her wrist that she was unable to remove, an Arab street trader having rammed them on unexpectedly in a bazaar. (They were very pretty, and she kept them for a few years before having them cut off.)

Marjorie was a gentle person, warm and sensitive. When, some years earlier, she had given birth to a baby daughter who died shortly after, she was devastated when the baby's grave had to be outside the sanctified ground of the churchyard, as it had not been christened. However, she later painted a reredos for the church, which includes the image of a baby grasping for a butterfly. The butterfly was highly significant for her, for when she had gone to visit the new grave, feeling utterly forlorn, a butterfly had danced along beside her until, arriving at the grave, it settled. She was a person of great faith, and she found the incident tremendously comforting.

Years later I, too, lost a baby. My father was desperately ill and Mother could not leave him. Marjorie was the most wonderful support and comfort to me in those first weeks. She gave me two maxims, which were immensely helpful. One was to help me deal with my grief by not examining it too deeply, too soon. "Imagine that you have to swim across a river. You have to put your clothes on your head to keep them dry. Don't attempt to inspect them until you are safely across."

The other maxim was one of Uncle Tommy's, which had been of comfort to her. "Religious experience is not a haven, not a ship moored to the shore, but the canvas spread to catch the winds of God."

She, my grandmother and my mother, were all the most remarkable and wonderful of people and, without achieving fame or perceived success, gave so very much, and enriched so many lives with so much love.

Uncle Jim and Aunty Mary were an oddly assorted couple. She was very tall and he was quite small. Mother always remained convinced that his small stature had been partly caused by his selfless devotion to their ailing older brother, Reg. Towards the end of his short life Reg was unable to walk but Jim, by then about nine or ten years old, carried him around on his back so that he could join in all the fun and games of the other children. Mother told me that Reg once said, "Was there ever a boy as lucky as I am?"

During the 1914 war Jim then lied about his age and engineered his acceptance into the army. After the war he married, and he and Aunty Mary, son Jimmy and daughter Janet settled in Solihull. He was the only person I knew who wore plus-fours. He and Dad sometimes played cribbage together, and he always called my father Bill, his given names being Frederick William, and I suppose Uncle Jim, unsurprisingly, preferred Bill to Fred.

Jim worked for his uncle, Percy Adie, and during the war I visited him in his workshop at Uncle Percy's factory on the canal behind Great Charles Street. He had a cramped little room in this old Victorian building, but here in place of silver-smithing he was now working on tools for manufacturing radar equipment.

Aunty Freda married Roy Wade, one of, I believe, three sons. I think he found the large, extrovert Dawes family somewhat overwhelming, and he always referred to himself as a 'fringe of the family'. This perhaps explains his seemingly strange behaviour when, having become engaged to my aunt, he joined the police force in China! Since he was an engineer by profession it seems a little odd. After entreaties from his fiancée he came back - after, I think, about two years - and they were married.

I think probably Uncle Roy was a man who was unable to cope with stress and, after struggling for years with gastric ulcers, he finally retired. A legacy from an aunt of his helped financially, and he seemed quite adept at playing the Stock Market. He and my aunt moved around quite a lot, living for some time in London, but also at one time, during the war, in part of a house in Leamington Spa, which contained a section of the most elegant double staircase - totally useless, but very impressive!

During the war years Aunty Freda worked in a munitions factory. She was an intelligent, capable, fashionable woman, she played bridge with a high degree of skill, and designed and made many of her very smart clothes, but she had never undertaken such employment before. However, due to her intelligence and dedicated professionalism, she ended the war as works manager.

Uncle George and Aunty Kay lived in a large house on the Hagley road in Edgbaston, having moved there from a smaller house where they had spent their early married years. He was a chartered accountant, but he subsequently became an extremely successful and wealthy business man, company promoter and founder of Neville Industrial Securities.

I would sometimes walk from our house in Harborne across 'The Tip', a cinder track that led across some few remaining fields and past a friendly horse, to the Hagley road and their house.

They had three sons, Michael, Howard and Nigel; Howard, the middle son, being ten years younger than me. In the period just before the War they must have been aged about 8, 3 and 18 months.

They were typical boys, and I remember watching in fascinated horror, on one occasion, as the two older boys tore through their parents' bedroom like a tornado, straight across the silk bedspreads in their shoes, scattering eiderdowns, their mother seemingly unperturbed.

Another time, unknown to anyone, the boys had got into the car parked on the sloping drive, and, playing with the knobs and levers, let off the brake. The first thing anyone knew about it was the arrival at the front door of a passer by to say that the car, and the boys, was across the Hagley road!

When the War broke out Uncle George bought a cottage amongst the hopyards at Hallow, in Worcestershire. Here he evacuated his family, travelling down to be with them once or twice a week.
The arrival at the cottage of the three small boys, and the unloading of the furniture vans became confused in three year old Howard's mind, and his recollections are of being transported rolled up in a carpet!

In spite of the cottage's isolation, Uncle George also had an enormous air raid shelter built as an added precaution.

Toward the end of the war the family moved back to Birmingham to a suite on the first floor of the Grosvenor Hotel, which Uncle George subsequently bought, and where the boys once again filled me with fascinated horror as they played near the open floor-to-ceiling windows in their first floor sitting room.

Ted was the baby of the family, and was in his early twenties when, in 1934, he met and fell in love with an American acrobatic dancer, Juanita Richards. He followed her round Europe, and in the end his perseverance succeeded, and they became engaged.

She was known as 'THE LOVELY JUANITA', having teamed up with the Polish/Russian Ganjou brothers, three strapping young men who swung, threw and caught her, as she performed aerial splits and somersaults as she danced, sometimes spinning her through the air across the width of the stage. On one occasion, one of her partners had dropped her but, although in pain from a fractured rib, she somehow managed to complete the performance.

She came to Birmingham to dance at the Theatre Royal, and the family went to see her dance.

When the curtains opened, the Russians, in pale blue tights, were lolling gracefully in a Rococo setting, either side of a beautiful clock, the pendulum of which was decorated with a delicate little figure in pale blue, which appeared to be made of porcelain.

Suddenly the pendulum stopped swinging and the little figure, dressed in a pale blue beaded leotard, with a matching close-fitting cap hiding her dark hair, stepped off and began to dance. And how she danced! She was magnificent. I had never seen anything like it before; nor have I since. She was so graceful, so balletic, and yet so brilliantly acrobatic, that one just sat there entranced. This was my first sight of Nita.

Later, she came round to meet us, a little figure wrapped in a coat with an enormous fur collar. No wonder she held my uncle in thrall!

She made such an impression on me that she appeared in all my school drawing books, and when the opportunity arose to see her dance again at the Birmingham Hippodrome, I leaped at it. I think, perhaps, Grandpa hadn't seen her dance, for it was Grandpa and I who careered off to Aston to the Hippodrome. I was eight years old.

When Grandpa and I were crossing the road to the theatre, hand in hand, I suddenly thought: "What do I do if Grandpa dies, for he's quite old and might do, and I'm all alone in Aston?"!

Anyway, he didn't die, and I once more sat entranced, as Nita danced in what was one of her few remaining performances, for she gave up her career and married Ted, and I was bridesmaid, my cousin Paul was page, and Ted's best friend 'Boots' Downie was best man. (After she left, the act continued with another dancer, but the name 'Juanita' was retained.)

Ted was terrified of Nita hankering after her life of dancing and, sadly, Nita allowed him to persuade her to burn all her scrapbooks and cuttings of her highly successful, though brief, professional life.

She came from Detroit and I believe her mother had pushed her, early, into professionalism. By fourteen she was teaching dancing, and by seventeen or eighteen she was dancing before, as they used to say, 'the crowned heads of Europe'.

Ted and Nita lived for a short while in Harborne, later moving to Tettenhall near Wolverhampton. In due time twin boys were born, but it was a small nursing home, the doctor was at a party and arrived in evening dress and where a Caesarean should obviously have been performed in view of her diminutiveness and the fact that she was carrying 2 normal sized babies, it was not. The result, tragically, was that one of the twins did not survive, and Nita had a thrombosis which kept her bedridden for some time. However in due course mother and child were doing well.

I used to love shopping for shoes with Nita; for many years she continued to buy theatrical style shoes, with incredibly high heels, and big decorative bows or buckles, and her little feet looked like dainty butterflies. She was five years older than Dennis, ten years older than me, and was more like an older sister than aunt. Once she saw me jumping on my bed, using it like a trampoline, and she stopped me - and demonstrated some more exciting jumps! I was still at an age when I fancied my chances as a ballet dancer, and she would show me how to do a standing splits against the door lintel, but one exercise she demonstrated seemed a physical impossibility to me. She would stand on one foot and tap the toes of the other foot, rat-a-tat against the ground at a phenomenal speed. If
I couldn't do that, she said, I'd never make a dancer.

    I couldn't and I didn't!

*

When I was about ten I developed rheumatic fever and was confined to bed for some time.

One evening, after a lot of whispering and giggling from my parents' bedroom, my father suddenly appeared in my bedroom doorway, dressed in a short-sleeved, old Chilprufe vest, my mother's silk knickers, with their elasticated legs pulled down almost to his knees, socks and suspenders, a Trilby, and his .45 revolver hanging loosely round his hips. He was a tall, thin man, and the result was absolutely hilarious!

Once again, I missed a lot of school, this time it was more critical, as I was approaching the crucial entrance exam for King Edward's. Anyway, after I had recovered sufficiently, the doctor recommended my being taken to the seaside to get my strength back, so Mother and Dad decided to take me to Western-super-Mare for a week.

We stayed at a hotel on the front, and the first day went out for a drive in the car. When we returned to the hotel I got out of the car and my legs gave way under me. I tried to stand up, but found I couldn't, and had to be helped into the hotel. I was able to get around in the hotel by holding onto the furniture. Mother later told me that people in the hotel referred to me as "the little cripple girl".

Each evening, after dinner*, we went for a cup of coffee, or in my case, chocolate, to a café further along the front.

*(In those pre-war, and war-time, days, dinner was partaken in the evening only on social occasions, or in a hotel. Normal 'working' week mealtimes were:-

Breakfast - almost invariably bacon and egg, toast, marmalade and tea.

Lunch - mid-morning- At school, milk and a bar of chocolate or occasionally cakes, from the tuck shop. Out in Town, coffee and cakes.

Dinner –mid-day- the main meal of the day, usually meat, poultry or game with vegetables and gravy followed by a pudding.

Tea - during the week usually 'High Tea', such as kippers, mixed grill etc; at weekends usually afternoon tea with home made cake and perhaps thinly cut sandwiches and tea, followed later by a light supper.)

One evening I was playing cards with some other children in the hotel and, not wanting to interrupt, Mother and Dad went off to the café on their own. When I found they had gone I was devastated and, putting on my coat, I struggled out of the hotel. I managed to progress slowly along, holding onto walls and railings, but then came to an area with nothing to hold onto. There were railings on the other side of the road and somehow, oh so slowly and with such difficulty, I managed to cross that road.

Mother and Dad were astonished when I finally made my appearance at their table, and mortified to realize how much it meant to me.

Gradually, as time progressed, the strength came back to my legs, and I was once again able to enjoy my tomboyish activities. However, unfortunately, when I was due to sit my entrance exam for King Edward's High School for Girls (my brother by now in his final years at the analogous King Edward's School) I had another attack of rheumatic fever, and was unable to sit the exam.

Such eventualities were provided for, and there was a substitute exam a few months later. Unfortunately I was once more ill and in bed, but it was decided that this time it probably wouldn't harm me to get up and take the exam.

I don't think anyone really expected me to pass, having missed so much schooling, and sitting the exam with a temperature, but I did pass, and I was absolutely thrilled. King Edward's School and King Edward's High School were considered two of the top academic schools and I was so proud that, as soon as I was well enough, I went into town with Mother and bought my black and green uniform and wore it!

1938, the year of the Anschluss, and, later, Munich, was a strange year. There was a sense of apprehension mingled with wishful thinking.

Because of events in Germany, it was decided to issue schoolchildren with gas-masks, and the possibility of evacuation began to be discussed. When a knock came on the front door it could as easily be a member of the Peace Pledge Union trying to get signatures for a petition, or a Jewish refugee, homeless, jobless and hopeless. When my mother invited one elderly Jew in for a cup of tea, to our astonishment, he burst into tears and hugged her, sobbing on her shoulder.

Everything was changing; by 1938 King Edward's School had moved from it's original building in the centre of Birmingham to temporary wooden buildings on the Bristol road, near the University, while the new school was being built nearby.

Personally, for Dennis and me also, it was a year of change. I was eleven and Dennis sixteen. I was at the beginning of life at a major secondary school, making new friends and scanning new horizons. Dennis was in his final year at school, surrounded by friendships well-established, and the horizons he scanned were in the sky. His burning ambition was to become a pilot.

A note in his diary in January refers to the possibility of his applying to Imperial Airways, while another reads: "Dad says he will pay for 'A' Licence if I get Higher School". He was in the Upper Science Sixth working for his Higher School Certificate, although his small diary at that time reads more like a social calendar. He and his friends seemed to be forever going to the pictures, playing cards, boating in the school dinner-hour, cycling and skating, and playing tennis.

Phillip, Dennis, Brian & Bill

There were five of them; Dennis, Vivian, Billy, Philip (Wishy), and Brian.

They formed a sort of association of the five friends, which was named the 'Quintuple Alliance' or Q.A.

It was Dennis's idea. Despite their different personalities, they were friends with quite a few similar likes and dislikes. The European political situation and Munich, and the threat of war, increased the possibility of the group being split up and losing touch.

Vivian was Chairman, Dennis was Secretary and Bill was Treasurer. 'Wishy' and Brian made up the other two members. They had a Minute Book and a 'Q.A. Song'. (Sung to the tune from the 'Vagabond King')

Dennis had it printed out:-

The Upper Science
Faced it with defiance,
They just said -
"To Hell with H.S.C."

Joint Compliance
Formed this fine Alliance,
They just played
The Hell with H.S.C.

Forward, onward through the years they go;
Thus united none shall say them "No"

The Upper Science
Face it with defiance,
They just say
"To Hell with tyranny".*

*Owing to the International Situation, this line shall be read as "To Hell with Germany".

Dennis also wrote poems and limericks about his friends. "'A Sad Love Story" (from life)' is about Brian, one of the Q.A. members.

We'll now unfold a sorry tale
    Of love and disillusionment,
And show how some poor fellows fail
    To find a life of sweet content.

Now there's a proverb you've all heard,
    It says; if you've been bitten once
You'll have more care; and it's absurd
    That Brian could be such a dunce.

For his is one poor sorry life
    Of errors and mistakes galore.
He's tried to find his future wife,
    (Perhaps he wants a Ma-in-Law.)

The story starts when he saw Pam
    Her subtle curves set him on fire.
Maybe he'd visions of a pram,
    Or nursery. What of Billy's ire?

Brian laughed at that; but Pam was cute;
    She knew that Billy's love was true,
So she gave Morgan, B. the boot,
    And said to him, "be off with you."

But even ere the words were said
    He'd succumbed to another's charms.
Curvaceous Mary turned his head,
    She spent an evening in his arms.

But this new passion quickly fled;
    He then met Thelma in the street,
And spent with her, it must be said,
    One night of love, so short and sweet.

A shapely girl in Harborne next
    To Brian's heart had found the key;
But his best smiles just left her vexed.
    She disappeared from sight, and he

Met Nita, put there as a plant,
    And being smart she led him on;
He found she was Knight's married aunt.
    Another hope of love is gone.

Now there's a moral to this rhyme,
    If you want fun, don't hesitate,
But hurry up and spend your time
    By watching Brian find his mate.

Another Q.A. member was the subject of a limerick:-

There was a young fellow called Billy
Whose method of courtship was silly;
    He spent his money on Zints,
    And Imperial Mints.
His friendships, though sacred, are chilly.

A friend, Teddy, had a very deep voice and spoke slowly, earning him the nickname 'Teddy Bear'. He also was immortalised:-

Our Teddy's voice is a delight.
    He's got lots of curly hair.
But it's a really horrid site
    To see a Teddy bare.

As was:-
Now Rowlands is awfully queer.
He's too thin to be seen unless near.
    When seen in the bath
    He's as thin as a lath.
He'll slip down the plughole, we fear.

Two weeks before his 17th birthday, Den was able at last to start his longed-for flying lessons at Castle Bromwich aerodrome, noting in his diary:-

"**Mon 4 April**
    Went round to Billy's in morning to take rackets back. Cycled to Solihull, usual Fascist gag. Flying in afternoon, 1st take off. Flew over Elmdon. Cycled to Grandma's in evening then round to Billy's.

Wed 6 Apr
    Flying, had new tutor. Did tight circuits. Chappie bought me tea at aerodrome, went round to Grandma's in evening.

Sat 9 Apr
    Tennis with Billy and Pam in morning, flying in afternoon, many planes; four complete circuits including first landings. Pictures in evening with Pam and Billy. Jessie Matthews in 'Gangway'.

Mon 11 Apr
    Dentist in morning, flying in afternoon, 45 mins, 3 Volunteer Reserve planes learning landings too.

Tues 12 Apr
    Cycled to school in morning to get books. Tennis with Pam, Billy and Nita in afternoon. Pictures in evening with Pam and Billy.

Wed 13 Apr
Flying in afternoon, not so bad. Went round to Brian's in evening.

Thur 14 Apr
    Flying in afternoon, pretty punk, if I may say so. I'm thinking I'd better take Bile Beans to wake up my flying (there was an advertisement at that time declaring "Bile Beans wake up your liver").

Good Friday - 15 Apr
    Gran came to stay."

    Gran became convinced that Dennis's fair wavy hair couldn't be natural. She mentioned it so often that he decided to do something about it. He therefore arranged with Mother that he would say he was going upstairs to his room to revise, and she would then invent some pretext to engineer Gran to go up to his room. When Gran entered the room she was greeted by the sight of Dennis sitting at his desk, surrounded by text-books, with setting combs pushed into all his natural waves! She came down to the sitting room triumphantly declaring, "I knew it!"

Mother had been ill for some time. Her weight had dropped to seven stone, and although, as ever, bright and cheerful, there was obviously something very seriously wrong. All the family were, of course, worried and distressed, and Dennis, who was still trying to organise his future career, didn't want to worry Dad, so made several visits to see Dad's brother, Uncle Tom, to discuss it with him. Uncle Tom dissuaded him from his beloved flying, advising him to seek a more secure career in accountancy.

And his brief diary notes continue:-

"Mon 25 Apr
Mother went to hospital. Took Pat to see 'Ebb Tide' (good).

Thurs 28 Apr - Birthday (17)
Tennis with Pam and Billy. Tea at Billy's and I bought salmon, tomatoes, cucumber, fruit salad, cream, meringues, bread and butter, and cakes etc.

Fri 29 Apr
Walk in park with Billy. Aeroplanes over B'ham, and Peace League sandwich men (Territorial week!)

Fri 6 May
Goodman and Jakeman *(two prefects)* objected to my parade in Old School tie, Basher, socks, suspenders and bathing slips (all true blue).

Sat 7 May
Went to see Mother at hospital. Won packet of cigarettes at darts."

Mother later went to recuperate at Grandma's at Moseley, and Den's diaries are brief notes, on chemistry tests, cricket matches, visits to Billy's and tennis, and, of course, visits to Mother at Moseley. Then, confined to bed with a feverish cold, and temporarily cut off from his friends and activities, he penned his feelings to Vivian:-

'Swansong written in bed while suffering from a bad cold.'

17.5.39 **DELIRIUM**

Dear Vivian,

      As, with youthful gaiety, and with energy of boundless mein, did we so disport ourselves that we must even have surpassed the thunderbolts of Jupiter for speed, and put to shame fleet footed Hermes - he of flighted grace.

      Yet see! Upon the morrow was I fatigued by such unwonted sport; soft bosomed Morpheus did claim me for his own, and in his opiate folds I did encompass a half rotation of this orbed sphere - and more.

Then were all worldly cares full momentless to me.

But, for all mortals, sad of character as we, there is but one eternal end. That was not mine! And so did I Return to my continual penance - like Proserpina, ever Twixt the dark and light, servant to both, yet longing for the one.

Yet such was my condition, tired by sportive waking, submissive by the spell of lingering sleep, I went my way all guardless, as a man in love.

      And now, the weather influenced by the Gods, three days of liquid cold and weeping blast in sequence followed; and on the third I succumbed to the clammy hands of sickness.
      Now with tortured head, and limbs of sweated wet, I lie in pain, the mock and plaything of each slowly stepping hour.

Dennis.'

'18th May 1939

SONNET

Dear Vivian,

Now, weakened by damp fever's wracking pain,
I hear the footsteps of a ghostly past,
Like distant shadows, born to die again,
Vague memories of a life that fleets too fast.

Parade in solemn pantomime, In mists
The vision fades. With bitter pulse and beat
A now fast failing heart, bravely resists
Death's strangling hand. But should my fevered heart
Change to cold lifeless damp; when I at last
Have gladly answered to the final call
And sunk to sleep in calm tranquillity,

I pray my friends, when speaking of my past
Consider well and say in equity
"We understand, and knowledge forgives all"

Dennis.'

*

And so by mid-summer, Dennis and his friends, having managed to settle down to some serious revision, took their Higher School Certificate and straight after were involved in the Pageant of Birmingham.

Den, Brian and Vivian were Knights in the Crecy episode; Billy was an Anglo Saxon slave. They used to meet at our house and dress in their armour before catching the bus to Aston Hall. The 'Knights' used to march in formation whilst the 'slave' rattled a collection box for the Waifs & Strays. They did quite well, too, and the 'Treasurer' handed over nearly £5 for the fund.

Dennis, Bill, Brian & Vivian

On one occasion I was taken along as a spectator, when they bought me my first Coca-Cola, which I didn't particularly like, but drank two bottles as it was breathtakingly hot.

By this time, I was just 12, and the boys began to include me in some of their activities, although at times I would be kicked out unceremoniously when I barged in uninvited. On these occasions Billy was always my ally and would try and plead on my behalf, sometimes successfully, as when Den had bought some records of their latest favourite, Hildegarde, singing 'You're an Education' and 'Tipi Tin' and I was permitted to remain to listen.

Dennis having noted in his diary on July 23rd that he partook of his last school dinner, we went to Pembrokeshire for our summer holidays.

We stayed in Tenby. Billy and his parents were staying in Pembroke Dock, and sometimes Billy would come out with us, and other times Dennis would go out with them. He and Billy nearly got themselves arrested on one occasion photographing flying boats in Pembroke Dock.

By the end of 1938, Dennis was making his career in accountancy with a Birmingham firm, Felton & Co., although he was still flying at every opportunity. We were frequent companions. Of course, most of the time we had our own friends, but often he would join mine, and even more often I would join his. On his birthday in April his friends Billy, Vivian, Brian and 'Wishy' came round for a Q.A. meeting in the evening, and I was invited to join them. At some stage they adopted me as 'Hostess', but whether it was on this occasion or later, I don't remember. I remember we had two pheasants for dinner - one 'high', one 'low'! It may also have been on this occasion that we attempted to 'de-bag' Wishy. He had a habit of leaving early and going on somewhere else, and this seemed the only way to prevent him!

Having reached the aged of eighteen, Dennis joined the R.A.F. Volunteer Reserve. Because of the uncertain international situation, from time to time rumours would circulate, many of them 'sightings' of German parachutists, and the boys, Dennis, Billy and Vivian, decided to lend a hand.

So one afternoon, Dennis put on his leather flying helmet, goggles and flying boots, and a dressing gown with a quilted collar, which looked somewhat like a foreign-looking flying jacket. For his 'parachute' he strapped a khaki haversack onto his backside and then he and Vivian proceeded to walk up Crosbie Road to the bus stop in Lordswood Road, talking animatedly in German, while Billy and I followed at a discreet distance, pretending not to notice and trying hard not to laugh.

By this time, I had become great friends with Esmé, a girl in my form, and she would quite often come home with me after school on a Friday and stay the weekend. We would go for walks, picnics in the car, and cycle rides but it always seemed to be Esmé who came out of things the worse for wear.

She seemed to be constantly going home in one of my dresses. On one occasion we were climbing through a barbed wire fence and she caught and ripped her dress. But the occasion that reduced me to hysterical laughter was once when we were climbing huge willow trees that overhung Edgbaston reservoir - we had been sitting in the branches looking at some photographs I'd taken, and deciding it must be nearly tea time began to climb down. I went first, and about two thirds of the way down shouted out, "Don't put your weight on that branch, it's .....", when, with a crash, down into the water went the branch, with Esmé on it! I couldn't stop laughing, but when I did manage to speak coherently, my first words were, "Are the snaps all right?!" Esmé was very, very cross!

At Whitsuntide, Mother Dad and I went on holiday to Sidmouth, taking Esmé with us, and leaving Dennis and Bill to look after the house.

Vivian joined them, and somehow managed to slip and break a bone in his ankle. The other two duly carted him off to hospital, where it was put in plaster, and, returning to the house they decided they should take a photograph.

We stayed the night at Weston-super-Mare on the way down, and, to our great surprise and excitement, Mother and Dad took us to Bristol aerodrome and we all flew in a De Haviland Dragon across to Cardiff and back. It was, of course, the first time any of us had flown. It was terribly noisy, but it was thrilling to look down and see the Bristol Channel with its lighthouse beneath us. On the plane was a boy who lived at Weston, but went to school in Cardiff, travelling to school by plane every day!

Mother, Dad, Esmé and I then continued down to Sidmouth to a hotel on the seafront. It was one in a Regency terrace of hotels, apartments and houses, and it wasn't long before Esmé and I had made the acquaintance of a boy named Kelvin, who was staying in a neighbouring hotel. Imagine our amazement when, next morning, before we were up, he appeared climbing in through our bedroom window! All the more astonishing considering that our room was on the top floor; he had climbed out of his window and walked along the parapet, passing several other rooms on the way. We felt it was far too dangerous for him to make the return journey, and so, in all our innocence, Esmé put on her coat over her pyjamas and escorted him downstairs and out through the front door of the hotel!

It was a good holiday, and the three of us swam and walked and talked, and by the end of the week Kelvin and I had promised to write to each other.

Saturday July 8th was the official opening of Elmdon airport. Dennis, as a member of the R.A.F. Volunteer Reserve (R.A.F.V.R.) was taking part in the flying displays. He had obtained tickets for Mother, Dad and me, and it was the most wonderful day. The new airport building was shaped something like a plane, with a curved glass-brick nose (which contained the curving stairs) and sweeping wings extending out from the sides, to protect passengers from inclement weather. I was entranced, and so proud of my handsome brother in his khaki green flying kit.

He took me to Elmdon again, on my own, and bought me dinner in the restaurant overlooking the airport. He pointed out how every plate put before one was always carefully placed so that the crest was at 12 o'clock, facing you. I was duly impressed. He later left me to watch him fly off, I knew not where, and when he came back he told me he had been to Blackpool and back, following the main roads and flying round the roundabouts!

I loved him so much, and was so proud of him.

*

On Friday 18th August Dad took his summer holiday, and we all set off for Newquay. We stayed the night on the way down at Pedwell in Somerset, at a guest house where we had stayed before, its bedroom walls covered in tracts, salutary pictures of biblical scenes and cross-stitched proverbs, and where there was one flickering candle in a brass candlestick to light the way to bed. We loved its other-worldliness and timelessness.

Earlier, outside in the still, quiet heat of the late summer afternoon, Mother and I had encountered a young father carrying his little daughter piggy-back, and had stopped to talk. He was a charming young man, and so proud of his little daughter, who was just learning to talk and could now say her own name. So we asked her what her name was, and shyly she replied, "Hosha Fosha!" We looked enquiringly at her father, who translated: "Hazel Fisher!" We never forgot Hosha Fosha.

Arriving in Newquay in time for lunch on Saturday, the weather was hot and sunny, and I intended to get in as much swimming and surfing as possible.

1939: August

Thursday August 31st

Our holiday is over. We're home again - three days before we should be.

We were having a wonderful holiday. Den and I had made lots of friends, and I had spent all morning on a pedallo with a boy called Alan and I bounced back into the hotel slightly late to find everyone in the lounge, listening to the radio, and looking very worried.

Den turned to me and said with forced cheerfulness: "Well, Pat, it looks as though our holiday's over."

I didn't understand, but gradually from the snatches of hurried conversation I gathered that the schoolchildren were being evacuated the next day.

Then – "War has been declared!" I thought.

After dinner we threw clothes - hats and shoes and bathing costumes - haphazard into the trunks and cases. Den came into the room where Mother was packing: "Mother, someone's borrowed our surfboards. They aren't there!"

We did all we could to get them back, and in the end we gave the porter 2/- so that he could send them to us as soon as they turned up again. We left then, and started the long drive home, stopping for tea on the way. There was a loudspeaker in the café giving a constant stream of information on the situation from which I realised that we were not - as yet - at War.

Back in the car Den was a dear; but he is. He tried to make me laugh, as he was sorry for me and felt I might be worried and depressed.

We arrived home at midnight, and I saw my dear Sooty and took her up until I got into bed.

Friday September 1st

Hitler marched his troops into Poland.

Next morning I was up early, and I dashed round to Mary Dutton's to ask her what I had to do and what I had to take to school. She was very helpful and, after a long hug to Sooty, we drove off to the school with all my belongings.

We picked up a girl on the way, and arrived at school all smiling and laughing. Den took a photo of me in a wonderful pose and, after staying around for about an hour Mother, Dad, and Den left me to myself and my friends.

At 12.00 we all piled into the buses, and went to the station.

An engine puffed by, and then an express train full of surprised and enquiring passengers who peered at us through the grimy glass of the compartment windows.

At last our train came, and we were very pleased when we found it was like a bus and had a passage down the centre, so it was possible to see along the train. However, the train was so long it was nigh impossible to see the end. In one half there were boys from Moseley Secondary School, and we were in the other half.

We ate plums and chocolate, biscuits and sandwiches. It was a very hot day and we were all terribly thirsty, as we'd been told not to take any bottles of drink. The French mistress in our section of the train carried a small flask of water and she allowed us to drink from it, telling us to take a little and swill it round our mouths.

As we got out of the train, district nurses came up with a jug and a cup, and from this the whole school drank some luke-warm, sweetish water.

Buses took us from the station to the old Pate's School, where we were given two days' rations, and then we were taken to our billets.

As Esmé hadn't turned up, I was billeted with a girl from my form that I had had hardly anything to do with. Her name was Margaret.

We were taken to All Saints' Villas road, where an old lady of 80 answered the door, when the prefect who escorted us rang the bell. She said that the government had told her that she must not have evacuees, and so we turned away.

As we waited for a car to take us back to the school, an old lady came up and asked if we were waiting for anything. As the prefect related our experience the old lady gasped and said: "The poor dears, they must come and have tea with me."

The prefect said that she was afraid we couldn't go, and when the old lady heard who had refused us she was very surprised and said that she was her best friend and had been very anxious to have two evacuees, and, worried, she hurried off to ask her about it.

The car came at last, and we were taken back to the school and given tea. By now everyone but us had billets, and the mistresses were very worried, and so were we, but at last it was decided that we should go in Miss Squire's road; Eldon road.

So we were brought here to a little white house, ultra-modern, where we were deposited. I don't like the people very much. They are small and fussy.

We were shown to our room and to our dismay discovered that we had to share a single bed. We were not even friends, but, after discussion, decided that the only way to deal with the situation was to sleep 'top to tail'.

That night there were lots of flashes and flickerings in the sky above the horizon, and I thought: "The Germans are here, and fighting is going on somewhere in the distance". However, in the morning it turned out that it was only summer lightning that had lit up the sky.

2nd Sept   5 Crosbie Road
Saturday   Harborne

My dear Pat

    We were very pleased to get your postcard today and to know that you seem to be fixed up in quite a nice house or at least Mrs Inman sounds nice.

    Dennis had to go today, but luckily I am able to come home from the works at night at present anyway so your Mother will not be so lonely at night.

    Gran is coming to stay for a time tomorrow so that will be much nicer and she will be able to give a hand with the dark curtains that we all have to put up to prevent any light from showing in the road at night.

    When transport is a little more settled we will try and come and see you some Sunday but we have to wait and see if we can get petrol etc.

    We are enclosing a 10/- note for you in the letter we are sending tonight, so that you may get yourself some bramble jelly or any other thing you fancy.

    I should give the money to Mrs Inman, or a mistress to keep for you and ask her then for so much at a time.

    I know I need not ask you not to waste it, but you must always feel that if you ever want anything, more money etc, just let us know and we will send you it whenever possible.

    I wonder if Esmé has arrived yet, I hope for your sake that she doesn't stay in Scotland.

    Your Mother is waiting to go and post this so that you will receive it on Monday.

    With much love
    from
    Dad

Saturday 2nd.

    We are to share the buildings of Pate's Grammar School. They will use them in the morning, and K.E.S. will use them in the afternoons, and also Saturday mornings.

As the Inmans would not allow us to play in their garden, Margaret and I played ball at the school. As we walked back to Eldon road, to my astonishment I saw a tall, fair boy walking along with a little figure in black trotting beside him.

"That's Grandma!" I said, and rushed across, calling her name.

By amazing coincidence she was staying in Cheltenham with her nieces, Doris Flower and Nancie Halliday, and their sons, respectively Raymond (the tall, fair haired boy) and his brothers Neville and Derrick, and Nancie's son Sebastian. It was wonderful to see her. She said they were staying at Rossley Manor hotel, and after a brief chat we left them, and returned to Eldon road and, on my part, feeling less lonely and isolated.

Sunday 3rd.

Miss Squire called to see us, and when we came downstairs we all went into the lounge. It was the first time I'd been in it. It's got a row of elephants going over a bridge on the mantelpiece; the elephants get smaller and smaller from front to back until the last one, which is tiny.

Miss Squire had been talking to Mrs Inman. Now she turned to us and said: "Well, how does it feel to be at War?"

I thought she was joking, and so did Margaret.

We went out for a walk later and met Miss Leighton and asked her, and she told us it was true.

When we came back the Inmans were out and everywhere was locked up. We looked under the mat, in case they had left us a key, but they hadn't. It started to rain, so we sat in the wood shed until it stopped.

After it cleared up we wandered up and down the road a bit, and then I saw someone who looked like Mother. I had never seen anyone who looked so much like Mother. As we drew nearer she waved to us, and then I realised it <u>was</u> Mother. It was just wonderful to see her.

We had to wait ages for the Inmans to come back, and after having a talk with Mr Inman she left with Auntie Edith, who had driven her down.

Mrs Inman was standing in the hall as I closed the front door. She looked at me and said: "Well, I don't suppose you'll ever see your parents again."

I felt awful.

Later that day Mrs Inman told me someone had come to see me. When I went to the door, there was Grandma.

She said she wanted to speak to me alone.

When we were alone she told me she didn't think my billet was suitable for me, and she would try and get me moved. Then she told me to ask Margaret to speak to her.

When Grandma had gone I went through the back way into the garden. Margaret was standing on the kitchen doorstep with her hands on her hips.

"Well, of all the –" she began, and then as I said "I'm sorry", and went into the kitchen, she put her arms around me and burst into tears. I was jolly sorry for her. She soon stopped, though, and laughed it off.

We've eaten all our two days' rations, they haven't given us anything else except tea and bread and butter.

Monday 4th.

I awoke feeling very groggy, and when I stood up the blood rushed out of my head and I felt faint. I stumbled through the door and whispered, "Mrs Inman" and when she came out of her room I told her I felt ill.

She told me to stay in bed, and got Margaret out to make more room for me.

I asked her to send for Grandma, and when she asked for her name, I found I couldn't say it.

"Well, spell it," she said. But all I could spell was my own name, then I tried again and found I was saying the alphabet.

"It's something to do with houses", I managed to say.

"Windows", suggested Margaret, and then, "Doors?"

Grandma's name is Dawes, so I nodded, and I think they really did think I was going mad. I know I did.

The address was on a piece of paper in the dressing table drawer, and they took it and went out.

After coming to tell me they had managed to contact her they all left the room and closed the door.

Eventually Grandma came.

Wonderful, bright, cheerful, clever little Grandma; and she told me to get up.

"I can't", I told her, but she said, "Oh yes, you can".

I said I was going mad, and she said, "Nonsense, it's a bilious attack. Bilious attacks always affect people like that!" *(Of course she knew it was not a bilious attack, but, in fact, shock.)*

And so I got up.

62

Raymond was waiting outside with the car and drove us to their hotel.

I was humiliated by being sick in his (actually, probably his mother's) car, (luckily, it was only watery stuff) and when Grandma had settled me on her bed, I was sick again and again, until I felt terribly weak and tired.

As luck would have it, Grandma was changing hotels that afternoon, and so eventually I was once more loaded into Raymond's car and we drove to the Suffolk Hotel.

At last I was able to undress and get into bed. It had turned into a fiercely hot day, and Grandma opened the bedroom windows wide and drew the curtains, gave me some warm milk and aspirins and told me to go to sleep.

I didn't wake up until six o'clock next evening, when I heard a newsboy calling outside in the road. Then Grandma came in and asked me how I was, and gave me some cocoa, and I went to sleep again and slept until this morning. And now I'm up again and sitting on the balcony in the sun and feeling much better and not mad any more.

At tea time Doris and Nancie came with Sebastian to see Grandma.

He's a dear little chap - I suppose about two, or thereabout - and he crawled under the table and played there with his toy - car, I think - quite happily while everyone chatted.

Eventually Raymond came to pick them up, and we all got to our feet, except Sebastian, who contentedly played on under the table.

"Seb-a-a-h-stion, come out from under the table", his aunt Doris commanded. As she stood there, with little wisps of hair falling down from her smart upswept hairdo, it just sounded so ridiculous I wanted to laugh.

Anyway, he happily complied, and off they went.

5 Crosbie Road

My darling Pat

I am so delighted to know you are with Grandma. Isn't it wonderful how she happened to be in Cheltenham. It is lovely to know you are with her, and I am so glad to know you are better. It is quite a good thing in a way that you were poorly as you had had a very strenuous time of it, and some very quiet restful days are what you want. I am sending your paintbox, and several things to Moseley as Grandma says she can collect them from there.

Dennis has had a week's holiday and has gone to Llandudno with six other R.A.F. men. He was so delighted about it.

Gran is here staying for a few days, and oh by the way the luggage arrived safely today from Cornwall, but the surf boards haven't turned up yet, possibly they will come later, as the trains have been so full.

Esmé rang up yesterday, she wants to see you. I expect she will be in Cheltenham one of the next days, or she may even be there now.

Well darling it is getting late and I want to write a little note to Dennis. He is at 'The Dorchester Hotel', Llandudno.

Dad and I just send you heaps of love, and hope to see you soon.
With love
From
Mother

P.S. I haven't yet received the long letter you wrote, but the posts are still a bit funny so it may turn up but I can't reply to anything you may have asked.

Wednesday <u>Sept 6th</u>   Hotel Suffolk
Cheltenham Spa

My dearest Dennis,

Mother told me that you had had a week's holiday at Llandudno. I am so glad. Do enjoy yourself, dear. I am in Grandma's room. It is pink and gold and extremely pretty. All the furniture is very old fashioned and sort of bow-legged.

I suppose you will set to work as soon as you come back. Hitler will wish he had never fought the Poles when you appear.

Attaboy!

I only wish I could carry on the good work and become a nurse. Then all our household would be doing something.

But instead I am stuck here. Enjoying myself in grandma's company admittedly. But just longing to do something.

As I said before do enjoy yourself and if you feel like sending me some rock, please send me a small piece. But don't feel obliged to send any.

This is my fourth letter today. I wrote 1 to mother, dad and you. Two to Esmé, and then I received a letter from mother telling me your address.

So naturally I am dashing this off at top speed.

I met some unknown relations. Raymond 18. Neville 13. Derrick 11. Ray is a little younger than you, and Nev a little younger than I.

They are very nice, but not half as nice as you.

I would love you to write me a long letter if you feel so inclined. But don't write if you are enjoying yourself and don't want to be bothered.

We can see seven different roads from our balcony.

I am hoping Esmé will come soon as grandma wants to get me billeted with her.

I hope you are having a lovely time.

Tons and tons of love

Pat.

Thursday   Sherwood Private Hotel
                                   Craig-y-Don
                                   Llandudno

Dear Pat

I hear that you have been removed from your billet and are now convalescing with Grandma Dawes. Not to be out-done I have gone for a holiday myself.

After you had gone on Friday, I heard a calling up notice over the radio in the evening. (I got my uniform in the afternoon) and went up and got my gas-mask
.Next day I reported at 9 o'clock in the morning and after a short medical examination, we received our pay for August, then after two games of table-tennis, a game of darts and a glass of mild we were told to have three hours leave in which time I had a five course lunch at Lewis' and then got my kit-bag from home and my flying kit from Elmdon.

Sunday I reported at 10.30 and left at 11 o'clock with the rest of the day free (all at 16/6 a day) and Monday I reported at 9.30 and left at 10 o'clock.

On Tuesday I reported at 9.30 and at 10.30 we were told that we could have a week's leave (with pay) and railway warrants to our homes. So myself and eight others have taken a holiday at Llandudno with our rail-fare paid!

I came up by myself on Tuesday evening and on Wednesday I went down to Porth-y-gent and saw Dorothy and Olwen*.

In the evening the other blokes turned up and now Llandudno wonders what has hit it.

By the way you will be sorry to hear that the crisis has affected my appetite very badly. In fact I am eating twice as much as before. On Sunday I had two dinners, one at Moseley and one at Hall-green and two suppers, one at 5 Crosbie Road and one at the Ensells.

If you want to write in reply I think you had better address the envelope as follows.

>Sgt. D. F. Knight,
>c/o F. W. Knight Esq.
>5 Crosbie Road,
>Harborne,
>Birmingham 17.

And mark the envelope on the top "PRIVATE, PLEASE FORWARD".

>Your wonderful brother
>Dennis.

Two sisters he had got friendly with in Newquay

5 Crosbie Road

My darling Pat

I was so pleased with the drawing and can see there must have been a lot of work in it.

Do you know I still haven't had your letter. I wonder whatever happened to it. Isn't it funny?

I am sending your paint box along today, as you are probably wanting it. The rest of your things I am sending to Moseley.

Gran sends her love. She has been helping me ever so much. Dad and I send you our dearest love,

from Mother. xxxx

Sooty is ever so well, and I am so glad you are alright again darling.

5 Crosbie Road

Thursday

My dearest Pat

Thank you so much for your lovely long letter. It took me quite a long time to read it out to Dad, and now I am sending it on to Dennis. By the way his address is not The Dorchester. It is 'Sherwood House', Craig-y-don, Llandudno. I am sending you a P.C. he sent.

I do so hope you get with Esmé. She rang me up as soon as she got back from Scotland and said she could be happy anywhere providing she could be with Pat.

I am writing this letter in great haste as we want to catch post for the two parcels of clothes etc. I will send you things from time to time.

Do you know if I were you and Margaret I should tell one of the mistresses how you were locked out of the house at Eldon Rd, and how you only had bread and butter, and most of all how they said you probably would never see Dad and me again. I don't like to think any other child could be told that, when it isn't true. I think it is positively dreadful of them, when you have only been sent there for a time for safety, and so that you can carry on with school.

Don't worry about us, we have got all our arrangements cut and dried and Dad says this dug-out is the safest place in Harborne. I don't feel a bit scared about it, but we are taking <u>every precaution and care</u>.

Should Dad have to stay at the works which he might possibly have to do, later on, because of the shortage of petrol, I think I should close this house for the time being and come to live at Cheltenham, if I could get a room - no matter how small, I wouldn't mind that.

Well darling I must go. This is not one of my long letters, it is just one to accompany the parcel. Give Grandma my dearest love and tell her everyone this end are well and cheerful, and I spoke to Aunty D. again this morning.

Sooty is very well and quite alright in every way.
With dearest love
From
 Mother

September   Hotel Suffolk
    <u>Friday</u>   Cheltenham Spa

My dearest Dennis,

I wrote to you at the Dorchester Hotel as Mother said that was where you were. But now I realize where you are so I am writing to 5 Crosbie Road because you made it clear that was where I was to write to.

Yours was a lovely letter, I thought it was so cheerful.

Mary asked me to send you her wishes for your good luck, and naturally I send mine.

I hope you had a <u>very</u> happy holiday, and I hope you saw Dorothy more than once.

I suppose you wore your uniform all the time you were at Llandudno.

How proud I should have been to be walking along by your side!

Esmé wrote and told me she was coming down today. But she has not arrived. Excuse my squiffy writing but grandma is doing my hair.

It is Saturday now. We are going to town to do a spot of shopping.

I have just completed a letter to gran. I don't know if you know, but the fountain pen I am writing this with cost only 3d.

If you would like one send me 3d and I will send you the pen.

I must comment again on your letter. It was lovely.

I am afraid we are going out now.

Love (and heaps of it)

clumsy Pat.

September   Hotel Suffolk
    Saturday

Dear Mother and Dad

Thank you so much for the clothes etc. I don't really need the panama any more. Can I throw it away? Please send my blue halo hat.

I expect you are all well, and if not I hope you will soon be better. Esmé wrote and said she was coming but she didn't. Later I received a letter from her <u>saying someone told her there was no room in Cheltenham and she would have to stay where she was</u>.

I got <u>very</u> het up and dashed off a lettercard and a postcard to her telling her Miss Baker had reserved a room for the two of us together. I told her it was quite alright to come, and asked her to come by train either tomorrow or Monday.

We went down to town today. I looked around to see if I could see anything to make for you but did not know what you liked. Write and tell me (please).

I sat on some wet paint and have got my buff coat striped with white now!

Did you know some famous person said the war would be over in 4 weeks? S'truth!

I had a very funny letter from Dennis which I will show you at Christmas.

I'm going to save up my firework money (which I definitely expect dad to give me as soon as November comes round) and buy big presents for you all. (I'm going to try and save that 10/- too!)

I can think of nothing to say although if I saw you I should be brimming over with news.

So - until we correspond (!) again

Tons of love

Pat

P.S.   Sorry gran had a longer letter but I started hers a few days ago. It won't be long till I write again. Tell gran to write.

10th Sept Sunday   Works Laboratory

My dear Pat

I had to come to the works this afternoon to see that some testing was done, so I thought I would pass away the time in writing to you.

I heard you say a few words on the phone to your Mother a few nights ago, it does make Cheltenham seem so much closer doesn't it.

I spent the morning blacking out the garage windows because when winter arrives and I want to do something or other to the car, it is illegal now to show any lights, so now I hope I shall be able to work there in more comfort with the lights on. I shall try it out tonight when it is dark to see if any lights show outside at all.

Your Mother went down to town the day before yesterday and bought two pairs of shoes for herself and some pyjamas and pants for me, as very shortly prices will probably go up.

We went down last night and I ordered a new suit as they too will be very much more expensive very soon.

Dennis is still at Llandudno. We expect him home again on Tuesday and I expect he will sleep at home that night anyway, after that I suppose he will have to report for duty.

Young Vizer *(the Vizers lived across the road from us)* has gone as a dispatch rider, his Mother said that later he expects to go out to Palestine to drive a 40 H.P. car, a nice job it will be won't it?

I took about 80 yds. of corrugated paper home from the works last week, so what with that and some green curtain material we bought, you wouldn't know we had a light on after dark.

We have mown the lawn three times since we came back from Newquay, but it still doesn't look quite right, not as good as when you did it, still if the weather keeps fine I may find a little more time to spend in the garden.

All the goldfish are still alive and look very well.

Sooty looks very fit and when I left for the works this afternoon was just about to finish a leg of mutton.

Your Mother and I have done quite a lot of walking lately as we are trying to save petrol, we both should be feeling very fit shortly.

Would you like us to send you the Picture Post & Illustrated occasionally, we could if you wish make up a parcel once a month say and send you all of them up to date, that is if they don't weigh too much for the post.

Your Mother wants to go to the post with some other letters so goodbye for the present.

Gran sends her love
With love from
Mother & Dad

Tuesday 12th

    Esmé and I were billeted with Mr and Mrs Thatcher. There were two kittens under our bed. She moved them. The cat's name is Tibby.

Tuesday   5 Crosbie Road
Sept 12th 39

My dearest Pat
I heard from Grandma this morning that you are in your new abode and that Esmé is with you. It seems almost too good to be true that Esmé is with you. Write and tell me everything about your new billet, whether good or bad as I want to know all. Tell me whether you and Esmé are sleeping together, what you do with yourselves, what you have to eat, how far it is to the school and well, just everything. Grandma says in her letter what a nice place you seem to have and how nice the people seem. Tell me what happened to Margaret and whether she is happy, also that girl who was billeted alone with the people out most of the time. You know, the girl who had been crying. Don't forget, I am so interested to hear. Tell me also who does your washing and mending for if it falls to the lady of your house, something must be done about it. If that is the case make it <u>all</u> into a parcel each week and send it home and I will put it all right and send it back to you. This I am afraid is very much a business letter but I am getting it all off my chest at once, and haven't half finished yet. Here is a bit more.

1   If you find your hair is a lot of trouble, I should have it cut, but keep the hair.
2   When it wants washing always go and have it done at a hairdresser.
3   <u>Don't</u> go out after dark, and <u>don't</u> go exploring any dangerous parts.
4   Be sure and help the people of the house in every way you possibly can, for two extra girls in the house must make ever such a lot extra.

And now for a proper letter -
Dennis has just been in for lunch, he looks very well and cheerful. He has been given some more leave as they are so full up with men at the moment that they can't cope with them all. Am sending you some little photos, you can keep them.
Of course we don't see much of anyone because of the petrol shortage and also the black-out at night, and we don't hear very much, because we are all so specially asked not to telephone. However we are all very well and cheerful, but I must say I am looking forward to the end of "this 'ere war", so that we can all resume our normal life again. Aunty Edith has taken up ambulance driving and is spending her time in practising on motor vans, and soon is to try a Midland Red bus.
What do you think I have bought myself? A bicycle!!!!! You see, already we are having to go and fetch our own provisions and I found I couldn't carry heavy parcels, so I have this bicycle with a bag on the back, and the bag off your bicycle on the front. As a matter of fact I have given your old bicycle in part exchange - a very small part - but when you come home you shall either have this bicycle or a new one. This is a Dawes full size ladies, but no swanky gadgets such as three speed or anything like that. It is quite nice looking, but plain and - well just very useful - I go into the village round Wentworth Rd, for safety, and when I actually get into the village, I walk, I want a bit more practice before I do anything else.
Sooty is very well, and seems devoted to Gran's bed, she is always there. Go through this letter, or rather the beginning of this letter, and answer my questions, and also tell me what has happened to Kelvin. Is he still at his own school? Also are the Winfield girls* in Cheltenham? Thank you very much for your last letter and in fact all your letters. Cheerio, and give my love to Esmé. I am so glad you are together.
Lots of love,
Mother
Our doctor's daughters, who also went to KEHS

September
Wed
                                                                        "Coltham"
115 Welland Lodge Rd
Cheltenham Spa

Dear Mother

    I received your letter this morning, but as I was in rather a hurry I did not read it immediately, but when I called on grandma I read your letter to her. (I called on her before school).

    The people we are billeted with are awfully nice. They are two brothers George and Arthur. A. is married to Mrs Thatcher, and George comes to stay occasionally.

    He is recuperating from a bad leg. He jumped over a wall and the top gave way. So he has been ordered quiet.

    Esmé and I are sleeping in a huge double bed. I am sure it is really a double double bed. Yesterday Esmé and I walked through the tiny lane next door to our house through the gate that led into the field. Past the farm where we fed Rover the sheep-dog, Ginger the race-horse, the hens and where we had meant to feed Tim the collie. (Please excuse me writing in pencil, but my pen needs ink.) Then we turned out of the field and down the road to Prestbury. There we caught the bus to Cleeve Hill (1d) then we roamed over the hills and ate biscuits. We came home and climbed into the house through the window as Mr and Mrs Thatcher were out: we dumped our clothes and went over completely new houses. *(The Thatchers' house was on a new estate which was still being built.)* Then we came home and had a lovely supper.

    I don't know if I told you but when we arrived we found the cat they had, had had kittens 3 weeks ago.

    We have lovely food. Raymond brought us some apples which we had baked and stewed for pudding.

    Margaret is still there and I think has a slight grudge against me. The girl who was billeted alone went to her friend's billet where she is for a month.

    Mrs Thatcher asked me for my washing today. She does it. I forgot what you said and now she's doing it.

    I <u>won't</u> have my hair off, although Esmé wants me to.

    Kelvin's school has closed down, but he is still there. You know he was going in for his School Cert. this next term, or was it the one after? Anyway he'll miss it.

    The Winfields are coming on the 19th.

Oh mother! I was going to write to you to ask you to send me my bike on the train. It is only 3/8d at the company's risk and 2/8d at your own.

There are such nice rides here. <u>Please</u> let me have a new one here, when I come back home on the train it could come with me.

So send me the money for it, or else send me a postal order or <u>something</u>.

Esmé is sending for her bike.

Yours was a lovely letter. Grandma gave me her photos of Den.

Please may I have a large one?

I'll pay.

If you possibly can come and see me do so because it's a marvellous place. A housing estate right plonk in the country.

Don't think I'm annoyed about the bike episode, but pleased that I can have a new one. 'Cos why not now (*rather*) than when I come back?

I am very afraid I must end off now because I have 3 more letters to write.

Lots & Lots & Lots of Love
    Pat

We have discovered that the New School, where we shall soon be going, is down the road, behind the houses, and there is a little lane between two houses that leads to it.

            Sgt.D.F. Knight
            R.A.F.
            5 Crosbie Road
            Harborne
            Birmingham 17

Dear Pat

I don't feel at all in the mood for writing a letter but I suddenly heard my conscience say, quite plainly, "You'd better write to that little squirt, Pat, and give her some good brotherly advice; otherwise she'll go and get herself into mischief - and that would be terrible!"

So here I am writing in a very bad humour, and in my glasses. I found my glasses upstairs and they make me look so distinguished that I simply have to wear them.

Doubtless you are all agog to hear news from home so just to pique you I shall tell you nothing of the sort!

I have just had my skates reground and now find that I cannot stop suddenly when emergencies present themselves as they feel so different <u>from</u> before.

I underlined the word "from" just to remind you not to make that unforgivable mistake, namely to say "different to". And whilst we are on the subject of grammar: I went back to the office on Wednesday to do a spot of work for my living. Now the income-tax johnny Mr Haines is about the only fellow at the office educated to my standard. For instance the other fellows all say "If I was you" and so on. Anyway it so happened that on Tuesday Mr Haines had been instructing another fellow, Mr McLintock, in the art of using the subjunctive in conditional statements. To which Mr McLintock, I believe, replied that no one would ever bother to think whether the subjunctive were to be used.

Anyway on the Wednesday Mr McLintock noticed that I was working on the papers of the Estate J. D. Burbidge deceased, so he said to me "What, isn't that finished yet". To which I replied "I wish it were." Mr McLintock bounded out into Mr Haines' office and shouted "Knight has just used a subjunctive. Think of it!"

I must break off now as the Queen is talking to me ------------ over the wireless.

She finished off her speech with the British National Anthem, the French National Anthem and the Polish National anthem.

I think I've written quite enough so Cheerio! and be careful

Love from <u>Dennis</u>.

It must be a month since I last wrote my diary (Dennis came down for the day and I've just seen him onto a bus, and now I feel a bit flat).

Since I last wrote, we've been to the farm quite a bit, and know the names of the animals. Ginger is a sort of racehorse. Tommy and Violet are carthorses. Tim is a collie and Rover a sheepdog.

Jack, a boy on the farm, showed us the racecourse, and told us the animals' names. We didn't like him much, but it was nice to have someone to show us around.

The Thatchers have a charlady called Mrs Lively, and one day she asked us to tea. When Mr Thatcher told us she lived in Bouncers Lane, we didn't believe him. But it's true! She lives in a sort of modern cottage, and when we arrived we were shown to the parlour, which had a huge dresser all down one wall, and on it were all sorts of ornaments: tea pots like cottages, egg cups like chickens, china flowers and children and dogs and goodness knows what else.

Her youngest son (17) came in and he turned out to be very humorous. Her daughter Rene (21) was tall and lanky, with glasses, but she too was amusing. The next person to come in was Joe, who was staying with them. He was a jockey, but as it was the wrong season, he had to work. The last person to come in was George, who was the eldest son (25). As we were having tea it turned out that George had a pig.

He said it was in the allotment, so we went to see it. We crossed the road and went through the garden of a public house. After climbing over a low wall we came to the allotments and there in a small corrugated iron sty was the pig.

He said it was a gilt which was a sow which had not yet had piglets. He said also that it was still young. But it was a horrible thing, and he gave it an apple which she dropped and he told us to give it to her. We would not and he laughed. When we got back to the house Mrs Lively showed us her hens.

Then we had a cheery evening, and at last George and Joe escorted us home.

Thursday
Sept 21st
                                                              5 Crosbie Road

My darling Pat
 I am wondering how you got on over your bicycle. Dennis seemed to think the one you and he saw would probably have gone by the time you went to say you would have it. I also wonder if Esmé has had hers sent on,

for yours won't be much use unless she has hers as well. When you both do get them do be very very careful about the traffic, and don't go into Cheltenham town on them, only go country runs and then only together for there are a lot of very undesirable people around these days.

Weren't you mightily surprised to see Dennis, and don't you think he looks jolly nice in uniform? He thoroughly enjoyed his day with you and Esmé and likes Mrs Thatcher very much indeed. He thought the position of the house charming and in fact felt ever so happy about everything. Poor old Barrie Matthews has a pretty rotten billet. I don't know what they are going to do about it, but he is such a dear boy that I hope he soon gets one more suitable. Vivian came to tea on Tuesday, he is now at the H.P. factory studying brewing chemistry. He tried to join up but was told to stay where he was for the time being as they had so many recruits they didn't know how to cope with them. Dennis also heard today that the Government don't wish to take boys of eighteen just yet awhile, anyway not for active service, so I don't know what they are going to do about him. The R.A.F. told him today that they hoped they wouldn't call on him for some good time yet, so Dennis says he doesn't want to knock about doing nothing whilst he is waiting, he is going to the office to go on studying whilst he is waiting, but I think he is supposed to stay in uniform.

You know someone burned two holes in his sports coat whilst we were at the sea. Dad claimed from the fire insurance as it was a new coat and got £1.19.11 for it. He wouldn't have claimed but for me.

Mrs Morris rang up yesterday, she said Ann wanted to know all about you and wanted your address. I told Mrs Morris I had sent on a letter from Ann to you, but didn't know whether you had received it as you have been poorly and have had so many changes of address. Ann very much wants to hear from you. Ann, Margaret and Ian all go to the same school, and Ann says it - the school - badly needs you there to cheer it up a bit.

I saw Grandma this morning, she is having a big dug-out put in her garden. The men are hard at work on it now. Uncle George has one in his garden big enough for twelve people, but I have seen it and must say I like our compact little one best. It somehow looks more homely.

Talking of homely - I have put a small net curtain across the kitchen window, it was so exposed and now that we are using that room so much it wanted to be a bit more private. I felt rather guilty about it for I know you don't like net curtains but really it looks quite pretty.

Sooty is still very well and is eating ever so well. How is your cat there, and her two kittens, they are so pretty, and look so healthy.

Please remember me very warmly to Mrs Thatcher, she is such a dear, do all you can to help her. I am so glad you and Esmé are with her.
Give my love to Esmé.
With dearest dearest love
from
Mother.

Wednesday   115 Welland Lodge Road
September

Dearest Dad,
Dearest Mum,
I went to the bike shop and reserved my bike, I am sending the bill to you.
The name of the shop is on the bill.
I have had the bill made out in mum's name, as I thought she would like a bill. I expect it will make her feel quite grown up. Does it mum?
Don't you think my writing has improved? It is like Dad's now- almost unintelligible. I have taken 4 photos of Ginger, 2 with Esmé, one by himself and one with the 2 cart-horses.
I have just written to Grandma I asked her to send me some - to make a - I am sorry I did not mean to tell you. I might as well now - no I won't!
Well I hope it is coming soon.
Please write very soon.
Heaps & Heaps of Love
Pat

Friday   5 Crosbie Road

My dearest Pat

Just had a beautifully written letter from you - just like Dad's writing. I am so glad you got your bicycle, am sending the cheque off straight away - I feel ever so grown up. Will send you a form for your bank to sign so as to refund money to Dad. Will send your list to Cornishes. Yours in great haste.

  All my love, Mother

(Before each school year began at K.E.S., we were sent a long list of books that we would need. It was something I looked forward to immensely, and it probably was a considerable influence towards my love of books.
Perhaps because of the international crisis and then war, it seems that the book list, or perhaps the ordering, had been delayed.)

Sunday   5 Crosbie Road

My dear Mother - Pat (my mistake?)

    I am very sorry you don't like my writing, but still you are not the only one, for the manager at the works could never read it and said I had better have a typist, and so of course since having a typist I haven't had much practice at writing.

    I suppose you have had the cheque for your bicycle. You had better let me have the receipt when you get it.

    We saw Mr & Mrs Dutton last night, they said they saw you last Sunday, and you looked as if you had lived in Cheltenham all your life.

    Your Mother and I went by bus this afternoon to Highfield Rd. and then walked to Moseley to see Grandma.

    They are building quite a good dug-out in the garden like ours but twice as long. They have also gas proofed the cellar, so I suppose if it is a wet night they will go into the cellar and if it is dry to the dug-out.

    They have rationed petrol now and until I know whether I am allowed any extra, over and above the 6 gallons per month, I cannot use the car for anything but going to the works, and the 6 gallons will only last me about 12 days, so I may be the next to buy a bicycle.

    Dennis was home to dinner today but has gone since.

You haven't said whether you have spent the 10/- I sent you, but in case you are short or want to buy any necessities I am sending you another in this letter. You mustn't get extravagant but I always want you to feel you have some to spend. I should buy a padlock for your bicycle, so many are being stolen, but you must never on any account be out on it after dark and <u>don't leave it around</u>.

If all goes well we shall try and get over to see you in about 3 weeks' time, that is if I can manage to get a whole Sunday off and I think it can be arranged. It won't be by car though, but by train, so in the meantime we shall have to find out how often they are running.

They have reopened the Harborne picture house, although we haven't been. They have to close by the way at 10 o'clock.

We have just been out in the garden tidying up a little for the winter. The goldfish are all still alive, at least all that were alive when we went to Newquay.

Remember me to Esmé.
With love from all
Dad

Saturday   115 Welland Lodge Rd
September 23   Cheltenham

Dear Mother & Dad (& Dennis if he is there)

I received the cheque and the other letter this morning. I am going for my bike this afternoon.

If you have time please look for my fountain pen. It is mottled black and gold I think. Please try and find it, this one is no good. It is the 3d one, and it has served its purpose.

I am bored stiff. There is nothing to do on a wet weekend. Although Mr Thatcher has a car it is only a very old one and tiny too. He is also at work and so we have to amuse ourselves.

It is jolly cold here when we wear summer frocks, but I want a fairly warm long sleeved something, not too warm.

By the way I have the bike now.

I am sending some dirty clothes soon.

Please write soon, a long interesting letter, also pop over and see me.

Esmé's bike hasn't come yet, but it is coming (I hope).

It is Sunday morning and I don't know what we are going to do this afternoon.

Ask grandma if she received my letter, because I want an answer soon as if she hasn't got it I shall get it from Woolworths.

Write and tell me if she has it. If she hasn't I shall probably want some pocket money.

To buy some stuff to make a rug. Will you like that?

Oh! I don't know what to say. I just go on writing 'cos I'm so bored.

Boredly Yours
Pat

P.S. Keep it dark but look! 100000000 times those each
xxxx
xxxxxxx
xxxxxxxxx
xxxxxxx\xxxxx
xxx

P.S. I have just received the gym dress. I don't know whether it fits yet. If it doesn't I'll send it back. Thanks awfully for it.

There was something else I wanted to say. Now what was it? - don't forget my pen.

Heaps of Love
Lots of Love and all the love in the world
Pat

Sept 25th Thursday   5 Crosbie Road

My dearest Pat

I am sending you the photo of Dennis. You can choose just whichever you like but only one. If you find you really need another frock, a warmish one with long sleeves you can get one, but don't get it unless you find you need it, and then get a useful one that would do for Sundays, something like the little blue-green one, only in a different colour and with long sleeves. Have you had the blue-green one cleaned yet, if not either send it home with next washing or have it cleaned there, because when last I saw it, it needed it <u>terribly</u> badly.

I had another awfully nice letter from Mrs Thatcher this morning. I like her most <u>awfully</u>, she really is a dear.

Well, darling I am going to write to Mrs Thatcher and Esmé now.
With all & all & all & all my dearest love
from Mother.

P.S. Dad has just said that he hopes to come over on Sunday week to see you. Won't it be lovely. Let me know if there is anything you want.

Dennis, having stayed with his friends in a hotel in Llandudno, returned to Birmingham and decided to stay at a hotel in Solihull, close to his old school friends and the aerodrome, believing that his call-up would come at any moment.

Thurs Sept 25   The Royal Oak Hotel,
High Street,
Solihull,
Warwickshire

Dear Pat,

Knowing how terribly sad you are apt to get the moment my back is turned or my attention is withdrawn I have snatched a hurried second from my labours to write you this epistle.

You remember the last thing you saw of me was happily catching the Birmingham bus, well when we'd got properly started I found I was on an ordinary bus and not a long distance bus at all! It took me two and a half hours to get to Birmingham.

I got so fed up with doing nothing that I finally went back to the office to do a bit of work, (keep me out of mischief and save money into the bargain) but today I woke up so late that I decided not to go to the office after all, so I rang them up and told them I wasn't coming as I had to report to the town centre at 11.30 A.M.!

I didn't say that it was tomorrow that I had to report and for pay parade at that!

And that brings me to another subject (Do you like the change in writing? I seldom keep to the same style all through a letter; it's so boring don't you think? Or don't you?)

Anyway to come back to our subject and talking of pay parades, I met a sergeant pilot from our Volunteer Reserve on the bus and he was evidently thinking of the pamphlet raids on Germany; anyway when I asked him when the next Pay Parade would be; he said "Paper raid? Why I believe there was one last night!"

As far as I can make out life in the R.A.F. consists of two things, Pay Parades and Paper Raids! S'funny isn't it?

Anyway it's time for bed so
Cheerio
With love from
Dennis

The Royal Oak Hotel,
High Street,
Solihull,
Warwickshire.

Dear Pat

I am writing this to you in very high spirits and the sitting-room of the Royal Oak Hotel.

I write in high spirits, not because of the stock of whisky and wines around me, but to tell you of my experiences as a skating ace.

I write in the sitting-room of the Royal Oak Hotel for no other reason than that I am sitting in the sitting-room of the Royal Oak Hotel, and as I'm sitting in the sitting-room I might as well write in the sitting-room as anywhere else, especially as a sitting-room is provided for the express purpose of providing room for sitting, and as I want to sit to be comfortable for writing I might as well make use of the sitting room in the sitting-room. Y'see? I mean to say, as I am sitting in the sitting-room of the Royal Oak Hotel it would be rather awkward for me to write in the dining-room of the George Hotel at the same time, and it would be foolish anyway, as as well as sitting room the sitting-room provides writing-paper;

Hence you find me, as I said before, writing in the sitting-room of the Royal Oak Hotel (and in high spirits).

And now having taken my time to get my position quite firmly fixed in your mind I shall have to leave to catch the bus to town.

Cheerio.

Well, here I am again sitting in the dining room at Crosbie Road one day later.

However to get back to where I started, No, not in the sitting-room, I mean in the first place. No I didn't say fire-place I said first place.

Anyway you will be glad to hear that I am now having lessons in dancing on skates and can almost walk. I have also done a little horse riding and theatre going in the meantime.

However I believe that in the near future I shall be posted to - who knows where? A little place by Neverneverhampton somewhere in ?!xy}g*land.

Cheerio for the present
Dennis.

October   "Coltham"
<u>Sunday</u>   Welland Lodge Road

Dearest Dennis,

I am sitting in the sitting room - ! No, as a matter of fact I <u>was</u> drawing in the drawing-room at 115 Welland Lodge Road. But the lure of your beautiful personality set me down and made me take up a pen and write to you.

I think the colours of your writing paper very cheerful. But what taste m'dear, what taste!

Mrs Thatcher treated us to the flics yesterday, and we saw "Blind Alley". It was very unusual.

Honestly Den, you are the loonyest loon I have ever come across. Sitting in the -
You said you were writing in high spirits. I should think, from what you wrote and the colours of the paper, that you were writing <u>after</u> being in "high" spirits. And the high spirits were now inside you. Tell me, next morn did you feel "low"?

Esmé and I have been riding a lot on our bikes, we have been about 20 miles but not all at once. Once we got up to about 25 mph.

I am listening to an RAF concert. Do tell me when you are called up where you are.

You lucky dog! To be able to go skating. If I come home for 1/2 term will you take me?

It's the "Hound of the Baskervilles" at the Gaumont this week, we are going to see it.

Lots and Lots and Lots of

Love Pat.

Tuesday   5 Crosbie Road

My darling Pat

I am writing this all lazily in pencil, as I have used nearly all the ink up in writing to you and must get some more tomorrow. I have just posted that card to you to say Grandma is sending you the rug things tomorrow. She has had an awful job in finding them as the house was so turned upside down when she was in Cheltenham. She still can't find the thing you do the rugs with - before I post this I will see if I have one, and if not perhaps you could get one in Cheltenham. I shall simply <u>love</u> the rug, and even if you only get part of it done we could finish it together at home, but get on with it as much as you can, whilst you are away. You are a <u>darling</u> to think of doing it. I shall love it.

Dad says he hopes to come and see you in three weeks time, we shall try and save enough petrol to come, but it we can't manage it we shall come on the bus or train. I had such a nice letter from Mrs Thatcher this morning, will you please thank her for it, she said ever such nice things about you and Esmé. You know you are very lucky to be there, it seems to be one of the very nicest billets in Cheltenham. Dad says he doesn't think this war will last very long. I don't think it will either, do you? We are already finding a little difficulty in getting sugar sent regularly with the grocery order, and of course coal, gas and light are all to be rationed almost straightaway - we shall all have to sit around in our coats.

By the way unless you write and ask for them I shall not send your green dresses back. I am sure they are not warm enough for you now. I have found a fountain pen which I think is yours, so I will send it along.

Has Esmé got her bicycle yet - I want to see yours, I expect it outdoes mine entirely, though I find mine very useful.

It is now Wednesday afternoon, nearly teatime. Your tunic has come so I will send it on to you straightaway if the post office is open. Hope it will fit you this time. If it is too long try altering buttons on the shoulders as that is such an easy way of shortening it.

Dennis is still around waiting to be 'posted', but he has <u>just</u> rung up to say his friend Baxter has <u>just</u> received a telegram telling him to go to Hastings. I think Dennis is quite envious, he says he wants to go and get on with his job of flying. He just loves planes, doesn't he?

I must go now and get the tea. I will send you the belt to the drill tunic tomorrow along with a photograph of Dennis, a big one that I have had especially done for you.

Goodbye for the present darling, and <u>heaps</u> and <u>heaps</u> and <u>heaps</u> of love from Mother.

Please give my love to Esmé and Mrs Thatcher as well.

October 1st   5 Crosbie Road
Sunday

My dear Pat

All being well you will see us next Sunday October 8th. We shall come in the car as I have quite a lot of petrol this month and shan't have again, as I had my tank filled before rationing commenced, so the only way I can use it up is to come and see you, as the coupons used are only for this month and must either be used or returned.

Dennis has had Vivian to tea here today, they are just having supper now and then Vivian is going home and Dennis back to his hotel at Solihull.

About the rug you are going to make, your mother says make it as large as you like, if it is too big for a rug then it will do for a bedroom carpet or if you are feeling very energetic for the lounge and dining room combined, or if you get tired it will do to stand the flower bowl on, on the dining room table. Daft aren't I?

*Your Mother, my wife that is, said something about black and gold and something else about bringing some back on Sunday with us, I expect you women understand what it is all about.

It is gold and brown I should like, only I have a little black wool and will bring it over (Mother).

Last night we went over to King's Norton to ask Margaret's mother if she would like to come with us, she was out but we left a note asking her.

This afternoon we went to see Esmé's mother *(this was quite an effort, as Esmé lived at Alum Rock, right over on the other side of Birmingham.)* to ask her if she would like to come along as well, she said Yes and is coming to stay with us Saturday night so that we can make an early start, and with luck we should be at Cheltenham somewhere around 11.30 am. Your Mother and I will take you out to lunch so try and find a nice place that is open on Sunday. I don't know exactly what Esmé's mother will do as we didn't think of asking her at the time.

We shall have to start back soon after 4 as we want to get back before blackout, but still I expect you will have had enough of us by then.

We went to Moseley this evening and on the way back came by KES. The girls school is full of soldiers and just as we were passing, they were changing the guard, and looked quite exciting, rather different to when you were there.

Sooty is as usual sitting on Gran's knee, no it isn't, Gran has just got up to get a bottle for her bed and has put it on your Mother's.

We are just going to have a game of rummy so must pop out and post this before it is too late.

With love from all
Dad

Oct 3rd   5 Crosbie Road

My darling Pat

Whoops and hurray for Sunday. Dad and I are so looking forward to seeing you again. We hope to be with you at about 11.30. Whoops & Hurray! We are bringing Margaret's mother with us and will leave her with Margaret on the way to you. I had a letter from her today saying how much she will like to come with us.

Whoops & hurray - darling Pat, I am glad Cheltenham is within distance of coming to see you. Wouldn't it be rotten if you were right down in Cornwall, or Northumberland, we couldn't possibly come then. Dennis is still around and about, but he doesn't sleep here, he just comes in each day for lunch, and today stayed for tea. He is quite disappointed each day when he finds he still hasn't been posted anywhere. I wonder which photo you liked. I shall be interested to know. Sooty has just jumped onto my knee and is nosing all around this letter. She is very well and I am taking great care of her. I bought her 3d of haddock today, and she ate the lot. Hope you haven't eaten any more green apples.

  Well darling, until Sunday.
  With all and all my love
  Mother

How is the rug progressing? I shall want to see it.

Sunday   5 Crosbie Road

My dear Pat
  And now I sit me down to write,
  to Helen Patricia Thingumibob Knight.
  Only a week today since we came to see you at Cheltenham, but what a difference in the weather today, rain practically all the time, in fact such funny weather that it was worth going to the works all day to pass the time.
By the way we never hear much of the "helpers" that were supposed to go with you. Are there any such persons, or is it the same as they said when they saw the first Okapi "There aint no such animal".
  I received my extra ration of petrol on Saturday for next month, it is for one gallon less than last month, so that if they do that every month, I shall have none at all in 10 months. By that time I shall be writing to you to borrow your bicycle, what shall you say about that.
  We thought how happy and well you both looked last Sunday and think how lucky you are to be with such nice people as Mr and Mrs Thatcher.
  We heard from Mrs Thatcher that Esmé has her bicycle, so that must be the reason we haven't heard from you this week, you must have been too busy riding to think of -riting.
  We went over to see Granma Dawes yesterday afternoon and inspected their new dug-out. It is similar to ours, only twice as long, fitted with electric light and all modern conveniences. It is big enough for a bed,

a table to play cards, or at a pinch Auntie Winnie could get her piano down.

I was stopped three times today by the sentry at the works and had to show my pass, I should have thought he would have recognised the red Rover by now as it is the only red car at the works.

The steamer you bought has proved most useful, your Mother put the dinner all in it and then went to church and at night we always fill it with water, to keep a supply of drinking water, should there be an air raid and the mains be cut.

So little happens here that I am enclosing a few jokes to fill up.

Sooty caught two field mice in the garden this week.

With love from both of us

Dad

Thursday   5 Crosbie Road
Oct 12th 39

My dearest Pat

We have finished lunch and washed up so now I am going to write to you so as to enclose my letter in the parcel of your laundry. It is a nice arrangement to have it home, it gives me a good chance of looking things over and mending wherever necessary.

We did enjoy our visit, I had a perfectly lovely day, but Dad, as you know, felt rather groggy. When I got home I took his temperature which was 100.4 so he went to bed with two aspirins and stayed there all day on Monday. But on Tuesday he was back at the works and is quite alright again now. We went to the pictures last night - the first time since war was declared, but there were not many people in the place, I think everyone is rather scared of air raids. When we came out we thought the door was closed, it was so dark it looked as if there was a dark door in front of us. It was quite fun really, Dad and I put our arms around each other's waist and just barged ahead. The picture we saw was "The Three Musketeers". It was quite amusing and lively.

Have you heard any more about coming home for half term? Let me know just what seems to be expected of you. I think you will probably be a bit bored here now, as it is considered rather dangerous to go far from home, we still don't know what old Hitler might have up his sleeve, Mrs Thatcher says you are hoping to go to Lewis' and the Ice Rink, but we shall have to see. Neither of those two places would be very nice should we happen to have a raid, and old Hitler might just be waiting to see if anything comes of this Peace proposition, and then might launch his attack.

I know I keep around here as much as possible, though I did go to town yesterday - chiefly to get your book and order some more photographs.

I hear Esmé at last has her bicycle. I expect you will have some jolly nice rides together now, but don't stay out when it is the least bit dusk, and do be mighty careful to whom you speak, and don't on any account go riding off with anyone who asks you to. You absolutely must have Mr or Mrs Thatcher to OK it first. This is not just being fussy, you and Esmé don't know of the rotten things that could happen to you, and you must be careful of what you are doing.

It is a perfectly glorious day here today, the sun is shining and everything looks happy and gay. Dennis has just come in and wants me to embroider the Quintuple Alliance badge on a chairback cover. He has drawn it, quite a big affair, and wants me to do it by Sat. as they are having a meeting over at Billy's. It isn't just going to be a rushed piece of work, and he is chattering about it all the time - you know, Dennis-wise! He is a funny creature isn't he?

How is the rug progressing? Have you done any more? It will take you ages and ages to do, but it will be simply lovely to have when at last it is finished. Don't forget to let me know what happens about the half-term holiday and don't attempt to cycle home. Now don't do this whatever you do, will you. You see I don't know how far I can trust you and Esmé where madheaded schemes are concerned. I haven't forgotten Esmé's dip in the reservoir, in her new frock. Give her my love and to Mrs Thatcher too, and tell Mrs Thatcher I was very pleased to have her letter. Well darling, are you still keeping your hair gleamingly brushed, it looked ever so nice on Sunday.

With heaps & heaps & heaps & heaps of love
From Mother.

Meanwhile, Dennis had written to Vivian:-

Posted 6/10/39

Phantasy

Oh! Vivian,
    What memories this happy name recalls,
    What visions of a sunny past,
    Of hectic hours in pleasure spent,
    Of simple joys, of laughs – and even tears.

But Vivian,
    The thunderclouds of war have broke,
    The bloated pomp of foreign martial power,
    Has scorned the promised word of Britain's wrath
    Has trampled simple folk and innocent
    Has plucked the flowers of manhood from the land
    And thrown them broken in the flames of Death.

Yet Vivian
    Think not of this,
    But more of further peace to come. When we
    May dwell in sympathy with foreign friends
    And live secure from fear of frenzied strife.
    To prosper and increase

Yes Vivian
    Then shall Dominion unrestricted sway
    And just omniscience care for all;
    Until our sons become of fighting age
    And war again shall scourge the land.

D.K.

*

Mrs Thatcher has a piano and she lets Esmé and me play it - or try to! She's only got stuffy sort of music, so Esmé and I bought "There'll always be an England" and "I'm gonna hang out the washing on the Siegfried line", and now she's teaching us to play them.

Sunday   5 Crosbie Road

My dear Pat

  Both your Mother and I were very sorry to find that you were much more interested in "Hanging out your washing on the Siegfried Line" than in writing to us.

  We shall be getting jealous of Mrs Thatcher soon, for she appears to be giving you a very good time and we have no piano either to try and tempt you back.

  Really though we are absolutely delighted that you are so happy and don't mind about you not writing, knowing why you haven't. I wonder if you will be coming home at half term, I suppose it rests with the school and if you do shall see you one of the next days.

  If you don't come, don't worry for we will come over and see you again one Sunday in the near future, next time though it will be by train for it gets dark very early now.

  We went to see the "Four Feathers" at the Old Picture House, Harborne on Sat evening, you were quite right in saying it was good, for we enjoyed it very much, although I don't think it is very suitable for these times.

  We had a morning gardening this morning and planted the shelter all over with rock plants, so that if they all grow it should almost be covered next year.

  We had three fellows from the works here Friday evening to play bridge, quite a pleasant time was had by all, except tho' that Gran hid four bottles of beer that they brought with them and they didn't find them, till they went home.

  If you do come for half-term I have managed to save a few gallons of petrol so shall be able to take you for a run on Sunday. And Dennis is trying to get his bicycle back, so that you can go a ride with Mother.

  With love from all
  Dad

Wed Oct 18th   5 Crosbie Road

My darling Pat
           This is my very best note paper, just kept for an honoured few. How do you like it? *(It was, actually, torn out paper from a 'Jotter' pad.)* By the way I should very much like to see a sample of your note paper as I haven't heard from you since the Sunday we were over. Is it that you are too much occupied, too lazy or have you been spirited away. Anyway write and tell me why it is, and jolly well hurry up too!!
           I am wondering what you are going to do about the holidays, and when they are. I think I shall have to leave it to you, Mrs Thatcher, and the school to decide what to do. Of course I should LOVE to have you home for a while, but I don't want you to run any risk, and it is certainly difficult to know what the Germans may do, I think it is the travelling that is the danger - once here there is always the dug-out which is very strong and safe. People say it is one of the safest places in Harborne. I haven't heard anything from the school yet about payment, they seem very long winded and haven't yet even sent in the bill for the school term, though we have written and asked them for it. Perhaps they are so delighted to have you with them that they are not going to charge us anything.
           Dennis is <u>still</u> around - in fact, at the moment he is in a hot bath, whistling away for all he is worth. Very hard work, service in the R.A.F. Last week I embroidered a large badge on a chair-back cover for his Quintuple Alliance. It is a fine thing and was duly presented to the meeting, which they had on Sunday over at Billy's. He also presented that naval sword, in honour of Philip joining the Navy, but the sword is to hang in the office - Dennis' bedroom.
           Vivian and Billy both want to join something, but have been told they are not wanted at the moment, so they are are trying to settle down to civilian jobs, but Billy's mother told me that Billy is finding it very hard. Barry Matthews has been home for a weekend and Dennis saw him. He is a Corporal now in the O.T.C. and has had his billet changed at Repton and is ever so much happier. It will be nice, oh so nice when you can all return home in safety.
           I must tell you Sooty is in her usual place on Gran's knee by the fire. I think she is at last really getting fatter, Sooty not Gran. Yesterday I trailed all over the village to get her (Sooty not Gran) something tasty and came back with a cod's head which I boiled and took all the bones out and gave to her. She has finished the lot. I am sure her appetite has grown just

because there is a war on and it is difficult to get things. I have managed to get two penny worth of it today, so that will carry on until Friday.

Well my child, I must go now, I have nearly used all my pad. Don't forget to write and let me know what is happening.

With all my everlasting love
from
Mother.

October 26th - came home from Cheltenham for half-term.

Wednesday   5 Crosbie Road

My dearest Pat

…..I wonder how school went down this afternoon after your very full time here. We certainly got lots in, didn't we, and it made a lovely week. I feel quite as if I have had a holiday. I enjoyed it ever so much.

Dennis says he saw a big bomber over Birmingham at about nine o'clock this morning, one that he didn't recognise and he wondered if it was a German plane. I think he was quite glad to know you had gone off safely without any mishap at the last minute.

I wonder how Esmé and Mrs Thatcher liked your frock. I am glad we managed to get that…..

Well darling
With lots and lots of love
from Mother

Sunday   5/11/39   5 Crosbie Road

My dear Pat

It seems much longer than last Wednesday since you went back, it was very nice to see you and now we shall have to wait till Xmas and hope you can come back then, although we hope to come over to see you before then.

Dennis had a letter from the Air Ministry on Friday to say he won't be called up for some weeks yet, so he is coming to sleep at home now, commencing tonight.

We went for a run this afternoon round by Middleton Woods, had tea at the "Happy Hour" and called to see Gran on the way home.

She will be coming back here in a week or so, as soon as she is passed fit by the doctor and has had a rest.

We came back from Sutton just after black-out time, it was raining and it was the first time we had really had night driving. It is no joke and takes twice as long as at ordinary times.

I am sending you another 10/- for pocket money, let me know when you want some more, but make it last as long as you can.

We went to the pictures again last night, it was at the Royalty, so you may know it wasn't a very good film.

I have finished reading The Citadel since you went back, you were quite right it is quite a good book, much better than I expected to find.

Well cheerio till next Sunday.

With love from
Dad

Wed. Nov 8th   5 Crosbie Road

My dearest Pat

Oh, it is a rough and windy day, everywhere seems to be rattling and shaking, leaves are flying in all directions, but the air is lovely and fresh with that Autumn, earthy smell. I walked up to the bank this morning, it was far too wild a day to venture out on my "fiery steed", and now I am here alone with Sooty - oh no, I am not alone - the window cleaner has just come! He will be blown off his ladder if he is not careful. Sooty was a naughty thing last night, she just wouldn't come in when we went to bed but ran off into the darkness. I gave her two chances, long chances but no, she preferred to stay out. She turned up for her breakfast this morning, but has been a sleepy thing all day. That is the worst of her if she stays out at night. She is very well and has partaken of a huge fish meal.

You will probably be surprised to hear that Dennis has gone back to the office to fill in time. He isn't expected to be posted for several weeks now, and got fed up with all the prolonged waiting.

I think the Woods have left, there were two big furniture vans there today and the men were stacking them up with things out of the house. The Hemmings won't like it if they have gone, for the rent from that house was their chief source of income.

Will you please thank Mrs Thatcher very much for her letter and give her and Esmé my love.

With dearest dearest love to yourself darling. (Darling Pat, you are a nice little codie, aren't you)

from
Mother

5 Crosbie Road

My dear Pat

You must excuse note paper but I am writing this whilst I am at the Works on Sunday, and it fills in my time whilst I am waiting for the work to be finished, at least the work this morning for I have to come back this afternoon for a short time.

Mr Holder and I take it in turns, he came yesterday afternoon and I come today, next week it is the other way round and so on, ad infinitum or for the duration, whichever is the shorter.

Mother and I went to see "Three smart girls grow up" one day last week, it was quite a good film in its way, very light and suitable for these hard times, but I am not very keen on Deanna Durbin although I must say she has a good voice and as long as you don't look at her whilst she sings, the effect is quite good.

We seem to go to the pictures more than ever since the war and the last week or two the Harborne picture houses have been crowded, people seem to have given up expecting air raids, may they all be right.

Dennis gave your Mother a present on Sunday, a brace of pheasants, they had them for dinner yesterday. They had quite a feed especially as on Sunday evening three fellows from the works came to play bridge and brought your Mother a bottle of wine, and as it wasn't finished Sunday evening we finished it up yesterday for dinner. Dennis said it was a bit like Xmas.

When do you break up for your Xmas holidays, have you heard yet? And has anything been said about the girls coming home for the holidays?

I expect in any case we shall try and come over to see you once before that, although as it gets so dark so very early now I doubt whether we shall come in the car, I expect it will be one of the first Sundays in December for the Sunday after next is stock taking here.

By the way what would you like for a Xmas present, think it over and let me know, money, books, anything as long as it doesn't cost too much. *(Gran wants to know what you want from her.)*

(It is now Monday - Mother.) Last night *(Sunday)* at about 7.15 your Mother and I thought we would go to Moseley to see Granma, and as I wanted to save petrol we decided to go by bus. We took a bus to Highfield Road from Harborne and then walked down Highfield Rd and crossed Calthorpe Rd to catch the bus to Moseley.

Your Mother said they only went every 30 minutes and as we didn't know whether we had just missed one or not, we prepared ourselves for a 20 minutes wait, however it seemed a very *(very, very - Mother)* long 20 minutes and at last when we were getting fed up, someone came along and we *(I, Mother, not Dad - Mother)* enquired how often the Moseley buses went. Oh they said, they don't run on Sundays, they were stopped when war broke out.

So we had to come back and you can tell the time it took for it was 8.30 when we arrived back, next time we would risk the petrol.

We have had some more sandbags placed round our dug-out, so that it looks like a miniature fort. Mr Reynolds when he had finished it today, stood back to survey his handiwork and said it was the best and strongest dug-out of its size he had seen, and he quite thought any small bomb would make no impression on it, not that we want to try it out in that way.

We have bought six very old wine glasses today from that shop in Harborne, they were exceedingly old and very cheap so didn't like to miss the bargain especially as Dennis is making me a present of them. *(Nice of him, isn't it? - Mother.)*

They look awfully nice in our corner cupboard along with the glasses you bought me and the other glasses Dennis bought.

Well cheerio till next week.
With love from
Dad & Mother.
By the way Sooty likes porridge and sugar and warm milk. Isn't she a queer one? This letter is getting too long. So once again
All our dearest love
Mother & Dad

Wed. Nov 15th   5 Crosbie Road

My darling Pat
              I have just come back from taking your stockings to exchange them.
              I wonder if Tibby's kittens have arrived yet, and if so whether they are as pretty as the last ones. When I went out this morning I just couldn't get rid of Sooty. She followed me so far up the road that I thought she might get lost, so brought her home and dumped her in the garden, and started on my way again. I hadn't gone very far when there she was again following me just like a little dog. Eventually I did get rid of her, but when I came home again there she was coming up the road to meet me, and mewing to me at the top of her very small voice, and she simply flopped herself in and out of my feet all the way home, and now she is asleep on the chair beside me, having first devoured a herring which I bought specially for her and cooked and boned. Spoilt little beggar! I do it because she is <u>yours</u>. I am sure, quite, quite sure she is getting heavier.
              You ask if Dennis goes to the office in his uniform. The answer is in the negative. Wasn't he a darling to buy me those pheasants and give Dad the sherry glasses. They are lovely things, very old and beautifully cut, and were very cheap considering how beautiful they are.
  They are the following shape –
Like them, Yes?

              Reynolds has built a wall of sandbaggs *(sic)* in front of the dug-out, and covered them with

roofing felt. A very worthy effort. Though not very attractive to look at, but I think we should be very safe from harm, if an air raid does eventually come this way. Have you heard anything about Christmas yet, we <u>certainly want</u> you, and I will see there is a pud for you.

     With dearest dearest love, Mother

Nov. 22nd   5 Crosbie Road

My darling Pat

     Nov 22nd, good gracious we are nearly on to Christmas. I have almost finished making the puddings, having chopped suet, stoned raisins, cut cherries, weighed currants, sultanas, sugar etc, all I have to do now it to put in eggs, and brandy, mix and steam which I hope to do on Friday or possibly even tomorrow. Then I must make a cake but it is such a business to get the provisions, currants come one week, mixed peel the next, sultanas the following, and so on. However I think I have just about collected all the necessary stuff, and now it is only finding the right time to do it, which will probably be next Tuesday. I haven't the brandy for the puddings yet but I hope to get Dad to go along with me this evening.

     I wonder if you will be allowed to come home. There is such a lot in the paper and on the wireless about how important it is not to have the children home for Christmas. I think it is partly the government are afraid, that if once the children return home they will not return to the safer districts. Of course that wouldn't happen in your case and I certainly want my "Codie", in fact I shan't have Christmas unless my darling is here, for with this dug-out and in this area I think we are very safe, as long as one sticks around here or Moseley.

     Dad is trying hard to save petrol so as to either come and see you or come and fetch you home. I wonder which you will decide. Also send a list of things you want from Gran and from Dad and me - you can have money if you like. By the way how should you like to to invest your money in these new Government Bonds, they are quite as safe as the bank itself, but you get a little higher interest, and into the bargain you are helping England. They are just as safe as the bank, not the sort you can lose. Dad and I think it a very good idea, but think it over and let us know, and you could ask Mr Thatcher what he thinks about it.

I wonder if the kittens have arrived yet, tell me when they do and what they are like. Sooty is flourishing and eating ever such a lot, just because it is awkward to get. She still follows us every time we go out. I thought it funny at the beginning but now I think it a nuisance, especially when it is dark and we are going to the pictures.

I have your blue-green dress back from the cleaners, but I shan't send it unless you ask as I think it a bit cool. Hope the new one is a success. I must go and get tea, so Cheerio. Please give my love to Mrs Thatcher and Esmé.

.By the way you put 15/- in for each separate bond and in 5 years each 15/- is 17/6. It would make quite a lot on your money and is positively as safe as the bank.

With dearest, dearest, dearest love from
Mother

P.S. What a delightful mess you made of your blouse!!!

Monday   Crosbie Road
23rd Nov.

My dearest Pat

I have just written to Miss Barrie for permission for you to come on Thursday, and now I am leaving it to you and Mrs Thatcher, but if there is an attempt at an air raid on the Midlands you are not to come. If you don't come Dad and I will come over and see you soon.

Will you tell Mrs Thatcher that I thank her for her cheerful letter, and also please tell her that she must ask for all money owing to her, such as for shoe repairs, hair cutting, slides or anything that you may need.

I am wondering if there will be a letter from you in the morning telling me whether to expect you on Thursday.

Please give my love to all.
With the very dearest love to yourself.
From Mother

Monday   5 Crosbie Rd.

My dear Pat

We have just been to the pictures to see "Gunga Din", have you seen it, is jolly good with Cary Grant. Victor McLaglen and Douglas Fairbanks.

By the way I can get a day off to fetch you home at Christmas, now which would you rather I did, come to see you say next Sunday week or come and fetch you home for Xmas.

Of course it all depends on whether you are allowed by the school to come home then, you had better write almost immediately and let us know what you wish and what the school are doing in the way of Xmas holidays.

Mother wants to know if you have been having an ink fight whilst wearing your green blouse, as she can't get the ink stains out.

Mother has bought a very swagger new hat, very chic, like an inverted saucepan with no bottom and worn upside down, it looks better than it sounds though.

Gran still wants to know what you want for Xmas and so do we, for you haven't answered my last letter yet, in fact I don't believe you ever trouble to read them, I expect you just look to see if there is a 10/- note in and then throw it away.

Well you had better read this for there is no note in it, because I haven't heard yet that you have spent the last, I hope not anyway as you shouldn't spend above 2/6 a week anyway, unless for necessities.

Well cheerio
With love from both of us, to both of you
Dad

Nov 9th - 23rd

Dear Mother & Dad

I am listening to ITMA, it is good isn't it? I should get Radio Times, there are such a lot of good things on the radio. I have just been doing the rug.

I spend most of my time reading David Copperfield.

E. and I rode to Tewkesbury and back, 20 miles in all. Do you think it is all right for me to cycle. Some people seem to think it is bad for growing girls to cycle too much. So I would like your opinion on the subject.

E. and I went for another ride up over Cleeve Hill the other day, I don't know if I told you.

Mrs Thatcher thought Tibby would have her kittens a week ago. They haven't come yet.

What would you like for your Christmas presents? I would like to knit them if poss. But I would rather give you something you wanted and not knit it than knit something for you that you didn't really want.

We had pheasant for dinner on Saturday, and went to Mr and Mrs Thatcher's friends Mr and Mrs Palmer and their son Michael on Friday. On Sunday E. and I went to Mr and Mrs Townsend. (Den will tell you who they are.) We had a lovely time - we went to the station to see Brenda (Esmé's sister) and Eric (Mr and Mrs Townsend's son, also Brenda's boy friend) off. The station was all blacked out. It was most scaring to be in all the black amid all the few red lights on the station without a gas mask. Yes! Did you know we don't have to carry our gas masks any more. It is very nice.

You lucky dogs!! Fancy seeing Gunga Din, I haven't seen it. E. and I went to see "Goodbye Mr Chips" and "The Castles" but we have to go to Mrs Binghams to tea on Saturday. Mrs Thatcher calls her Polly.

Mrs Thatcher is making gloves for soldiers and Esmé is making her father some gloves.

We don't yet know whether we shall be home for Christmas.

By the way, you know the U.G.S. well E and I are making vests. The wool and pattern is provided. So we are all doing our part!

The ink on my blouse is because my pen (black one) leaks. Very sorry and all that, but it doesn't show so it doesn't matter - does it?

Did you receive my letter - I have written to you since half term haven't I?

Tell gran I would like money please, from you I would like books or book coupons or money. I don't mind at all.

Don't get the books yet, if you are getting me books. I must make a list first.

Am I to spend not more than 2/- or 2/6 a week. I hope it is 2/6. Because of Christmas presents and wool etc.

It is 7 now, we haven't had tea yet, we are listening to the wireless.

Would dad like me to knit you (dad) some mittens? And what about you mother? (By the way the mittens are for the car.) Well I have got to write to Den.
    Cheerio
    Heaps
    100 per cent of best love
    Pat

P.S Hello it's Thursday now - Tibby has just had her kittens. You know so far she has had two. Well Mrs Thatcher came in and said "Tibby has excelled herself she has had 3"!! and when we went to see them Mrs Thatcher pointed them out and found she had 4!! Tibby has had one since.

P.S.2 This isn't so nice. It's about a bill. I sent one to you with a letter quite a time ago. It was all torn and was for about 14/5. It is for milk and books (second hand). R.S.V.P. as quickly as you can.

Sunday   5 CrosbieRoad

My dear Pat
    I have just finished reading your letter again so that I shan't forget to answer any of your questions.
    First of all I am sending a pound note to pay for the milk etc and you may keep the change.
    You seem to have a much more exciting time than we get here for you appear to go out to tea several times a week, well it makes it more interesting for you and enlarges your social horizon.
    To answer another of your questions, I very much appreciate your offer of mittens for the car but Gran has knitted me some blue gloves so I shan't want any more thank you.
    A few cigarettes will be very nice or a magazine, anything you like.
    Your Mother had better answer her questions herself when she writes. *(A knitted tea cosy would be nice - Mother.)* As to cycling twenty miles, a lot depends on the speed at which you rode, whether you walked uphill or not, if you went slowly and walked up steep hills and rested

before you started back that distance shouldn't hurt you but it would really be better to stick to shorter distances I think. *(I think 20 miles much too far - Mother.)* I don't know whether you have heard from Dennis that he has been posted to St Leonard's on Sea.

He leaves somewhere around midnight on Tuesday and Mother and I shall drive him down in the car.

He won't finish his training there, but he doesn't know where he will finish, still he may probably be down there for some time. He is having a party on Tuesday evening and inviting 7 or 8 young people to supper, Mother's buying two ducks for the occasion and they are also having an Xmas pudding. *(Not yours, just an extra one - Mother.)*

I should think they will allow you to come home at Xmas, I wonder if we have to write and ask as we did when you came back at half term, we shall be very disappointed if you can't come, still if you don't come, I shall get a day off and we shall come to see you.

Mother and I went to Uncle Jim's last night and drove both ways during the blackout, luckily it was a moonlight night and but for rain wouldn't have been too bad at all, but even then if a pedestrian is on the road it is impossible to see him. Mr Holder and I have a shilling bet on, the loser pays if he is the first to hit anything in the blackout when he is driving even if it is only the curb and let me tell you, you can't see the curb at times. *(Nearly hit it last night - Mother.)* It is dark coming back from the works each night now, so I have to be very careful and Mr Holder asks me every morning whether I have lost or not. *(I bet Dad asked Mr Holder - Mother.)*

I have coupons for 39 gallons *(of petrol - Mother)* to last till Jan 31st and about 5 gallons in the car, I use 30-32 gallons going to the works so shall save some to come and see you or fetch you as the case may be. *(Hurrah - Mother.)*

We have had a bridge party here the last three Friday nights, they come here because as long as Gran is at Sutton I don't want to leave Mother alone in the house at night. *(No thank you - Mother.)*

Dennis has been very busy marking his flying kit this afternoon, at least he was until Vivian turned up and now I think they are busy planning the party for Tuesday night. *(I had to complete the marking - Mother.)*

Don't forget to send us the list of books you would like for Xmas in plenty of time because letters seem to take such a long time to come, you had better send it in one of your next letters. *(Yes, and Town is beginning to get very crowded - Mother.)* Would you like books from both of us?

By the way I am sending 30/- in this letter, the 10/- note and the change from the pound note I hope will last you till Dec. 31st.

Mother has just finished boiling 5 Xmas puddings, so there ought to be some left for you when you come. *(My Goodness YES - Mother.)*

Dennis and Vivian are just writing out the menu for the party on Tuesday, the two principal items according to them are: -

'Og's pudden

Tripe

I have seen the present Dennis has bought you for Xmas, my word it is a "snorter", it cost oodles and oodles and looks simply - wow. No you are wrong it isn't what you thought. *(No, wrong again, 'tisn't that either, but as Dad says, it certainly is a SNORTER - Mother.)*

Well cheerio

With love from

the parents

Hope you approve of my additions.
Lots and lots and lots of love from us both – Mother

Nov 30th   5 Crosbie Rd.

My dearest Pat

Huh! I wish I had a typewriter to do my letters with, though I should never be able to get such a good result as you made of your letter to Dad and me. I will look for your brown socks and if still here will post them along to you. How about fetching you? Sat. Dec. 16th would be a wonderful day to come, Dad could arrange to have the whole day off, which is my birthday and what! oh what! better birthday present could I have than my Pat, unless it was my Pat and Dennis.

I have already posted the letter to Miss Barrie saying we want you for the holidays. Do we want you - well I ask you?

You seem to have had a very nice time at Mrs Bingham's, also with the Townsends. Fancy you going to the race course, great swank, even though you did not approve of the jockeys' clothes.

I haven't Dennis' address for you, though I have a letter from Hastings waiting to be forwarded on to him. He had a lovely party, and I did it beautifully for him.

They started off with grapefruit, followed by two roast ducks, sprouts, apple sauce, potatoes etc, followed by plum pudding, and custard sauce, stewed pears and whipped cream, followed by coffee in the little Crown Derby coffee cups.

The table napkins were all folded in the glasses, I had got all my best silver out, best table cloths, china and glass, and a big bunch of roses (out of the garden) in the middle of the table.

There were three girls, two Bettys and a Peggy, and Vivian, Billy, Bob Smythe, Raymond Raby and best of all Dennis. Vivian made a speech and they all drank Dennis' health in sherry, then Dennis made an amusing speech, about the 'fair sex', and they all drank to the ladies.

Then Billy produced your telegram, which I had kept for the occasion as Dennis was out when it came. Bill said, that during the day he had been entrusted with a telegram from the girl who was dearest to Dennis and who loved Dennis more than anyone else. Den was delighted, he flushed with pleasure and said "How like Pat, how dear of her". I then produced Den's present to you and made the girls gasp - yes gasp - with envy, and the boys all agreed it was a beautiful present. Of course it is just possible Dennis may be here to give it to you himself (ask in your prayers) but if he is unable to be with us, we will pack him up some good things and let him have them down there, for he would have quite a good time with his friends.

I am very very proud of him, as I know you are, but won't we give him a party when he comes home for good.

When we come to fetch you I will try and bring Sooty, if she is available, but in any case Dad says he can take you back by car, so you could show Sooty to Mrs Thatcher then should we not be able to find her when we come.I do so hope poor Mrs Thatcher has quite recovered from the effects of having three teeth out.

Give her my love and thank her for her letter and tell her I do so hope she is better, with no more toothache.

Well my darling, not long is it before you will be home. We shall be into Dec. by the time you receive this. No, don't <u>buy</u> me a tea-cosy. I just thought a knitted one might be rather a good idea, and don't get Dad the fancy case, just plain cigarettes, or chocs or toffees.

Well, my darling, as I said before, don't forget to let me know about Dec 16th as soon as possible.

With dearest dearest love from Mother

Sunday   5 Crosbie Rd.

      My dear Pat

          You are a bit of a - *(darling - M)* you know, I asked for Dec 16th off to come and fetch you and then you write to say it isn't the 10th - *(16th - M)* - it is the 20th. Now make up your mind which day *(you have already said 20th - M)* - it is and I expect I shall be able to manage it. *(Jolly well have to - M)* I expect Mother wrote and told you she had written to Miss Barrie asking if you could come home for Christmas. *(Yes she would have the letter on Friday - M.)* You can tell Esmé that she can come back with us and when we do come I expect we shall reach Prestbury all being well somewhere about 11 o'clock *(Hope earlier - M.)* We shall probably get 2 or 3 days holidays at the works as well so all being well we should have a very nice Xmas.

Dennis I am afraid will probably not get home at Xmas as he won't have been down there very long, still he may, and if he doesn't he probably will early in the New Year.

Mother tells me she told you all about Dennis' party and how we took him to the station after 12 o'clock at night. *(Didn't say much about this - M.)* He was very pleased with your telegram *(I'll say he was - M.)* Billy made a speech and handed it to Dennis when they were all having supper. Billy said it was a telegram from the girl who loved him most, I think *(know - M)* that it's true too, don't you. They all had good appetites, for they ate a tin *(3 tins - M)* of grapefruit, two ducks, two dishes each of potatoes and sprouts, a Christmas pudding and then stewed pears *(and cream - M)* besides rolls and butter etc.

We went over to Moseley this afternoon and then on to Sutton to fetch Gran, and here we are all sitting in the lounge.

Lesson should be returned today, I think. What say you?

      With dearest love from Mother
      and dearest love from Dad
      and dear love from Gran.

Fri Dec 1

748099
Sgt. D. F Knight
No 2 Flight R.A.F
Alexandra Hotel
Hastings

DearMother & Dad,
  I've quite a lot of news to tell you so I'll begin at the beginning and go straight through.
  We left New Street at 12.30 (I hope you got home O.K.) and for the greater part of the journey we had a compartment to three of us. We stopped at Coventry, Daventry and Rugby, where I had a cup of tea and a ham sandwich (I also ate the bananas and biscuits and we could have done with the meringues - what became of them?)
  From Rugby to ? I had a little sleep on a board on the floor of a guards van and from ? to London I slept on six kitbags on the floor of the compartment.
  We got to London at 3.45 and as it was a long way up the platform we put our luggage on a porter's truck and pulled that. Arrived at the top of the platform we put our luggage on another truck and Chapman and I sat on it, while a porter coupled it on to an electric trolley and the rest rode on that to the taxi rank.
  A taxi driver drove us five at a time in two journeys, kit included, to Charing Cross at 1/- a head and thence to a Lyons Corner House for nothing but a tip which he was very loth to take. We spent 1 1/2 hours at the Corner House, and then did a one hour Cooks tour round London to Charing Cross. We left Charing Cross at 8.30 and Chapman and I got a compartment to ourselves, and half-slept all the way to St Leonards. Several people came to the door but when they saw us lying at full length apparently asleep they found other compartments...... Food is much better than O.T.C. camp food (perhaps as it's Sgts. mess), beds quite comfortable (palliasse, 4 blankets and straw pillow on steel sprung camp bed), and water is always piping hot [so far!], and we are lucky in having a basin in our room.
  With love from Dennis

(The rest of the information here appears in the following letter to me.)

Marine Court & New Sun Lounge, Hastings & St. Leonards-On-Sea. 3296.

Sunday.

748099
Sgt. D.F. Knight
R.A.F.
No 2 Flight
Alexandra Hotel
Hastings.

Dear Pat,

    I am sitting on the verandah of the hotel, in bright sunshine, on the second floor, in front of our room, on the sea front, upon my kit-bag, in peace and comfort, watching the sea and - aw! But this could go on for ever.

    I am having quite a good time here and at the moment I am in very high spirits.

    I shall not discuss the topic of the war; because, now I am on active service, it seems so very far away and I hear so little of it that I have got quite out of touch with it.

    When I got down here on Wednesday I was dog-tired and felt very depressed, but now things are very different.

We started from B'ham at 12.30 on Tuesday night and got here at 10.45 on Wednesday morning with scarcely any sleep and a mouth tasting like a cardboard box, so you can guess how we felt.

On Thursday I saw Gordon Harker in some film, I forget which but it was quite good. By the way I expect you think you are reading the second page but actually this is the third, the second is opposite. Or didn't you make that mistake?

Friday we were doing drill when our corporal (fancy a corporal being in command of a flight of Sgts!) fell us out for fifteen minutes. We had just fallen in again - only just - when the C.O. came up and not knowing we had just had a break said 'Oh you might fall your men out for a quarter of an hour Corporal'. So we went and had a cup of chocolate and a cake at a nearby café.

There are five initial training wings of four squadrons each, each squadron being about 250 men either Sgts or L.A.Cs.

No. 1. at Cambridge
No 2 in Lancashire
No 3 at St Leonards (300 yards away)
No 4 at Bexhill (3 miles away)
No 5 here at Hastings.

No 4 & 5 are not full just yet. All this is military information so don't shout about it, though of course it is not secret.

About 11.30 on Friday morning I was vaccinated and twice inoculated. This was <u>absolutely</u> painless. It didn't even hurt as much as when Dr. Winfield did us. Not a bit. Though our right arms were rather stiff next day.

I believe, however, that our vaccinated arms (left arms) start swelling in about a week's time.

Several fellows collapsed, some with fright and some with the effects. Some collapsed even as long as five hours afterwards and one or two even collapsed before the inoculation - just with fright.

The first night I and two others went to bed at 7.30, five minutes later Baxter came in from No 3 I.T.W. but one fellow never saw him, he was already asleep!

We are lucky in being on the front of the hotel, and in having besides two small verandahs, a wash-basin with constant hot water.

There are six steel spring camp beds in our room but no furniture. We are quite comfortable, however, having equipped ourselves with coat hangers, towel rails etc.

　　　　　I am just going for a walk on the sands, so cheerio!
　　　　　Lots of love
　　　　　Dennis.
P.S.　　I think I shall be back for a day or two at Xmas, so BE THERE.
Den

Civilians -

- RAFVR Sergeants

The night sky acquired a deep fascination for me.

Everywhere was in total blackness, and, looking up at the sky it seemed so vast and deep inky black, sparkling with a myriad of glittering stars; I began to ponder on the vastness and splendour of it, and the implications (and impossibilities) of infinity and what, then, lay beyond infinity.

This constant wonder was the cause of one of my nightly 'discourses' with Esmé

December 4th.   115 Welland Lodge Rd

Dearest Den,
      I am sitting on the sofa in the lounge, listening to "News of Paul Temple", warming myself by the fire, listening now and then to Mrs Thatcher talking, looking at Tibby and her kitten - and most of all Oh Most Wonderful Brother!! writing to you.
      There is a fine empty house in a road off the Prestbury Rd. just the other side of Prestbury. At least I expect it was once upon a time, but the house isn't there - just the bare foundations. But the grounds - ooh!! We first of all came in in great style through the main gate. Then we explored the lodge, Esmé found a long gold chain on the stairs. When we were coming out again Esmé opened a door which she thought led into one of the rooms. However when she opened the door she gave a gasp of surprise. The door led outside!!
      We wandered round the grounds and came to a garden wall arrangement. The other side was another "empty" house.
      We were tiptoeing noisily to the door. Esmé was going in when I noticed something awful!!
      THERE WAS A PITCHFORK LEANING ON THE WALL AND <u>IT WAS NOT RUSTY</u>.
      I could not call out to Esmé, so I just watched her walk into her fate - so to speak - she was just going through the door when she gasped and whispered "There's a man in there", at that we ran. Heedless of the noise we made we ran blindly. Suddenly we saw a little overgrown path winding between the wall and the trees. We swerved left and broke through the "tangled and dripping undergrowth", in other words the grass.

On the left were two bamboo plants each about 15 ft high. We cut ourselves four huge stalks off these plants each and marched past the farm where we had lost our way and Esmé had asked a dark gypsy-looking farm boy astride a carthorse the way and then came home.

Oh Den! What lovely paper that paper is you wrote to me on (would you like to send me some?) And what nice ink!

(I hope you don't mind my generousness with exclamation marks.)

By the way most marvellous brother what would you like for a Christmas present? Anything you know, you can mention - but of course I don't say you will get it.

You know I am getting quite eloquent. I make a speech to Esmé nearly every night. Last night it was about the planets, eternity, space and boxes - oh no that was the night before!! Last night it was Esmé's father's and mother's names.

A long time ago it was darkness and youth - all sorts of things. And she just lies there and listens until I have finished and then she breathes deeply and turns over and goes to sleep - and do you know what?!

SHE TALKS IN HER SLEEP!!!!

The other night she said it was cold, a long time ago she said something about horses and sirens. It is ever so exciting to wake up and hear her talking!! The other night she said something like "Are you cold?" I said "What?" But she was fast asleep, talking in her sleep as usual.

You know Jean Smith that came to tea with Joan and all of them on my birthday? Well she is billeted the other side of the farm in Newborne Lane. It is parallel with Welland L. Rd. S'nice ainit?

Oh it's 'Monday Night at 8' now. Do you have a radio?

I don't suppose you would like me to knit you some socks or gloves. I don't say I should be able to finish them by Christmas, but I would love to knit you something.

It's Inspector Hornleigh now.

I think I shall be back at Christmas. I shall be <u>very</u> disappointed if I am not. If you can't get home for Christmas but come home sometime in January I could get a week-end off and come and see you.

Oh Den!! It's snowed. The ground is all white, by the way tomorrow is today now - in other words it's the 5th.

Has it snowed in Hastings? If so how much?

Mrs Lively thinks George has a big sledge in the outhouse - oh no just the runners. Still I could fix them on my sledge. It would be nice if Esmé and I could go tobogganing down Cleve Hill.

You MUST come home for Christmas! So I can snowball you (if there is any snow) and I want to shew you the toboggan slide down the alley into Carless Avenue.

Cheerio

All the love in the world

and   all " luck "   "

Pat

P.T.O. I didn't make that mistake about reading the wrong page but Esmé did.

Wednesday   R.A.F.
                                                  Alexandra Hotel
                                                  Hastings

Dear Pat

I have just had your letter and am making a point of answering promptly, though I am afraid that from now on my letters will become shorter and fewer as I have a rather large writing list (swank!) and I am having such an enjoyable time (so far that I don't feel much in the mood for writing.)

From your letter it seems that you have been having a pretty gay time of things, down here it's really quite good fun.

Reveille (that means "get up") goes at 6.30 and I get out of bed at 7.15; breakfast is at 7.30 and I get down at 7.45. But I don't miss my breakfast as you can arrive for breakfast up to 8 o'clock.

As far as snow is concerned I hear that they have also been having snowstorms in B'ham. But we have seen none down here. In fact, as I told you, last Sunday it was so warm I sat on the verandah. We've had a little rain, especially in the evenings but on the whole the weather has been very good.

As far as Xmas leave is concerned I may get four days at home, but I am not certain. I hope so very much though.

I have been learning morse down here and can actually receive at 3 words per minute!

I am enclosing one sheet of paper as I can't spare any more.

Lots of love

<u>Dennis</u>
P.S   As far as knitting is concerned, I should be very glad if you would knit me a pair of R.A.F. mittens as a Xmas present.
   D.

Wednesday   5 Crosbie Road

My darling Pat

   The days are flying past, and in two weeks, only two weeks, you will be home.

   I went to town this morning and met Grandma, and we each got a photo frame for Dennis' photograph. When I produced Dennis' photo for fitting, the girl said "Oh, what a beautiful boy, isn't he lovely". I said "He certainly is lovely".

   When in town I also managed to get the ingredients for the completion of the Christmas cake, which I hope to make on Friday. I could get neither sugar or icing sugar in Harborne, but managed to get it from Barrows, when I explained I wanted to make a cake for my evacuated daughter and air force son. I have everything for it now.

   Do you know that Gran is staying with us again, she is in her usual position knitting and Sooty is in her usual position on Gran's knee. Gran says Sooty has grown enormously. I wonder if you will think so, she certainly eats enough. The other evening we couldn't find Soot, so decided we should have to go to bed and leave her outside. I had been out and hadn't put my little blue feather hat away, so pulled out my hat box with my three best hats in it, and it struck me it felt rather heavy, but I didn't take much notice, opened the lid and out jumped Sooty. My hats, oh, my poor hats, Soot had certainly scrimmaged around before finally making herself comfortable, but Dad and I couldn't help laughing, we were so astonished.

   I haven't come across your socks, but they are too cold anyway.
   All my love, Mother

Gran and Dad each send their love, also mine to Mrs Thatcher and Esmé.

Dec 9   CrosbieRd.
Sunday

My dear Pat

We have just been down town to see off your big brother for he came home on weekend leave and had to leave by the five o'clock train today.

He had five friends in to tea yesterday, the same people he had for his party when he was posted, that's all but Bob Smythe and his sister. He couldn't get in touch with them as they are not on the phone.

They all had a good time and all of them were showing card tricks etc.

Dennis has grown since he went to Hastings and his uniform is getting too small for him, he will be positively fat if he goes on and then they won't have him as a pilot. That would suit you, wouldn't it.

If Dennis comes at Xmas he is going to have his party again so that you will be there and you will see all their parlour tricks and some of them are quite clever.

You appear to have many more adventures over there than we do here, in fact after I get home from the works it is dark, at least it is dark before I start home so that you can imagine we don't see very much here.

We haven't even been to the pictures this week as Gran is with us.

I went to play cards on Friday night at High Tor with Holder and Co and didn't get home till 12.15 and imagine my surprise to find Mother and Gran still up, but I was more surprised still when I heard another voice from upstairs and who should it have been but Dennis, who had rung up whilst I was at High Tor to say he was coming home and when I arrived home, he hadn't long been there.

Well one more week and you will probably be back here. Hurrah!
With all my love
My sweet little dove
Dad

ALEXANDRA HOTEL

Dear Pat,
    Thanks ever so much for your letter, I am afraid that I am rather late in replying but I went home this week-end and so had no spare time at all in which to write.
    First of all with regard to your offer to knit something for me, it is ever so nice of you, but actually I can't think of anything I really want.
    However if you are in any difficulty in thinking what to get for my Christmas present, here are some suggestions. Of course you might think of something better but these are just suggestions.
    Anything to eat.
    R.A.F. handkerchiefs.
    Or whatever you can think of.
    I am hoping to come home for four days at Christmas in which case I shall try to hold a small party of the Q.A. on the day after Boxing Day.
    I have just been inoculated and so have 48 hours free of duty but unfortunately we can not go out until 4.30.
    Last week we had a very easy maths test, I and about 7 others got

100% and yet do you know 2 fellows actually got 0%!

    The following day I was on parade and we were being inspected by the C.O, the assistant C.O, the flight sergeant and our sergeant. Now the two previous days I had forgotten to clean my boots and this day I was so late getting up that I had only time to clean my greatcoat and cap and left my tunic unpolished.

    The Flight Sergeant stopped and put my collar straight and then the C.O. said to the Sergeant "Take that man's name". I thought 'Good Lor's what have I done now', but it turned out my name was being taken for smartness on parade!

    The sea is very smooth today but sometimes you get very strong winds and high seas, in fact one day I got blown off my feet on one corner and found myself running down the street before I could stop myself.

    On Friday I managed to catch the 2.12 train from Hastings and so was able to be on the skating rink in Birmingham by 7.35.

    I even had my skates sent down here so I could go direct to the rink, without first calling in at home.

    With lots of love
Dennis.

Wednesday   5 Crosbie Rd.
12th Dec. 39   Harborne
                                                               Birmingham17

My dearest Pat

    I wonder if this will be the last letter I shall write to you before you are home for the holidays, as Dad will probably write his usual Sunday letter and if I have anything to say I can add it to his epistle. Just think one week today and my darling Pat will be home. Hurrah, oh hurrah and hurrah, and five days after that, it will be Christmas Day. I have the cake all ready made waiting to be iced - that I think I shall leave until you are home so that you can advise me. You haven't said yet what books you want, but no matter, you and I can have a day in town and we will give you the money and you can buy your own present though you can not own it until Christmas Day. Have you made Gran any roses - she would love them for her present from you, as also should I. In fact they would be nice to give to any grown up that you feel inclined to give a present to - or rather to whom you feel inclined to give a present.

What did you think of Dennis coming home on leave so soon, and after our grand send-off party. He looked awfully well and strong, and was nearly bursting the buttons of his tunic, and will have to get a larger size before he comes again. We certainly seem to have a fine and efficient air force. Sir Kingsley Wood says it is the finest in the world, the machines themselves are the finest as also are the men who fly them. Bless them!

What did you think of the Bremen getting safely into a German port. It is a pity we couldn't have captured her, it would have caused such a stir in Germany, to have had their finest liner captured by the hated British. Have you heard that there is to be an air raid warning all over England on Sat next at 12.30. Dad says they are to blow the "All Clear" signal first just to reassure people, then they will give the Alarm signal followed later by the "All Clear" again. We didn't have a practice when you had one, in fact, we haven't heard anything at all, excepting the night after war was declared when there was a very 'half-hearted' alarm, which later proved to be a mistake.

You want to be very careful indeed when crossing the road when it is the slightest bit dusky. Mr Felton senior was crossing from his car, (which was on the wrong side of the road) to the office, and the light was just beginning to fail and he was knocked unconscious by a car and taken to hospital. It was found he was not seriously injured and later he was allowed to go home, but it was a mighty near shave.

I must write to Dennis now, we still do not know whether he will be here for Christmas but we certainly HOPE so, and he thinks it is quite likely.

Well my darling, Gran and Dad both send their love, and Gran has just said she hopes you won't disappoint her over the roses.

With dearest love, Mother

Please give my love to Mrs Thatcher, and expect us to fetch you and Esmé in the car, as Dad is sure he can arrange it.

December 12th - 14th   115 Welland Lodge Rd

Dearest Dennis -

I answered your first letter, and then you answered my answer to yours and now you have just sent me a letter apologizing that you were late in answering my letter. So you had forgotten that you had answered my letter and so you answered mine twice - this is how you started answer no 1.

Dear Pat

I have just had your letter and am making a point of answering promptly -

This is how you started answer no 2.

Dear Pat

Thanks ever so much for your letter. I am afraid that I am rather late in replying –

Oh! Dear Dope of a Dennis!! Good name - what?

Now I want this clear. In letter no 1. you said you would like me to knit you some R.A.F. mittens.

In letter no 2. you say you can't think of anything you really want (me to knit). Which do you mean?

Mrs Thatcher had a tooth out yesterday, and having teeth out affects her so she stayed in bed all today and we got the breakfast and did our bed and swept the step and scrubbed it, and brushed the carpets and laid the fire - I laid the fire and you ought to see it now, it's a beauty! By the way it is 7.15 at night. Then we cleaned the kitchen and made Mrs T some Bovril - then we got our dinner - ooh! it was a nice dinner. We had sausages and tomatoes fried together in a lot of fat, and we had some baked beans put in a saucepan and heated them up with tomato sauce and we had mashed potato. That was fine, and after we had mince pie and some lovely creamy custard we had made - we made it creamy by boiling it up twice - it made it a bit lumpy though, so it was good you weren't here.

Then we went to school and we were late as we had had to wash up and we explained why we were late and all was fine.

When we came home we were looking out of the window when we saw a plane come over. It was very low, about 300 ft., it went round over the racecourse and turned and came back again at about I don't know what, because I was dashing downstairs to have a better look at it, then it turned

121

again and came over at about 250 ft. It made for the racecourse getting lower as it neared.

I yelled to Esmé and she yelled to me "It's going to land!!" and we grabbed our coats and just dashed out of the gate up the lane along Newborne Lane, down the lane to the racecourse, across the course to the other side near the stadium where the soldiers are, and there we saw it!

Oh Boy! It was thrilling. We saw them all - well 5 - clustered round a wheel, while they were so occupied we crept up and hid behind a jump. We quietly - oh! I can't tell you how thrilling it was! - we quietly raised ourselves up and peered over the jump.

We could see them clustered round the plane. We stayed there quite a time, and then we crawled along the length of the jump, just around it - and then we saw two soldiers walking away from the plane. They looked as though they were walking towards us so we crouched against the jump with our heads lowered, the soldiers passed and we moved round the jump and crouched against the fence, slowly raising ourselves to look at the plane again. It was a bit dangerous there, so we crawled back again.

Then we peeped over the jump again. (It was now getting dark.) Out of the dusk we saw two figures looming - we crouched flat against the jump and stayed there in a breathless silence - then a voice cut the dark: "Halt! Who goes there?" We crouched, still silent. The two figures receded into the distance (I could see this by peering through the lattice of the jump).We then decided it was so dark we had better go home, and so we crossed the field, but we were confused in the dark, and you can see on the plan how we lost our way a bit.

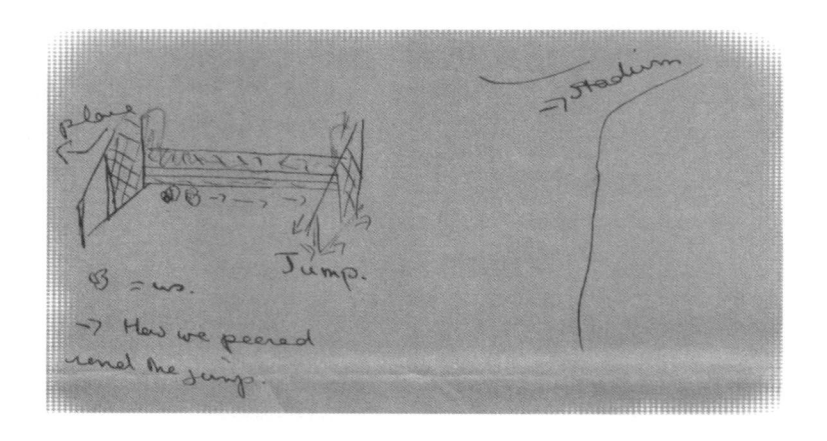

When we got to the blue blob on the line there was a shrill schrietch (is that how you spell it?) and a huge bat flew overhead.

We hurried home, and did the blackout and got the tea.

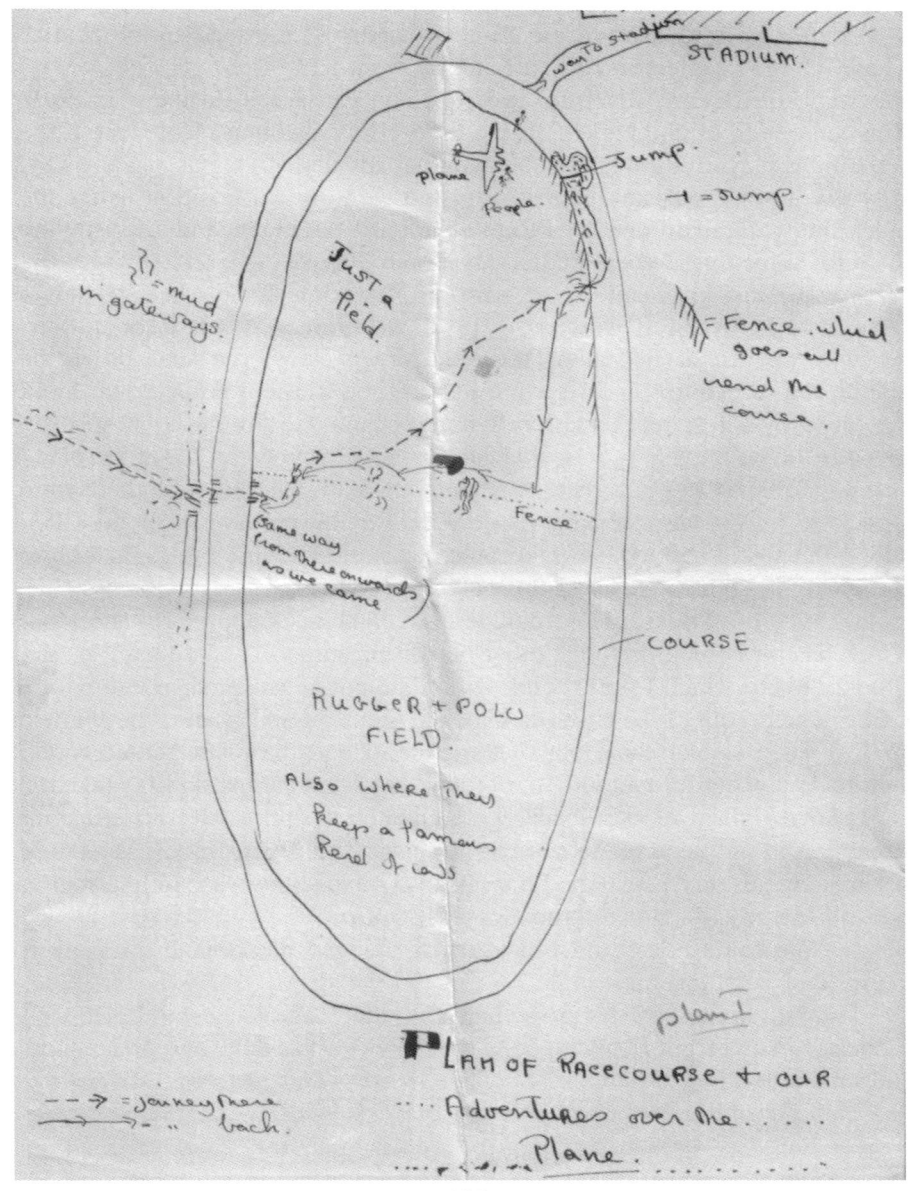

Hello! This is Wednesday now - Listen!

We got up early this morning and had our breakfast (Mrs T is all right today) then we made our bed and put on our coats (Esmé put on 3 pairs of socks), then we started out for the racecourse.

Well we took my camera and went across the mud to the course. There I hid my camera in my scarf and we went on.

We went a different way from before. You can see it on the plan no 2. Tim came with us and barked all the time. He was a nuisance! Just as we were in a precarious position he would bark and give our place away. Anyway no-one took any notice of us and we took our position where the black line with arrows ends. I took a photo of the plane, and after staying there for some time we started to come home.

We had got to the sweet shop in Newborne Lane when we saw a biplane come over. It was terrifically low. Barely 200 ft I should say. Anyway we just dashed along the road, down Newborne lane, down the lane to the racecourse and we were just in time to see it come down, miss the fence by a few feet and slowly come nearer the ground as it sped on towards the buildings. It drew up near the mono as you can see in the plan.

The pilot got out (there was only one man in it, although there were 2 cockpits). And we walked across the field to our previous position - Tim still with us, still barking. A man came out of a field with 2 dogs, and these came with us so now we had 3 dogs all barking!!

After quite a time the pilot came back and got in and a tall R.A.F. chap - belonging to the other plane I presume - swung the prop. and I took a photo which I don't think will come out because when Esmé took it (the camera) out of the case she knocked the lever and opened the shutter.

Then smoke came out of the exhaust and the plane turned round and made a beautiful take off (the ground was very lumpy and the take off very short) right over our heads, we could see the pilot with his streamer streaming in the wind as he passed over us - Oh! It was nice! We could see his goggles and I imagined his set lips (I expect he was smiling really, but still I let my imagination run away with me).

We came home and I saw a high winged monoplane - I think it landed, but I am not sure.

Well I am sorry this is such a short letter - Did I say short? Oh well it doesn't matter - but I have to copy this letter - at least the aeroplane part - and send it to our dear parents - So Cheerio

Lots and Lots of Love

Pat

P.S. We have had our letters about coming home so now it's up to YOU.

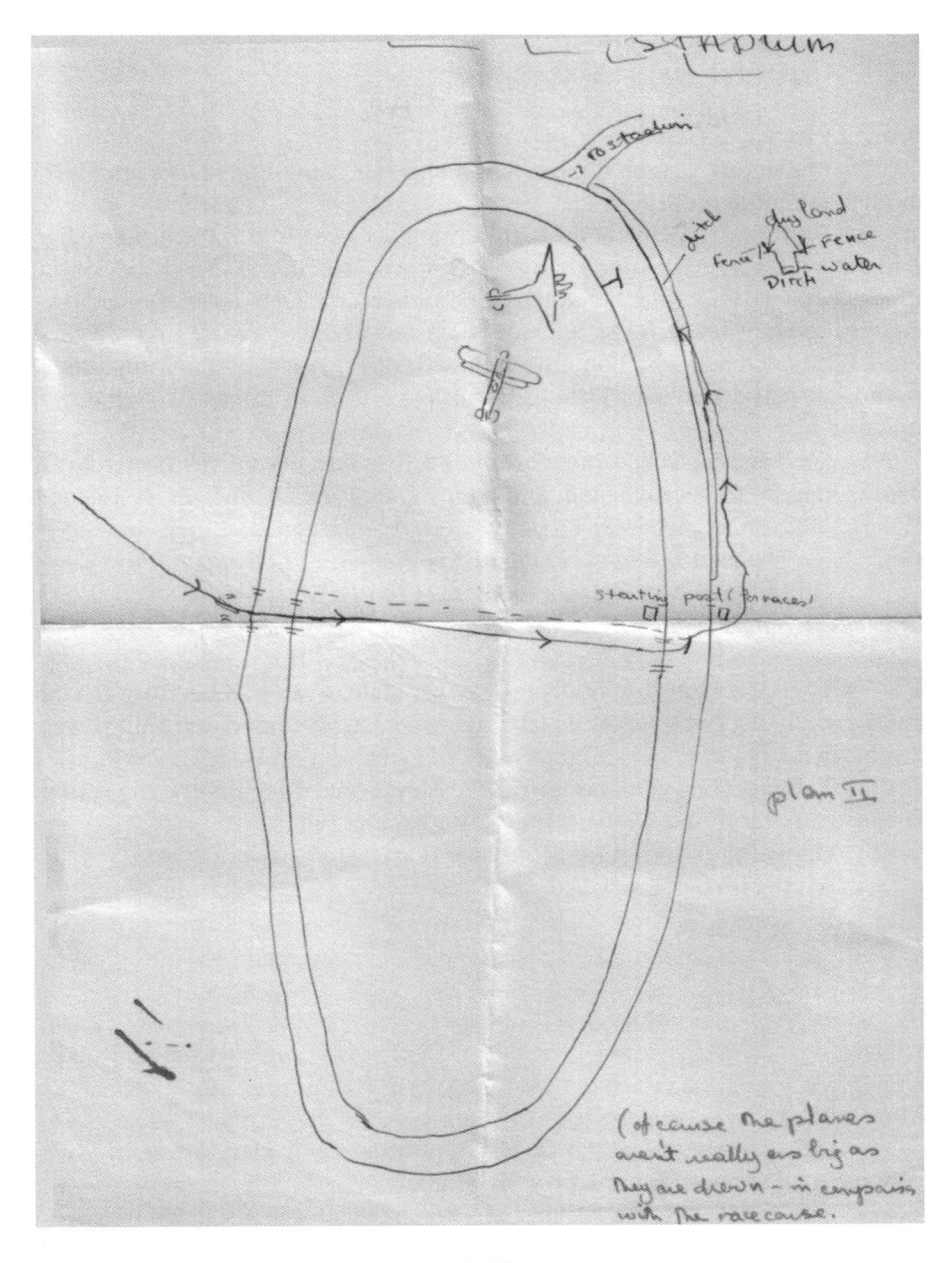

Dec 14th   You know what
                                                  goes here

    Happy Birthday to you!
    Happy Birthday to You!

Dearest Mother & Dad
    I have just written 9 pages to Dennis, and now I have no paper left, so I have to write on this.
    By the way Esmé and I were talking to Miss Orton about leave etc - Esmé's father has joined up - the navy, he thinks he'll be on a minesweeper - and told her about E's father and Den and she said we should have got leave to go and see them before they went. I then asked her if Dennis couldn't be home for Xmas could I get leave to see him when he did get leave, she said I could if his leave was 48 hrs or over, but not under 48 hrs.
    Well we have had our permission to come home. Hurray! Now Dennis has got to get his leave, and then we shall be all fine. Now Listen! This is an adventure we had.
    ..... *The next section is copied from the letter to Dennis.*
    On Monday Mrs T had a tooth out.
    ..... *The remainder of the paragraph is copied from the letter to Dennis.*
    Then we went to school and we were late as we had had to wash up and we explained why we were late and Miss Orton smiled and said it was alright then.
    Talking about Dennis growing, Mrs T and Mrs Lively say Esmé has grown fatter round the face, they say I have grown.
    Oh well, not long now till I come home.
    All the love in the world
    Pat

17 Dec   5 Crosbie Road

 My dear Pat
    Where do you get the knack of writing such nice letters, it isn't from me, so I suppose it must be your Mother.
    The females of the species always have a lot to say anyway so it

must be a feminine trait. However it was a very interesting letter, but I must warn you not to play tricks like that again, as the soldier might easily have fired after he had challenged you and you didn't answer, for they are told to do so, and several people have been shot already.

It is also a <u>very serious</u> offence to take photographs of anything to do with the Services without permission, so don't do anything so foolish again, however adventurous it may seem at the time.

We shall be over to fetch both Esmé and yourself on Wednesday Dec. 20th at somewhere around 11 o'clock, maybe earlier, maybe later but be ready waiting for us, for we want to get straight back again and don't forget to bring your ration book with you, as rationing begins soon after Xmas.

Mother had a telegram from Dennis on her birthday on Saturday to say he was coming home on leave on Friday Dec 22nd, so you will both be at home together, so that will be very jolly won't it.

I don't know how much he gets but he said when he was home before, he thought it might be <u>six days</u>.

We went out this evening and bought a box of crackers in anticipation, the time is getting so short.

You never sent that list of books you said you would, so we haven't bought your present yet, but perhaps you would like to choose for yourself when you come home.

With lots of love
from Pater.

Thanks ever so much for your lovely cheerful letter, also the card. I had a very nice birthday and a festive telegram from Dennis. Hurrah, isn't it near now.
I will bring enough sandwiches for all our lunches, Esmé as well.

With dearest love, Mother.

18 Dec '39   RAF
                                                        Alexandra Hotel
                                                        Hastings

Dear Mother & Dad,
    With your permission I should like to hold another quiet party on 27th December to celebrate Pat's homecoming and my departure.
    I shall invite only about a dozen people not more than eight of whom shall I expect to find it possible to come. As some of those invited are in H.M. Forces you should not have too much difficulty in procuring butter for the occasion. By the way Baxter is almost definitely coming, you haven't seen him, but you spoke to him on the phone once.
    By the way did Felton and Co. ring you to get my address? as I have just had a Christmas present from the staff. 100 Turkish cigarettes of my favourite brand, very decent of them don't you think?
    Well I am about to rush off some of the invitations so cheerio!
    With love from
    Dennis

Just before we went home for Christmas Mrs Thatcher presented Esmé with Wuthering Heights, which she had long wanted, and me with a fountain pen that I'm now using to write this.
    Next day, **Thurs Dec 21st**, we came home and the following day Den came home on leave while I was icing the cake. He went skating in the evening while Mum, Dad and I went to the cinema, and Sooty followed us and hasn't come home yet and I'm afraid she's been run over.

Saturday 23 December 1939

    Den went riding in the morning and was bitten by a horse. In the afternoon Vivian and a friend of Den's came round with some fairy lights for Den's party. I had never seen him before and I think he's very nice. His name is Raymond.
    In the evening Den went carol singing with Vivian and his girl friend Olive and got 6/6 from 10 houses.
    Christmas morning we spent at home, opening our presents. Dennis gave me his Christmas present to me - a magnificent pink silk

quilted dressing gown. As Mother and Dad had said, it certainly was a "SNORTER"! We spent the afternoon and evening at Grandma's and had a lovely time. As usual, quite a lot of the family were there and Den did some conjuring tricks.

Boxing Day Den took me skating and Mother and Dad came to watch.

Ray and his brother Dennis were there.

Extract from Den's diary:-

"Wed 27

Morning preparing for afternoon.
Afternoon - see Minutes.
Saw Christine home - she's very pretty.
Bill stayed night."

Den's party was great fun. His girl friend Christine came. It was the first time I'd met her. She's very sweet, small and dark haired with enormous eyes and a tip-tilted nose. At the end of the party Ray pulled off a piece of mistletoe and kissed her under it. Dennis was annoyed, I could see. Then Ray kissed Mother and me too - FLIRT!

Anyway, Dennis took Chris home.

Thursday 28 December 1939

When I awoke I found there had been a deep fall of snow. Bill and Den pulled me on a toboggan round to Ray's to return the fairy lights. Ray and his brother Dennis were waiting for us behind the hedge and pelted us with snowballs. We took up strategic positions and gave them as good as we got. It was great fun.

When we were all covered in snow, with it running down our necks and hanging in our eyelashes, we left them and after lunch Bill went home.

Den went back to his unit and I tobogganed.

1940

Aged 13 ½

List of Illustrations

Page

- 133   Dressing gowns
- 155   Corporation Street, winter 1940
- 157   Postman and Clerk of the Weather, winter 1940
- 160   Billiards diagram 1
- 161   Billiards diagrams 2 and 3
- 163   Billet plans (Mrs Jones')
- 173   Dad's 'sherry letter'
- 175   Vivian, Dennis and Bill
- 176   Vivian, Dennis, Pat and Chris
- 187   Pat at Weston-super-Mare
  Mother and Dad at Weston-super-Mare
- 209   Billet plan (Mrs Millard's)
- 230   'Handsome Hero'
- 238   Bomb crater diagram
- 239   Dennis in officer's uniform
- 251   Oil bomb diagram

Monday 1 January 1940

I had a postcard from Grandma, and one from Kelvin which he made himself. Went to town. Bought some overshoes for mum and me. Had coffee with Aunty Kathleen and Grandma.

In the evening we went to the pictures to see Beau Geste. It was very good.

Bought Mother & Dad 50 cigarettes.

Tuesday 2 January 1940

Mother went to the hospital. I went to Moseley for dinner and tea. Came home in the blackout. It was bitterly cold and I had to wait a long time for the bus going down.

Wednesday 3 January 1940

Mother came upstairs with Sooty in her arms - Yes! She's back. Took her to the vets, found she had kidney trouble. He gave us some pills that we have to give her.

Friday 5 January 1940

Den came home on leave.

He told us that he and his room-mates had had a room-inspection, and had received an 'Excellent' for it.

He reckoned that it was largely due to them all having bought themselves smart dressing gowns which they wore instead of R.A.F. tunics when relaxing in their room.

Saturday 6 January 1940

Made the pudding.

Went to town with Den, then called at Bill's office, but he wasn't there. So Den rang him up.

I met mother in the dress department of Lewis's and got a coat. A light brown swagger with a dark blue lining to the hood.

Christine came to tea. Den took her to the pictures, and I had my hair washed.

Sunday 7 January 1940 *(most of this information is in letter to Den, Jan 22, p121)*

Billy and Vivian came and stayed for dinner, and then another airman came for Den, to take him back to Hastings.

Wednesday 10 January 1940

I got up very early and had breakfast. Then I got all my things together, and after saying goodbye to Sooty got in the car and started off for Cheltenham. It was very frosty.

When we got to Welland L. Road we found they were making it. We stopped the car far down the Rd and walked up to the house. Mrs T. gave mother and dad a cup of tea and some soup and then they went.

Thursday

5 Crosbie Road

My dearest Pat

This is just a very hurried note in answer to your letter. I have collected everything you asked for and want Mrs Bonehill to post on her way home, hence the haste.

Now, about going to church - Dad and I both feel Mrs Thatcher is right, and that you should go. You see when you were at home you used to come sometimes with me, and sometimes with Mary Dutton, but now you seem to have given it up altogether. You see Pat, it is just this lack of thought and lack of going to church and general "Have a good time idea" that has caused the world to be in the dreadful mess it is today. God is waiting and waiting for people to turn to Him. You and Esmé both have someone dear to you in danger. Go to church next Sunday and don't go in a critical mood, just go with the idea of thanking God for all He has done for you, for the safety of us all, for the happy Christmas etc. and then ask for His help for the world as it is today. We all need it so terribly badly, continuously, and yet people just turn to Him when they are in special need, and then forget Him. Pat, it is all wrong - think of Dennis and copy him and pray for him, look how happy he is, how good and how everyone says what a splendid influence he is. This is a serious sort of letter, but Dad and I urgently want you to go to church.

    With love to Mrs Thatcher and Esmé.
    With all my love
    Mother

Please thank Mrs Thatcher for her letter

Jan 11th   115 Welland Lodge Rd

Dear Mother and Dad
    I have remembered some more things that I need, but that's not all I've written this letter for -
    Esmé and I went for a walk after you had gone. We went to the blacksmith's at Prestbury, he was blowing up the fire with some huge bellows. He did two horse shoes, and shoed a horse's two fore hooves.
    There was a nice little - well not so little, boy with very determined lips and an awful jagged tear in the lower part of the seat of his trousers. He was very worried about his horse, and when he had gone we asked the blacksmith why he hit the anvil in between when he hit the shoe. He said it was just habit and all blacksmiths do it. He says that when he is being

helped they do that to keep in time, and he supposes that is why. He says that horse had never been shoed before. He only did the two fore feet for that reason.

After dinner (Esmé said it would be stew or rabbit, and it was rabbit) we changed and went to school.

When we got there they said that there was no school and we were to go to the pump room. We did no work, and came away early.

I met Mary, and she came our way home and saw where we are billeted and then we saw her home. On the way she told us that she thinks we are coming back after Easter, I hope so!!

I said to Esmé we might live at home and anyone that went through a danger area might have an armed guard. So Esmé said that I wouldn't have one so I said I'd go right through Town and back to Harborne. Then they laughed. But this is beside the point, I do hope it is not a rumour about coming back. I don't think it is. We might stay at the University hostel, that would be safe, <u>and</u> fun! Then we could come and see you each weekend, and thoroughly enjoy ourselves. I should like that very much. I do hope they do it. It is quite feasible, don't you think?

I'll tell you what else I have forgotten now

Towel - ordinary one
All my knitting
My cyclist's diary
William & A.R.P. (not very necessary)

I think that is all.

This is for Dad. I saw a book called 'Lilliput Annual.' It is all the books put together, and cost 4/6. It looks very nice, do you want it?

Mrs T says we can tidy the bookcase and try and find her medical books. What fun! We are going to do it tomorrow.

Hello! It is Friday now. I received the parcel this morning, thanks very much for sending <u>that</u> promptly. I am sorry you have to send 2 parcels, but I will pay you back when I next see you.

Isn't it THRILLING about coming home for good at Easter? Of course, as I say, it may be a rumour, but Mary said she or someone else (I'm not sure which) heard Miss James telling someone.

But for the fact that Miss Barrie says she doesn't know what we are doing, I should say it isn't a rumour. But because of what Miss Barrie says I am not at all sure.

I do hope Mary is right though. She is much more independent now, she went to Gloucester (9 miles away) and got her bike and cycled all the way back. (A thing her father would never have let her do before.) It is a full size bike, like mine. Hers, too, is a Hercules, without a 3 speed however.

Unfortunately for me I have a chain guard which makes my bike heavy.

I undid it once, but there was one piece which it seemed impossible to get off. I may have another attempt some day, but I don't feel very hopeful about it.

I have just put the kitten in the stationery box. I put the lid on and then put the box in front of Tibby. When I took the lid off, Tibby was very surprised and licked her kitten heartily to show her affection for it.

Esmé and I are going to ride out to a little church about 4 or 5 miles away. If it is low we are going there. If not we are going to Holy Trinity next Sunday. Miss Orton says it is the nearest low church.

There is a frost again today, but the sky is a lovely blue and the sun is shining away.

The kitten has just been responsible for a puddle in the corner. Tibby is chasing her around now. Tibby got on the back of a chair and waited for the kitten to come in. They are both fighting on the back of the chair now. Ugh! School this afternoon. I hope it doesn't last long.

Mary, Esmé and I (and Jean if she has time) are going cycling sometime. I don't know where or when at the moment, but soon I expect.

If you cannot read my writing please write and tell me.
With
ALL
MY
BEST
LOVE
from Pat

P.S. The buttons have been taken off my green dress when it was cleaned. Will you ask them about it? Or shall I buy some more?

Monday 15 January 1940

There was a terrific frost and a thick wet mist.

We went down for team practice, and in the end couldn't see the other goal it was so misty. We chucked it up almost 5 mins after half-time as it was so bad, and Esmé, Mary, and I went to town.

We came back and had dinner, then we went to school. After school we went to the racecourse and slid on the water-jump. Tim came with us and was very disappointed when we went on the ice, for he did not trust it.

We had tea, and then I did some parlour tricks.

We told 2 stories, and then went to bed.

5 Crosbie Road

My dearest Pat

I am afraid this will only be a note as Dad is still in bed with Dr Winfield coming to see him each day. He has been really very groggy but feels and looks just loads better today, in fact I think he will soon be up again now.

As luck will have it Mrs Bonehill is bad with 'flu, and had to leave her work and go home on Sat. and hasn't been since, and I myself haven't been any too grand, with a little temp., only 99, but I haven't felt very good. Sooty is flourishing again, jumping up and down off chairs and window ledge and enjoys a game with a ball of wool once more.

By the way I think I have the buttons off your dress, so don't get more. I will post them next time I am out, but shan't make a special journey, as I don't want to go out more than absolutely necessary until I feel quite myself again. I also want to send your stockings, the fawn lisle ones.

The weather here is just ice, more ice and snow, much as you seem to be having in Cheltenham.

I am delighted to hear you and Esmé went to church and found the service more to your liking. Keep it up for I am convinced that the world never needed prayer more than it does today.

Just because I am writing in pencil, don't think it is because I don't feel well. I am in Dad's room and a pencil was handy and saved me a journey downstairs.

Please will you thank Mrs Thatcher very much for her long letter.

And now I must write to Dennis and will enclose a letter from him, but don't be anxious about yourself for Dennis has had both sorts of measles and mumps.

With dearest love
from
Mother & Dad

Den wants you to keep his letter in a safe place, so don't forget

Usual Address

Dear Mother, Dad and Pat,

In the twenty hours I have been down here the craziest things have happened. The journey down was uneventful and we all, with the exception of the driver, got quite a little sleep before we got to Hastings. We ran into quite a bit of fog which held us up somewhat but apart from that everything went O.K.

I went to the guard room to present my pass as soon as I got in, and the guard said "Flight 2, Ah Yes! you're in quarantine!"

I went upstairs and found that Chapman of our room was down with measles and had been removed to the military hospital, and another fellow on the same flight is down with mumps (Better take full precautions with Pat).

This morning the whole flight had breakfast brought to us in our rooms and then the fun started. First we heard we all (our flight) had to parade at 8 o'clock for sick parade. Then we heard that all the flight with the exception of our room and the other infected room would have to parade. We stayed in our rooms and saw the 8 o'clock sick parade move off. Before it had gone 100 yds it halted, about turned and came back as news had come through that the Medical Officer would not arrive at Headquarters till 9.30.

Then a man arrived to fumigate our room. (This about 8.10.) he told us that if he fumigated the room we should all have to stay out of the room till 4 p.m. We then told him that we had had orders to stay in our rooms till further notice. So he went away without fumigating. Half an hour later he came back and orders came that, we were to go out and stay out till 4 o'clock whilst the rooms were fumigated. Our room went for a walk round the town, the other room for a drive in the car and the rest of 2 Flight went on sick parade at 9.30 and then did normal lectures.

When we came back at mid-day we were told we could stay for lunch if we had it half an hour after the rest of the Squadron. So I got my skates and we all went to Brighton ice rink for the afternoon.

We came back at about 7.30 and were told we were to go on medical parade at 9.30 next day (Tuesday).

In the meantime, the other room had mooched round Hastings in the afternoon and then at 4.30 had gone on sick parade. The M.O. told them they were all right so they came back and went in to tea. They had just got their tea when the assistant C.O. came in, said they were all in quarantine, sent them up to their room and their tea was sent to them. The had just had tea when the Flight Sergeant came and told them they were out of quarantine and were to go to an evening lecture on Signals. They had just got downstairs when a fresh order came through from headquarters saying they were all in quarantine and back to their rooms they had to go. Half an hour later they were told they could leave their rooms but were not to mingle with any other people.

And to top all that at the Signals lecture the rest of the Flight had to attend after tea the lecturer never turned up so after 15 minutes the Flight Sergeant came and told them all to go out.

And if that doesn't shew lack of organisation, what does.
Cheerio with love
from
Dennis

P.S.   Anyway the skates came in useful!

Sunday   5 Crosbie Road

My dearest Pat

Well here I am in bed now. I have been since I last wrote to you. Dad is more or less up again, getting up late and coming to bed early and has been doing the best he can with the cooking etc. Mrs Bonehill turned up yesterday and put things straight a bit, but poor Dad has had to be cook, nurse and washer-up again today.

I wonder if you are frozen up at Coltham. In spite of a constant fire in the bathroom the overflow from both the bath and the basin are frozen and we can't get rid of any water. Yesterday Mrs Bonehill put some sprouts and potatoes ready in water for Dad to cook today and they were frozen into a solid lump just like a mould, and all the milk was in a solid lump and had to be thawed before one could do anything with it. It hadn't just lumps of ice in it, it was just one solid lump, I'm afraid the poor goldfish will be frozen.

Sooty is very well, but I haven't let her out of doors yet, she keeps coming upstairs to have a look at me and meows just as if she is trying to tell me it is quite time I was up.

Don't forget to write to Dennis, he so loves letters.

With love to all and dearest love to yourself

Mother

Friday 19 January 1940

We did our prep for an hour and then went to town. On the way we met Tim, Rover and another dog.

They followed us to town. When we got to Pittville gates the other dog turned back. Then Tim ran in front of a man on a bike and the man skidded to avoid him and fell off his bike.

Past the Gaumont Rover turned back and we tied Tim on our gymslip girdles because he had kept nearly getting himself run over.

I got a toothbrush and called in to see about a new nib, it cost 2/3 so I am going to think it over before I do it.

After school we didn't go out, but at tea time we discovered that Mr and Mrs Thatcher are going down to Bath to live. So we shall have to change our billet.

We knitted, did homework and listened to Babes in Arms.

Friday 19   Usual address.

Dear Pat

I expect that Mother will have already sent you my last letter to her and so I will refrain from repeating the news contained therein.

Suffice to say that although Chapman developed measles in the last week-end I was home, no one else here has caught it and we are now all out of quarantine.

Wednesday we had breakfast in bed and then mooched around Hastings all day, and had the excitement of seeing a mine which had been washed ashore.

Friday we had inoculation in the morning after our usual medical examination; and after pay in the afternoon we had no further duty.

Saturday we went skating in Brighton in the afternoon and saw Band Waggon in the evening.

Monday afternoon we had to go to a lecture on the pier and when we got there it was on 'fishing'. This important lecture was followed up by a film show on "The Principles of Aviation".

I am afraid that I have nothing else to talk about except to say my billiards is improving

    so Cheerio!
    With love from
    Dennis

Sunday 21 January 1940

Went to church.

The snow is still on the ground. The meat was frozen, so was the milk. When I went to the bathroom the water in the bath was frozen, and when I tried to make it go out it wouldn't because the pipe is frozen.

Esmé put her inner tubes in. (They had been frozen.)

22 Jan 1940   115 Welland Lodge Rd

NOTICE
read this letter before you
read any of the odd pieces of paper
that are enclosed with this.

(On a small envelope)
Don't open this till you have read page 3 of the letter (when you will read the small piece of paper which also must not be read till you have read p.3.)

Dearest Den
      I hope this reaches you as it leaves me, in the pink. With heaps of love from - Pat.
      Now isn't that a nice letter - what? You want me to say some more? Well, I do think that you might have liked it - Eh? Oh you want me tell you some news.
      So - here goes.
      When you went Vivian and Billy washed up. Then I had a pain to which Mother added an aspirin and a hot water bottle. While I was recovering Mother and Dad went out for a walk. When they came back I had completely recovered, done the black out, and read several chapters of "The Red Badge of Courage".
      I helped mother get the tea which consisted of egg and chips, and while I was eating it the phone went, and when I answered Billy spoke. He said that he had just rung me up to wish me a nice journey and to hope Mrs T. would be pleased to see me.
      Vivian was on the phone too and when Bill asked me whether I was going to see Jack and Jill Vivian said "Oh no, she doesn't want to". Bill thought I said I didn't want to under Vivian's voice. So he said "What? Don't you want to?" I sweetly explained that I did want to go, so he said "Well then we'll see about it".
      But Vivian said that he thought you would want to go alone with Christine? Well? Dear Dear Den!! Anyway, if we get a large party you and Chris could be at the end and no-one would bother you. No suree! They'd all be gripping their seats staring open-mouthed at (turn to small piece of paper).
      * The stage. Caught you there, or didn't I?

Well, now you've read all the scraps of paper .... You haven't? Well read them now. - Ah! Now you're ready to carry on.

When Esmé came the day before we came back Bill rang me up again. Again to say goodbye, but Vivian was not there that time. He asked me to write to him and he says he expects we will meet again before Easter.

Mr George Thatcher has come to stay the weekend. Esmé and I are going out tomorrow (Sun.). We have to motor out to the Davis's parents for dinner. You know Jean Smith? Well she is billeted with Davis's.

We have just been to church. It is now a week later. I'm sorry to have been such a long time sending this letter, but I could not remember your no. and I left your letters at home.

Mother and Dad forwarded your letter. Mrs T almost insisted that I should burn your letter, but I wouldn't and didn't. So I still have it safe and sound.

Yesterday we went to the Gaumont to see 'Stanley & Livingstone'. Have you seen it? If not you must. It is <u>very very</u> good. Spencer Tracy was Stanley and you know what a good actor he is.

Do you think we shall come home at Easter? Or do you think it's a rumour?

I have heard the same story from 2 different people, but then they both may have heard it from the same person. I hope not anyway, because I shall be glad to get home.

Mr & Mrs Thatcher have to go to Bath to live in about 2 weeks time, so we will change our billet. I wonder where we'll go?

I have started to finish your mittens now, so you will probably get them by your birthday!

I will do my best now to get them done soon.

The sooner I finish this letter the sooner I finish your mittens, because I will get on with them as soon as I have finished this.

I am glad you have had both mumps and measles so you probably won't catch them. Gosh! I wouldn't have thought you could have gone to Brighton ice rink, and as for those poor fellas who kept being ordered about in different directions - gosh! They must wish they'd joined the Navy!!

Oh well if I don't end soon I shall use too much paper, and that would be --

Lots of Love

Pat.

I received your letter this morning. You seem to be having a fine time. Carry on -

Heaps of Love, Pat.

MOSELEY,

22nd January 1940.

Dear Pat,
    I hope that you will be pleased to hear that I have been lucky enough to secure six tickets for Emile Littler's 'Jack & Jill' starring Arthur Askey, Billy Bennett and the O'Gorman brothers. The tickets are dated Monday 25th March (i.e. Easter Monday) and they are Matinee ones, the performance starting at 2.00 p.m. and finishing about 6.00 p.m.
    Therefore will you please mark, learn, and inwardly digest the date and put off any engagements with Boy Friends to some later date.
    Vivian and I phoned your Father last night and he gave full permission for you to come. If however you know that it will be absolutely impossible for you to be there - in which case Viv and I will never speak to you again - please let us know miles in advance - if you dare.
    The six tickets will be split up as follows:-

    Females:- Pat (that's you)
                Betty Smyth
                'Bobby' (Vivian's 'flame')
    Males:-   Dennis (I think you know him)
                 Vivian
                Your humble scribe (that's me).

    Well and how is life going along at Cheltenham. I do hope you did alright in that fearful Biology test they were going to greet you with.
    Now Pat I know you have got oodles of spare time so I shall expect you to use some of it this week in writing me a letter. Now its no good making that fuss: fill your fountain pen and get down to it.
    Trusting that you are in the very best of health and spirits and that you will pardon my abominable scratchings out.
    Cheerio,
    <u>Billy</u>.

Jan   115 Welland Lodge Rd

Dearest Mother & Dad

    I have enclosed a letter about the milk bill which I have paid. Please pay me back.

    Do you know what? Well unless Mr Thatcher has his salary raised to stop him we will have to change our billet. Yes sir! And Mr and Mrs Thatcher have decided that brother George's business in Bath is not running properly, so Mr T is going to be a partner in it.

    And we will have to change our billet unless something unforeseen happens, I wonder where we will go to? Somewhere where they have better regulated meals anyway.

    How's Dad? I expect he is almost up if not up.

    I hear that you have heard that we have been to the Davis's parents to tea. Jean Smith is billeted with the Davis's.

    Mr Davis (Jr) used to be a racing driver, and he goes along at a fine speed even in the black-out. He is a very good driver, however, yes, a really good driver.

    Anyway, to get on with the story. When we got there we went with Mr Davis (Jr) and his brother to get some sticky buds.

    On the way back we decided to go over the empty house we had passed on the way up. We were scouting round when Esmé put her hand against a window pane and peered in.

    The window pane gave way with a loud crash, and we bolted!

    Then we went down to look at the spring from where all the people of that village get their water. It was very clear, and we each sipped a little and wished.

    Then we went to have a look at the cows being electrically milked. They did not seem to mind at all.

    Then we went to see two dams in the river, and noticed that although the ice was about 6 inches to a foot thick the river still flowed beneath. Where the water surged through the lock gates was a kind of waterfall. All beautified by icicles. I climbed down and broke off some icicles which we threw at the ice.

    Then we went back to the house and we had tea. After that I did all the parlour tricks that I knew. And we went back.

Mr Davis (Jr) admired the hood on my coat. (Jean says he often teases her by saying "If you don't stop bullying me I'll change you for Pat Knight.")

I hope we get someone like him to fight. I think he is awfully decent.

They say this is a very short term, so we may not have a half term. Anyway the holidays are nearer when it's a short term. However we have exams this term which I must pass.

I do hope I shine in the subjects I need to be a nurse. I am really going to try hard this term and try to do my best. Because if I am not a nurse there is nothing left for me to do.

I think if and when I specialised I would like to take up fever nursing and go to North West Africa or somewhere like that.

Talking about Africa, have you seen "Stanley and Livingstone"? If not you must see it. It is <u>awfully</u> good. Spencer Tracy is Stanley, and you know how good he is.

If it's on again I shall see it again, and we have already seen it <u>completely</u> through twice. We didn't come out of the cinema till 7.30, and we went in at 2.15!!

The snow is still on the ground, but we don't go sliding in the evenings any more. It is too darn cold for one thing!

A chap put a thermometer out and it registered zero!
Oh well, I can't think of any more to say.
    Heaps and Heaps of Love
    Pat

Tuesday   5 Crosbie Road

My dearest Pat

I have just had your nice long cheery letter. I am still in bed, as my temp. was up a bit last night and Dr Winfield wouldn't let me get up. However I hope to get up this evening, for I feel <u>really heaps better</u> today.

Grandma is here looking after my wants, and very nice too (for me).

I am terribly sorry to hear you have to leave Mrs Thatcher, but hope you will still be with Esmé and will find a nice billet. Will you ask Mrs Thatcher to tell Miss Orton (or whoever is the right one to tell) or tell her yourself the special importance of a <u>dry house</u> and <u>aired</u> beds for you because of your tendency to rheumatic fever at this time of the year. This is most awfully important and I want to know that it has been done, else sure as ever you will be in serious trouble again. Don't be silly about it, ask Mrs Thatcher what is best to do about it and let me know what has been done. <u>Don't</u> just trust to luck. Is there anyone I can write to about it before it is too late.

The billeting officer must know that you have had rheumatic fever twice recently. Tell Mrs Thatcher I would be eternally grateful if only she will see that you are landed somewhere suitable, and help her all you can with her preparations for a move, and don't forget to thank her very much for all her care and kindness to you.

Yours with the best of luck and all my love
Mother

P.S.　About the rheumatic fever etc, you can show it to anyone you think advisable. I think I should give it to Mrs Thatcher.

Dear Mother & Dad,
Miss Jaques says she knows one or two billets, but they are all separate. And Esmé and I could not be billeted together. She is going to try and find a billet for us; on Friday and Tuesday we are going to see if she has one.

So we may not even get a billet together, let alone a dry one. If it is damp however I will report it at once to Miss Orton (who is absent at the moment) and get moved, or have the bed aired or something.

I am sorry, Mother, but don't get worried. I <u>promise</u> on my honour if it is the least bit damp I will report it.

But after all the two billets I have been to since I've been here have both been as dry as a bone, so <u>please</u> don't worry. It worries me far more whether I am going to be billeted in C'ham at all.

This is not a long letter, but it is (to me) a vital one.

I had a letter from Bill this morning. He does write nice letters. He has got 6 tickets for Jack & Jill.

Mr & Mrs Davis took us (Jean, Esmé and me) to the flics last night. We saw 'Where's that fire', 'The Saint in London' and Graham Moffat in a personal appearance on the stage of the Gaumont.

Then we came back in the car. It was grand fun - I will tell you about it when I come home.

But again, I feel guilty about the new billet - please write and say I needn't go through that business, because I honestly wouldn't be surprised if we didn't get a billet.

Also it would go all round the school, and I would be the laughing stock behind my back. <u>Please please please</u> don't worry, and say I needn't bother - oh please.

Thanks awfully for the letter. I have a lot of prep to do, so will write proper letter later. Heaps of love
    Pat

Jan   5 Crosbie Road

My dearest Pat
    I have just had your letter and want to scribble a reply before Dad leaves for the works so that he can post it.
Alright darling, don't worry. Trust to luck and try and get billeted with Esmé. If by any chance you can't the only thing to do is to try it out and make the best of it using your spare time for studying, real studying - for the School Cert. isn't very far away now and you will certainly need that for your nursing. If you then found you were still unhappy you can always come home and either go to the Edg. High School, or to King's Norton's King Edwards High School. It is absolutely up to you, so whatever happens don't get too fed up or lonely. There are always other alternatives, and of course there is always a chance that you will be billeted with Esmé again. If the worst comes to the worst, there is every chance that that rumour about you all coming back soon, is correct. Actually, I have heard it here, quite apart from your letter, but it is only a rumour, so don't bank on it.
Well Cheerio and the very best of luck
All my love, Mother.

PS   Vivian rang up some days ago to enquire whether you would like to go to the panto with them. Aren't they all good to you? You seem to be the mutual friend of all Dennis' friends. Have you heard from him lately, he seems in the best of spirits and very happy but he <u>does</u> so love to receive letters.

Thursday 25 January 1940

After we had had our tea we went to see Mrs Lively. We found she had flu, bronchitis, and burst taps! She said that one night she heard the dog barking, and when she came downstairs she found it shipwrecked in its basket amongst a rush of water.

25 Jan   Thursday   Usual Address
                                                               St Leonards

Dear Mother & Dad,
    On looking back I should imagine that the cryptic sorrowfulness of my previous letter must have given you a completely wrong impression of my position here.
    If I remember rightly, the chief content of the letter was a sad beseeching for letters from home. This arose from the fact that one of the fellows in our room has, on the average, about three letters daily and as I had gone for three days without any letters at all, I dashed off my letter to you.
    About two days later I found out that it was only natural that I had a sparsity of letters as I had only written two replies since I came back here from my last week-end.
    I don't know whether I have already told you but another fellow in our room has chosen to go sick, this time with German Measles.
    This means that it is most unlikely that I shall be home this week-end but I am hoping to come back the one after.
    Owing to our isolation we are having a grand time, our daily time-table being somewhat as follows:-

6.30 Orderly comes and wakes us
6.40 Fast asleep again
7.20 Wake up for breakfast which is brought to us at about 7.35. We get up at any time that pleases us. The M.O. comes to see us at about 10.30. We are allowed to go out for a walk between 11 and 12 and also 2.30 till 3.30. Lunch is brought us at 12.30 and tea and supper at 4.30 and 6.30.

Tuesday I got up at 9 o'clock.
Yesterday I got up at 2.45 p.m.
Today it is 9.45 and I am still firmly ensconced in bed.

A week ago we had a 10" fall of snow which thawed one day and then froze hard. But for the last few days the weather has been grand.

On one or two occasions I have been to the Brighton ice rink. (The last time we went to see 'Band Waggon' afterwards, at the Hippodrome.) And I might say that the country looks really grand, we have had some really perfect blue skies to set it off. It's really worth going to Brighton if only for the train run.

I am sorry to hear of the difficulties you have been experiencing at home in the way of illnesses. However I believe that you are getting over the worst now, anyway here's hoping.

Lying in bed, I can if ever I feel in need of inspiration, look out of the window to see: a bright cloudless sky, a sparkling sea and now and then a bunch of seagulls - what more could I want?

Anyway here's hoping you will soon all be well again
With love from
Dennis

Sunday 28 January 1940

A terrific freeze. All the rain in the night froze. We knitted and washed and darned all morning, and in the afternoon we slid down the path up the passage and through the gate breaking icicles all the way.

As we went through the gate Jean was coming towards us with Joyce and her friend. They wanted to see what it was like in the lane. We went on slowly, it was so slippery on the path, and the little blades of grass were encased in short fat icicles that crackled and crunched as we walked.

Jean caught up with us and we went down Newborne Lane, that was great, and 3 soldiers came up in a car.

As we were slipping and sliding along, we started talking about how difficult it was for us to get a new billet, and Jean said she'd ask Mr and Mrs Davis, who she was billeted on.

Then we walked past the Burgage to Mrs Lively's. As we were going up her path a gust of wind blew us off the slippery path onto the cabbage patch.

We went up to see George and his pig, but he's changed the stye and we went to the old one.

Monday 29 January 1940

It snowed in the morning, and the ice was not so slippery.

I was doing my hair, when there was a knock on the front door, and when I answered it there was Mrs Davis with snow blowing all about her. She said she'd heard that a Mrs Jones would like to have two girls billeted on her.

I quickly plaited my hair and we went round to see her, but she said her husband, Davy Jones, was a jockey and they went away too often.

We went back and Esmé went to the post. Mrs Jones came along and said she'd been thinking it over and she would have us.

Went to school in the afternoon and told Miss Jaques about the billet. She was very pleased.

Wednesday 31 January 1940

Got up at 7.30 and said Goodbye to Mr Thatcher. Did geography homework, and then carried all our stuff to Ridgeway, our new billet. We had dinner with Mrs Thatcher, and then went to school. We had Maths, and then we went to Miss Jaques and got our billeting paper.

We went back with Jean. By that time a thaw had set in, and the snow and ice on Cakebridge road was melting fast. We went up the lane and had a snowball fight. The snow is always best when it's thawing. Then we went to Mrs Thatcher's and collected the odd things left and went to Mrs Jones'. We had tea, and at 6 Mrs Thatcher went home.

We wrote letters. Our room is at the back and has much the same view, only the house is lower.

Wed: 5 Crosbie Road
31st Jan 40

My dearest Pat

I have been thinking about you so much this morning and wondering how things are progressing. I am so very glad to know you have found a new billet in Welland Lodge Rd and are still to be with Esmé. I think you have been quite remarkably fortunate.

Now listen - listen intently and don't forget what I am about to say. First and foremost I want you to thank Mrs Thatcher for all her kindness to you. She has been simply splendid in the way she has looked after your well-being and allowed you to use all her rooms, chairs and things just as if you were at home. It is a very, very big thing, you know Pat.

Secondly, I want you to promise to <u>never</u> on any account criticise adversely anything at all that may have happened during your stay with Mrs Thatcher. It would be very very bad form and ungrateful - doesn't matter what it may have been - if anything. This is very important. Only speak well of anything that happened there, and don't criticise anything that may not have quite pleased you.

Thirdly, will you please thank Mrs Davis from me, for any part she has had in finding you this new billet - don't forget.

Lastly, Mrs Thatcher tells me what a charming home Mrs Jones has. Remember to take great care of her wallpaper, furniture etc, and change your shoes, to save her new carpets. These things mean so much to people.

And now to get along with my letter, for this isn't only to be a sermon - but <u>please</u> remember what I have told you.

Oh, by the way, I am in bed again. I got up Thursday, felt bad on Sat: - came back to bed Sunday, and here I still am, though I am better today and hope to get up a bit tomorrow. Dr Winfield has had an awful time trying to get round to his patients through the snow. On Monday he couldn't manage to get here at all, yesterday he got here late in the evening and had had to walk from Lordswood Rd. He said that on Monday he got in two separate snow drifts, one took him 1 1/2 hrs to dig himself out, the other 3/4 hr. We have been in a state of siege here - no Tradesmen of any description have been able to call since Sat. We have had no bread, milk, greens, meat or groceries delivered, and Dad has to go down to The Ivy Bush to Wathes, C. & G. to bring in enough milk to keep us going for a day or two. Mrs Bonehill comes in for a few hrs each day to tidy up and give me some food, and she goes round the village collecting what she can on her way here. Oh, yes - it is a 'game', I can tell you. We seem to have it particularly hard just round here, as Sutton and Moseley are still getting supplies of bread and milk, though I don't know about other provisions.

Dad says there were sea-gulls at the works, driven inland in search of food. Mrs Bonehill says there were people buying fat from the butchers this morning to give to the birds, and we have given them food. Poor little things, they certainly need looking after. I should think the poor goldfish must be frozen into a solid mass.

Dad and I hope to come over and see you soon and we want to meet Mrs Jones. Dad has been forced to save enough petrol as it has been impossible to even get his car out of the garage during this arctic weather. Well darling, I hope you will be very happy and comfortable.

With all my love
Mother.

Thursday   Usual Address.

Dear Pat

AD REFERENDUM.

Full knowing and aware, I do not stoop to make amends or offer, with a contrite heart, excuses for the tardiness of this epistle. Nor am I fain to mollify your wrath with subtle flattery.

"Procrastination is the Thief of Time."

Since man's primordial birth, reveréd sages, bestowing wisdom on a clamouring mankind, declared those quoted words and found belief.

Inspiréd bards, from quivering strings and eager throats, gave back reply: no doubt or questioning to mute the cry.

The world considered, then, unanimous, opined deep-founded verity; and down the wheeling ages none has risen to dispel this fallacy.

Till, obdurate, one soul alone, disciple of Truth's golden art, I gird me with the armour of a righteous cause.

"Procrastination is", they say, "the Thief of Time".

Yet, each second of a task undone is but a second saved for other duties, perhaps of greater worth.

Convinced of this, ponder awhile that mayhap the hours I spent in other pursuits upheld a worthier cause than even that of fellowship between us.

And now my conscience satisfied, assured of understanding on your part and sad fatigued by tedious composition I bid adieu.

Finis, gaudaemus igitur.

With love from

<u>Dennis</u>.

Mother sent me some newspaper clippings about the terrible weather they had had.

THIS WAS CORPORATION S

SNOWED IN!

7,000,000 TONS IN ONE WEEK-END

BIRMINGHAM'S ARCTIC CONDITIONS

MOST SEVERE SPELL ON RECORD

£1,800 PER DAY TO CLEAR STREETS

Long after this war is over, Birmingham men and women will call to mind how, during the last weeks in January, they had to shovel their way out of their homes and plough knee-deep through the snow in quest of transport which either did not run at all or was long delayed. They will tell how suburban roads were impassable, so far as vehicular traffic was concerned, and how for days on end there were no deliveries of bread, milk and coal, and they will dwell in memory upon many other unfortunate aspects of one of winter's severest moods for nearly half a century.

In two to three days over 7,000,000 tons of snow fell upon the city to an average depth of 16in., the deepest fall since 1895.Following as they did upon the tribulations of an exceptionally severe and protracted frost, the sharpest for 45 years and one which sent the thermometer slumping to 11 degrees Fahrenheit, these conditions proved a sore trial to all classes of inhabitants, and particularly those who had to be out and about performing manual tasks which are essential to the life of the community.

The transport systems of the City – trains trams and 'buses - were disorganised, and roofs of houses and business premises collapsed, rendering homeless 30 families.

Many aspects of the situation have already been recorded in the "Mail", but what was not set down owing to the limitations of censorship regulations, was the burden of the snow, which blocked the roadways to harass and inconvenience thousands of persons and incidentally to add to the financial burden of the city, a bill of £20,000.

POSTMAN AND CLERK OF THE WEATHER

The horse came into his own again during the severe weather. Top picture, taken on January 29th, shows a Kings Norton postman setting out on his rounds; lower picture shows Mr Kelley, of Edgbaston Observatory, digging a way through the snow to get to his instruments.

Sunday 4 February 1940

After dinner Esmé and I decided to ride to Gloucester. We got all the things ready, and started off.

We passed the aerodrome and saw all the camouflaged buildings. Then we passed Rotol and thought how grim and forbidding it looked in its dark camouflaging. As we were about 3 miles from Gloucester it started to rain. With heads down and wet legs we sped on, and at last arrived at the Townsend's. We dried ourselves and had some tea, and then started off again. As we passed some soldiers camped in the low swirling mist we whistled and shouted to them as we rode on. It was very dark when we reached the Prestbury Rd and we had to walk our bikes.

Monday 12   5 Crosbie Road

My dearest Pat

Here come your clothes at last, I only got them back from the laundry on Sat, and then had to look them over for mending, so do hope you have been able to manage. I am going to ask Mrs Bonehill to post on her way home. Hope the I.R.A. won't be active – 'twould be very awkward for you.

Dennis came home on leave Friday evening and went back after dinner yesterday. He had Christine to tea and supper on Saturday and Billy, Vivian and Christine to dinner yesterday. Now his ambition is to get leave at Easter, so that you can all go to the pantomime together.

What are you doing about half-term, shall you come home? Do we have to write to Miss Barrie? And how long do you get? I should certainly like you to come home if you can, yes sir - that I would. Let me know what is happening and what Esmé is doing about it. All being well we hope to come over to see you on Sunday, in fact, unless you hear to the contrary, we shall come, and we will bring a picnic lunch for us all, and you and Esmé as well, if she would like to join us. The only thing that would prevent us coming is the weather, for if the roads were snowbound or ice-bound, we could not come. I will send a wire on Sat, if we are not coming. Well darling, I am rather writing against time as Mrs Bonehill is almost ready to go, and I still have to pack the parcel.

Grandma was on the phone this morning and both she and Gran ask me to send you their special love. Dad didn't write anything yesterday as he was again busy at the works.

With all my dearest love
Mother

February 1940						748 48099 etc

Thursday (or is it Wednesday?)

Dear Pat

In spite of the fact that I find that you owe me a letter, or is it two?, I have decided to write you a letter on my very best paper, and in my very best writing.

By the way you may or may not know that when Gran knitted me a pair of gloves she had not enough wool to finish the last little finger and so she had to use some of your wool. And do you know that out of all the many home knitted things I have seen in Hastings, that wool of yours is the first I have seen that is the correct colour.

I am hoping that it will just be possible for me to get back home for Easter Monday, in which case I shall, of course, be able to come to the pantomime with you. By the way the pantomime list is now as follows:-

Vivian & his friend Olive
Billy
Yourself
Bob and Betty Smyth
Myself and Christine

Bob, myself and Olive, however, may be unable to come but we are hoping for the best.

Last Friday I went home for the week-end and ordered two pheasants from Macfisheries. These had to be sent specially by train from Worcester as there were none in B'ham. On Saturday morning I went to a lecture at the Chartered Accounts Institute with Bill.

Thursday (it really is this time) -

On Saturday afternoon Christine came round to tea and in the evening we went to the Warley to see 'Double Crime in the Maginot Line', a very awkward film to follow the meaning of.

On Sunday morning, at Christine's suggestion, I got breakfast for Mother, Dad and Gran, they were so surprised that they fell in with my suggestion that Chris might come round to lunch (I had already asked Bill and Vivian, on condition that they did the washing up).

I might add, although I think it unnecessary, that the lunch was a complete success.

When I got back here on Monday mid-day, after staying Sunday night in London, we were treated to a lecture of British Law and Administration by one Pilot Officer RAGBAGLIATI.

We have also had two very interesting lectures by our C.O. on the History of the R.A.F.

Did you know that Napoleon used 'captive' observation balloons and so did the Americans in their Civil War; and did you know that each year (for the last 300 yrs) the King has to get permission to keep an army and a R.A.F. in peace time as, according to British *Statute Law, it is illegal for the King to have an army or R.A.F. in peace time!

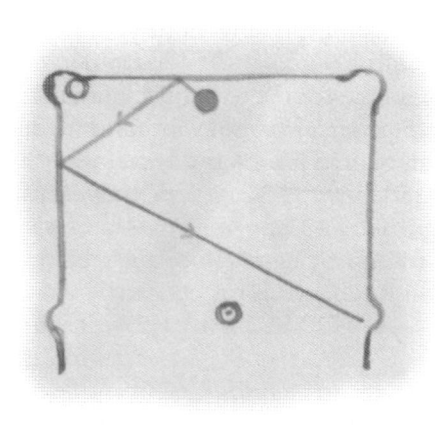

* Statute = Permanent

The night before last I went out with Baxter, and though we played *(billiards)* for an hour he beat me by only one point.

At one time in the game I was losing by 20 or more when two fellows who were leaving stopped to watch me make my shot, I will now break out into diagrams and details. So hold tight!

My ball was the one in the centre and it was my intention to hit the red on the left hand side and then cannon onto the white by the top left pocket.

Actually I made a very bad shot and my ball hit the red on the wrong side and went anywhere but whither I had intended. Judge my surprise therefore when the red rocketed across the table along the red line shewn and went straight into the middle pocket, to the accompaniment of cries of 'Good shot' from the two fellows watching.

From this moment I scored in great fashion and caught up the twenty in no time.

This was nothing, however, to the fluke I made playing against a fellow in this room at the same billiard table about three or four weeks ago.

The balls were arranged as shewn below and my intention was to cannon as shewn by the blue line.

(I am afraid that the billiard table is a little out of shape.)

My ball is the one with the spot at the bottom of the table and the shot was a particularly easy one.

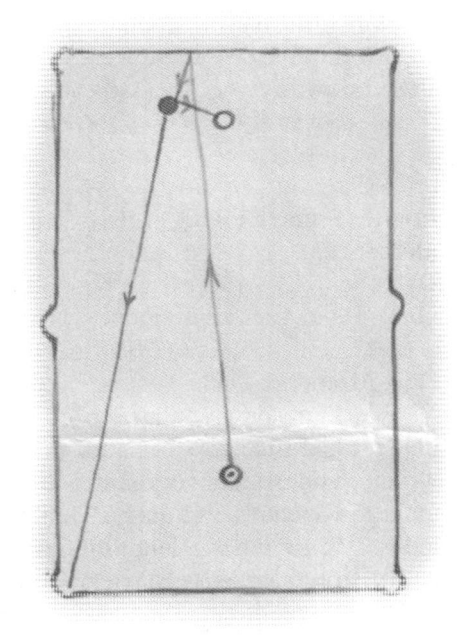

Actually what happened was that my shot went a bit wrong and my ball passed straight between the two others!

It hit the cushion, came back and hit the red and then the white (a cannon = 2 points) and the red went straight down the table into the bottom pocket (3 points).

Was I surprised!

And some people who were watching looked surprised and murmured "Oh, very pretty shot", or something like that. It so happened that I made a break of 11 points and next turn made another pretty shot and so they thought I was a much better player than I was!

    Well I must hurry if I am to post this before afternoon parade.
    With lots of love
    from
    <u>Dennis</u>

Friday 16 February 1940

    Went to netball. Did homework, went to school. At recess Mrs Hopkins told me off about standing after she'd told us to sit down which wasn't fair because there were lots of others standing and anyway I thought I'd sat down.

Friday (Friday? <u>FRIDAY</u>!)   "Ridgeway"
                                                             106 Welland Lodge Road
                                                             Cheltenham

Dear Mother & Dad

    I am sorry you have been kept waiting so long for a letter, but I just haven't had time. As a matter of fact I am skimping my Scripture prep. to write to you, so feel very gratified!

    I haven't written to Den for about a month, but I've started his letter. Please write a letter on Sat. and bring with you on Sun. It is to get permission from Miss Barrie to come home at 1/2 term. She must get it by Mon. you see.

    George's pig has had 8 piglets. They are pink with white hairs.

    We have met a painter whom we call "Handsome", his name is A. McCarthy, is <u>very</u> nice, and we have had lots of adventures with him. I'll tell you about it when I come home.

    Our new billet is very nice. Mr and Mrs Jones are young, and Mrs J has offered to take us to a tea-dance, but don't mention it when you come, because we don't want to go. Not without a partner, and Esmé and I wouldn't want to dance together.

I have been put down for the junior team practice, and I am getting real good at Netball now.

Pat Ball has got chickenpox, and cinemas are now out of bounds - isn't it a SWIZ? And it is 'Five came back'. We have thought of going on the sly - we may yet. I have been trying to persuade Esmé, but we have been getting in rather a lot of rows recently (for not wearing our hats in the road and for leaning out of the form-room window, and waving to the painter, and for making a row in the form-room) all of which we consider quite harmless things and stupid rules are broken by doing the above, and the rules deserve to be broken - anyway we have decided to reform, and that's why E is undecided about going.

I don't like to tell you any news, because I want to tell it you all when I come home. I'll bring my diary which I hope you'll find very exciting (some 'opes!)

By the way when you come on Sunday this is how you'll find the house.

There are 2 blocks of houses from the corner.

I think you'll find it quite easily-

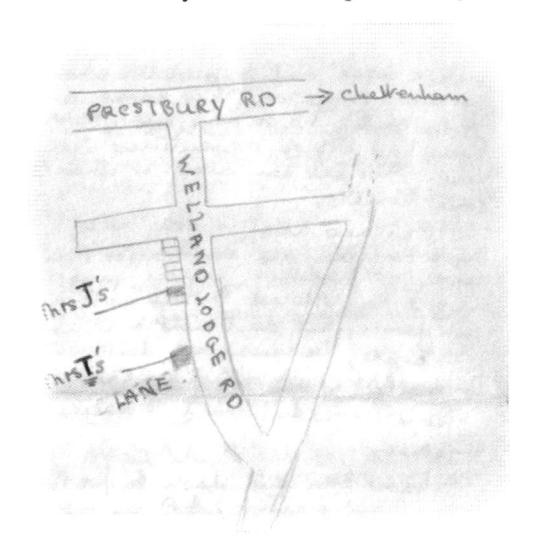

Do you think Den will get a leave at 1/2 term? I hope so, because I don't see him as often as you do. Do you like this paper? 2d from Woolworths - 8 envelopes into the bargain.

Mrs Jones is a marvellous cook - her pastry is - beautiful.

She wants to have you to dinner on Sunday, it's pork. Isn't it nice of her? I want to have my eyes tested at 1/2 term. There's nowt wrong with them, but I feel that I ought to.

We've seen 'Handsome' again today. He's terrifically nice, and he's rather shy. He's about 5' 10. He has a moustache (a very nice one) and his hair is dark, and starts growing right away from the temples. Esmé keeps getting her autograph book out and looking at his autograph.

We both think he's marvellous and worship him more than any film star. I cannot say any more about him because words cannot express how nice he is!

No, honestly though, he is awfully nice and I wish we were in B'ham so that we could talk to him instead of just looking at him and smiling and winking through a window.

Well, to get back to earth again, there is a terrific gale blowing outside and I love gales. I am praying to heaven that it won't snow tomorrow, so you can come on Sun.

I've got to post this letter so
Cheerio
Lots of Love
Pat

P.S. I'm sorry I was so long writing to you.

Mother rang up and said they could not come on Sunday because of the snow.

Sunday 18 February 1940

Had breakfast at 11.30. Had just finished breakfast, washed up and sat down by the fire when Mrs Jones came in and said dinner was ready. We were 1/2 way through dinner when Mr Jones said "Roll on tea-time!"

After dinner we wrote to Den and Mr Edwards and I enclosed Den's mittens and Esmé, Mr Edward's gloves.

On the way to post them we called at Mrs Thatcher's - oh the house is upside down! In the evening Mr Jones said he would take us to the pictures tomorrow - Hurray!

106 Welland Lodge Rd
Cheltenham.

Dear Den

Well here are your mittens at last. They are my first attempt at ever knitting on 4 pins so you will have to overlook the various mistakes to be found everywhere. They'll keep your hands warm anyway; I hope they fit, because I am not expert enough to alter them. Please forgive me for not having written for such a long time, but I have been very busy moving, and - well you know how time flies - or don't you?

I hope to be home for 1/2 term next week-end, will you be on leave? I hope so. A girl in our form has developed chicken-pox. And now cinemas are out of bounds; and it is 'Five came back' this week. Still we may break bounds and go. I do want to see it. But not 1/2 as much as I want to see you again!!

It is very nice at my new billet, and I think the Jones are very nice. N.B. I have just received your Valentine greetings telegram - thanks awfully; you are a dear -

I suppose you know Mr Jones is a jockey? He is not riding at the moment because of the weather. The house is called after his first winner. He is quite a famous jockey.

<u>Friday</u>. We come home on Sat. morning, and go back on Tuesday. I am just longing to see you again, so you've <u>got</u> to get a leave at Easter if not at 1/2 term. But I hope you get back for both.

I have thought of a new way to do my hair. I don't think it will work, but I am going to try it at home at 1/2 term.

George's sow has had 8 piglets.

I received your letter the day before yesterday. Phew! What a long one, I shall never send you one as good as that.

Mr Jones is taking us to the pictures tomorrow evening - yes, I know it's out of bounds, but we're going in plain clothes and wearing our hoods so no-one will recognise us.

The film is called I don't know what, but George Formby is in it. Unfortunately we missed the 'Five came back', but I hope to see it in B'ham.

It has been snowing, and has prevented mother & dad from coming down on Sunday. There are drifts up to your knees by the farm, and I had a lovely time in them yesterday.

In the afternoon we went to town, and went here there and everywhere - then we went to see George and his pigs, but George wasn't there, and 3 of the piglets are dead. We couldn't see the sow and the 5 other piglets because the sow might jump up at strangers, and land on another piglet and kill that, so we went through the allotments.

When we got outside we snowballed posts, and we didn't hit one. So Esmé said "Watch me hit that window". She raised a handful of <u>soft</u> snow and threw it and crash!!, it hit the window and broke the glass!!

A woman had just come out of the house and Esmé went up to her and the little boy with her said "Ee! Mum, that's our window!" The lady didn't seem a bit worried, and Esmé apologised and offered to pay for the window.

Is there any snow at Hastings? Esmé & I are going home by train because of the snow.

Do write and tell me if you think you'll be back at 1/2 term. It is <u>next week-end</u>. You <u>must</u> be home then. Please forgive me for not writing for such a long time.

      Lots of Love
      Pat

P.S.   If you do have a leave next weekend please bring your skates so we can go skating.

<u>Tuesday 20th Feb</u>. 1940   748099 etc

Dear Dad,

I have just had a letter from Pat, enclosing a pair of mittens which she had knitted and which, by the way are one of the first pairs I have seen which are the correct colour.

She seems to be very excited that she is coming home this week-end. As I have said before, and also as you suggested, I shall not be coming home for some short while.

Today we had some interesting information of the Borkum Raid, details of which I can, if you are interested, tell you next time I come home.

I am writing this in the guard room, not because I am under close arrest but because I have the misfortune to be on guard tomorrow and tonight.

At about 4.30, just after I had first gone on guard, there was a loud rumbling bang which rattled all the windows on the front and apparently came from out at sea. I am wondering whether it were a mine exploding, perhaps I shall know from the papers in the near future.

During the last week-end everybody from our room, except Chapman and myself, went away on a long week-end pass and left us to lead a life of laziness and luxury. We got up late, went to bed early, used everybody's beds for throwing our belongings on etc, and at 8 o'clock, or thereabouts, each evening we regaled ourselves with toast and butter and ham (or crab), fruit etc, and (I) having got into bed Chapman heated up some more cocoa and we had more toast etc and chocolate.

I think I mentioned this in my last letter to mother, but we also bought some artificial roses and daffodils (the roses smell just like the real thing) and also a broom, coal scuttle, shovel, and brush for the room. In point of fact my part of the room is already beginning to look like a luxury flat.

This however does not impair the efficiency of our work, apart from tending to make us late on parade in the morning when we like to make the most of the comfort of our beds.

As I have little else to say I think I'll stop now; I have to go out on guard again anyhow.

Dennis.

P.S. As the Government suggests that paper should not be wasted, may I suggest that you use the back of this sheet for scrap paper, and the other two sheets for whatever use suggests itself to your mind.

Wednesday 21 Feb. 1940

748099 etc
St. Leonards-on-Sea

Dear Pat

I have your letter containing the mittens to hand for which "I thang you". (*A catchphrase from a radio show, I.T M A*) They are, as I have said before, the correct colour, and do fit. Although, until I start flying I haven't really very much scope for using them.

At the moment I am on guard duty. It is now 12.55 a.m. (just after midnight) on Wednesday morning and I am duty guard for these two hours. But as everybody, with the exception of one fire picquet who goes about looking for fires, is asleep I am just sitting in the guard room writing.

I am afraid that I shan't be able to get back this week-end but I am hoping that it will just be possible for me to get back at Easter; after all, you know, we <u>are</u> at war, and I <u>am</u> in the service, and you <u>can't</u> always get leave when you want it.

I am afraid that this letter is neither bright, long nor witty but who wants to be bright, long and witty on guard duty at 1 o'c in the morning.

Actually, though, it's not too bad.

With lots of love from

Dennis.

Friday 23 February 1940

Went to Netball. Went to town and got Mrs Jones some flowers, went to school.

Saturday 24 February 1940

Got up early, packed. Went down to Landsdown. Met Jean, Mary and Norma. After waiting a while the train came in, and we just went to the nearest carriage and opened the door and walked in. We walked along the corridor, and passed 1 compartment. In the next was 1 Army officer. We all peered in and then opened the door and went in. He helped me put my case up and we all settled in. He was very nice, and showed us his badges and what they meant. E and I got his autograph, he was on leave, going up to Derby, he is billeted at the racecourse.

He was a Terrier before the war and was called up on the outbreak of war. We talked for a long time and at the last stop before B'ham an inspector came in and told us to go and that these were 4 reserved carriages. Lt. Alexander begged him to let us stay, but we had to go. After tramping up and down corridors and many adventures we went to the luggage van where we stayed among the luggage. Mother met me, and we were walking down the platform when we met him. I introduced them, and then went home. Went to see grandma, says how much older I seem.

Sunday 25 February 1940

Had a bath and washed my hair. In the afternoon went to Middleton woods. Had tea at the Happy Hour - what a happy hour! Cut out a blouse, played cards.

Tuesday 27 February 1940

Got up early. Said goodbye to Dad and Gran and went to the station. We waited in an awful crush, and then got the train with Jean, Esmé and Olive.

Thursday 29 February 1940

Alarm went at 7, got up at 9.30, went to netball. Went to school. Mr Jones won 2 races.

Tuesday   5 Crosbie Road

My dearest Pat
    I expect you wonder where your usual Sunday letter is. The fact is Dennis came home on a short week-end leave, Dad was called to the works Sunday morning and did not return until nearly two o'clock, and I came to bed as soon as I had washed the dinner things as I still feel rather groggy and my temperature will persist in going up each time I have been up for about a day and a half. It is my silly antrums that are doing it, but anyway they are trying a new treatment, so I hope to be like a two-year-old before I am much older, in the meantime Doctor Winfield advises me to stay in bed.
    Dennis had quite a nice leave in spite of my bad behaviour. Sat. morning he saw Billy and Vivian in town, and Sat afternoon went to Christine's to tea and supper. Sunday he went to Billy's to dinner and tea, spent the night in London with an air force friend, and I haven't heard from him since. I have made up a little poem in his honour.
    Sooty sneaked out last night and didn't return in spite of prolonged calling from Dad, but she was on the doorstep this morning, none the worse

for her night out. She spends nearly all her time up here with me, she certainly likes company, and I must admit I like having her around.

We hope to be over quite soon to see you, will let you know when. Don't you think it would be a good thing to bring some of your surplus books and things back with us and so give you less to look after. Please thank Mrs Jones for her letter.

Yours with all my love, Mother

(Of course, besides writing, Mother phoned me from time to time, but at the beginning of March she phoned me to break the awful news that Sooty was dead.

She had developed incurable eczema, and they had had to have her 'put to sleep'.

I was terribly upset and Mother said she would be writing to me to explain in more detail what exactly had happened.)

March 5th   5 Crosbie Road

My dearest Pat

First and foremost, before I forget, don't forget to write to Dad for his birthday on March 13th. Secondly, I have written to Miss Barrie, so all is O.K. in that respect.

I wonder how you are getting on with exams, very well I hope, but time will tell, it will be interesting to see your report .... I hope! ... Now I must tell you about Sooty. One of the last days I noticed a patch on her side that was quite bare. I thought possibly she had been fighting but feeling the responsibility whilst you are away Dad and I took her to the vets. He said Sooty had a skin disease, which was very hard to cure in cats and was very irritating. However I tried treating it, giving pills, and rubbing in lotion and boracic powder, but the patch got bigger and more angry looking, and another patch came over each eye and I rang up Harborne dispensary and told them about it, and they said the kindest thing would be to put Sooty to sleep, as animals hardly every recovered and if they did they were always very likely to develop the disease again so we took her along before the patches got too irritating or sore. Christine said their dog had the same trouble and got in an awful state before they finally gave up treatment and had it put to sleep.

The vet said Sooty never would have made a strong cat, and would probably have gone on from one thing to another. When the war is over, we shall have to see about getting another pet, not before, the meat difficulty is too great. Sooty was lucky in that respect, she never went short of anything.

Dad has just said he has been trying to save enough petrol to take you a run or two at Easter. We took Dennis, Christine and Vivian to the 'Happy Hour' to tea on Sunday.

By the way, have you and Esmé seen anything more of the lieutenant. Don't trouble to write if you are studying for exams, or if other letters are waiting to be written, for I heard you on the 'phone so know all is well.

 Dad and Gran both send their love.
 With dearest love
 from Mother.

Wednesday 6.3.40   2 Flight
                   AlexandraHotel
                   St Leonards on Sea

My dear Pat,

Although I find that I have not had a letter from you for many a long day, I have decided that this must be due to the fact that you must be enjoying yourself too much to find time to write.

I should like to say that, so far from finding no use for your mittens, I find them very useful, and wear them all the more as you knit them.

In fact the real reason for me writing this letter was to say how much I find them useful; and also to remark that they are the correct colour - I forget how many times I have said this before.

Well! As I have a lot more letters to write, I'd better say Cheerio! I'll write again as soon as I have more time.

 With lots of love
 Dennis

Monday 11 March 1940

Brenda rang Esmé up to tell her her father was home on leave. So Esmé is going home.

Wednesday 13 March 1940

Esmé went. I knitted and did my prep. Looked out of the window and saw lots of soldiers in the field and with lorries and cars parked around the hedge. Got my dinner, because Mr Jones was at the races, then went to school.

13/3/40   5 Crosbie Road

My dear Pat

In your last letter you accuse me of not writing to you for a long time, but on the other hand your own letters are few and far between.

Still "qui s'accuse s'excuse" as the monkey said when he stole a piece of sugar, or if he didn't he might have done.

The two books you gave me were very interesting and I enjoyed reading them very much and now Gran thought they looked so nice that she has taken them both upstairs to read in bed.

Dennis sent me a packet of Pavlova cigarettes. Gran gave me various presents too numerous to mention in a short letter but including scissors, scarf, shaving soap, handkerchiefs and sweets. Granma Dawes sent me two packets of cigarettes and Mother is taking me to town on Saturday on the spree.

I have given public notice to your Mother and Gran that as it's my birthday, I am going to have at the least 4 glasses of sherry tonight, so quite likely your Mother will have to put me to bed.

You will observe as my letter proceeds, how the bottle of sherry is progressing, not progressing, I mean diminishing.

Poor old Rover has been out of commission for over a week now poor dear, she leaked badly and so has had to go back to Coventry for an operation.

As you can see the censor has been at work hence the blue pencil.

That is the result of another glass of sherry.

I am afraid you will have to come home by train for two reasons, firstly because it is extremely unlikely that Rover will be out of hospital by then and secondly if I fetched you, it would use all my spare petrol and as you will be at home for 3 weeks *(4 isn't it, Mother)* you are sure to like to go runs on Sundays and that would then not be possible.

I may go half shares with Mr Richards and use his car one week and mine the next and so save a week's petrol every two weeks. I applied for my supplementary ration of petrol last week end for April and this time we had to prove there was no alternative means of getting to Oldbury.

I said there were no buses on Sunday mornings and as "I was an old man of nearly 50 with shrapnel in my leg from the last war, they shouldn't expect me to walk".

I am waiting now to see if my plea works. Mother and I have been invited to Moseley for next Sunday dinner (a couple of ducks), don't you envy us?

We have decided that as we can't get about so much due to the unfortunate times in which we are now living, we are going to move the rockery hedgewards, or in other words where the herbaceous border now is, and then there will be room for two deck chairs by the pool and you and Mother and I can then sit and watch the goldfish disport in the pellucid waters of the lake.

The sherry is now commencing to work and Morpheus is closing my eyes and

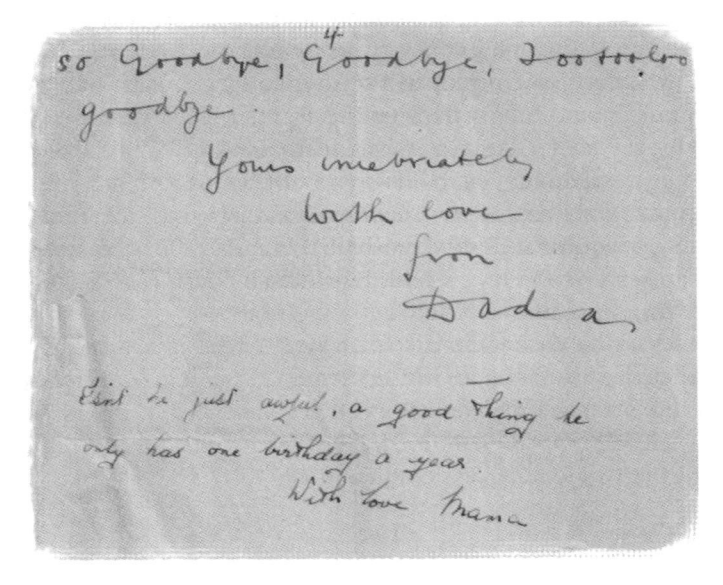

so Goodbye, Goodbye, Goodbye, goodbye.

Yours inebriately
with love
from
Dada

Isn't he just awful, a good thing he only has one birthday a year.
With love Mama

Sunday 17 March 1940 - Palm Sunday

We went for a walk as it had stopped raining. We passed the racecourse - I think the soldiers have left.

Fourteen planes have been over Scapa Flow - 1 civilian killed, 3 or 4 others injured - because they watched the battle instead of going into an air-raid shelter.

Sunday
2 Park Road
Moseley
Birmingham

My dearest Pat

Such a short while now till you are home. I am writing this at Moseley as Grandma has just treated Dad to his birthday dinner of roast duck etc. etc. followed by liquor *(sic)* chocolates and all helped down with sherry. Yes sir, we have had a very good war-time meal.

Yesterday I treated Dad to the pictures in the evening and dinner at The Burlington, which consisted of hors d'oeuvres, soup, fish and mushrooms, roast duck, ice cream, coffee, all helped down with Chianti; all very nice and enjoyable in these hard times.

By the way don't forget to bring your ration cards with you, and don't bring any more clothes than you can get in your suitcase. I should come in your grey coat and skirt, and hooded coat. It would be a good way of bringing those. I should leave all school clothes behind including school coat, you won't need that. Also I should make a parcel of all soiled clothes, and whatever else you could send and POST them on. It is wonderful what a lot once can send in this way, and it would make your case lighter for you to carry.

I will be on the station to meet you, I have the time of the train from Miss Barrie. If there is any difficulty in seeing each other on the station wait for me and I will wait for you at the bottom of the steps. Rover is still at the works, but Dad is hoping to get it back for Easter. He has quite a bit of petrol saved through being unable to use the car.

Please thank Mrs Jones for her nice letter, we shall hope to see her in the near future. Dennis hopes to get leave for Easter, but isn't definite about it yet, although he says he will get leave anyway whilst you are home.
Until Thursday and then hurrah!
>With all my love
>Mother.

Thursday 21 March 1940

Went up to Jean's. Mr Davis took us to the station in the car. Found Mary in the train and spent the time in the corridor with the soldiers showing off. Arrived B'ham.
In the evening Viv came and said "Is Den in?" I said "No, I don't think he's getting a leave" and at that moment the QA song was heard and in came Den!!!!

Friday 22 March 1940

Went to the village with Den, got rations. In the afternoon Dad took us to see his stack being pulled down. *(It was considered a landmark for enemy bombers.)* Came home, Chris, Bill and Viv came to tea.

Monday 25 March 1940 - Easter Monday, Bank Holiday

    Went to the ice rink with Den and Chris. Her brother Jeff took us, and we arrived there at 10.00. We found it did not start 'till 11, so went round town. Went to the art gallery, but there was only a small part open. Then went to the rink for an hour. I am greatly improving and Chris, under the expert tuition of Den, improved terrifically during the session.
    Came home and changed and went to "Jack & Jill", of course we were first. Very good show. Den, Chris, Viv and myself went round to Bill's for the evening.
    Den and Chris went to Matthews while Viv, Bill and I washed up.
    Came home - Den's leave expired, Den went back to -- !!

Tuesday 26 March 1940

    Bill came round to fetch his things, took me to have coffee at Pattersons. Later, as I was seeing him off he looked at me and said "You know Pat, you are pretty - at least not pretty - beautiful!" What could I say? I don't know, except I know I blahed something about mirrors and other simple things.

In the evening went to Royalty to see "Thunder Afloat", very good!

Friday 29 March 1940

Had a letter from Den saying he thought he could come home for a pass. Later a telegram saying - Anticipate unavoidably procrastinated arrival" - then Viv rang up to say he had German measles and had had a telegram from Den saying - Arrive New Street 7.30 - Mother and I went down to meet Den.

Saturday 30 March 1940

Went skating with Den and Chris, Den had Chris round to tea in the afternoon

Went to the village, Den wouldn't speak on the way back and then went into the middle of the road and picked up a piece of rhubarb which he carried in front of him - Den and Chris went to the flics. Bill rang up.

Sunday 31 March 1940

Den, Chris, Bill and I went rowing - at least Bill and I did while Den and Chris walked round the reservoir. All went to Bill's to tea in the afternoon. Called on Bob Smythe but they were all out. Then called on Barrie Matthews, his cousin Jimmie was there, and his sister and her young man.

Went to the station to see Den off, he kissed Chris goodbye.

Bill and his father took Chris and me home in the car.

Thursday 4 April 1940

Went to town, met Grandma. Got a bathing costume, had dinner, did some more to my dress. Rang up the Smethwick baths. Then Bill, I had a long talk with him. Bet him a meringue that the Bournville lane baths are rotten. I expect he'll win.

Friday 5/4/40

Dear Pat

I think that actually, in spite of the fact that you were the last person to write, you still really should be the person to write. However out of my generosity and goodness of heart I find it in me to write to you.

It seems quite probable that (as I expect Mother has already told you) I shall be getting a week's leave from 17-24th of April - Hip! Hip! Hooray!

Of course, it is not definite yet but I think I stand a good chance.

A few fellows have had the luck to be posted to Rhodesia for flying training.

Only a very few fellows are going but those few that have been lucky enough to be posted should have a pretty good time of it out there.

As yet I have heard no news of my posting but all the fellows with names beginning with the letters A-H are going to Prestwick, Perth and Fairoaks. So I am expecting to go somewhere about May 20th.

By the way about the Rhodesia I shouldn't tell too many people about it until it is published in the papers - you are the only person I have told.

Naturally in view of my posting leave I shall be unable to attend Billy's birthday party, as it is too much to expect both a week's leave and a week-end pass as well.

Actually the last few days my mind seems to have been utterly devoid of ideas for writing so I am afraid that this letter may seem unnecessarily short. However I feel sure that you would rather have me finish in this fashion than to say, "I must hurry to catch the post now", so Cheerio!", because that would be an obviously lying way of trying to get out of writing and seem polite at the same time, and would deceive no one.

Cheerio!
With lots of love
<u>Dennis</u>

I received a formal invitation to the A.G.M. of the Q.A. from Dennis at Hastings.

Sunday 7 April 1940

At 10.30 Chris, Bill and Peter came round. Went to Bournville lane baths.* Had a fine time, came back, Chris asked mother and me to tea on Friday.
*I won the meringue!

On Sat 13 April Dennis came home on leave.

Sunday 14 April 1940

Bill, Peter, Chris and Den went swimming. I only watched because I had a cold. In the afternoon went to Bill's party. Went to Bob Smyth's, Philip *(by this time an officer in the Navy)* was there. Went boating. Bill and I went in one boat. Phil and Chris in another and Den and Viv in another. We had a grand time. Phil's hat went in the water, and at one time Phil was moving his boat with his rudder and only one oar.

We went aground once or twice, and at the end we all went aground and Bill and I got an oar. Then Phil tried to get another, and Den then got into the boat with Chris.

After tea we went for a walk. Bill, Phil and I went together and Den. Viv and Chris went together. A sailor saluted Phil and then we came to a river, Phil and Bill jumped across. We waited till the others came and asked Viv and Den to jump across. This they did. Then they all jumped back. The river was about 10 ft wide - It was a grand evening.

Bill gave me the meringue he owed me.

Saturday 20 April 1940

Hitler's birthday! Den and I celebrated our birthdays and we also had the annual general meeting. Had a grand time. Ray, Bill, Bob, Phil, Den, Chris, Viv, Teddy, Myself. Bill and Den ran a race. There was a presentation of a box of chocolates to mother.

The boys all got in a line. Den was back to front and Teddy (Bear) Gray stood at ease when the others stood at attention.

It was a marvellous party.

Sunday 21 April 1940

Went swimming with Raymond, Bill, Chris and Den. Ray and Chris sat and watched. While we were in the water Viv came and he also watched. I taught Bill to dive.
Went to Moseley in the afternoon. Den went back.

Tuesday 23 April 1940

Got up early. Went down to the station. Got a seat on the train with Esmé and Jean.

Wed: 5 Crosbie Road
April 24th

My dearest Pat
Well, how goes it at Cheltenham? I have already vacuumed your room, put new sheets on the bed, and altogether prepared it for your next homecoming. One day has already gone, and I must begin to save for the rest of the things you seem to need. Have you yet written to Mrs Thatcher, if not <u>do so</u>, make an effort and get it done.
It seems funny without you today. I shall be very glad when you are home for good. Didn't they allow us a long 3 mins on the 'phone last night.
      All my love darling
      from Mother

Wednesday 24th April   748099 etc

Dear Mother and Dad,
I think that in view of the foreknowledge of increased postages I shall write to both of you at the same time to save for future letters.
Firstly I should like to say that I had a very good journey back -

Billy came to see me off from the station and I met several friends on the train.

I got a good meal at the Strand Lyons Corner House and I also ate two oranges and some sandwiches on the L.M.S. train.

Strangely enough in spite of the train journey I woke up exceedingly fresh on Monday morning and in the very early hours of the day it became apparent that a minor heat wave was in the offing.

In the afternoon Nevill Reeves and I went for a run along the front in our running kit, climbed up the cliff at the fishing village and sunbathed on the top of the cliffs. We then ran the whole of the distance back, a distance of about two miles or more.

By the way it seems possible that I shall be posted on May 13th to Desford Aerodrome. This is - I'll be honest with you, although I was going to give you the impression that it is further away than it is, just to surprise you at a later date - 30 miles, as the crow flies, from Stephensons Place; if crows do fly from Stephenson Place.

This will mean that if ever I do get a slack week-end, if I <u>do</u> get posted there, that I should be able to get home from about say 5 o'clock on Saturday till say 7 o'clock on Sunday. But this is all wishful supposition.

One point that is definite however is that owing to a very marked excess of numbers in the pilot section of the V.R. quite a large percentage <u>are</u> getting demoted.

However let's hope for the best.

And now as I am on guard and am just going on duty I must end now

With love from
Dennis.

April 26th　　　　　　　　　　　　　　　　　　　Ridgeway
　　　　　　　　　　　　　　　　　　　　　Welland Lodge Rd
Friday

Dear Den

I want to try and get these cigs to you for Sunday. I hope I succeed. They are the easiest present, because I know you smoke them occasionally and hoping the reason you smoke them only seldom is that you like them, but cannot afford them (which I know is not so - you lucky -!) I got them for you.

Tell me if you like the pen. It is a beauty really, just like yours, but yesterday I got an autograph and the nib is awfully wobbly and 'clicks' when I write. I hope to get back for Whit, but we are not allowed to go to the pictures - something to do with German measles or something. Anyway I shall go just the same.

I went swimming yesterday at the spa baths. They were tiny and the water was a horrible color. E & I were the only ones in, and we tried out all sorts of newly invented strokes. We got home late for dinner, but just made it to school.

We have a horrible lot of homework, and I am just about fed up with my stay in Cheltenham. How are you getting on at - down South?!! I bet you feel fed up sometimes. I hope to get back for my birthday as well as Whit, but it's going to cost rather a lot! Do you know I've only got 4 1/2^d to last me 'till I get my pocket money!

I'm afraid if you are to get this by Sunday I'd better finish. As it is you may not even if I finish now. Still I'll do my best.

Lots & Lots of Love
Pat

Friday & Saturday

Dear Mother & Dad

We had a grimy journey down, and a hectic time on the bus trying to cart our cases upstairs. It was hard work! We are in bed now at 9.35. At least I am in bed. Esmé is sitting on the edge of the bed dressing one of those things on her heel that I had.

The light is going out now so cheerio until I pick up the pen again!

Hello! Here I am again. We have had three days of school now. Every day I feel as though I'm on holiday. Everything is so warm and peaceful (?) here, and then we go to school or bed, and it doesn't fit in at all.

Mr and Mrs Jones have come back, just.

I am afraid I have not written to Mrs Thatcher yet; in fact you are the only people I have yet written to. But only wait a bit, and then you'll get results.

I have left my socks in the right hand drawer and belts in left one. Also I would like another towel and tennis racquet, if it doesn't cost too much.

I hope to get back at Whitsuntide. I am going without lunch at school (which consists of 4 biscuits, dry, soft and thoroughly horrible, and which costs a penny) to save for some new shoes. I still have 1/2 pint milk at school which is quite enough.

Please send some money, as I am broke all but 4 ½^d.

You know the lovely pen I got, I am writing with it now. But I got an autograph yesterday and now the nib 'clicks' the whole of the time when I'm writing. I am terribly disappointed and don't know what to do. It writes fairly well as you can see, but what can I do? At the moment I am heartbroken. I wish I was home so you could comfort me, as I write the pen gets better and better, so perhaps by the end of a fortnight (when I next come home) I shall not need the comforting words etc.!

Anyway please write and comfort me.

It is 11.40, and I have got Den's cigs., but I have not written to him yet. I suppose I had better start pretty soon.

Well, I wrote to Den, and have posted it and his cigarettes and gone to school,

Please send a fortnight's (5/-) pocket-money as soon as poss.

I had to finish there as tea was ready. It is Saturday now, and E & I are going swimming now! I'll write again soon.

With All my very best Love
Pat

P.S. <u>Please</u> send the money as soon as you possibly can.

Sunday 28 April 1940 - *Den's birthday, age 19*

Didn't do anything much in the morning. In the afternoon took our tea up Cleve hill. Went through Queen's wood. There was a very steep part where we had to carry the tea between our teeth. It <u>was very steep</u>.

When, at last, we reached the top, we lay down among the gorse in the warm sunshine, and shielded from the wind, and ate our sandwiches and played with our fingers among the few dead leaves paving the rabbit run through the gorse. Just near where we were sitting, we saw two skylarks, and lay watching the sky, all the time munching away. How long we lay there I don't know, but it must have been near an hour.

Monday 29/4/40
(The morning after the night before)   748099 etc

My dear Pat

Please excuse the paper, but as I am writing this in a Signals lecture, it is the best I can get.

Thanks ever so much for the cigarettes, they were a very sensible present and certainly have come in useful.

I could have got home for my birthday, but I didn't think it was worth £1.50 travelling fares, especially as I am hoping to be posted to Desford on May 13th - only 35 miles from home, 5 miles from Leicester.

I enjoyed my birthday very much; it was lucky it was a Sunday, wasn't it?

I got up at about eight o'clock and had breakfast. Fresh grapefruit, bacon and egg, bread, butter and marmalade. Then I opened two of my presents after which there was a church parade.

I opened the rest of the presents after church parade - yours got here in time, but I saved them all till Sunday.

In the afternoon I went to a classical music concert at the White Rock and in the evening I went to another concert with a friend.
The first part of it (community singing) was broadcast from 6.30 till 7 o'clock; I wonder whether you heard it?

Actually I was rather lucky, as I should have been guard-commander on the pier from 6 o'clock on Saturday until 6 o'clock on Sunday but I got somebody else to do it for me for 5/-. Actually he wouldn't have done it if it hadn't been my birthday.

By the way will you be back for Whitsun? or will you stay in Cheltenham? I expect you hope to get back.

Well! as I think I'd better take a little morse, I'll say cheerio!
With lots of love from
Dennis.

P.S.   I have just noticed a large notice in the room which reads:-

OUR PATRONS are earnestly requested to assist OUR CONDUCTOR
BY MAINTAINING
SILENCE
DURING THE PERFORMANCE.

Saturday 4 May 1940

Went to school. Went to town. Lots of soldiers. One said "Mind my hair!" as he passed me, and another said "Miss Goldilocks!" Grrr! Came back, had tea and went a walk across the racecourse. Met a very interesting man who told us all the history of cottages, churches, castles, monasteries etc in Cheltenham. He knew Twist *(our school head-porter)*. He was awfully nice.   Came back. Mrs Jones says mother rang up. I am to go home for a week. Also Mrs Jones says we are not to see Jack and when Mr Jones came home Mrs Jones took him straight upstairs for about 5 minutes! I wonder what Jack's been up to!

Horrible rat!

Mother is going to ring Tuesday.

Sunday 5 May 1940

Had nettles for dinner because Mrs Stevens *(the greengrocer)* had no greens.

Went for a walk over the Cotswolds. It was <u>very</u> hot, and the path was dry and stony. Sat down on a lump and had tea. Made our way down. On a low common, or green heath Tim decided to investigate a rabbit hole. He dug away and poked himself into the hole. We brought him away but he went back again, he was right in the rabbit hole all but his tail. As soon as I tried to get him out he snapped at me, but after he came out quietly and we tied him with a piece of string and led him.

Went through another wood. Lost Tim twice because he chased rabbits.   Disturbed several ant-hills.   Went back across the racecourse. Went to the car park entrance, it was shut so had to go back and go through ordinary way.

May '40   5 CrosbieRoad
Sunday

My dearest Pat

It is a most glorious sunny afternoon and I am sitting out in the garden writing this, the sunshine is too good to be wasted. Dad has finished the rockery at the back of the pool and crazied it, and there is enough space for three deck chairs, it makes a lovely cosy corner. The garden is beginning to look most awfully pretty, flowers everywhere.

I was sorry to miss you last night on the 'phone, but of course there is always that risk, and after all I was glad to know you were out for a walk, and all I wanted to tell you was that we are hoping to pick you up on Friday morning to take you for a week's holiday somewhere. I am going to write to Miss Barrie now and ask permission for you to be allowed to come away for a week with us. I will ring you up Tuesday evening to let you know whether we have heard and what we are doing, also I would be glad if you could find out from Miss Barrie yourself, whether it will be alright, and then you will know what to expect. (Ask her.) Only pack necessary things, I will bring summer frocks and anything else I think of ready for you and we shall want you all ready packed when we call on Friday. Please tell Mrs Jones that all being well we really and truly hope to meet her on Friday.

I haven't time for more now, but can only hope nothing will turn up to spoil our little plan. Hope you approve.

All my love darling
Mother.

Thursday 9 May 1940

Did some washing; prep, cleaned my shoes. Went to the food office on my bike while Mrs Jones pressed my blazer. Went to school.

Chocolate for lunch!

Came back got tea, cleaned bikes, packed.

Friday 10 May 1940

Mother and Dad called for me and I found we were going to Weston.

When we arrived at Weston, Valerie, my friend from childhood days was walking along the front. We went for a walk together.

There are a lot of soldiers at the Lake hotel. They were washing and vimming plates, when we passed they said "Hallo girls!" In the evening a lot of soldiers went up past the hotel with mugs.

Hitler invaded Holland and Belgium.

Saturday 11 May 1940

Woke up to find soldiers on the roof of the bandstand opposite, with a Bren gun, looking out for parachutists etc. Went round to Val. She had not seen the gun. Went on the pier. Went swimming with Val and Merial (her sister).

Sunday 12 May 1940

In the afternoon went to Kewstoke woods with mother and dad and had tea at the toll gate. There were a lot of airmen in the woods.

In the evening listened to the band and went for a walk.

Wednesday 15 May 1940

Poured with rain. Had tea at a café overlooking the winter gardens. Three airmen came in and sat at the table behind. They were very young and very refined. They ate an awful lot and joked about one's moustache. The one airman had to pay for the whole spread.

Saturday 18 May 1940

Got up early. Dad brought the car round before breakfast. Lots of soldiers in Winchcombe. When we got back Uncle Roy and Aunty Freda came round and gave me some soap and cakes for a birthday present. In the evening I went to the pictures with Val, who had also come home. Val went in the middle, because she thought she'd sprained her back. Later she found that it was only her roll-on that had rolled up!

Sunday 19 May 1940 - My Birthday, Age 14

Woke up to find Mother wishing me many happy returns and giving me some gloves and 2/- from Gran. Washed my hair. Chris came. Invited her to Middleton woods in the afternoon. At 2.15 I heard an awful racket and dashing downstairs saw Den. He is now at Desford and thrilled to death with everything, he is now flying and has to cycle to all meals etc. as the flying field is so vast. Went round for Chris. She was very surprised to see Den. Went in the woods and then had tea at the Happy Hour. Went home, packed etc.

Monday 20 May 1940

Went to C'ham, met Mary Jennens on the train, found Den had sent me a Birthday Greetings Telegram –

"ON BEHALF OF H M ROYAL AIR FORCE MAY I WISH YOU MANY HAPPY RETURNS OF THE DAY. SGT KNIGHT".

School. Went for a walk in the evening.

(Mother began to suffer increasingly from more or less constant pain in her head, and symptoms of some sort of chronic infection.

At times she was able to lead her life normally, but at times she was so ill or in so much pain that she was forced to lie on the settee ,obviously suffering severe pain, or retire to bed with a low fever.

She did not feel well enough to see me off on the train to Cheltenham, so Dad had asked Aunty Freda to do so.)

5 Crosbie Road

My dearest Pat

    Aunty Freda just rang up to say she saw you safely on the train, complete with two K.E.H.S. girls. As a matter of fact I know you are quite competent of catching the Cheltenham train yourself, but Dad seemed quite concerned upon your behalf. I have just noticed your emergency food card and am enclosing it in case you have to return it to the food office.

    I am writing this sitting up by the pool, the sun is glorious and I have come away from the house as the painters have arrived and are very busy burning off old paint. I hope they hurry up and finish the job.

    What a nice birthday we had yesterday, wasn't it lucky for Dennis to be home, don't forget to make your diary up to date, and also when you have a chance a letter to Mrs Thatcher wouldn't come amiss. She wrote you such a lovely long letter.

    Well Pat, we had a jolly week and hope to have you home for good very soon. Please remember me to Mrs Jones (if at home) or Mrs Jones' mother, and love to Esmé.

    With dearest love
    from
    Mother

P.S. Heard from Aunty Freda the sad tale of the extra fare, just see what a fourteenth birthday does!

May   Tuesday   5 Crosbie Road

My dearest Pat
    Grandma has just been over, she expected you would have been here, and has brought your birthday present. It is a 10/- note. Very nice and acceptable, and she sends you lots of love and all of the very best wishes.
    We sent Dennis' bicycle off this morning, and now have to wire him to let him know it will be at the station.
    Well, I haven't anything to tell you, I am still feeling pretty groggy and Dr Winfield was here again today. He is going to Cornwall tomorrow for three weeks, so Mrs W. *(his wife, also a doctor)* is coming tomorrow. It is quite a time since I saw her.
    Hope your cold is better.
    With dearest love
    Mother

Dennis' address is

    748099
    Sgt. D. F. Knight
    No. 7. E.F.T.S.
    Desford
    Leicestershire.

Friday 24 May 1940

    Did prep, went to school. Went to the pictures to see "Dust be my Destiny" and another film with Wallace Beery in it. The King's speech was broadcast, and then we had community singing. Esmé and I bought ourselves Community Song books so that we knew all the words.
    It was such fun, with everyone singing at the top of their voices, like a big, jolly party!

Monday   5 Crosbie Road

    My dearest Dennis *(crossed out)* Pat
    I have just finished writing to Dennis and packing up his shirt and one or two things and it made me put his name again - I hadn't properly got my thoughts quite transferred.
    Your laundry arrived home today so I am posting it straight on to you also your blue dress (last year's).
    Dad has joined a special home Defence Corps, against parashootists *(sic)*, it is A & W's Corps, and he spent the whole of Sat. afternoon and Sunday morning practising shooting.
    His time is already terribly filled up with extra war work, but he is giving up his little bit of leisure as well. One week out of every three he is to stay at A & W's all night. Now, about coming home for a week-end. Do we have to write for permission - we should <u>love</u> to have you. Let me know what - if anything - we have to do and then COME.
    with all my love darling
    from Mother.

P.S. Please give my love to Mrs Jones and Esmé.

I put your soap in your bedroom the day you went away, and have also put your 10/- note from Grandma in safety

Tuesday 28 May 1940

Went to tennis. Rained. Had 4 games. I am improving. Went to school. Had an air-raid practice. Had another air-raid practice later. At the same time as the 2nd one 3 companies of soldiers marched past.
    In the evening went for a cycle ride round town. Very boring. Esmé nearly knocked an airman over and I was nearly knocked off my bike by a car coming along on the wrong side of the road.
    KING LEOPOLD OF THE BELGIANS HAS WITHDRAWN HIS TROOPS. THE B.E.F. ARE ISOLATED.

Wednesday 29 May 1940

Went to rounders match. We won by 1/2 rounder. Went to school. Did nothing much rest of evening - we are bored stiff and detest C'ham - there is <u>nothing</u> to do.

THE BELGIAN GOVERNMENT ARE MUSTERING AN ARMY AGAINST LEOPOLD'S WISHES.

THERE IS VAGUE TALK OF US BEING EVACUATED TO CANADA.

Saturday 1 June 1940

Went to school, hurried back. Mr Jones took me to the station. Met Nancy, Mary, Olive there. Caught the 1.59 train. Very full, had to walk the train to find a carriage. Found room in a dining car. Three Canadian M.Ps sitting next, had revolvers, were huge. Mother met me, went home and had a grand tea - strawberries and cream, sugar buns. Went to the pictures. The garden looked very pretty.

The B.E.F. have been and are being rescued from Belgium.

Sunday 2 June 1940

We took Christine to see Den flying, called for him later and had tea at the George Inn at Hinckley. We crossed traffic lights at red and stopped guiltily by 2 police who were looking at Identity cards, and they just told us to go further down the road to 2 more police. When we got there Chris hadn't got her card - there was nothing on Den's and they didn't look at mine! They asked for a box of chocolates which we gave them, but they handed them back.

Monday 3 June 1940

Got up early. Dad took mother and me down to town. Got a pair of blue shoes and a blue gas mask case to match. Caught the 9.48 train back.

June 3rd   5 Crosbie Road

My dear Pat
 This is just a hasty note to tell you that on no account must you take your camera out with you. One of the men at the works was arrested today at Stratford-on-Avon <u>for just walking along the streets with a camera slung over his shoulder</u>. Also don't go anywhere near where there are sentries, or near the race course. Two men were shot yesterday, one fatally and the other is in a very serious condition, and they thought they were perfectly safe - they just didn't hear the sentry in time. Things have become very serious in the country recently, so **TAKE NO RISKS**.
 What a successful morning we had. I hope the shoes are as nice as they appeared to be, but in any case, even if they are not your fit or are uncomfortable in any way, they would fit me.
 With all my love
 Mother.

Write to Den when you have a chance, even a note is better than nothing.

Monday   5 Crosbie Road
10/6/40

My dear Pat
 It seems more than a week since you were here and I understand that Mother's writing to Miss Barrie to ask if you can come home for next weekend, unless of course things get too hot, the war I mean not the weather.
 Gran came again yesterday for a stay and will be here next time you come.
 We haven't heard from Dennis since we saw him last Sunday, but Mother rang up Christine this evening to wish her many happy returns of the day and she said she had had a letter today from him.
 By the way let me know when you want some more pocket-money and I will commence and save again.
 The eggs in the little box tree have hatched out and the mother bird is very proud of her family, occasionally father comes along to inspect the

family, but only occasionally, he is probably out, very busy looking for food for them.

The young blackbirds at the top of the garden have already disappeared.

When we went for Gran to Sutton last night we were stopped by the police twice, once going and once coming back and asked for our identity cards, and according to the papers tonight they were stopping them in town as well today.

I must write to Dennis tonight to tell him I took a parcel of tarts *(this word is Tarts - Mother)* to the post tonight but had to bring it back because the post office was closed..

So cheerio
With love
Dad

Gran sends her best love, *('dear' should be the word - Mother)*.

7-11 June '40   Friday-Saturday - Sunday Mon. Tue

Dear Mother & Dad

I am saving (?) as well as I can to come home next week-end. But the weather is so terribly tropical heat here that there is a great temptation to go swimming twice every day. So far I went swimming Mon. evening - Wed. evening and Fri morning. I am going tomorrow afternoon with Nancie (Esmé has gone home for the week-end as her father is on leave) and we're going to stay in all afternoon, have tea there, and not come out till 8!

Sun.- I went swimming yesterday, and now I am beautifully burnt.

I am going to church or rather chapel this morning, and I was going swimming this evening but I have discovered I have only 9d left (not counting the 4/6 I have saved to come home) and it costs 3d to go swimming, and I want to go on Mon & Fri, so I am not going this evening. Instead I am going to do my prep, and then go up on Cleeve Hill with Mrs Jones.

I have got to sleep at Mrs Millard's tonight and tomorrow night, and perhaps the night after - blinkin' swiz I call it!

Please write to Miss Barrie by Friday for permission to go home - I am <u>definitely coming. I simply loathe and detest this place.</u>

<u>Tuesday</u>. This is getting quite a diary! I slept at Mrs Millard's (I only sleep there, I don't eat anything) last night, and found she is very nice. She has a little boy of 5 years old, his name is Roger. Yesterday morning a parcel came for me from Den. If you have seen it tell me in your next letter what you think of it. If not say so and I'll bring it home to shew you. It is a <u>wonderful</u> present, and I hope it will last me all my life. It is very beautiful, and must have cost him a fortune. It is very useful too. I wonder if you know or can guess what it is! *(It was a tooled leather writing case, and I still have it.)* Please don't forget to write to Miss Barrie for permission to come home, and if you ever want to ring me up I have decided that between or around 10.00 to 10.30 is best, because we are not allowed out after 8 o'clock now, as there are 1000 soldiers come to Cheltenham, also Norwegian sailors (wounded), the soldiers are supposed to be English, French and Belgian - they all look alike to me!

Exams start in July, so I shall have to start swotting. Miss Barrie came round the other day to find out who wanted to take what in the Lower V.

      You can take either:
a)   German (if you are good at French)
b)   Greek (if you are good at Latin)
c)   Geography (if you are good at neither)

I want to take German, as most people do, but as I am no good at languages I shall most likely have to take Geography.

You can tell Gran that I'm not half so skinny with my letters as she is, she doesn't seem to like me much (you can tell her!) as she seldom writes and always retreats to Sutton when I'm around!!

Anyway when I do write I make it a long letter. But still I had better end now.

      Don't forget Miss Barrie -
      I'll be seeing you this next weekend
      Lots & Lots & Lots of Love all that's left over from this*
      Pat

P.S. We aren't having any 1/2 term holiday as the troops need the trains - I don't think it's fair, but still I suppose it is <u>really</u>.

      See you Saturday I hope!!

Please let me come, I have saved 4/6 plus 9d to spend before then. I am looking forward ever so to coming home.

Wish Christine very many happy returns from me, and tell her I didn't even realise she had a birthday!

Send my love to Gran.*

Mon.   "Ridgeway"
                                                           59 Welland Lodge Rd

Dearest Den

As you can see I am using your wonderful present. I have decided to use the R.A.F. notepaper up, and to use this only for very special people and purposes. Thanks <u>terrifically</u> Den, if only you were here to thank. It doesn't look half what I feel when put onto paper. But when I next see you I'll thank you again, and properly.

It was rather funny how I got this. I was expecting a parcel from mother with my washing in, and when Mrs Jones said there was a parcel for me, and I opened it and found this - I just couldn't believe my eyes. I knew at once it was from you; it's just the sort of thing you would do. Send a beautifully elaborate telegram, or letter, and then take one's breath away with a simply marvellous present which is really to be treasured.

Your letter accompanying it was so modest too! You didn't say "I hope you will like it" or anything of that kind, you just send a short, simple, modest letter that makes one worship the present even more. I am afraid this letter may seem a bit poetic to a big, strong he-man like you! But it 's just how I feel.

You won't receive many letters on this paper, not many people will because I am going to be very stingy with it. It is beautiful paper, and when the end of the war is nearing and everyone is writing on wall-paper (and the other kind I won't bother to mention!) I'll write a very special letter to one or two people on this lovely paper and they'll think I've come into some money!

But it is much too good to use just for writing home asking for my washing, or a bit of pocket money to go on with, and that kind of thing; so I shall use that other very nice paper you gave me - the R.A.F. notepaper, and now I feel really luxurious!

I have a padded silk dressing gown, some very nice notepaper, and some very best notepaper in a <u>beautiful</u> writing case - and all from you!

I wish my pocket money would stretch a little so that I could buy you presents half as good as yours for me.

I hope to get home next week-end, do you think you will get the Sunday off? Or did you get last Sunday? I am trying to save enough money to come home every other weekend. That makes it practically like being a weekly boarder at a boarding school. We don't get our half term holiday now, because the trains are too full of soldiers, but I can go home for weekends instead.

We are going to see "Gulliver's Travels" and "Just William" on Friday - have you seen them? I am sleeping at a Mrs Millards for 3 nights as Mrs Jones has a visitor. I only sleep there, I don't eat or do anything there.

I must end as I haven't enough news to fill another piece of paper. I promise to write again as soon as I have time - and thanks again for the writing case - Thanks Den.

Lots of Love, Pat

Saturday 15 June 1940

School. Dashed down to the station and got on the train. Walked the train to find the others. Saw a train full of wounded presumably from Dunkirk. Mother was on the steps at the station. Went back and had tea and then went to the pictures to see "The Wizard of Oz".

(As Dad would arrive back from the works at 5.30, not having eaten since mid-day, it became our habit to have tea then, and go to the pictures straightaway after, as cinema performances were continuous.

The result was that we invariably arrived in time to see the last twenty minutes or so of the main film before watching the performance - B-film, news and advertisements - before then watching the main film from the beginning, up to the point where we had come in, when we would then make our exit and go home!)

Sunday 16 June 1940

Had eggs for breakfast then made the pudding, messed about all morning. Read and sewed all afternoon. Dad went to the works, but came back for tea. Had cherries for tea.

Went to Moseley. Had some fruit salad and cream.
Came home and read. Went to bed. Dad went to the works.

Monday 17 June 1940

Had bacon and egg and tomato and potatoes for breakfast.
Said goodbye to dad. Went down to the station with mother. Caught the 9.48 train with Nancie. There were about 5 soldiers from Dunkirk in the corridor, and we had a fine time. At last we arrived at Cheltenham. School. Messed about in the evening.
France has laid down arms.

June 18th   5 Crosbie Road
Tuesday

My dearest Pat
  I am returning your washing mended and washed but find two of the socks are odd, perhaps you have the other two. I am also sending you some cotton wool to stuff into your ears should we have a raid. I may grease it already for you or may send it plain, I shall see what I think when I come to pack. Put it <u>straight</u> into your gas mask container, then it is always ready, also you can give Esmé a piece if she likes as so many people have had their ear-drums broken by the noise in France, and everyone has been advised to always stuff their ears at the beginning of a raid and to take cover immediately even if the raiders sound to be a good distance off as they can move so quickly and people get hit by falling debris or anti air craft fire before they realize the raiders are anywhere near them.
Isn't it funny to be writing all this in a letter to you. I am sitting in the garden on a lovely peaceful sunny afternoon and the birds are twittering and singing all around. Two of the baby birds in the little box tree have learned to fly, or "flutter" around. The other one seems a bit lazy or timid and still sticks to the nest, though of course it may be the last one hatched out, for the last egg hatched four days after the first one.
  I wonder what you are doing about the summer holidays, we shall

have to wait and see what the government suggests, but I suppose in any case you will be leaving Cheltenham.

Don't forget the cotton wool. Do it <u>now</u>.

All and all my love darling

Mother.

Thursday 20/6/40

Dear Mother and Dad,

I am sitting in a deckchair making the most of the cool of a country evening - on guard duty. I am about half a mile from the aerodrome and it is my job that no suspicious characters pass the barrier.

We have just heard for what types of planes we have been recommended. There are three kinds of recommendations: for Twin Engine Planes, Single Engine Planes, and single seater fighters. Actually I had hoped very much to be recommended for fighters, but you have to be pretty hot at flying to go on them.

Out of our flight of 25 only 5 were recommended:- Jackson, Johnston, Barry Kneath, Land and of course myself.

And now, as you did not take any notice of the other names may I point out that Johnston is the Birmingham fellow who brought me up in the car from Hastings, and Barry Kneath is the friend of mine who took those photographs of Hastings.

It may also please you to know that as a fighter pilot we have a longer training period than any other - if we pass!

I think that I can thank Dick *(Flight Lieutenant)* for this, he concentrated on making me a fighter pilot from the start and he's certainly taught me some useful tricks and acrobatics.

You know that Air Raid we had on Tuesday night? Well! we were standing by with loaded rifles and fixed bayonets in the trenches from ten past twelve until twenty to four in the morning. We heard anti-aircraft fire all the while but only as a very low dull reverberation of the ground.

Next morning I woke up, looked at my watch which said 7.15, and had a bath. Fully dressed at 7.30 I noticed the bungalows were very quiet and that planes were flying around; so leaving the bungalow I asked a passing sergeant the time, to find, to my consternation that it was 9.30!

However, all ended well and the mere result was that I got this two hours guard duty - which from 6-8 o'clock on a night on which we are not allowed out anyway is no fatigue at all.

Especially as by doing this guard I miss the Duty Flight parade at eight o'clock!

With all love
Dennis.

Friday 21 June 1940 – Longest Day

Did prep. School, finished early and missed out one lesson. Dashed back. Met Mary J and Doreen Ford at the crossroads and cycled to Dean Close Boy's School. Saw " The Merchant of Venice" performed by the boys. <u>Very</u> good.

Portia	Very handsome
Antonia	VERY good, fairly handsome
Shylock	played by a master
Lancelot	very handsome

Bassanio and Lorenzo were both quite good. Lorenzo was like Robert Donat when he was 18. Jessica very good.

Narissa – was a small boy. He tripped and bounced across the stage, and once when leaving the stage (which was open air) he gave a little jump. He was terribly funny with his big, boy's feet protruding from under his robe. Cycled home.

Saturday 22 June 1940

School, came back and discovered that Eric had rung up and said he was calling for Esmé to take her to B'ham. Anyway I went too. When I got back they were very surprised to see me. Dad was at the works. Had a very nice evening cutting flowers and reading and talking.

Dennis had moved once again. This time to Grantham.

Sunday 23 June 1940

Christine came round in the morning. At about 1 o'clock Den rang up, and we decided to meet him at about 3 o'clock at the barrier at the aerodrome.

Called for Christine. Got as far as Market Bosworth, or some such place, and then got lost.

(All the signposts had been removed for security early in the war, and people had been told not to give directions in case it was parachutists in disguise. Unfortunately for us the locals had taken the advice seriously to heart! While we were wandering around in circles we saw a plane practising emergency landings and take offs in a field and wondered if it might be Dennis. When we finally met up with him, we found out it was.)

We asked 3 boys lounging in a doorway, a man telling someone else the way and then arrived in a tiny hamlet. We were then despairing as it was nearly 4.00, and we were afraid that Den would not wait. So Dad got out and asked and mother got out and asked. Dad asked 2 people who said they did not know, he then asked if there was a police station in the village, they said they did not know, then he went somewhere else. Mother and Dad both came back triumphant. "Turn right" says Dad, "Turn left" says Mother - we did not know what to do. We turned back and asked a tubby shrunken bow-legged little cow-man. He set us on our way and soon we were at the barrier. Den wasn't there. We asked the airman on guard who said he'd just gone to get a cup of tea. Two airmen came by and we stopped them and asked if Knight was coming and one went back to find out. Soon Den came and we all went and had tea at Hinckley at the George Inn where we had it last week.

Dropped Den at Coventry. I was too late for Eric. Chris and I got supper. Mother wasn't at all good and went to bed.

Sunday 23/6/40   748099 etc

Dear Pat

I am expecting to be moved from here next Sunday - where I shall go I cannot say - I expect to go to Anstey (near Coventry) or Yatebury, first of all for two weeks training in night flying and formation flying and from there I go to a F.T.S which may be anywhere in England.

I have been lucky enough to be recommended for single seater fighters - only four out of twenty five in our flight were lucky and I happened to be one of them.

I had my 45 hour R.A.F. test here on Tuesday - the examining officer is a very moody fellow, sometimes he's very chirpy and sometimes damned irritable. Anyway I got into the plane for my test and he taxied to the end of the field and turned across wind to wait for a plane to land. The plane landed and still he waited!

I sat there waiting for him to turn and take off - or at least ask me to do so, when he suddenly said "Look at that bird!" I looked and saw a skylark hovering about thirty feet off! Having looked at the bird I prepared for the take off but he did nothing until he finally said "Jolly little fellow isn't he?" "Yes Sir" quoth I. A few seconds later the bird moved off down the field, and as I expected the examiner started the engine up to turn into wind - but did he? No! He followed the bird to the boundary and stopped there watching it until it finally flew over the hedge. And not until then did we take off!

With lots of love
Dennis

(This letter must have been written and posted before Dennis flew in the afternoon.)

Monday 24 June 1940

Said goodbye to Gran and Mother. Dad took me down to the station in the car and I got on the train with M.J. Terribly crowded. Leaned out of the window and saw 2 sailors who waved to us. Looked the other way and saw some soldiers, they waved to us, and more soldiers looked out, and waved. School.

Tuesday 25 June 1940

Tennis. School, after school went for a ride with José.

Raid last night on Midlands. Five people killed in a town in S.W. England.

Tuesday   5 Crosbie Road

My dearest Pat

I am still in bed but thought I would send you a note to say, the operation* has been postponed for at least a month as Dr Winfield says that if I had it sooner than that after this attack I should probably end up with blood poisoning. Isn't it a nuisance? I wanted to get it over and done with especially as it gives me so much pain in the meantime.

I hope you found your two school dresses alright also the orange flower one, but everything was done in such a rush, wasn't it?

What do you feel like doing this week end? I should leave coming home I think, just to see what is going to happen in the way of air-raids. There seem to have been some warnings over the Midlands. Though so far we have neither seen nor heard anything unusual.

Have you had your name put down for enquiries into the Canadian scheme? Do so <u>straight</u> away will you - for if the whole school went I should certainly like you to go with them. Eh! What a TO DO! it all is. Aunty Marjorie and Margaret are thinking of trying to go to Australia, though I doubt if they will be allowed now as I don't think they can take their money out of the country.

I must write a note to Den before he leaves "that strange place difficult to locate."

Please give my love to Esmé and to Mrs Jones, and tell Mrs Jones how deeply grateful I am to her for all she has done and is doing for you, especially as she must often feel very over-tired herself just now *(she was pregnant)*. All my love darling, Mother.

If you have to go to an air-raid shelter at night, go very warmly clothed as it becomes <u>very</u> cold after a while.

<u>Wed</u>. it is now. Dad went to the works all day yesterday, came back for tea, then went back at 10 o'clock last night and doesn't return until 10 o'clock tonight,

We had an air-raid warning last night at about 11.30. It lasted until 2.30, so you had better not come home this week end. We had better see what the "German Gentry" intend doing first.

I didn't really know whether to go up to the dug-out or not as I am still in bed but anyway I wrapped up extra well and went. I am going to ask Dr. W. what to do, when he comes today, which is the lesser evil of the two. I wasn't the least bit frightened but just felt calm and collected only I didn't much like my family being so scattered. Dad at the works, and you and Den away. Have just had a lovely surprise from Dennis, a big bunch of luscious black grapes and two boxes of strawberries. Very delicious, especially as I am still not hungry for ordinary things.

    All my love, Mother.

*   *(Mother was so unwell and in so much pain, it was decided that an operation might be the solution. When it was finally performed, it was a tonsilectomy.)*

Thursday.   59. W.L. Road
27th June   C'ham

Dear Mother & Dad
    This is only a note to say I'm alright, and the sirens went on Tuesday night. I slept all through the raid.

    Esmé looked out of the window and saw a bomber silhouetted against the moon.

    Jean dressed hurriedly and crawled in the ditch.

    June was up 1/2 the night, and Mrs Jones' sister said there were German bombers over Burford trying to find the aerodrome (which is <u>not</u> at Burford - clever chaps these Germans, always find their target!)

    Gloucester had an air-raid too - and the night before.

    Please write for permission to come home. I'm resolved to come home before July is out.

    Mrs Jones says we are too much trouble now Mr Jones is working at the aircraft factory, as it means her cooking 2 big meals a day. So we are going either to Mrs Millard's (in the same rd) or we are trying to go with Jean, but I don't think it will come off.

    I must end now as I have to go to school.
    Lots & Lots of Love
    Pat

(Friday 28th June)

Dearest Pat
    Just a hurried note to you and Miss Barrie. I am still in bed. I am still rather dud though better than I was. I have asked Miss B. for permission for you to come each week end to help me though that doesn't mean we should expect you each week end.
    Please give my love to Mrs Jones and tell her I am not surprised to hear she finds it too much under present conditions, she wants a little extra care, not a little extra work.
    If you come tomorrow, just look out for car at station entrance because I anyway shan't be there and Dad may be back at works, so if car isn't there come straight on bus.
    All my love Mother.
    Just had your letter. I guessed the Germans had paid you a visit just so that you wouldn't be jealous of us or Den. Nita had the Germans right overhead.

Saturday 29 June 1940

    School. Dashed back, changed, had dinner and met Jean and Mary. Went to the station and met Nancy. The train was very full so we put our cases in the luggage van and walked the train, through 2 carriages full of B.E.F. from France, could get no further, so Nancy and I turned back. We got to the end of 1 carriage, then two B.E.F. stood up and offered us seats. We sat down, then Jean and Mary came and Jean sat down. Mary sat on the arm. One soldier was reading a book called "Under The Red Flag". At last arrived at B'ham.
    Went to bed, and about 1/2 hr - 1 hr afterwards the sirens went, got out of bed, put my coat and shoes on, grabbed a blanket and went up to the shelter, the searchlights were going and it was all very thrilling. Stayed in the shelter for a long time, then Mr Ensell, Dad and I got out to see how things were going. We watched the searchlights, and walked around, and then heard an explosion (like a bomb dropping) and after that some sounds of gunfire. We dashed back into the shelter, and had to move gas masks, rugs etc. Anyway we stayed there for 2 hrs then at last a faint sound was heard - we listened intently - to me it seemed to come from UNDER the

shelter; anyway it was the all clear sounding in the distance. It grew nearer and louder, and at last all the sirens were going and we heaved a sigh.

5 Crosbie Road

My dearest Pat

    I don't know your new address, but shall post this to Mrs Jones in the hope that it will reach you. It seems from the letter Miss Barrie sent you are almost certainly coming home, at the latest on the 26th of this month *(July)*. I am so glad, I think it will be better in every way, though I could have wished my operation was over and done with. It will be rotten to have to leave you almost as soon as you are home. Never mind though - you will be <u>home</u> and that is the chief thing. I contemplate paying you a weekly wage if you will undertake certain household duties. I put your 10/- in your bank this morning, thought it was better than leaving it around in the house and you can get it any time you want it.

    Mrs Taylor came this morning with some lovely flowers Christine had bought for me, one bowl of yellow ones is in the hall, and the other of pinky-mauve are standing on the lounge hearth. They look just lovely.

    This afternoon Dennis Raby came to bring a book back that Dennis had lent him. He came in and stayed talking for two and a half hours! I like him very much, he has high ideals, and a terrific love of England and Our Empire. He has joined the R.A.F. and has passed his medical exam as a pilot, and goes down south to begin his training on Monday. Do you remember skating with him that time, he seemed very nice then but improves upon knowing.

    Mr and Mrs Vernon are in the midst of having an air-raid shelter made, it seems as it will be a "super" thing for they have enough stuff there to build a house. I mean to go across one of the days to inspect what is being done.

    Dad was at the works all yesterday and all night and won't be home until 10 o'clock this evening. I hope we shan't have a disturbed night with sirens, we haven't heard them since you were here.

    Dad wants me to tell you he hopes to be able to fetch you and your belongings, and of course Esmé and her belongings to Birmingham, but we are <u>still</u> waiting for the car to be repaired, though the All Electric rang up today to say the spare parts had at last arrived. I will let you know more about this as soon as we know if the car will be available and if we can scrape enough petrol together for the journey. I really don't see how you will ever be able to get your stuff home unless we can fetch you and it.

Hoping you and Esmé and Mr and Mrs Millard? are all well, oh and also the boy, I forget what you said his name is.

With all my love
Mother

Sunday   5 Crosbie Road

July 7th 40

My dearest Pat

Time is getting very short before you will be coming home. Dad thinks he will be able to fetch you on Sat. July 20th. or Sunday July 21st. He is almost sure he can fetch you, but well, you know how uncertain things are these days. In any case - if the worst comes to the worst, you would have to bring what luggage you can and we should have to fetch the rest later.

I haven't yet heard when the operation will be. I expect just about the middle of your coming. Absolutely <u>rotten</u> I call it, but anyway it is a very bright spot that you will be home. Gran is very pleased about it. I had such a very nice letter from Mrs Millard yesterday. I am going to write to her, she sounds awfully nice. You have really been very very lucky with your billets. Have you written to Dennis lately? I think he will be into the fighting very soon now.

Mr & Mrs Vernon's dug-out is getting along at a pace and they hope it will be finished by Tuesday. I will enclose a 10/- note for pocket money. Dad is as usual at the works. Gran sends her love.

All my love, Mother.

Christine is coming in this evening.

Tuesday 9 July 1940

Revised. School. Latin and English exams - Latin was <u>terrible</u>. Had tea. Went down to the fish and chip shop with Mr Millard in the car. On the way back saw a sack of coal in the rd - about 1/2 cwt, we picked it up and put it on the back. Went to bed at 11 and had not been in bed long when we heard a plane, leapt out of bed. There were 8 searchlights playing on nothing. Then suddenly a terrifically powerful and wide beam swung across. It is supposed to be a Birmingham one, the searchlights did not pick up the plane, but followed it towards Glos'ter.

73 Welland Lodge Rd
C'ham

Dear Mother & Dad

I received the pocket-money, and it's a good thing because I owed Mrs Jones 9d, and I had only 3d.

We break up on July 27th. You need not write to Miss Barrie for permission for me to come home, but you have to write to Mrs Millard just to say that I'm going.

Mrs Millard is, as you think, very nice. They have taken us to the Lido and are going to take us to a variety show. Mrs Jones is going to take us to the pictures, and Mrs Millard is buying us some strawberries if we pass 8 exams.

We had the History and French exams today, I hope I did well in French. It does not matter so much about History. It is Latin and English tomorrow. I honestly only expect to get about 23% in Latin. I am trying to do my best, but it certainly is hard.

I do wish I'd been home to see Dennis Raby in air-force uniform. I thought you would like him. I only hope he doesn't fly a plane like he drives a car! He is too dare-devil - so is Raymond.

Mr Millard keeps a hen and 7 chicks. There were 15, but 8 died of the gapes - whatever that is. It is caused by drinking too much water, when they first came out of the incubator.

The balloons were up at Risington, and we think we saw a German 'plane terribly high. Bristol had a daylight raid, so it is quite possible that it was a German.

Esme and I play quite a lot of tennis at school. By the way here is a list of exams :

History *	French *	Monday
Latin x	English *	Tuesday
Scripture	Science *	Wed
Maths * x	Hygiene * x	Thursday
Geography *	Maths * x	Fri

The ones ticked *(asterisked)* are the ones I've got to do well in. The ones crossed are the ones I expect to fail in, and the ones underlined are the ones we've had. I do hope I do well in Science and Maths.
Oh Boy! 1 week and exams will be over - Hurrah! One more week and we'll be home for a weekend, cheers! One more week and we'll be home for good! (we hope) oh whoopee! etc. etc. I'm just going to bed as it is 25 to 10. By the way here is how to find the house.
Tue. We have had Latin and English now. I am sure I have failed in Latin, but hope to have done fairly well in English.

I'll see you next weekend July 20th -

Lots & Lots of Love
Pat

P.S Latin was the most ghastly paper I ever had in my life - ugh! It was <u>terrible</u>!

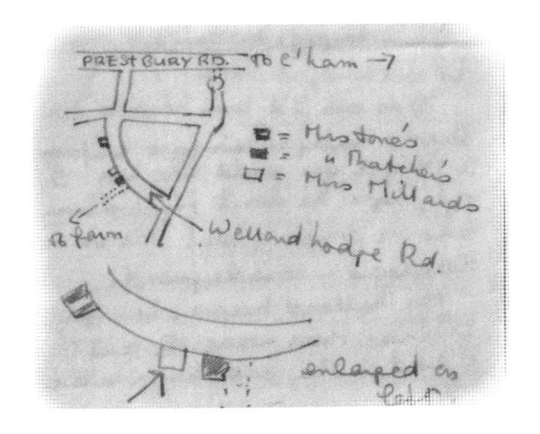

July 11th 1940   5 Crosbie Road

My dearest Pat

Thanks very much for your letter, and will you please thank Mrs Millard for hers. Now about the coming home business. Will you come home next week end July 20th unless air-raids get so severe that Mrs

Millard advises you not to come. Dennis hopes to get leave then, just week end leave and naturally wants you to be here. You will have to come by train as Dad is on duty that week end and can't possibly fetch you. He hopes to be free the week end of July 27th. and all being well will fetch your luggage then. Now look here, I unfortunately expect to go into hospital on July 31st. for my operation, so I suggest that when you come home on the week end of the 20th you remain here, as otherwise I should see so little of you before you go. If you would rather go back until school breaks up you can do so, and I shan't mind. It is just which <u>you</u> would like. I will write to Miss Barrie and ask permission for you to leave Cheltenham on the 20th July and if you want to go back well - you can, and we could fetch you the following week end. When you come, don't overload yourself with luggage as you <u>can't</u> bring all and if Mrs Millard will allow you to leave your things we will collect all the following week end.

    Understand I am writing to Miss Barrie, so find out what she says.

    Your room is all ready awaiting you - your wardrobe cleared out, and coat hangers waiting to be filled

    With love to All.

    Mother.

Sunday 14 July 1940

    In the afternoon packed up some tea and went for a run in the car. We saw Brockworth aerodrome - it is wonderfully camouflaged. We passed lots of soldiers, balloons etc. We could see a lot of balloons from on top of the hill. We went on, into a <u>private</u> swimming pool; some soldiers were coming away, so we thought it would be all right. It was a lake with an island and a raft, and no one in. We had a bit of a swim, and then came out. On the way back to the car Roger said he did not feel well.

Tuesday								5 Crosbie Road

My dearest Pat

I was so pleased to get your card and to know you can come on Friday. I had a letter from Miss Lander this morning telling me you can come Friday evening on the 6.45 train. Mind and leave yourself <u>plenty</u> of time to catch it. Dad and I will be at the station to meet you, we will find out the time it (your train) will arrive and we will meet that train at the top of the steps of the platform on which you arrive. Now <u>don</u>'t bring much luggage, we can fetch that next week, and as for your bicycle Dad says, make arrangements for it to be sent by train (in advance). Have it fetched from your house there and delivered to this house here, send it straight away.

Love to all. Mother.

Don't forget to thank Mrs. Millard and Mrs Jones for their kindness in having you. The money is for your ticket and to pay for bicycle.

Tuesday 16 July 1940

Went to Netball tournament.

Went to town. Got the ticket - 3/6. The amount of troops, equipment and ammunition on the move is tremendous! The whole of the time vans full of soldiers, armoured cars, despatch-riders, tanks, light artillery etc. are going in and out of the town, everywhere there are lorries under trees, and round corners - everywhere.

School, after school went swimming. It began to drizzle while we were in the water. We did not stay in very long, cycled through town to the fish and chip shop - got 1d worth of chips. Cycled home. Saw John, Dennis and Geoff at the cross-roads and talked, got back about 10.15. Mrs Millard was terribly annoyed.

Meanwhile, Mother and Dad had a letter from Dennis at Grantham.

16 July 1940   740899 etc

Dear Mother and Dad,
    I think that the main topic of the day is the possibility of a pass this weekend. As yet nothing is very definite although it seems probable that, unless the situation changes within the next few days, I shall be able to get home for Saturday and Sunday.
    I still haven't quite got over the type of meals we get here - take Sundays' breakfast, for instance,

        Two servings of grapefruit
        Two boiled eggs
        Bread, butter and marmalade
        Four cups of tea (two heaped spoonfuls of sugar each)

    Tea:
    Fried egg, two rashers of bacon and chips - excellently cooked.
    Bread, butter and jam
    Cake (very good - fruit)
    and Tea.

    My favourite breakfast includes egg and two rashers of bacon - which we get about three times a week. Today, however we got bacon, fried bread and baked beans.
    I don't know how much butter you get - I hope you are as well off as I am.
    I get about 2/3 of a Bryant and Mays match box at breakfast and tea - and about half the size at lunch. If I take more I leave it, so what more could I want?
    I flew down to Desford yesterday and circled the aerodrome at 2,000', I then did steep turns over the forest at the same height - I felt very 'pukka' in my Battle, I also flew east a little way and could see the Wash fairly clearly, although the light wasn't very good.
    I'll ring you up as soon as I know definitely about the week-end.
    With love
    Dennis.

Wednesday 17 July 1940

Packed. Went down to see Mrs Jones. Went to school. I shall be sorry to leave Cheltenham. Went to see Mrs Jones again. Saw Mr Jones and said goodbye to him.

Friday 19 July 1940

Mrs Millard took me and my case down to the station. Left it in the cloakroom.

School. Left early in the middle of the art lesson. Felt queer as I left the school for the last time. Turned round and looked back and said "Goodbye" to it.

Dashed home and changed. Got a few things together. Got on my bike and cycled off. On the way down it started to rain, and before I had got far it pelted down. Settled about my bike and asked where I could dry. Went onto the platform which was crowded with airmen and soldiers. One train came but it was a goods train - another came and as we were getting in someone shouted "It's the Bradford train" and everybody got off. Very few people were actually on. An engine, and then a goods train came through, and then 20 mins late the B'ham train came. I got into a 1st class carriage, and got stuck in a corridor between 3 airmen. Then a 1st class compartment door opened and a soldier invited me in. When my case was in the rack and we re-opened the door and invited the 3 airmen in, there were 3 soldiers and a terrific lot of kit already in the compartment, so it was terribly crushed. The airmen were very interested in my report, and one spent most of his time reading the French exam paper, they were Scotch. When we pulled in at B'ham he carried my case out for me and said goodbye. I was met by Mother and Dad.

Saturday 20 July 1940

Den came home on leave last night.

Sunday 21 July 1940

Messed about in the morning. In the afternoon went to Moseley to tea. After tea saw Dennis off. Met Murphy and Vandervorrd (2 other pilots).

Vandervorrd was Dutch, tall, well-built and fair. I admired him very much. I hope I see him again.

Friday 26 July 1940

Did the house, cycled to Bearwood. Got some beans to pickle. Cycled to the village. In the afternoon, cut the hedge a bit, then went to the Smethwick baths with Janet. Did some more to the hedge.

Dad has put his revolver and some bullets in the back of the desk, and told us how to use it should there be an invasion.

Saturday 27 July 1940

Did the house. Went to the village with mother*. Had dinner.

After dinner I cycled to the village. There were quite a few soldiers and LDVs (Local Defence Volunteers) in the village.

*Many very nice remarks were made about me and my hair. I am glad I did not have it off.

Sunday 28 July 1940

After dinner went to C'ham to get my things back. Saw lots of soldiers in C'ham. There are army lorries all round the edge of the racecourse. In Pitville park annexe are lots of tents, and in the field opposite, (the other side of the Evesham rd) were more tents. When we got to the Millards we found that Roger had a rabbit - a pet one, a lovely grey Angora.

Sunday 28/7/40. 748099 etc

Dear Pat,
I suppose that you are now enjoying your summer holidays; and giving Gran a heap of work to do into the bargain.

We have been having a simply grand time here - I expect that you will have heard a great deal of it already from Mother or Dad. Today I flew up to 12,000 feet on a height test, the idea is to see if you are O.K. up there without oxygen. Its surprising what a lot of country there is and how tiny the towns and villages seemed from that height.

I then did some solo forced landing practices and precautionary landings. Before actually landing on a precautionary landing you have to fly across the forced landing field about 20 feet up with the wheels up - its great fun I can assure you.

By the way do you know that the last time I had a letter from you it was 12th June and in spite of your busy life I should very much like another one from you. I hate asking, but - well!

With lots of love
Dennis.

Wednesday 31 July 1940

Mother and I went shopping on our bikes. After dinner Mother had a bath and packed. Dad came home and Dad, Mother and I went to the hospital. People (doctors, nurses etc) kept thinking I was the patient. Mother's room is very nice, she has a wardrobe and a dressing table, and hot and cold water in her room. She has a bathroom of her own.

Saturday 3 August 1940

Did the house. After dinner Dad and I went to visit mother, fairly good. On the way back (in Broad Street) picked up a soldier who wanted to go to Dudley. He had 48 hrs leave as his father had a haemorrhage.

Sunday 4 August 1940

Made my bed, washed my hair and dried it in the garden while I read "Turnabout". After dinner went down to see Mother. She is much better today. While we were there Mr Strong, the consultant, came in. He is a tall, fairly slim, dark man with a drooping mouth, and a faint bluish suggestion of a moustache following the curves of his mouth.

He examined mother's throat and said it was much better. Afterwards we went to Grandma's to tea.

Because it was considered dangerous to stay in the Ear, Nose & Throat Hospital, in the heart of Birmingham, as soon as Mr Strong decided Mother was fit enough to be moved, she went to Grandma's in Park Road, Moseley, to recuperate.

Because of the possible danger of air-raids, a bed was made up for her downstairs in the dining-room.

Monday Aug 12th
                2 Park Road
                      Moseley
                      Birmingham

My dearest Dennis

  Dad & Pat have been over to see me, and are just starting off for home. I can hear them and Grandma talking in the garden, ah - now the engine starts up and they are off!

  I want to thank you very much for the lovely box of chocolates. I shall eat them and let the garrulous visitors be garrulous, as I think they (the chocs) are far too good for garrulous visitors. It is very sweet of you to have sent me such a nice present. Yes, I think you are quite worth owning as a son, in fact I just couldn't imagine a nicer one.

  Let me see - I wrote to you on Thursday just after arriving here, well that night we had an air raid warning and what with the journey home and the getting up in the night, I had a temp over 102 degrees on Friday and the bleeding had started in the throat again. Gosh, I did feel bad, but anyway I am <u>heaps</u> better again, my temp is normal and I sat out of bed for two hours this afternoon, in the sunshine in the window. The front garden is a mass of colour and I quite enjoyed it, I am sure I shall go along swimmingly now, and am even fit for an air raid again tonight, though I prefer that we don't have one. What positively <u>wonderful</u> work the R.A.F. are doing - you must be very very proud to be a member.

  I think Pat and Christine have really decided to go away together to Chipping Camden on Thursday. They are going by train complete with bicycles and then if the invasion should begin and transport become difficult they could, if necessary, cycle home. Pat ought to be alright with Christine and it would make a nice little change for both of them.

  All my love and thoughts Laddie
  Mother

Tuesday 13 August 1940

Did the housework. At 2.30, Chris came round. Went to see Mother, she wasn't quite so good. At 4.00 we went to town and had tea at Kunzle's - 4d for one tomato sandwich. Walked to the Paramount. Saw "The Bluebird." Went home, the A.F.S. station is getting on fine. *(The Auxiliary Fire Service had taken over the Wood's empty house next to the Hemmings.)*

At 11.20 I was woken by Gran and the sirens. I jumped out of bed, and put my mac and polo-necked jumper and wellingtons on. Then, grabbing my gas-mask, I said "Goodbye" to Gran* and dashed into the shelter.

We waited in silence, and then heard the low drone of a plane. It was definitely a German because the intermittent beat of the engines could be heard quite distinctly. Straightaway there was a terrific explosion somewhere not far away, and the A.A. guns thundered into action. All the time explosions were going on, and once a loud explosion happened just near. I do not know whether it was a bomb or one of our guns. There was an A.A. gun near, and every time it barked the shelter vibrated. Many of the explosions were terrific, and the noise was awful. But I cannot think how the noise bursts one's ear drums. Somehow the noises and explosions seemed to go straight into the brain without passing through any outward channels to the brain.

The plane went away and then came back again, 4 or 5 times. Each time it got just as warm a reception as the 1st time, once or twice warmer!

After two hours, when the guns were barking, bombs were exploding, and the drone of engines filled the night - when it sounded as though a tremendous thunder storm was raging overhead - <u>the All-Clear went</u>!! Three sirens went wailing through the night. Of course we stayed in the shelter. Then, a while after - not long - these 3 sirens sounded the warning note, while all the explosions etc. were still going on. At 3.15, after 4 hrs in the shelter the all clear went. I tottered back to the house, and Gran and I had a cup of tea.

N.B. persons in house - Gran and me
         "   " shelter - Mr and Mrs Ensell and me.
(Dad was on Home Guard duty at the works.)

* *Gran suffered such severe claustrophobia that she would not go into the air raid shelter*

I hated Dad's works. When I was little I even had nightmares about it. It wasn't his laboratory. No, that was O.K., and I knew he loved his work. But outside his lab. was the huge chemical works that absolutely terrified me.

There were enormous overhead pipes and tanks of chemicals and buildings housing strange sounds, shapes and smells.
In fact a strange and unpleasant smell was everywhere, even outside the works itself, where huge pipes criss-crossed the road. Underground there were pipes as well, and Dad occasionally had to supervise their inspection.
On one occasion he arrived home unexpectedly early, looking pale and shaken with a big lump on the back of his head. He gave my Mother a sort of sheepish grin and said, "You nearly didn't have a husband today!"
We were shocked. It was his way of leading in to what had obviously been a near disaster.
Apparently, he had gone to inspect a huge vat that had contained some chemical, to make sure it was all right for the men to go in to to clean it out.
He climbed up the ten foot ladder to check it. Unknown to anyone, fumes had accumulated in the vat, and, as soon as he had reached the top of the ladder, he was overcome, and crashed backwards unconscious onto the floor. Thank God he didn't fall in. As it was he was quite badly concussed and very shaken.
He did, in fact, come home one day, terribly upset, to tell us of a horrible disaster.
There were two kilns on the plant. I've no idea what they were used for, but they were constantly kept lit. Sometimes the door to the kiln might be left open, and a passing worker would give it a push to shut it. On this occasion, unknown to the passer who pushed the door shut, there was a workman inside, making some repairs to the still-hot kiln. There is no need to say more.
So I hated the place. And when the war came and I thought of him - and all the other workers - in this awful place, it was a frightening thought.
Right outside his lab. were water tanks full of phosphorus, and nearby stood a huge tanker of chlorine. Around the works were small bell shapes made of thick steel. They were just a little larger than a man in size, and, when Dennis and I had gone to the works with him on the occasion of

the demolishing of his works chimney, I had asked Dad what they were. They were, in fact, one-man air-raid shelters. Should anyone be working in this awful place during a raid, and the situation get 'too hot'. they would retreat into the claustrophobic confines of these steel bells.

Thursday 15 August 1940

Air raid.

Monday 19 August 1940

Air raid.

Tuesday 20 August 1940

Air raid.

21/8/40

740899
Sgt. D.F.Knight
Officers Mess
12 S.F.T.S
Grantham

Dear Mother,

We got back here on Sunday night to find that 6 L.A.Cs had been billeted with us, making the house terribly crowded, and next day we were told that the houses are to be inspected twice weekly.

However Dennis as usual was lucky and, in company with about nine other sergeants in our course, was invited to the Officers Mess.

I now have a large room with two windows to myself with writing table, book-case, wardrobe, chest of drawers-cum-dressing table, bedside lamp etc. and a batman to do all cleaning for me. Another advantage is that we now get full dinner at night instead of supper.

So far as getting a commission is concerned, however, it means damn all.

I got my Log book back from the C.F.I. on Monday and found to my real surprise that I had got "Above average" again.

Yesterday Land (a friend of mine) and I had to take each other up for instrument-flying practice. It seemed very strange going up with a fellow pupil in place of an instructor.

Today Jessop and I in one plane and Land and Cawthen in another went up for camera gun practice. We flew side by side and 'fired' at one another from the rear cockpit. After an hour we landed and changed positions so that the fellow who had been piloting could have a shot at shooting.

With all love
Dennis.

Thursday 22 August 1940

Air raid.

Friday 23 August 1940

Air raid.

Sat Aug 24th '40   2 Park Road
                                                   Moseley

My dearest Dennis,
    Well here we are after a very crash-banging night, a real old noisy cracker. I stayed in bed, and nurse made tea in which Grandma joined. We had music the whole of the time in the way of anti-aircraft fire, German engines and a light sound of shrapnel falling on the roof of this house, all <u>very</u> thrilling, though very sleep disturbing. I intend to have a nap this afternoon after a lunch of roast chicken which smells mighty good. Dr

Winfield has just been and is very pleased with me, he says he really believes I am beginning to get on at last and I am going to sit out of bed for a bit, nurse is staying until Wednesday and I hope to be able to do a few things for myself by that time. I was terribly interested and not a little amused to hear of your move. May you always fall on your feet, laddie as you seem to have done so far. Dad and I were very proud that you again have won the praise "Above average". We understand what it means in a service that has such a high standard. Congratulations.

Dad is going to take a machine gun course. Bless him, he is ready to do anything to help our cause to a speedy victory, for in the long run we shall be victorious. I am absolutely confident of that, and a great deal of thanks and gratitude will be due to the R.A.F.

Pat, Dad and Gran are all alright after their disturbed night though the "To-do" was more over Jim and Mary's way so Harborne was not quite so noisy.

With all my love and dearest wishes
Mother

Saturday 24 August 1940

Air raid.

Sunday 25 August 1940

Woke up at 12.15 am, got up and had dinner. After tea went to see Mother.

Air raid. A great many planes over. Very little (practically no) gunfire from us. The raid started about 9.40 pm and it ended 4.40 am. There was a break in between. Many bombs dropped. Much damage done around town. Delayed action bombs - therefore streets prohibited. The market hall was blown up. While we were in the shelter we saw a red glow in the sky - that was the Market Hall on fire, it was burned to the ground.

We learned later that the firemen, unable to put out the fire, opened all the cages that they were able to reach and let out the animals. There were reports of stray dogs and cats roaming around the town for days after.

Monday 26 August 1940

Did the housework after getting up at 11.30. Went round to Christine's in the afternoon, and we went to see mother.

When I went to bed, as soon as I had turned the light out the sirens went. Dressed, went into the shelter. Many planes came over. Heaps of bombs dropped, counted about 150. After a long time Mr Ensell said "There's a red glow in the sky over there" - (the direction of Moseley, slightly to the left) - "Would that be a fire?" We looked (Dad and I) and decided it was a fire - a very large one, the sky was brilliant red, and it flickered. We got out of the shelter, and looked, and then went and opened the back gate and stood and looked at the fire - previously we had heard 3 fire pumps go from the A.F.S. station. While we stood there we heard talking, and we went and saw 7 or 8 firemen standing with top boots on, steel helmets and their respirators on their chests.

Tuesday 27 August 1940

We tried to phone Moseley, but the phones were dead. When we drove over to see Mother we were absolutely horrified. The house opposite had gone, and there were mattresses and bedsteads and things all round Grandma's house and garden that had been flung across.

Air raid.

Tuesday

                   2 Park Road
                      Moseley

My dearest Dennis,

Very many thanks for your letter, which I received about a couple of hours ago.

Talking about air raids, we have one almost every night. Last night we had <u>the</u> <u>dickens</u> of one, they seemed to concentrate on Moseley. A house just across the road was completely demolished, killing six occupants, an incendiary bomb dropped just outside the French window next door to Grandma's, fires were started up everywhere and bombs were just showered around. We spent the rest of the night in the telephone bogy hole as I was not well enough to come hurrying out to the shelter. Tonight we are starting off in the shelter, in fact I am already installed, and very comfortable I am, lying on a full length mattress. Do you know yesterday, part of a bedstead, clothing, a broken clock etc, etc, were flung right across the road into this garden. Bricks and mortar were everywhere, part of a mattress was flung on the roof, a car was turned completely upside down. Golly, it was a to-do. *(In fact, before retreating to the telephone room, Mother was blown out of bed [she was still sleeping in the dining room] and the nurse, who was sitting with her, momentarily thought she had been blown in half.)*

It is now Wednesday evening, we of course had our usual air-raid warning last night from 9.45, to 5 o'clock this morning, but it seems that most of the bombs fell on open ground on the other side of the town. During the night Bernard Howel, an old K.E.S. boy came to see us in the shelter from time to time, just to see we were alright. He is a Home Guard man, and was so awfully cheerful, and kind. He says he will come every night so we are not to worry about anything.

This is a fine shelter. I wish ours at home was bigger, so that we could lie down instead of sit up. Everyone around is very friendly and cheerful, and even on that awful night we laughed and joked and drank tea. We had several screaming bombs, which we didn't find in the least any more disturbing than the other bombs. Every time one came whistling down Aunty Winnie said "Oh Lilly, listen, there is the All Clear". She is quite daft.

Dad is here and is about to escort me to the dug-out, so I will end now. He is going home early for some sleep and I want him to post this. He says Pat is amazingly good and is standing things remarkably well. I had a lovely sleep all afternoon. Must end now.

    With dearest love and <u>all</u> best wishes
    from Mother.

Wednesday 28 August 1940

Air raid.

Thursday 29 August 1940
Air raid.

29 August 1940

Officers Mess
12 S.F.T.S.
Grantham.

Dear Pat

I hear that you have been having a grand old time with Air Raids this last week or so. I was rather surprised to hear that they had been over as often as they have, as - touch wood - its been fairly quiet here, and even though on Tuesday night we had a few bombs dropped on our night-flying field we haven't had any warnings. One bomb didn't go off anyway.

It's just half past eight, and I am writing this, sitting in my pyjamas, I shall go straight to bed as soon as I have finished.

I wonder if you remembered anything I said about going to bed early - What? You've been too busy but are going to start next week? I was afraid of that.

Actually, if I were you I should be in bed by 7.30 at the latest every night except Saturday. And I really mean that.

This may sound a very fatherly letter but I do wish you'd take my advice, I'm usually in bed by 9 o'clock and we haven't had any warnings here ---- yet!

I suppose you'll be starting school again soon, are you staying in Birmingham? I have heard that the army are taking over the new school on Bristol Road - is that right?

With love
Dennis.

Friday 30 August 1940

Air raid.

Saturday 31 August 1940

Air raid.

Sunday 1 September 1940

Air raid.

1/9/40   Grantham

Dear Pat

Maybe I hadn't heard from you for a long while, but your letter was worth waiting for.

I'm glad to hear that you are at last getting the shelter to yourselves (though won't it seem quiet during air raids now), but surely it isn't quite large enough to lie down in, is it?

We were night-flying last night and had a couple of air raid alarms. The first time we got the warning I was just taking off and consequently I had to make a very hurried circuit. When I had landed and had got to the night-flying hut there was a sudden Atatatatatat, Atatatatat of machine gun fire and Bup-pup-pup-pup of cannons as a German flew low over head.

There was a terrific rush out of the hut, half of us to the shelter and half to watch the fun. Streaks of light like successions of brilliant shooting stars went up the sky as the cannons fired. And smaller streaks shewed the machine guns. Suddenly, just like a squib going off the German started to use a machine-gun.

Those outside the shelter decided it was wiser to get under cover and those inside started to come out to see what the fun was about. Result was confusion on the steps.

After it got quieter we became very interested in a light to the north which appeared to be circling over a spot on the ground and as we watched we noticed another light beneath it. We watched for about five minutes and then went back into the hut when about 3/4 hour later the all-clear went and we started flying again.

What? Oh! the lights? Well they turned out to be a couple of stars which weren't moving at all.

We had another short warning later on, but nothing whatever happened.

With love
Dennis.

Monday 2 September 1940

Air raid.

Sunday   2 Park Road

My dearest Dennis

    Well we are still here intact and things have been a bit quieter around here since the whiz-bang! However we all go to bed in the shelter all being settled by about 9.30 for it is at about 9.45 that the "visitors" usually arrive and play around until "fourish" in the morning. However I don't think they care much for the reception they get these days, as our R.A.F. boys always seem ready to greet them and give them a warm welcome!

    Grandma has packed Aunty Winnie off to Nancy's at Cheltenham, and a good thing she did for the very next day Grandma herself crocked up with a temperature 100.6 and water on the knee. Fortunately I still have nurse and Grandma is heaps better today, but you should see the procession that goes to the dug-out at night - talk about the halt and the lame - well we do look a crew, for my legs are still like cotton-wool, we only hope a tram won't pass whilst the procession is in progress. Pat is a useful soul in the evening - yesterday she boiled me a lightly boiled egg and toast, made Grandma a cup of tea which was all she wanted, and some biscuits, and nurse some sardines, toast etc <u>on a tray</u>, so that she could pick it up and carry it to the dug-out if the "visitors" turned up a trifle early. The dug-out is all fixed up with beds for four - it is topping. Dad is trying to get one like it for us at home, so that we can all go to bed and not worry about sirens etc. He is seeing Reynolds today about it, I think Ensells are going to do the same in their own garden. We seem to have annoyed Hitler with the raids over Berlin, he doesn't appear to like to receive the treatment he meets out to others. What the country would do without our Air Force Laddies I don't know.

    <u>Sunday afternoon</u>. Grandma is very much improved, Dr W came in and just about started having a look at my throat when - Air Raid Sirens! My poor throat etc got neglected, he hopped home to his air-raid post, we all retired to dug-out. It was just dinner time so whilst Grandma and I were being helped downstairs, Maud got lunch all ready on trays and we had a picnic lunch outside in the dug out*. This is the second mid-day raid we have had lately, last time the R.A.F. got the plane - and I think they must have done the same this time as the "All Clear" went within the half-hour. We finished our lunch and back we tramped, poor Grandma on her gammy knee and me on my cotton-wool legs, both in night attire having to come

across the front garden. What a game! but really no one seems very shocked. Hitler would be quite disappointed if he could see everyone carrying on just their usual old way.

Monday. Just received your letter, very many thanks, it amused me so much. Pat and Dad have just arrived and are reading it. I am going along well but still spend nearly all day in bed, Aren't I a Goup.
All my love and thoughts, Mother.

(Apparently, when the Air Raids are really going full swing, with bombs dropping etc, Maud has a habit of jumping up and lisping, "Would you like a nice cup of cocoa, Mrs Dawes?"!)

Thursday 3 September 1940

Air raid.

Thursday 5 September 1940

Air raid.

10/9/40

No. 12, Flying Training School
Royal Air Force,
Grantham,
Lincs.

Dear Mother,
I got your letter this morning, I'm so glad to hear that you are progressing favourably, if slowly.
By the way the final authorisation for Wings came out on Friday and on Saturday we went to Leicester to see Dick, our old flying instructor. He was very pleased indeed to see us. We met his mother - his wife is now back in New Zealand.

I'm afraid that as all R.A.F. leave has been cancelled, as since Sunday, I shan't be able to get back for a week-end for some while. However it will give you all the more time in which to get well, I hope to see a marked improvement when next I see you.

I flew over to Wolverhampton Friday, but unfortunately as Nita's house is just inside the prohibited area I couldn't get as low or as close as I should like to have done.

Anyway Nita tells me that she saw me, which is the main thing. Think of it! Grantham to Wolverhampton via Stafford and back including time for taxying (10 minutes) in 1 hour 5 minutes. And it takes 4 to 5 hours or more for the single journey by bus.

I have just written to Commander Langley to tell him that I have got my wings, do you know whether King Edwards have come back to Birmingham yet? I sent the letter to Vivian to address for me, poor Vivian if ever there's a job I can't do very well at my station he does it for me.

By the way, Barry Matthews has joined the Home Guard - it says something for the Science side of King Edwards;- Vivian, Barry and John Davies in the Home Guard, Philip in the Navy and myself in the R.A.F. and all under military age. It's a pity the classical side isn't the same, Barry and John are only seventeen*.

I wonder how Bob Smyth is getting on now, he is so very keen. I wrote to him last month but, if he is at sea, heaven knows when he will get my letter or I a reply.

With all love
Dennis.

---

*Bill and Vivian had both tried to join up at the outbreak of war, but the services were so snowed under with men in training that they were told they were not required at present.

Bill wanted to join the Fleet Air Arm, and Vivian the R.A.F.

Whether or not the feeling of frustration at Dennis and Philip soon to be entering the fighting while he, Bill, was office-bound and unable to help in the war effort, affected his mental state, I don't know, but in the summer of 1940 Bill had a nervous breakdown and was away for several months.

Saturday 14 September 1940

Am writing this during an air-raid, the time is 8.30, and the sirens went 1/2 hr ago. I am sitting on my "bed". It is a mattress laid on the floor of the lounge by the desk, it is covered with 3 red blankets. I am wearing my "siren-suit"! being slacks and a long sleeved green jumper. Nothing much has happened yet, If any guns fire or anything like that I shall go to the shelter.

All Clear at app. 11 pm (I am not quite sure what time). Dad was on Home Guard duty at the works.

Sept 15th
                                                    2 Park Road
                                                       Moseley
                                                     Birmingham

My dear Dennis

Very many thanks for your letter <u>and the wings</u>. As if it were necessary to tell me not to lose them, when I prize them so highly. I even take them to the dug-out each night for safety. You don't know how intensely proud I am of 'My Lad with Wings'. I am even reading a book by that name, and all because of you. What did you think of the "bag" of 185 Jerry planes yesterday. Was it not a positively marvellous performance! Yesterday Dad took me to Crosbie Rd for my first outing and we picked up two aircraft men for a lift. We naturally talked about you, and they being Scotties said "Ah, we are only very small fry, 'tis the flying section on which the life of Britain depends just now. They are the Laddies!" They were so Scotch we had to translate everything they said, in fact some things we never did understand. We still have rather half hearted raids - last night we had three separate warnings, and another one just as we were about to have breakfast. We could hear no aircraft, so we just carried on, but ready and on the alert, and anyway before we had finished our meal the 'Danger Past' signal sounded.

I do so hope you don't meet any stray German formations on your solo flights - oh - er - what if you did!

I am getting much better, but still I am keeping nurse another week, to save Grandma doing things. I wonder if you will be home this weekend. Anyway until I see you Laddie dear,

With all my love
Mother.

Dear Den

Congrats! I told you when you gave me this writing pad that I would only use it on special occasions. Well, I'm using it! I think you're doing fine. You are still my handsome hero – comme ca!

In fact much more than ever.

A lot of girls at school have asked how you are getting on, and I have (very proudly) told them about you getting your wings. Veronica says her father often quotes you, eg. "Dennis says so-&-so"!

We are at school at the new one, but the boys have to use 3 of our labs (we have 6) and therefore we haven't quite the run of the school.

N.B. We have (as yet) no rules! However Miss Barrie says if she is knocked down when coming out of her room she will make a rule that there is to be no running in the corridor.

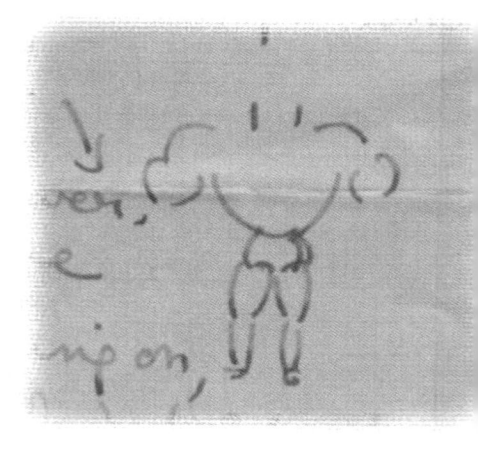

Well I have hardly left enough time to catch the post so cheerio for the present - Best of Luck

Lots of Love
Pat

Miss Barrie was a wonderfully understanding, witty person. She was J. M. Barrie's niece, very Scottish and twinkly-eyed.

Once, at the old school, Esmé had been pushing me on the milk trolley when, rounding a corner, we almost bumped into Miss Barrie. We

waited for the wrath to come, but she merely smiled and said, "Put it back when you've finished with it, won't you"!
Sunday

    My dearest Dennis
        My heartiest congrats upon your success and reaching the fulfilment of your hopes and wishes, for my part though you know of old how I hate this flying business but as you're really intent to have a whack at the Germans <u>may</u> you bring <u>many</u> down and come back safe and sound and tell your children in the days to come how <u>clever</u> Daddy was.
        Good bye my boy for the present and all luck be with you.
    My dearest love
    Gran

Monday 16 September 1940

    Got up and had breakfast. Dad was just starting the car when the air raid warning went. I went out to see what he was going to do, he said he was going to the works. He had forgotten his gas mask so I had to fetch it for him. At about 5 to 9 the All Clear went (the warning went at about 20 or 1/4 to!)
    There is now a raid on, the warning went at about 8.30 pm.

Wednesday   5 Crosbie Road

My dearest Dennis
    I have addressed my letter 'Crosbie Road' but of course I am still at Moseley. Pat and Dad came over to see me yesterday evening and Christine brought me a most glorious bunch of pink carnations yesterday afternoon, they are very lovely. I want to tell you how much I enjoyed your grapes. I had every single one myself and they were real good. I don't know how much you paid for them dear, but they were worth it I enjoyed them so much. I am still going along, very slowly it seems and today I

surprised everyone by having a bit more bleeding in the throat. I don't seem to behave at all in the orthodox way but never-the-less I am getting along though it is so slowly. Nurse is still here and I have been advised to keep her for another week.

    We have some quite lively midnight parties, with cups of tea or Horlicks or something. I am getting quite spoilt. I am hoping we shall have a quiet night tonight from German visitors as Dad is on all night at the works, and I don't much relish raids when I know he is there and Pat and Gran are alone at Crosbie Rd. However the weather doesn't look too good for raiders, quite a high wind is springing up, so I hope we shall be left in peace, though Birmingham seems to have a great attraction for them, there are so many objectives.

    - Well laddie, how are the wings, have they burnt a hole in your tunic yet? Dad and I are terribly proud of you, and you looked so clean and keen and youthful and so much The Type that will save Britain from destruction.

God bless you laddie always
    Mother.

Thursday   Grantham

Dear Pat,
    Believe it or not I am writing this in the back seat of a Battle. We've just been on a practice reconnaissance and Land the pilot is flying me back.

    Land strangely enough (my co-pilot) [we've just been 'shot up' by a Spitfire] is a Chartered Accountant and even more of a coincidence was recommended for fighters at Desford, got 'above average' both at Desford and I.T.S. here and is in the officers mess.

    We're just passing an aerodrome with about 12 Battles parked around. They're all dummies and the aerodrome is merely ordinary fields made to look like a camouflaged aerodrome.

    Well we're just slowing down to land now so cheerio!
    Love
    Dennis.

22/9/40   Grantham

Dear Mother and Dad
    I have just seen my flying report for my course here. Actually I shouldn't have seen it, but .... "An above average pilot, keen and intelligent with a natural instinct for flying. Does not get flustered when things go wrong. Recommended for Fighters or G.R".
    I though you might be interested - Eh?
    With love
    Dennis.

    Den came home on leave. He has got his commission. He is now a Pilot Officer.
    I went into Town with him to get his officer's uniform. We went to Burberrys. A lot of it, of course, he has to be measured for, and it will be sent on to him.
    It was all most exciting! And I felt so proud.

Tuesday 1 October 1940

    Stayed away from school to see Den off to Sutton Bridge.

Oct: 1st   5 Crosbie Road

My dear Dennis,
    As you may guess I am wondering very much <u>who</u> you will find and what you will find at your journeys end this evening.
    I shall be most impatient to open your letter when it arrives, and I am sure the rest of the household will be no less impatient. Gran is just opening the groceries - your little lot, 1/2 lb.lard, 1/2 lb. butter, 1/4 lb. tea, 1 lb. sugar, 8 ozs bacon - very generous, aren't they?

We shall be able to be very lavish. Pat has been home and had her lunch, and gone off to school. She will be in time for over an hour of school, and can collect her homework. She told me how luckily Aunty Freda and Grandma met you. Aunty Freda rang up in the middle of lunchtime, to tell <u>me</u> all about <u>you</u>. She is frightfully thrilled about it all, and says she envies me in having you. She told me what she advised if you come across one Messerschmit, and what if you came across more than one. I told her of my advice of a nice little flight to Aberdovey. Aunty Freda says you look quite two or three years older than when she last saw you. She thinks it is because you have acquired 'pilot's eyes'. My lad with wings, with pilot's eyes.

Well dear, I hope you will find everything "good", and if not your old friends, some just as good new ones, and now for the thrill of addressing this letter to you, and I hope I shall very soon have a letter from you telling me all about everything.

    Yours with dearest love
    Mother.

2/10/40   <u>Sutton Bridge</u>

Dear Mother

We actually had a peaceful night's rest again last night, without an air-raid, but I believe that we do get more bombers over here than at Grantham.

I have not been up yet - may go up tomorrow - we have instructions that, should we see any German bombers, we are to shoot them down even though we still are training.

It is quite bewildering to hear the number of languages spoken here - but it does remind one that we are not the only pilots left to fight Germany, even if ours are the only machines.

As I am in rather a hurry to get to Kings Lynn to do some shopping I'll close now

    With love
    Dennis

Thursday   5 Crosbie Road

My dearest Dennis,
    Thank you so much for your letter which arrived this afternoon. I was so glad to get it and to know a little bit of your new surroundings, but you said nothing about your journey. I wonder how you got on and at what time you arrived, it is all of such interest to me. I am glad to hear Shimmonds is there and wish for your sake Land had arrived as well, but expect you will soon find other friends, I shouldn't think it is very hard amongst pilots. They all seem particularly nice fellows. How interesting it must be to find yourself one of so many different representatives of the common cause, it isn't as if the men of each country are simply fighting for their own country alone, but all are in it together fighting for the one reason, Right against Force and Brutality.
    When you write, do let me know how you like being amongst such a cosmopolitan crowd. Personally, I think I should very much like it, and it must broaden one's outlook immensely.
    What is the food like? is it as good as at Grantham. You will certainly need it if you have to be on the look-out for German planes. Well laddie dear, "Here is <u>luck</u> to you when you do".
    We had three air raid warnings during the day yesterday, but only once did we hear the sound of engines when I was in the village, I was just near the Harborne baths, and my goodness didn't the siren there make a noise. I was on my way home and a lady (living up at the corner house of this road on the same side as this house) came up and spoke to me *(I was later (1943) to be introduced to her son Ray, who was by this time a P.O. Observer in the R.A.F.).* She said she had often wanted to speak but hadn't liked to, but she wanted to say how much she admired Pat, you and me. Pat and me for our cheerful, happy faces, and you as one of our young defenders of the air.
    Last night we had no warning of any sort, it was a misty slightly foggy night and it seems that all aircraft was pretty quiet. Nevertheless Dad, Pat and I went to bed in the dug-out as we always intend to do. It is really quite comfortable and warm and we all sleep perfectly well up there. Well dear, I want Pat to post this on her way to the pictures.
    With dearest love and all best wishes, Mother.

Monday 14 October 1940

After tea had an air raid warning as usual. ˙Slept in the shelter.

Tuesday 15 October 1940

In the morning, as I came up from the Air Raid Shelter and went into my room, I saw that gran had put a bolster down my bed, threw my coat onto the bed, and the bolster TURNED OVER AND LOOKED AT ME!! It was Dennis!! He had arrived at 4 am (the train was supposed to arrive at 10 am).

(He had been given 24 hrs leave, as he was posted from Sutton Bridge to Filton.)

Messed about and then Mother, Den and I went to Moseley to have dinner. Aunty Freda, Kathleen were there and Uncle George and of course Grandma. Had a marvellous time. Jugged hare and rabbit*, onion sauce etc. Uncle George took us all except Aunty K to town. Dropped us just outside Baileys. Had my eyes tested. Den went to the office. I have to wear glasses for reading, but they look quite nice. After tea Den took me to the pics to see "My Two Husbands", very good. While we were there the film went pink, and the lips moved but no sound came forth, then a young girl walked onto the stage and said the alarm had gone and if we wished to leave would we please go. We stayed, and saw the film through. On the way home, we saw a lot of A-A *(anti-aircraft)* shells bursting in the sky in front, so ran home. Shrapnel was pattering down all around us. How I wished we had had our tin hats with us! Slept as usual in the shelter. Den on top bunk, Mum and Dad and I on bottom. A lot of A-A fire and bombs. One of the worst we've had yet, All Clear 4.00.

* In the middle of this dinner there was an alarm. Went on eating - All clear a short while later.

Wednesday 16 October 1940

Den got up at 6.00, and had his breakfast. I got up and had mine just as he was going, Said goodbye to him, and he went off to catch the 8.00. Went to school, At 8.00 while I was doing prep the alarm went. Went to the shelter. A lot of guns and bombs etc. Slept all right - All Clear 1.30.

Thursday 17 October 1940

Went to school, took a red hospital blanket in case there is "a Blitzkrieg" while I'm at school. After tea put the beds straight in the dug out, was doing my prep when at 8.00 the air raid warning went. I was already changed so got my supper, and tidied my books up a bit.

While we were all having our supper there was rather a loud bomb-burst, so went up to the shelter. There was a lot of gunfire, and in a lull we went back to the house. We thought we saw a fire but it was the moon. (The above was written on the roof of the shelter.) We are now in the shelter for the night. There have been heaps of explosions - mostly A.A, but some bombs. The planes have been over many times, the guns are firing now and the planes are overhead. The lights keep flashing as the guns fire. There are 7 casualty lists, 4 fatal and 3 injured, put up daily outside the police station. Districts are Holloway Head, Edgbaston and Kings Heath, Sparkford and all those districts. New Street station has got it too.

Friday 18 October 1940

Esmé told me about last night's air raid with her. They had 8 bombs in her road, and on the way to school she passed a crown of people round a tree, looking up. When she looked up she saw the remains of a man.

After tea changed, knitted 2 rows and the sirens went. Went up to the shelter.

Saturday 19 October 1940

Got up. Made a box for the shelter to keep things in.
Bad night as far as raids were concerned. Lots of gunfire etc.

5 Crosbie Road

Dearest Den

We have had 3 air-raid warnings today. Nothing happened, however, as far as we are concerned. The night before last was very hectic, and very close!! It started, as usual, just before 8, and immediately after the A.A. fire began. We certainly gave those jerrys a pasting! Then 2 large bombs fell somewhere in the town direction, and one or two more fell in roughly the same place. Suddenly, when we were very engrossed in our A.A. fire right above us, we heard a whizzing sound. It got louder and louder, and then suddenly stopped. We looked at each other blankly for a moment, and then Dad said "I think it's an unexploded shell". I said it sounded louder than that, more like an aerial torpedo. Anyway we had 3 more whizzes the same, only not half so loud. I think they were pieces of shrapnel falling quite close - next door perhaps.

Then there were a lot of bombs, and flashes and A.A. fire - going on all the time, so loud and close that the shelter shook.

Then there was another whizzing sound - louder even than the first, coming nearer and nearer, (and we all ducked and waited for the bang!). I quite expected at the least to have some earth and stones hurled at the shelter, but it suddenly stopped. I said I was perfectly certain that *that* was an aerial torpedo, but we found out later that several delayed action bombs had been dropped in our district (they think Fitz-Roy avenue).

Next day (yesterday) I cycled to Court Oak rd because our milkman said that a shop had been hit and a woman and a little boy killed. I cycled past the Court Oak and on until I came to the place where the bus stops by that roundabout, and we turn right to go to the Warley.

I was just about to turn back as I had seen no damage, but I saw crowds and crowds of people in the road we walk up to the Warley. I turned right, and went up and saw 3 houses had been completely demolished. Another house next to these three looked as though a giant hand had taken hold of it and twisted and smashed it. 8 houses away the rooves of the houses were still damaged, and opposite these houses, about 10 yds away from the smashed houses was a huge crater in the road. it was simply terrific, but not very deep, about 8 ft - perhaps more. You know how there is a long grass island all the way up the road, about as wide as the road either side? Well the crater stretched right across the one road and onto the grass island

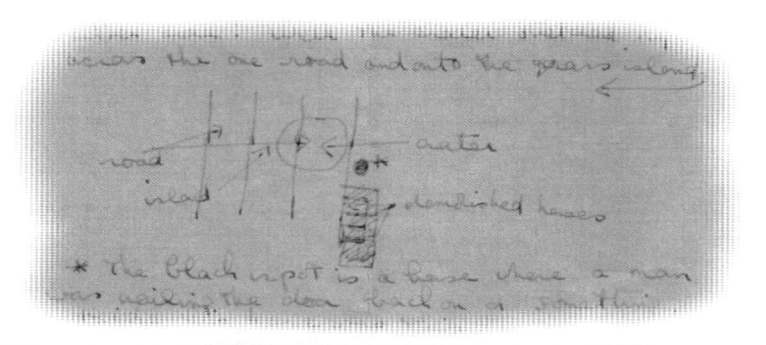

* the black spot is a house where a man was

nailing the door back or something. Outside his house was this huge crater, making it difficult to go out of his front gate.

On the way back down the rd I noticed near the bus-stop, a rescue van, and a space very close to a shelter where I presume there used to be a shop. All the way up the road, and round the corner and down the other road the houses were propped up with long props. The glass was broken in nearly all the houses.

Esmé had 8 bombs in her road the night before our "do."

Well, I hope I'm not morbid! How are you getting on? We expected a letter but thought the reason we didn't get one was probably because you were too busy settling in etc. Have you called on Miss Bladen yet? I shouldn't if I were you, though, because she's awfully deaf, and always interprets you wrongly!

Dad is at the works tonight, so I hope they do not have a bad raid. Since we have had 3 today I should imagine they are preparing for another attack tonight - spying out the land!

I suppose you have had no raids, but perhaps it is S. Wales where they are always getting the raids. I can't think of any more to say, except good luck!

Love
Pat.

Sunday 20 October 1940

Dad's night at A&Ws. Mother and I were in the shelter when we heard footsteps and Den walked in! He was in his officer's uniform.

Monday 21 October 1940

School. Den brought Chris and Vivian round in the evening and there was a telegram waiting recalling him.
There was an early warning so they went home. Spent the night as usual in the shelter.

Friday 25 October 1940

Den turned up to complete his wasted leave, that night was a bad raid.

Saturday 26 October 1940

Went to town*. Den and I dashed up to Nita's; there was an air-raid while we were getting dinner, tried toasted marsh mallows.
Went home. Very bad raid. Many bombs on town.
* When we went to town the damage was bad, but not as bad as on Sunday 27th.

Sunday 27 October 1940

Did prep in the morning. In the afternoon we (Dad, Mother, Den and I) went to Wishaw to see Aunt Helen, Uncle Frank, Uncle Fred and Auntie Popsy and Freda. Aunty P's brother has just died of shock from air-raids. Wishaw seemed frightfully peaceful after B'ham. Uncle Frank seems much more cheerful now Aunt Millie has died. Aunt H is getting more deaf than ever, but is a real old sport.
She says she loves to go to the top window and look out at the gunfire etc of B'ham - of course she cannot hear it.
Came home. The damage in town is terrific. Made a detour at Broad Street just near "The Hungry Man", Great Charles Sreet is an awful mess, and all the way to Wishaw we came across bombed houses, craters etc. We hadn't seen anything like it before.

Monday 28 October 1940

Mary came and said we ought to hurry as there was a crater in Pritchatts road, and we might have to make a detour. We did not, the bomb was exactly outside the entrance to the University, the wall was very cracked. There was a crater in the field a way back.

Tuesday 29 October 1940

Went to school, an incendiary bomb in Pritchatts road, just near the crater. An incendiary bomb through the roof of our school. Landed in the art store-room.

Wednesday 30 October 1940
Said Goodbye to Den. Went to school. Two air-raid warnings. Came home, changed, Esmé and Hazel did not turn up at school today - hope they are all right.
It is 6.50 and the sirens have just sounded.

Thursday 31 October 1940

Went to school. In the Maths lesson the warning went. At about 3.30 (1 hour after school) the All Clear went. Slush (Madame Schlumberger) had just given us some French books to read as we were bored. Went to the bike sheds and found M had gone. Was just wheeling my bike out when the warning went again, the mistresses would not let us go, so took my prep to the shelter. Did some German. Miss Martin gave us a piece of pear each. (Jinks, Fish, Mack, Jean and Gill and me, there was one piece over so J. Mercer had it.)
Miss Wallace came round with barley sugars. At 4.30 (app) the All Clear went, got on my bike and went home as quick as poss.

31/10/40
                                                            Royal Air Force Station,
                                                            Filton
                                                            Gloucestershire.

Dear Mother,
First of all, I am enclosing the ration card, which I could not find - having eaten you out of house and home I hope this will be the

wherewithall to replenish your larder. Actually, by all the rules and regulations it can only be used by you.

I was very sorry in a way to pack you off home yesterday, but you looked so very tired and it wasn't much fun waiting there, was it?

I have now managed to move into the same room as Land which is much better, especially as it's about half as large again as the last one.

I think that I scarcely need say that I enjoyed my leave very much - in spite of air raids - but now I'm well and truly back in the busy hubbub of R.A.F. life. Today at about 11.30 I saw a film on treatment of prisoners in Germany and since then billiards, letter writing and perhaps, this evening, a trip into Bristol. However too much work makes Jack -and Dennis - a dull boy so the R.A.F. organise entertainments in the evening. Last night for instance there was an excellent dance and two or three nights before a concert. What a life!
With love
Dennis.

Sunday   5 Crosbie Road

My dear Dennis,

We had an absolutely sirenless night last night, one almost felt there was something missing. I see we gave it <u>hot</u> to Berlin, the hottest raid of the war they have tasted. Talking about tasting, did you know Uncle George couldn't bear the thought of a good joint of English beef going to waste, so risked the bombs, dashed in to "Glenarm" *(Grandma's house)* and carried his prize to safety. It amused me, - just the thing Uncle George would rescue. However, all is well that ends well, and your rug was escorted to Pattisons, Harborne, yesterday, by Grandma and Aunty Kathleen. Aunty Kathleen wanted to see your face when you received it, but I wish you could have seen hers, she looked so delighted and proud to give it to you. I hope when you write to thank her you will realize the terrific amount of work she has put into it, and also that it would be a very costly thing to make, I only mention this in case you being a 'mere man' may not understand the magnitude of her gift. I have no news whatever to impart. I went shopping in Moseley and three places in town yesterday, and ordered a pair of gym shoes, a green school blouse, Dad's shirts, and two dug-out mattresses to be made to measurements, and yet I never left the house, I did all by 'phone. Hope they are a success when they turn up.

Gran had a letter from Austrey yesterday, they say what a terrible time they had in their first and only air raid. They were all in bed, and when the bomb dropped the plaster in Sybil's room shimmered down, and Sybil and Joe jumped up to see if their two children sleeping in the next room were safe. They found them sleeping quite peacefully, which was lucky, as the bomb only dropped seven miles away! Wotcha think about that!

With all my love and dearest wishes
from
Mother.

Friday 1 November 1940

Air raid.

Saturday 2 November 1940

Air raid.

Sunday 3 November 1940

Air raid.

Monday 4 November 1940

Air raid. Rained all day.

Tuesday 5 November 1940

Air raid.

Wednesday 6 November 1940

On the way from school discovered that soldiers were moving into a house in Pritchatts Road. Quite a lot of soldiers in the village. Rained all day.

Heard a whistling bomb, at least not a proper whistling bomb but a whizzing one, that means that it was close.

Thursday 7 November 1940

 Air Raid. Went to school. Rained.
 In the raid I was in bed in the shelter, and when the guns fired my bed bounced up and down.

9/11/40   504 Squadron

Dear Mother,
 I have just arrived back from the pictures in Bristol to find my pyjamas laid out to warm in front of the fire. It was such a cosy sight that I could not refrain from writing you of it.
 ..... I have flown very little recently, although three days ago I flew a pilot to Pembrey in a Magister, and then brought the plane back empty. It was a very pleasant trip, along the coast all the way.
 We are having, so far, a remarkably easy time here. Even the squadron has only been up once, and no sooner had it got up to 25,000' than it was ordered to land again as there was nothing doing.
 However, we are seldom at a loss for anything to do. and, even above billiards, reading or walking, sitting in the ante-room doing nothing holds primary place in the list of most practiced and most enjoyed entertainments.
 We usually get a couple of dances and a concert each week, but so far I have not been to one, although I expect to next week.
 With love
 Dennis.

Sunday 10 November 1940

Made pastry, had dinner and then at 3.30 Mother and Dad decided to go for a walk. So I then went to Mary's to see if she would come with me, when it started to rain. I came back. I'm fed up with the rain, it has done nothing but that for about a fortnight - and it hasn't even stopped the Germans. At about 4.00 Mother and Dad came back and we went in the car to Meadow Rd to see a bombed house. When we got there we could see nothing damaged, so that was another rumour! Then we went to Bearwood near the Bear Inn to see where a time bomb had exploded. Dad said he thought it was a house that had been pulled down, and not where a bomb had exploded.

It is now 8.30 and there is a raid on. Mother and I are in the shelter with the light on, Dad won't come. He says it is only a chance in a million that we should be hit - yes, but there is that chance! There is a lot of A.A. fire going on, and a plane directly overhead.

It was announced on the 6.00 news that Neville Chamberlain is dead. Poor man! I am sorry for him.

Wednesday 13 November 1940

Went to school. At the end of recess the warning went and we all went to the shelters. At 2.25 the all clear went. Came home. Did a bit of gardening. Gran, Mother and I all in the garden, the warning went. The balloons all went up. A while after a plane was heard, and looking up we saw it a little to the left of our garden. It was just cruising around but there were many short bursts of machine gun fire. The A.A. gun fired, and it went over town direction. Then another plane came and cruised around. Gran said "Come down to this end of the garden, it will machine-gun you!" but we stood on the roof of the shelter and watched.

Our 4.5 got 2 shells jolly near it, and the firemen who were all out in Wentworth Rd cheered like the dickens - so did Mother! We heard a lot of machine gun fire, and found afterwards that one was bombing Austins and they were machine gunning it. (We learned later that it was the Cadburys workers they were machine-gunning as they came out of work.)

Wednesday.   5 Crosbie Road

Nov 13th 40

My dear Dennis,
    You have been very good to me with your letters lately, thank you very much. Yes, I got the coupons safely - you funny thing -, you needn't have troubled though, for we seem to manage quite well with everything, and so far haven't had any real hardships to put up with, in fact we would willingly share with you any extra rations if by so doing we could get you home on leave more frequently.

Dad got his full Home Guard uniform yesterday and has put his ribbons up, and very proud I am of him - yes, my two men-kind are certainly doing their stuff.

    We had a most thrilling afternoon today. *(There follows a description of the air-raid described above.)* It, in fact, they, circled around between Harborne and Northfield, and once went over Dad's works district, but it almost seemed as if the display was put on for the Harborne district. Laddie, it really was thrilling, but I wish they had got the plane.

    The news is pretty good this evening, though I wish the Jarvis Bay and her gallant captain could have reached port in safety. It wouldn't surprise me if the Americans were in the fray before very long. Dad had a very nice summer holiday on Monday though it poured with rain. We spent the day shopping and he bought a pair of grey slacks, - very nice, and ordered a Harris Tweed sports coat, also very nice. I bought a pair of blue brogues, very sensible. We had a meal at The Burlington, and met Christine there. We had chicken, done with mushrooms, onions and small carrots, followed by ice cream and coffee, and swilled down with a bottle of Sauterne. Christine had to rather hurry hers to get to the Queens (hospital), but we dawdled over ours.

    I suggest Dad has an autumn holiday soon. It is seven forty-five, and our nightly visitors are late. I think I must go and change in readiness for their arrival, so as I said before, I must go now.

    With our dearest love and all best wishes.
    from Mother.

Thursday 14 November 1940

Went to school. Had a raid.

Had a bad raid in the night, at least Coventry did - 1000 casualties. The pictures in the papers are awful. Two incendiaries were dropped on town, but the gunfire over town was <u>terrific</u>. We put up a marvellous barrage. Once a plane came directly overhead, and you could see the white puff of smoke still lingering in the sky long after the plane had gone.

Aunty Freda rang up next day to say they found a piece of shrapnel on the bedroom floor.

Friday 15 November 1940

Very frosty. Went to school. At Pritchatts rd skidded and fell off my bike. Made a hole in my blazer, my blouse and my stocking, and twisted my handle bars, dented my gear-case and broke the 3-speed - Nice work!

When I got home changed, and took my bike to be repaired.

There was an air-raid too, lots of incendiaries were dropped very close - but that's all.

Saturday 16 November 1940

Got up, had breakfast. Messed about and had dinner. After dinner went down to get my bike but it wasn't ready. Came back and went to see "Dr Cyclops" with Chris, not too good. Had tea and then went back with Chris, she took the eggs. (The 'egg man' delivers eggs to our door in a huge basket, and at the moment we can have as many as we want. We have a dozen and now get another dozen for Mrs Taylor. He has a chicken farm out near Shirley, and so far rationing doesn't seem to have affected him.)

Went to bed early, 9.30. There was a short raid at 7 which lasted an hour. There was an even shorter one about 11 which lasted 10 minutes, I think.

504 Squadron

Dear Mother

We are still having a very pleasant time here, although we are not doing very much for our money. Yesterday we were in Bristol by four o'clock and after we had done a little shopping we had tea and then went to the pictures. We then had supper and came back.

I got up as usual at twenty five to nine this morning and, having had breakfast, went across to flights to see if anything was going.

By the way Hitching and Jessop share a room in a semi-detached house in a road by the aerodrome boundary. The house belongs to the R.A.F. and several sergeants live there.

As it is only about fifty feet from the dispersal hut, our normal day's work consists of sitting in basket chairs in Hitching's room reading, writing or playing cards.

It seems very strange spending one's day in a suburban house.

This afternoon I was going up to practice with two members of the fighter squadron. The idea was to practice formation flying and tactics but of course as we were an operational flight it was up to us to tackle any Jerries we might be directed to chase. My instructions were that in the event of a dog-fight I was to get out of the way above the fight and get a grandstand view to give me a chance to learn the dodges that we and Jerry employ.

"On no circumstances" was I to attack "unless the enemy was a single machine and the other two had used up all their ammunition".

Don't they take care of us?

However as we were talking of what we should do a message came over the radio to take off and intercept an enemy bomber coming south towards us.

We rushed out and took off in a great hurry and having got to 10,000' a message came over the radio saying "Enemy plane out of sector, continue your training flight".

So I missed my grandstand view.

I'm afraid that you aren't living up to your save waste paper principles, and so I am returning to you two sheets of blank paper that you enclosed in your last letter.

With love
Dennis.

P.S.   I tested to see whether there was any writing in invisible ink on them, but No!

Tuesday 19 November 1940

School. After tea did prep, had just started when the sirens went. Brought my work downstairs; had just settled again when it got rather bad so went up to the shelter, then it got very bad. The planes came over incessantly, and we put up a terrific barrage. I saw 3 balloons come down in flames, and Dad saw some machine gun fire, which Mother and I heard. Three bombs dropped very close and the searchlights were out searching the sky. It was <u>very</u> hectic, there seemed to be fires all round. Suddenly there was an explosion of flame in our garden, over near the garage.

Mother swears that I grabbed my tin hat and leapt out of the shelter shouting something like, "Come on, Dad, we've got one!" But I don't remember that.

Anyway, I got the stirrup pump and with Mother's help started pumping. But Dad had an unorthodox, but much more effective treatment, and, grabbing the snow shovel picked up the incendiary and threw it onto the rose border and threw soil over it.

Meanwhile Mother and I turned the water onto the canopy tent, which was still out in the garden, and was blazing well.

Between us we put everything out, and then realised there was a fire somewhere up the road.

We all went to the front of the house, and there were people scurrying around everywhere. Apparently, a stick of incendiaries had been dropped straight down our road.

Everyone had coped and put them out - with one exception.

Half way up the road the roof of a house was on fire. We were told an incendiary had fallen through the roof and they needed a ladder.

Dad and I rushed back and got our ladder, but by the time we got back the whole house was well and truly alight and beyond the help of ordinary civilians.

That is a bit of an ironic statement, because the house was occupied by an army officer - a major, I believe - and his batman. When the incendiary first fell, and was discovered by the major, he sent his batman to fetch a hose.

The only thing wrong with that move was that the batman arrived back with the complete hose, unattached to any water supply!

Next morning town was <u>terrible</u>, there was no gas, no papers, no trains, and an oil bomb on the way to school. I can't describe the raid as it was, maybe the papers when/if they come will put it better than I.

Wednesday 20 November 1940

No papers in the morning, as the stations are bombed.

Went to school. Got nearly as far as the University when we were met by some K.E. girls who said "No school today - there's a delayed action bomb, come again tomorrow!" So we went home.

Thursday 21 November 1940

I am in bed with gastric flu. I shall get up tomorrow. It is now about 2 pm, the sirens are just going. They went a little while ago, and then we had the All Clear. Mother has just told me there was a little boy ill in bed, and a bomb dropped on the bed and his mother can't find any of his remains! Isn't it awful.

Nov 21st   5 Crosbie etc

Dear Den

As you are almost sure to know, we had a very bad raid on Tuesday night. It started before 7, and I hadn't time to do my homework. I tried to work a bit downstairs, but it got so bad that we had to go up to the dug out. Mother & Dad saw 2 balloons come down in flames, and I saw those 2 and another. Dad saw tracer bullets very low over Christine's way, and it turned out later that the Germans were machine-gunning the people as they put out the fires etc. The searchlights were searching the sky all night long, and the planes came over incessantly. Squadrons at a time. Dad forgot his coat and said he would get it in a lull. But there wasn't a lull, and he got so cold that he had to go and get it with the planes overhead.

There were fires all around, and the sky was just one mass of red. The majority of the A.A., and the bomb-dropping was over Smethwick district, town, Moseley, Selly Oak and directly overhead. We put up a fine barrage, but we didn't seem to do much.

We heard a lot of heavy stuff drop, and 2 of those whizzing bombs. Dad was in the house when one fell. It just whizzed down frightfully loudly, and then landed with a terrific explosion. That was the nearest large one we had. I think Mother is writing to you, maybe she can make it sound as bad as it was - I can't.

Anyway, next day I went to school, and had got to the University when a prefect stopped me and said that there was a delayed-action bomb at the school, and we were to come again next day! On the way back we passed an oil bomb in - I think the name is Somerset Rd. Anyway here is a plan.

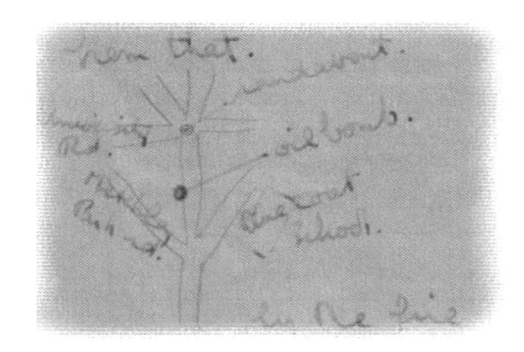

Perhaps you can tell from that There was thick yellow all over the road, and an awful smell. It was pretty skiddy.

When I arrived back I didn't feel too good, so sat by the fire with a blanket round me. While I was like that I heard Mother exclaim and dash to the front door. I followed her, and had the shock of my life to see Grandma carrying 2 cases being helped in, and the first thing she said was "My house has gone!" Luckily we had some dinner ready, and she ate it and felt better after it, I think. It's her Moseley house, it hasn't quite gone, but all the windows and doors were blown in, and she can't get into 1/2 the rooms. She went into that room with the huge mirror in it, and discovered all the glass was smashed out. The doors are wrenched off cupboards, and the kitchen ceiling is fallen down.

Mrs Carter from across the road is very worried about all the valuables, as anyone can steal them. (Her house is badly damaged too - so is Mrs Hemmings - next door to Grandma's, and Mrs Blooms - next door to the bombed house.) By the way another bomb fell on the bombed house, or rather in the crater (there goes the saying that a bomb never hits the same place twice) and threw all the debris into the road. All the houses in Park

Rd are damaged, but not as badly as those I have mentioned. They think it's a land mine that's caused it.

Mother rang up Aunty Mary, because Aunty Kathleen said their house was damaged, and discovered that all the doors and windows had been blown in there. Uncle Jim and another warden were helping to put out fires or clear away debris or something, when the Jerrys started machine-gunning them, so they sheltered in their doorway, and a bomb fell and the blast blew the door and the lintel in and Uncle Jim and the warden with it!

Apparently town was nothing before compared with what it is now! Grandma says it is awful. New Street and Snow Hill railway stations are "out of order" and Holloway Head end of the Bristol Rd is barracaded off. In fact everywhere is barracaded off!

Last night the raid was bad again, but compared with Tuesday it wasn't so bad.

Well, I'm sorry you missed your sight of Jerry versus British fighter, better luck next time! However, it does lengthen your period of training!

Best of Luck.
Love from
Pat.

P.S. Mother has just received your letter. I discover you like my favourite - no 36. I am going to have that one.

In fact, Grandma's house was looted. Apparently a large van drew up and several men openly loaded it up with all Grandma's beautiful antiques, silver, pictures, ivories, etc, smoking and talking and acting in a completely casual manner The few neighbours remaining thought that it was a group from the large family taking the valuables to safety.

Friday 22 November 1940

Went to school. Had 2 raids while at school. Came home. Had a raid.

At about 7 had another raid warning. Things started straight away. Went up to the shelter, and worked. The searchlights were out, and incendiaries had started big fires in town. I got my camera, and tried to 'snap' the searchlights. Each time I got them in focus they switched across the sky to some other lot of planes. Or else the gun near here fired and made me jump like the dickens and nearly drop the camera and jump back into the shelter.

After a while went to bed, and woke up about midnight. Next moment there were 5 whizzes, ever so loud, and 5-6 explosions - very close - then Dad said it was very red, and looked like a fire. So they both got out, and next moment I heard them exclaim and say there was an oil bomb in the gardens at the back, and it looked like Dr Winfield's! One of the whizzes landed just across the road from Christine's, and severely damaged 2 houses, damaged 2 more, and made a large crater in the road. In the paper next day the air raid was said to be nearly 12 hours long.

Saturday 23 November 1940

Discovered our water was off.

Sunday 24 November 1940

Water still off.
Did a spot of prep. Went to the Taylors to tea. A warning, but no raid.

24/11/40
                                                                                       P/O D.F. Knight
                                                                                       R.A.F.Station
                                                                                               Filton
                                                                                               Glos

Dear Pat,

Firstly, thanks very much for your letter, I wish I could write them as long but I don't get very much to write about and it's very hard to think of something fresh for each letter.

So very hard, in fact that I wrote to Grandma, Christine and Vivian identical letters the week before last I was so hard put for original things to say. But don't tell any of them that for Heavens' sake.

Oh! By the way, if anybody is thinking of buying me Christmas presents and is hard put for ideas here are a couple of suggestions you might publish.

Letter Knife: points to look for, I'd like the blade to be fairly narrow and pointed so that it will easily slip into the corner of a letter; but strong enough not to bend.

Pyjamas: Blue; elastic top for 29"-30" waist - I prefer this to cord; fairly long in arm and leg; definitely long in jacket so that it will not slip out of pyjama slacks - you remember Daks have rubber pads round the waist to stop shirt riding up. Why not pyjamas the same? Provided, of course, the rubber will stand laundering.

Book ends: Smart; strong; won't fall over when you lean a book against them; *won't slip sideways when you lean a book against them; will stand packing in a suitcase when moving from place to place.

That's about all I can think of at the moment. Do I hear you saying, "And a good job too"?

So Grandma's house has gone at last, I suppose there's not much I can say that will do any good.

By the way, as you see, I am sending along with this letter a copy of the "Aeroplane" with my name in. I want you to pay particular attention to the half page cartoon about the Spitfire fund.

Your letter sounded very exciting indeed; but in the thrill of air-raids (said the elder brother as elder brothers will) don't catch colds!

With love
Dennis.

* It's surprising how many book ends have these faults.

Oct. 24th 1940. *(Sic, actually Nov)*   5 Crosbie Road

Sunday

My dear Dennis,

As I believe Pat told you in her last letter we have been having a pretty lively time around these parts. I know she told you that Grandma's house has been damaged, and in fact all glass broken and roofs damaged in all houses around that area, and there has been a good deal of damage around Uncle Jim's, in fact, he and three other wardens were taking shelter on Tuesday night from German machine gunning, (a new and pretty little habit they have adopted as the wardens are helping injured). As I was saying, they were taking cover when two large bombs were dropped in that little lane just opposite them, and the blast blew the four men, plus the door and the lintel all in a heap in the hall. Every window was broken and a few frames blown in as well, but Uncle Jim and his three companions were unhurt though a bit shaken, as you may guess.

Friday night proved to be the hottest night we here have yet had, and Dad and I dressed and remained so all night. There was an oil bomb, or something of the sort which shrieked just over the dug-out and landed in one of the gardens between here and Lordswood Road, I think Dr Winfield's garden. It wasn't an ordinary incendiary bomb, it caused what looked like a large fire, but the firemen were on to it in a second and had it out immediately. St Mary's Road received a direct hit, and one house at least is completely demolished and one or two now have been evacuated, and Ravenhurst Road came in for a high explosive, just on the corner by Christine's. There is a huge crater in the road, and you know where Uncle Ted lived, well not the next two houses to his, but the next two are very severely damaged, roofs, walls and everything, though they are just about standing. They look very pathetic, such dear little houses, with curtains still up and furniture in, but I doubt if the people would be able to do anything about, as the houses are tottering.

Aunty Kathleen had eight incendiary bombs in their house and garden on Friday night. The roof was on fire, the landing and hall all at the same time. Uncle E, Aunty Kathleen, and nurse all did their stuff and got the things out, but whilst still finishing in the hall a collection of shrapnel came through the roof, and caught them. *(It later turned out that they were victims of one of the first of the exploding incendiaries.)* Aunty was slightly cut in two places, on her thigh, nothing at all really, but Uncle had a lump of shrapnel in his back, one in his shoulder, one in his arm, and one in his ribs. He was operated on yesterday for the removal of the two largest pieces, the other two will be left alone for the time being at any rate. We have a packed suitcase in the dug-out, ready for emergencies for ourselves, as we are continually having calls for clothes, blankets etc, for people who have been bombed out of their houses or who have had to leave because of unexploded bombs. (Just struck me, Modern Warfare - A letter from a Mother to her son in the forces.)

Your letter to me was all about photographs and how hard it was to find a German to tackle. Ha, ha, we live in strange times. You will be pleased I know to hear Pat is as brave as anything, in fact she doesn't seem the least bit frightened. Her chief worry last night (when the sirens sounded, and then the All Clear came without any incident whatsoever), was that a whole lot of fireman who have arrived yesterday at our station from a distant county, would think things had been exaggerated, and that Birmingham wasn't having much of a time after all. I think she wanted a good show for them to write home about.

Dad is at the works all day today and it is his night on duty, so we shan't be seeing him until tomorrow night. We are going round to the Taylors to tea, as both they and we feel we should like a little change, but Pat and I, being on our own intend to come home very very early.

Well laddie, I must go and get ready to go out to tea now, it is a glorious day almost like spring and I am quite looking forward to the little walk across.

With dearest love and all best wishes
from Mother.

(Letter from Dad, finished by Mother. The first part of the letter relates incidents already mentioned.)

Sunday
24.11.40.

Dear Dennis,

..... I have managed to save about 6 galls of petrol during the last two months, so one of the next week ends and if the weather is fine, I want to take Mother and Pat for a nice long run. We might possibly go to Leamington to see Aunty Freda, but it's very indefinite.

Last Sat. I was orderly officer and didn't get home till 2 o'clock on Sunday.

Today Sunday I am orderly officer again, so I am about due for Sunday off next week.

One of our fellows who lives at Selly Oak has just been into the office with some bottles to fill with water, as they have been without since Wednesday.

We had none yesterday morning, so when I went home yesterday I filled 4 x 2 gallon stone jars at the works and took them with me. However it had come on by then, but went off again later in the day and then came on late in the evening.

Anyway I shall leave the jars at home for the time being as I have been loaned them from the works, and always keep them filled.

I haven't any stamps with me, so will post it tomorrow night when I go home and if there is any more news will incorporate it in the above.

Dad has come back with a cold tonight, Monday and feels lazy. He is going to stay indoors tonight all being well. I went to Moseley today to try and clear up. Oh the mess, there have been 2 incendiaries and four high explosives within the radius of 4 or 5 houses at Park Rd, one falling exactly on the place where the Smarts house was demolished, there is an unexploded bomb still in Park Hill, and as for Moseley village, there is scarcely a shop left undamaged. Russell Road is roped off again, as also is Priory Rd, and that little tiny lodge house in the trees by the old church, just at the corner of Priory Rd has had a hit, and is tottering, and evacuated. I wonder laddie dear, was last night's raid anywhere your way? We are wondering also about Aunty Dorothy as they had a very severe raid there on Sat. I believe, and she didn't phone this Sunday as she usually does. Probably nothing more than that the telephone was awkward.

All my love, and God be with you
Mother & Dad.

Monday 25 November 1940

Went to school. Were told that there was an evacuation scheme, and anyone wishing to go was to arrive at school at 9.00 tomorrow. Those not going were to arrive at 10.30 instead of 9.45.

Believe it or not - no raid.

Water started at 7 pm to run.

Tuesday 26 November 1940

Water still off - comes on each night.

Went to school at 10.30, only 21 girls went. There is a notice that all water must be boiled for drinking, cleaning teeth, gargling and washing-up.

Friday 29 November 1940

School. We are going to be inoculated against typhoid.

Sunday 1 December 1940

Did prep in the morning. In the afternoon went in the car to Kidderminster, through Droitwich and back. Very pretty everywhere.

Passed many peculiar green camouflaged factories - all alike - along one road that wound through the country - Most peculiar. Police on guard - guns on roof etc.

Monday 2 December 1940

Went to school. As I turned out of Crosbie road 2 firemen on motor bikes and a brown fire pump went past. I turned out behind it, and there were many more grey pumps behind me. One passed me, and the driver looked out of the window at me, then I cycled behind it, and after a second or 2 the firemen on it became aware of my presence. They shouted to me, but I couldn't hear what they said, then they told me to hang on the back. I didn't, then they told me again, then I asked them where they were going. I couldn't quite hear their answer, but it sounded like "home" or "London". They turned off at the Duke of York, and waved goodbye.

There was a raid warning at 6-something. It didn't last very long.

Tuesday 3 December 1940

Went to school, when I came back I went to the village. On the way I met one of the firemen. He said the firemen were from Yorkshire, Sheffield and Norwich. They were the ones I saw yesterday, they were going home.

Sure enough because they had gone we had a bad raid - not 1/2 as bad as Friday, though. There was a very big fire down town, but it was out fairly soon. The Germans went before midnight because of bad weather conditions.

Wednesday 4 December 1940
    School. After the 1st 3 lessons did handwork. Had a warning. Came back from the shelter, and were just going to the science lecture when we had another warning. That lasted about 3/4 of an hour.

    Had another warning when I got home, all clear went before tea. Had another warning at 10 to 7, it is still on.

Thursday   5 Crosbie Road

My dear Dennis,
    Where have you got to laddie? We hear of a severe raid on Bristol, then a raid on the south west, and I should just like to know 'my lad with wings' is alright. As a matter of fact I am not really anxious, for I know I should hear from the war office if you had been hurt at all, and besides which, Aunty Freda has just 'phoned through to know if we are all in the land of the living and she said what a nice letter she received from you yesterday. Christine rang me this evening and wanted to know if I had heard from you, as she was wondering if you were alright. As a matter of fact we are in the midst of an air-raid now - had to leave off and go to the shelter, it is now Friday afternoon. As things turned out I don't think any bombs were dropped around here last night, but one never knows and there were many planes over, and quite a bit of gun-firing and shrapnel around.

    I am just back from town, I went to get a few crackers for Christmas in the hopes you may be here. I haven't made the Christmas pudding but have all the necessary things in for it, and now, what do you want for a present, is it to be money, or is there anything else you would like.

    Do you know we are still provided with greens out of the garden. I haven't had to buy any since we started cutting the cabbages, and they are beautiful hearted things. I only have about eight left, but still have two large marrows intact.

    Did you have your photograph taken, I haven't ordered any of the others until we see what this is like. You will be pleased to hear uncle Eustace is home again and very little the worse for his experience, but according to aunty Kathleen there has been a lot of damage around their district. Maud has just rung up from Grandma's and says that now the windows are blocked up and plaster etc cleared and Johnson has been at work, the house looks ever so much better, and if nothing further happens to it, I am quite sure it will be able to be put into complete order at the end of the war. I am so glad for Grandma's sake, quite apart from ours.

I must write to Grandma, she is so worried about the planes that pass over the cottage* en route for Birmingham and she wants me to write and tell her just exactly how everyone is, plus their homes. Hoping to have a letter from you in the very near future.

Yours will all my love and dearest thoughts
Mother.

Your book 'Flight' just arrived, you are in Oct. 31st as well

*   *(Uncle George's cottage in Hallow, Worcestershire)*

Thursday 5 December 1940

We were inoculated for typhoid. At the end of the day our arms ached like the dickens. There was a warning just when we were in the cloakrooms getting ready to go home. It was awful in the shelters. Anyway after a long while the all clear went, so home James! and don't spare the horses.

Dec. 12th. *(sic, actually 5th)*   5 Crosbie Road,

My dearest Dennis,

Dad was so pleased to get your letter and I have been up to the bank this morning in response to your request. You had £19.15 put into your account on Dec 2nd. - nice for you, isn't it? By the way - don't forget you owe me £1 - nice for me, isn't it? We have had two short sharp raids the last two nights, mostly incendiaries, and both started in the early evening. Dad was late coming from the works in the first one, and he said incendiaries were falling to the right and left and in front of him. He nearly left the car and went down a public shelter but didn't like the idea of deserting his car so put on his tin hat and hoped for the best. He arrived home without mishap and found your letter and a nice tea awaiting him. I have just been making the Christmas cake, what chance have you of leave? Though I am not at all sure Dad will be here for Christmas Day. However - we must just arrange things to make the best of it.

    I went over to Grandma's on Monday. The windows have all been filled in, and the doors blocked up and Grandma and I cleared up the lounge and made it look really quite presentable.

    - Tuesday morning Mrs Carter rang me to say all windows and doors had been blown out during the night. They seem fated around that district. We have just had our fourth warning today, so I shouldn't be surprised if we have somewhat of a "to-do" tonight. I have even taken the snap albums to the dug out, as I treasure them so much because they depict pre-war days. Now, about your Christmas presents, pyjamas, book-ends, and paper-knife, the first one Gran is providing 1 pr, - the book-ends Dad and I have already got, and Pat is trying to get the paper knife - What else do you want laddie, should anyone ask, and do you want us to send them on to you, because we ought to do it within the next day or so, the postage is so funny and besides, I wouldn't be surprised if the 'jerries' try and bomb the post offices nearer Christmas, or even if they don't especially try for post offices, the post offices may come in for a bad time, and I want the book ends to arrive intact. I must go and make the dug-out beds, I left them for Pat to help me with them when she came home, but she has just arrived and her arm is stiff after being inoculated for typhoid, a precaution because of the water - we boil it all for safety. If you know when you are to come home on leave let me know, so that I can make preparations, food and dug-out. Hoping to see you soon.

    With all my love and dearest thoughts 'my lad with wings'.
    Mother.

Friday 6 December 1940

    School. My arm was a lot better. In the evening Mr Richards came round with a Polish girl to introduce her to us. She is going to stay the week-end.

6/12/40

R.A.F. Station,
Filton,
Glos.

Dear Mother,

I am sending your birthday present a little early for two reasons. Firstly with Christmas mail prevalent it may be delayed a little in the post and secondly as perhaps the electricity may be cut off, it will help to keep you warm at night in the shelter.

By the way I haven't been able to have my photograph taken yet as I don't know of any photographers left in Bristol, except one which is closed for repairs and when it does eventually open will shut every night at 5 o'clock.

However, when the opportunity arises I'll get my photograph taken, in the meantime order that one I asked for and post it down here to me please.

By the way it seems from your letter that you still seem to regard it as probable that I shall be home for Christmas, in actual fact I think that this is rather unlikely, but it is impossible to give any opinion at the moment one way or another.

Did you get my letter to Pat and also the copy of the 'Aeroplane' I sent you?

It seems that the C.O. wants us all to get in 35 hours on Hurricanes before we become operational; up to date I have done 21 hrs, an average of 10 a month since I left Grantham so it seems that unless something unusual happens we shall be nearing the end of January before we go on to operations.

On Monday night we had an incendiary on the Mess which burned out the dining hall, but luckily we put it out before it spread.

We now have our meals in the ante-room and are using the card room as the ante-room.

Well here's wishing you a <u>Very</u> happy birthday and many more of them.

With love
Dennis.

P.S   Don't forget to use the present!

Saturday 7 December 1940

Helena Drimma (a Pole) came to stay for the week-end. She is 19, average height, dark, with her long hair done into a page-boy bob in a fish-net snood. She is engaged to the son of the Polish ambassador, he is a soldier in England, her parents are in Turkey. Her best friend remained in Warsaw, where Helena says, it was not too jolly for girls to be.

We had to go down to the police-station in town to get permission for her to stay with us and also for her to come for a run tomorrow. Mother and I stopped in the car, while we were waiting two peculiar-looking individuals came out of the police-station, raised trumpets to their lips, and heralded a grey-haired man into a large Rolls-Royce. All the traffic was held up until it had driven away.

In the evening Dad felt bad so went to bed.

Sunday 8 December 1940

H. went to church.
Slept in the shelter as usual although there was no raid.

Monday 9 December 1940

That night Den came home on 5 days' leave. He is going East.

Tuesday 10 December 1940

Went down to Moseley with Den. Met Grandma at her house, and also Aunty Kathleen and went to Pattisons at Moseley to have lunch. Then went down town and called in at Bill's office.
Came home and had tea.

Wednesday 11 December 1940

Treated today as though it were Christmas day. Had roast duck, green peas (tinned), kidney beans (salted), roast potatoes, and Christmas pudding (the ingredients having been carefully and tediously collected from various shops). I gave Den 50 Players and 1 tin tobacco, and Dad and Mother a bottle of Sauternes.

Later in the afternoon Chris came round, and we had a Christmas

Cake (the ingredients of which had been got in the same way as above).

The sirens went rather early, and Den took Chris home. Later we went into the shelter. There were many bombs dropped, some very large fires over town, and our Ack-Ack was pretty fierce. The raid lasted 13 hours, from 6.30 till 20 to 8. Den found the nose-cap of a shell buried in the lawn next morning. It was a very fierce raid, but I slept quite well and so can't say <u>very</u> much about it.

Thursday 12 December 1940

Went to school so that I could have my 2nd inoculation. They were much longer doing it, and our form wasn't done until recess. My arm wasn't so stiff, but later I felt the same as before, only my arm didn't hurt as much. When I went to bed at 8.30 I couldn't lie on my right side because I was done in my right arm. So I slept very badly, my head was hot and pulses were throbbing in my head and neck. My ears were aching, there was a sticky saliva on my lips, and I could only lie with my mouth open, moving about to try and get cool. At about 5 Mother and Dad went down the garden to the house (we had had another raid) and then I slept till 8.30, when I got up I had a rotten head;
N.B. On the way to school there was a barrier across the High Street by the police station, and a barrier across another road and a barrier across the road the Bluecoat school is in. We had an incendiary in the music room. It made only a tiny hole, and just charred the floor.

Friday 13 December 1940

My head was pretty foul when I got up, but I had an aspirin and later went to town with Den. They have removed the D.A.* from near the Green Man, but at the main post office we had to turn off and go a long way round, and at last came back onto the Harborne rd. Called in at Bill's office. He told us to reserve seats at the Lancaster. So we did, and soon there was an awful clattering downstairs and Vivian came, then Bill and Colin came. After dinner Den went to see Vivian off. I left Den in town and came back. On the way I noticed that after the barrier in Harborne there are many shops with their windows broken.

I went to Sadlers to cancel the "Flight" and passing Pattisons noticed that the glass was completely broken in one window.
*Delayed Action bomb.

Saturday 14 December 1940

In the afternoon Den, Chris and I went in the car to Bill's to tea. He had Colin there already (they were in Home Guard uniform). We walked down Swanshurst Lane in the rain and the 3 boys went to see Pamela (the house next door, but 1 has been completely demolished) but she was not in. There are many houses damaged, and about 7 either completely demolished, or just twisted remains. We next went around to Matthews. We discovered that, as usual, it was "full house". Barrie's cousin Jimmy had had their house bombed - they were in the shelter and therefore all right, - and he and his family were staying with the Matthews. Also a girl and her young sister were staying there, as she had got a job there and her parents were in London.

After a while all the boys went to help salvage stuff from their bombed house, and after a while Viv came and we went as well. They all (excepting Bill) called on Pamela on the way back, but after a while they all arrived, and we had tea. While we were having it the sirens went, so after a glass of ginger wine we all went home.

Outside our house Den had a bit of a talk with me about Bill, and told me to be careful.

He seemed a bit worried - Bill does seem to be different, since his breakdown.

Sunday 15 December 1940

In the afternoon Dad took Mother, Den and me out in the car. We went past Austins. It is a huge place. At Worcester we turned off, and went to Uncle George's cottage. Grandma was there. It is a lovely place, very small. It is really 2 cottages made into one. It is very cosy. There is an electric water heater, and an electric pump for the water. We had tea there, and then went down to the river. At about 5.30 we went.

On the way through Worcester 2 soldiers asked for a lift. Unfortunately we weren't going their way, but we took them as far as we went.

Monday 16 December 1940 - Mother's birthday

Went to school. Went to a lecture on astronomy. Discovered that we break up tomorrow instead of Wed.

Tuesday 17 December 1940

Went to school to break up. Before I went Den left. It was still dark when he went.
Broke up.

18 December 1940

Dear Mother, and Dad,

I arrived here safely yesterday afternoon, the train was only forty-five minutes late and I was able to have a good lunch of turkey and Christmas pudding before going to find my ship.

I can't tell you much about the main points of interest until the journey is over - for two reasons - one because it would, naturally, be unwise and secondly because I don't yet know half the information anyway.

I met Jessop and Hitching, and the two other sergeants this morning and we shall quite probably go out together this afternoon when I go to post this.

I went to the pictures last night and much to my surprise we did not get any air raid warning at all. I hope that you were as lucky.

At about ten o'clock this morning a barrage balloon suddenly burst overhead and the whole of the front half of it collapsed. It looked quite prehistoric as it sank in the morning mist just inland.

We have had cabins allotted to us, but as soon as we get to sea we sleep on an upper deck, and only use our cabins in day time, in case of torpedoes.

So far as my kit is concerned, as I am keeping it all in the cabin I shall be able to use stuff out of the twenty pounds until we leave the ship.

This means that I can use my dressing-gown, bedroom slippers, and clean shirts etc right until I leave the ship.

I was so glad that my leave was extended so that I was able to stay for your birthday, it made all the difference to my leave didn't it?

I suppose that this letter may reach you before Christmas day, so here's wishing you a very happy Christmas and many of them.

With all love
Dennis.

Thursday 19 December 1940

Went to town with Mother. Bought me a lovely winter coat with a padded lining. Also a coloured scarf to go with it. In the afternoon I just knitted and read.

Auntie Nita and Dick came around. She gave me my Xmas present. It is a bottle of scent.

Uncle George and Auntie K sent me an Xmas card that is also a Savings book. It had 2/6 worth of stamps in!

Uncle Roy and Aunty Freda sent me a 1/- postal order.

Wednesday 25 December 1940 - Christmas Day

I went to church. Came back and had dinner. Had some very nice presents. After listened to the wireless. It was very interesting. We heard the children in America talking to their parents in England. Then we had tea. After listening to the radio for a while we played some games and then sang and made up limericks until about 11.00.

Thursday 26 December 1940

Slept in. Went round to Christine's in the morning. In the afternoon we went to Stratford in the car. Chris came too.

We had tea at a charming café. Very old, and packed full with Czech soldiers. There was also a South African airman and several English airmen. When a Czech private came in and sat at a table next to two officers he clicked his heels and bowed a tiny military bow. There were many types, and they were very interesting to watch. There was one rather sinister looking officer who talked the whole of the time we were there - was talking when we came in, and was talking when we went out.

We came home and played bagatelle, then we played cards.

Dec 26th, 1940

Dear Mother, Dad and Pat,

As it seems probable that we shall be calling in at *(rectangle cut out)* on our way down, I am hoping to get this letter posted there.

Owing to the length of the trip I am afraid that, in all probability I shall arrive at my destination with two sets of dirty clothes, and no clean stuff to change into.

However I am getting some laundry done for me on the ship and I am hoping this will see me through.

I should have been badly off for handkerchiefs, though, had it not been for the gift of the Pyramids I gave myself as a Christmas present. *(He didn't. This was, in fact, a clue for us as to whereabouts he was going. I didn't realize until much later that the Western Med. was 'closed' and that their course was taking them round Africa)*

Talking of Christmas, I do hope that you enjoyed yourselves to the full. At least I heard over the radio this evening that there were no raids over England either on Christmas Eve or Christmas night.

Our Christmas morning was not too bright, in fact due to the cause that the kitchen staff were otherwise engaged my breakfast consisted of cereal; my lunch of a ham sandwich and a glass of water.

The other two meals made up for this, however; we had Christmas cake for tea, complete with marzipan and icing.

Dinner started off with the usual soup and fish followed by turkey, york ham, sausage etc, Christmas pudding, mince pies, fruit, nuts and, of all things, crackers!

I think that, with the course we are taking, it will be a good fortnight at least before we complete our journey; so that by the time I have discovered my new address and have let you know it will probably be well into February.

And quite possibly your reply will come in time to greet me on my birthday.

By the way, I have made no arrangements with Felton & Co. about my pay; if ever you are in that way perhaps you could see Mr. Leslie or phone him.

If possible I should like them to pay it into my account at the Municipal Bank; they could pay in through the Head Office. Anyway I leave it to you.

Rather an amusing thing happened on the 20th.; Jessop, Hitching and I were talking on the deck one morning. I happened to say "Any more of that, Jessop, and I'll throw you overboard", in what was intended to be a menacing tone of voice. A boy (in the Navy) who was passing at the time, suddenly stopped in his tracks and looked rather surprised. It turned out that his name was Jessop and apparently he wondered whether I was referring to him.

I must say that life at sea gets pretty boring, so boring in fact that I usually go to bed at about eight thirty or thereabouts. And as I do not usually get out of bed again until seven thirty, I can scarcely complain of lack of sleep.

With the advent of the finer and warmer weather of southern latitudes (comparatively southern at least) we are now having gym in the open for an hour each day.

This not only serves to break the monotony but also makes up for the lack of exercise which until now we have suffered.

Perhaps you remember the story I told you of the Major who bought me a Benedictine on the train up from Bristol? I am nearly positive that he is travelling on this boat, although I am not certain.

The likeness is so great however that I think there is little doubt as to his identity.

Two days before yesterday (it is now the 27th) a sub-lieutenant came up to me and asked me, "Were you training at Birmingham before the war?" When I said "Yes", he replied "I thought so. I was one of the mechanics at Elmdon!" It makes the world seem quite a small place doesn't it?

I am rather sorry now that I did not bring my camera with me, however I hope to get all the photographs I want from fellows who have brought their cameras. It also means that they take the risk of inadvertently taking pictures of the censorable type.

Which reminds me perhaps you could do something with the films in my camera; if you have not yet done anything. It seems a pity to waste them even though they are a year old. perhaps you could ask Mr. French, (*the chemist*), if they are still of any use. If so there are 3 unexposed films in the camera and 2 unexposed rolls of film in the case. (*We did as he suggested, and the unexposed films came in useful, as we were unable to buy film at all during the whole of the war.*)

I might warn you that the camera is rather awkward to open. Perhaps again the advice of Mr. French would be helpful.

I'll write to you again in about ten days time and I will try to cable you an address in about a fortnight. Meanwhile perhaps if you were to write a letter addressing it to "Mr" (and not P/O) c/o Post Office of the town where Auntie Marjorie used to stay it might reach me!
With all love
Dennis

Saturday 28 December 1940

Went to town with Chris. On the way back we heard planes, and looking up we managed to see 5 planes very far apart going along very slowly. It was hard to see them because they rather resembled the balloons.
When I got home I saw 2 more.

Sunday 29 December 1940

Bill came round at about 11 and took Chris and me in the car to his house. After dinner Colin arrived, and then Vivian, Bob and Brian turned up shortly after. We played Truth and Dare. They kept on pestering me to know if I was in love with a small, dark haired fellow from KE*. Brian asked me if I had to save my life by kissing someone in the room, would that person be Bill. Bill asked me if I had ever been kissed by Raymond.
They asked Christine if she considered herself in love. She said "Yes."
Chris had to play the piano to get her forfeit back. I had to kiss the boy who I thought would make the best husband. They turned out the light. I said I considered Vivian the best, and he did not want to be kissed and I did not want to kiss him, so in the end I was let off.
* ie Bill

Tuesday 31 December 1940

Chris, Mother and I went to town. I got a brown coat, and a tweedy skirt, and a scarf. I had to leave the coat to be altered. Chris went so as to be in time for work, then I left Mother, and went to Bill's office. We were going downstairs on the way to the Lancaster, and were saying how nice it was Colin not being there, when Colin appeared! We went down to dinner, and Colin sat (at our request) at a different table. Bill showed me the seating arrangements for the panto.

<u>Males</u>
Bill, Raymond, Colin, Vivian

<u>Females</u>
Chris, Bobby, Jill and me

<u>seating thus!</u>-
Chris   Ray   Me   Bill   Bob   V   J   Colin.

 Vivian came in, and I had a quiet argument with him about Raymond. Bill and I went to Bill's office, and Bill locked the door, which I wasn't particularly pleased about, 'cos Bill is a bit strange at times, these days. We talked for a long time about Raymond, the Q.A., Bill's joining the Fleet Air Arm, and other things during which time several people tried the door. At last Bill (thinking that C and V were trying it), opened it and in walked Mr Jefferies!
 Phew! We went downstairs and met V and C, We went to book the seats, but could not get through.
 Bill said he would dive into a tank of water for £5*. I said O.K., but he said (hastily) that he did not want to deprive me of it.
 Went round to Taylor's for the evening. Talked in Chris' room in the firelight. Mrs Taylor brought up tea and cakes.
 Dad met me 1/2 way home.

*He was referring to the 'static water tanks' which were placed at strategic intervals around for the firemen to use in the event of the mains being bombed.

1941

Aged 14 ½

List of Illustrations

Page

289 The Good Neighbours' League letter

290 The Good Neighbour's League letter, 2nd page

294 Dennis sailing in Ismailia

297 Bob, Vivian, Chris and Bill

305 Christine

307 Pat, with her hair up

Wednesday 1 January 1941 - New Year's Day

Went to town and called at the office to see Bill and we went to the Lancaster and had a cup of coffee.

After saying goodbye to Bill I went to Lewis' and got my coat. They have altered it very well, and it looks very nice.

Chris came round in the evening. There was a warning, but we took no notice. After I had gone to bed I heard a plane, after the all clear and another warning had gone (I had slept through most of it). Went up to the shelter. My bed was very cold. The all clear went, then another warning, then a loud explosion. I slept through the rest of it until about 7.00 am when I heard the all clear.

Wednesday 8 January 1941

Got the lunch. After dinner dug up the lawn to plant potatoes. I only managed to do a little in about 2 hours.

Friday 10 January 1941

Went shopping. Called at Wrensons's and Dobneys, then at Macfisheries, but they had no rabbits and were expecting none. After dinner cycled to Marsh & Baxters for some sausages. Had to wait about 15 mins in a queue.

Sunday 12 January 1941

Had a bath, Just after the bath Bill rang me. Talked for 3/4 of an hour. Chris rang. Had dinner. Pork! They are selling it in meat shops now. After dinner I dug up the lawn some more. Bill rang up again. Had tea, knitted, read and wrote my diary.

Saturday 18 January 1941

In the afternoon went to the panto. There was quite thick snow on the ground and it snowed all day.

Ray called for me and then Chris. Met Bill; Vivian turned up late. The show was very good. Went to Ray's to tea. At about 9.00 Bill had to go home because of the trains and the snow. Betty (a girl who had come round), Raymond, Chris and I saw him to the bus-stop.

He nearly kissed me but couldn't quite pluck up his courage - thank heaven!

Raymond took Chris and me home.

Sunday 19 January 1941

The snow was over a foot deep. I went to get 3 pints of milk, and then to Raymond's with the eggs. He was clearing the snow away. He said I looked very sweet. Inside he said I had some snow on the back of my coat, and said he would brush it off for me, he then put his arms round me! I had 1/2 apple with him. He threw my 3 bottles of milk into the snow and had an awful job finding them again.

When we decided to go he could not find his wellingtons, and two kids had moved them round the corner and I had to go and fetch them.

We went to the dairy and got 2 more bottles of milk. On the way back he asked me if I loved Bill! Of course I said no so he said did I feel any affection for him - I said no. So then he said "Will you ask me to the wedding" so I said "You usually ask the bridegroom to the wedding!" He said that one should seal an engagement with a kiss, but - that sort of thing's not done!

Monday 20 January 1941

The snow was about 2 feet deep, and it was snowing when I went to school. I walked, and the road was like a cart track. Near the university there were deep drifts. When I got to school it was late, but it had not yet started. Finished school at 12.30 and were told not to go until Thurs as the coal used to heat the school was snowed under.

In the afternoon Mother and I had a talk about Bill. I was wondering how to let his attentions drop. It was very awkward to think of a way, because of his state of mind. But I have no feeling for Bill except pity and sympathy and friendship. He has altered so that even that friendship isn't quite so strong. But people must be thinking about Bill and me because of Raymond's remark yesterday. So I am going to try to extract myself from a rather troublesome net.

Tuesday 21 January 1941

Did a bit of work. After tea went round to Raymond's, he wasn't in, but at last he came in, and remarked again about my hair and how he liked it done that way. Had a cup of cocoa, and a cake. Ray and I had meant to go to Christine's, but it was 8.30 before we had started out, so we rang Chris and told her we would not be able to manage it. Ray saw me home. I told him about Bill and me, and at first he acted the fool, but just before Wentworth road he became serious, and he gave me some advice!

He came in and had a cup of tea. - also announced our engagement!

Wednesday 22 January 1941

Chris came round at about 4. I went round there to tea. Ray rang up, and about 7 he came round. Went to Christine's room and talked. Ray saw me home. Chris came too. At the door (before I had knocked) Ray said to Chris "Do you think I had better kiss the child goodnight?" Chris remarked that it wasn't much to do with her, and at that Ray entered the porch where I was standing. I turned my face aside, but he took it between his hands, and - well it was the first <u>real</u> kiss I have ever had!

Thursday 23 January 1941

Mary came round and said that there would be no school till Monday because of the coal. Went to the village. The butchers have had no meat since Monday. Helped get Dennis' room ready for Aunty Dorothy.

Friday 24 January 1941

Chris and her parents came round for the evening.

Ray rang up and said Dennis (Ray's brother) was on leave, and would Chris and I go round there as he could not come round as he (Ray) had a chill on his liver.

It was a foul night, but quite fun when we got there. Ray had a terrible old pair of slippers on which we tried (?) to burn.

Den said that I had altered since last he saw me.

27th January 1941.   MOSELEY

Dear Pat,
    I phoned Raymond this evening and asked him if he would come to tea here with you and Chris next Saturday.
    Of course now that Ray is coming you will have no qualms about having to face a boring afternoon listening to me generally making a sentimental ass of myself: and just think of the bus ride back to Harborne with such a gay and handsome male escort. You lucky girl!!
    Will 'phone Thurs. or Frid: Be Good, especially with Ray around.
Love,
Billy.

On one occasion Bill dedicated a poem to me.
It seems as appropriate as anywhere to locate it here.

Oh Helen Patricia Knight
For thy love would I fight
With claw tooth and nail,
And not once should I fail,
For were I to lose thee
Naught else could amuse me
Save to die.

On a Pedestal High
Have I put thee so shy,
Here enthroned you must stay
Thru' the long night and the day
For were you to fall,
T'would rob me of all
Save to die.

Friday 31 January 1941

School. At tea time Dad said he had had his bonus, and a - rise! He gave mother £3 and me 2/6 as our bonuses - (or should I say bonos?)

Monday 3 February 1941

School. As it was snowing I walked. Did quite a lot of swotting in the afternoon and evening.

Planes came over in the evening. They keep on coming over now; they are ours, of course, but I wonder why they come.

Tuesday 4 February 1941

It was very slippery so went on the bus. Chris came round to see about sending a cable to Dennis. He is at Imailia which is on the peninsula of Sinai. I wish I could go too! I often wish I was 2 years older so that I could leave school and be a nurse. The only catch in that is that if I was a nurse I should live away from home, and in case of an invasion I should not like that! Talking about invasion reminds me that we had to try our gas-masks on - they are expecting the Germans to use gas -

There was a warning, but nothing happened as far as we are concerned. Heard planes, but that's all.

Wednesday 5 February 1941

Went to school on the bus again. Came home and read Gone with the Wind (I'm nearly 1/2 way through) while I ate my dinner. I had pigeon, or duck or something. I don't have meat now because it is very hard to get.

In school today Esmé said where did we get the tinned cherries that I was eating from. I told her they were out of mother's store.

Yesterday she had an egg for the first time in weeks, and that was in a pork pie! Mother gets 4 dozen a week but only keeps one dozen herself, Mrs T, Mrs R and Mrs Bonehill (our "woman") have the others.

Thursday 6 February 1941

Stayed in bed. Mother thought I had measles so rang up Dr Winfield and asked him to come round tomorrow.

Friday 7 February 1941

Still in bed. Dr Winfield came. Told me to take M&B 693 and gave me some cough mixture.

Sunday 9 February 1941

Still in bed. Dr Winfield came. He said I might get up a bit this evening.
Oh! Why am I in bed now? Raymond may be called up any day. I want to see him before he goes. Oh, it is so boring to be in bed, looking forward on all these hours I may have to stay in bed. Still, I am getting better - it isn't as though I have got to stay in quarantine for ages, or anything like that.

Monday 10 February 1941

Still in bed. I'm bored, bored - bored. Chris came for a short while. She's coming again tomorrow.
I feel all right - why can't I get up? I'm desperate. I think of all the bad words I know, and if I wasn't a lady I'd use then - trouble is - am I a lady? - I think I'd better pretend I am. It's a lovely day, but I'm still bored, depressed, glum, moody, melancholy, low, blue, and generally deflated - although I feel inclined to burst - *!?-3/4!*.

Tuesday 11 February 1941

Dr Winfield came. He seems to be fairly pleased. I am to stay in bed, he'll come on Thursday. Maybe I can get up then.
Early in the morning there was an air raid warning.

Wednesday 12 February 1941

Still in bed. I feel a lot better today. I hope I shall be up tomorrow. Did a little work in the morning. Had a few half-hearted attempts at Patience. <u>Patience</u>! Don't make me laugh. There's no such thing; and if there is I have yet to find it. I hope Chris comes this afternoon, and yet if she does I shan't want her to see me as I've put some cold cream on my face, and it is shiny.

At about 9.00 Ray rang up to see how I was. I hope to see him on Sat, or if poss Fri - I wonder if I shall!

Friday 14 February 1941

Had a Valentine - found out later (by a roundabout method) that Jo and Esmé sent it - they thought I would think it was from Raymond - a suspicion which I entertained - however it was not his writing.

Saturday 15 February 1941

Got up fairly early. It was a lovely day. Mother went to hospital. Dr Winfield came. He said I could go out. I went to the village to get the meat. I could only have the lamb as the beef had not yet arrived.

After dinner messed about in the garden waiting for Chris.

Ray rang up. He said he's had 3 Valentines, and if he'd remembered what day it was he'd have sent us one.

Sunday 16 February 1941

Had breakfast in bed. Got up and had a bath. After dinner I messed about until 3.30 when I went to Christine's to tea. Ray rang up at about 6.30. He said he had a cold, and couldn't come. We tried to persuade him, and then he said he'd come sometime tonight - perhaps.

In the end we went round to dig him out. We took the eggs. When we got there we found the root of the trouble - his mother. She was furious with Ray and said if he came back with a bad cold she would not ring up his boss to say why he was not there. We didn't know what to do, what attitude to take, whether to laugh or be serious - it was awful!

Ray came anyway. We had a fairly nice evening, but there was the shadow of Mrs R on it!

Then Mother rang to say Dad was coming for me in the car. I offered to take Ray back. Afterwards Dad was furious! Wow! What a night!

Saturday 1 March 1941

Ray drove Chris and me to Bill's to tea. After tea went for a walk and when we got back Bill's father adopted a defeatist attitude, and then the warning went. Driving back it was very dark, no headlights on, of course.

Thursday 6 March 1941

      School. Before lessons started Miss Maikin said "What's the matter with you?" to the class in general.
      We complained that we were depressed and that school was dull.
      She said she'd talk about it later. We spent the whole of the Latin lesson (double period) talking about it.

Sunday 16 March 1941

      Lovely day.
      Messed about, went to Taylors at about 4.00 with the eggs. Stayed to tea. Had a boiled egg as there were no cakes.
      There was a raid warning about 10.30, one plane, or one lot of planes came over, and about 20 mins later the all clear went.

Sunday 23 March 1941

      Went for a run in the car to Stratford. Chris, Mother, Dad, Aunty Dorothy and myself. Past Henley we braked to avoid running over a dog. And got a puncture and broke the shock absorber.
      Had tea in Henley as we did not go on to Stratford.
      When we got back we saw Uncle Tom's car outside our house. Uncle Tom, Aunty Edith, Kathleen and Gran came out of the house when we arrived.
      Uncle Tom drew Dad aside, and then suddenly Gran started to cry. What was the matter? Then Dad came up and showed us the telegram saying that Dennis was missing and believed to have lost his life.
      I don't believe it! It is inconceivable.
      We took Chris home. She was absolutely knocked out. She went and looked at Den's photo and cried and cried and looked so sweet and so sad.

      On the previous day, Saturday 22nd March, Dennis had been on interception patrol between Malta and Sicily, and had been shot down.
He was posted as missing, believed killed.
And later, the following report appeared in the paper:-

Press Association.

> A communiqué issued by the R.A.F. Middle East Command, said that in Saturday's raid on Malta one of our fighters was shot down by a Messerschnmitt 110, which in turn was destroyed by another of our aircraft. German and Italian reports claim that seven of our Hurricanes were shot down, and that the raiders scored direct hits on shops and anti-aircraft positions.

(Letter to Mother from Grandma)

March 24, 1941   Sundown
                                            Bickerton Rd
                                            Headington
                                            Oxford

My Darling
    Words of course cannot express my feelings when I heard your clear, sweet, <u>calm</u> voice on the phone last night telling me that Dennis your only son (and what a son) had given his life for his country and for us. I marvelled at the way you are already fulfilling Dennis' great wish that you would "carry on". What a wonderful thought and comfort it must be to you and Fred to know that in every way you have allowed Dennis to plan his life, even to his glorious end, or rather beginning of his new life, his influence will always be with us - young, brilliant, guiding.
    Dennis several times told me how wonderful it was to have a Father and Mother who understand him so well and considered his wishes in every way.

Give my fond love to Pat, she is like Dennis so will do her best. Also much love to Mrs Knight and Christine. Fondest love to you and Fred my darling, you have a glorious cross but very heavy to carry. God bless and help you both.

From Mother.

Tuesday 25 March 1941

School. In the evening I called for Chris and we went round to Raymond's for the evening. A dog followed us into his house and lay down by the fire - it was a black and tan long-haired bitch.

Raymond was alone - he was on the phone to Bill when we arrived.

We had some coffee etc. and went home to my house. Raymond cheered mother up a bit, but Chris looked very white.

Mother kissed Raymond goodbye, he did the same to me, but as mother was there it was short and sweet.

On the way home Raymond made Chris depressed by saying he didn't really believe there was as much chance as he had made out.

I believe there is.

(Letter to Mother from Aunt Marjorie)

25.3.41
                                                  Sundown
                                                  Bickerton Road
                                                  Headington
                                                  Oxford

Darling Gladys

I am dumbstruck and full of tears before your grief and your great sacrifice. I just stand by and ache and ache and can do nothing.

Dennis has gone on the Awfully Big Adventure. He was so marvellously equipped for life - but he was so gloriously equipped for death, more, much more than most of us twice his age.

In our blindness and human love we cannot get free of the tragedy of it all and the seeming waste, but who can speak of death in a destructive sense where Dennis is concerned. He is beyond the border, beyond all hurt, with so much to do before him and <u>endless splendid</u> influence behind and endless affection.

This is your and Fred's son. We do all <u>thank</u> you for him. He made the Great Sacrifice very nobly, very willingly. He knew and chose his calling in the day of need. And if you are proud of him, so is he of you who understood him <u>so unselfishly</u>.

Good shall come out of it. The world is shaken to its foundations this time.

All the time, behind a panorama of pictures of you all, actual or imagined, is the memory of a cartoon I saw at the beginning of the war. It reached across two pages. On the left across gas and flame and destruction reached the huge monster of total war; on the right was a mono-plane with the rings on its wings. The pilot's head showed against a halo. It was called "Saint George and the Dragon."

Saint Dennis was a Patron Saint as well. With such a name: Dennis KNIGHT - do you wonder that I see him continually as that pilot in all the paraphernalia of flying kit.

Hundreds and thousands of people in time of sorrow ask beatingly, incessantly - why us! Why Dennis! Why me! - that precious youth should be used so cruelly is wrong - so much in the world is wrong. But you and Fred and Dennis and Pat, despite all physical trials are a riveted tower of strength and stand together in spirit against all adversity.

It is so hard for Fred after fighting through the last ghastly war; but I am not afraid for either of you, you are both such splendid people, and have clear vision. I have always admired you as well as loved you most terribly much. I have always feared something big for you to bear: you are such 'big' people.

There is a 1/2 hour 'war' service in All Saints on Monday evenings. David Porter knew of your sorrow and he had seen Dennis' plane making double circles round 'Sundown' last summer. He might have known him intimately, the gentle sincere way he prayed last night. Nobody but we and he knew for whom these prayers were. He remembered you all and gave thanks for you all and he felt it all very deeply.

I kept thinking of <u>you</u> Gladys, the Mother of Dennis, over and over.

Will you please give my love to Mrs Knight. I am glad she is with you. She will feel it greatly.

In love, and sorrow, and admiration and thankfulness for you all
Marjorie

Margaret sends her dearest love. She has told me it makes her feel despicable, doing nothing.

I have never met Christine but oh dear, I do feel affectionate towards her.

Mother sends her dearest love and says she would love to come to you any time even if it means returning to Worcester on the bus.

25.3.41
TheOld Vicarage
Maxstoke
Warwickshire

Dear Mrs Knight

The sad news conveyed to me by Mr Knight (Beal & Co) has worried me terribly. No one seems to be free from trouble and I can well imagine your shock. How we are able to stand up to the worries is at times past comprehension! I suppose we must be brave. I had such high hopes of your son's success, to me it is almost like losing a son - I was so extremely fond of him. Is there no hope of his being alive? I should so like to hear from you if you could tell me any further news. But perhaps writing is too much of a strain at the moment - if so I shall understand. What a trial it must be to you all. I cannot but express to you and your family my very deepest sympathy in your heavy loss.

At a later date to suit you - I should so like to have a chat.

Yours very sincerely

I Leslie

Wednesday 26 March 1941

School. In the evening went round to Christine's. She looked pretty white and 'down-in-the-mouth'. I took her for a walk. The searchlights were playing round the sky. We talked about many things on the way back and when we arrived at her house and went up into her room. Also on the way home. We talked about sixth sense, and all the psychological sort of things.

It was a lovely night, and we stood for a long time at the bottom of Highbrow looking at the stars. We saw a shooting star and wished.

Before going away on active service, Dennis had said to Mother, "If anything happens to me, I should be most annoyed if you grieved for me".

She tried to keep her word to him, and faced the world bravely and seemingly cheerful, but in her private despair she flung her grief onto paper in an anguished cry:-

Vainly I strive, in mad dissatisfaction
To tear away the ropes, that bind us to this little life
To find the purpose of it all
The reason for the wars, the sweat and strife

Shall I not know, until the greedy claw of death
Tears off my body from my striving spirit
Then, must I still wait and batter at the Gate of Truth.
Dull fruitless hours go sliding by
And still I stand and wonder why
I came onto this earth.
Was it just to live my life and then to die?
And pass into eternal nothingness.
Did God, if God there be,
Create this thing called man
To seek the eternal Life and Truth
Or just to live his span
Of three score years and ten
Then to dissolve and know no more.

Oh, God, in passing through my years of life
Let it be shown to me
That all is not in vain
There is an everlasting Love
That follows on this Life of Pain.

And, on a small piece of paper, in Dad's writing, are the following words:-

Into the mosaic of victory, I lay this
Priceless piece, my dearest one.

Thursday 27 March 1941

School. Jo wished on one of my eyelashes, and I knew what she was wishing. Miss Orton and Miss Waterfield both said how sorry they were. Barbara Jones said her parents sent their love etc. Esmé said her mother did. On the way home Joyce Griffiths cycled up to me and said her parents sent their love etc.

Friday 28 March 1941

Mother is worried about Dad, he is taking things pretty badly.

Our neighbours in Crosbie Road united in writing and signing a letter of sympathy, which I reproduce overleaf.

Crosbie Road,
Harborne,
Birmingham 17.
1st April 1941.

Dear Mr & Mrs Knight,

    As neighbours of yours, we feel that we must convey to you an expression of our deep sympathy in the anxious time through which you are passing.

    Believe us, when we say that you are very much in our thoughts and prayers during this agonizing time.

    We have all been grievously shocked to hear such terrible news about Dennis; we trust and hope you will find comfort in the knowledge that he was doing his very brave and just duty in the struggle against the dreadful evil which confronts the world today, and we send you our heartfelt sympathy in this time of bitter trial.

    Yours very sincerely,
    The Good Neighbours' League.

H Ensell
E Ensell
M. & Mrs Jagger
K. Jagger.
M R Commander
Ethel M. Vizor
Harry Vizor

A Rotothaur
H. Robotham.
Mr & Mrs Daniel & daughters
Nellie G. Heath & family
Wm Shotton and Anne Shotton
Mr & Mrs Smith & Family

Rose Mitchell
Fred W Mitchell
E. A. Clamp
Kemp
Archie H. Grimley
Violet K. Grimley
Lilian Gibbs
Frank Gibbs
Amy Jeffrey
Joan H. I. Jeffrey
J. Jeffrey
H Watts
E Watts
The Misses Findon
Mr & Mrs P. A. Loudham

H. J. Vernon
Mary Smackman
Marie P. Vernon

Rev. J. N. Connell
M. Elsie Wood
J Staley Wood
Dorothy A. Taylor & Father
Mary J. Standfast & Nieces
E & E Culwick
Mr & Mrs Dutton and daughters
Miss I. Thompson and family
Mr & Mrs John H Houghton
Mr & Mrs W. G. Ziry
U. Ueters
Cate: Rhoda Eastwood
Mr & Mrs G. A. Marsh
Mr & Mrs A. J. Brookes

Although in March we had received the terrible news that Dennis was missing, believed killed, I wrote in my diary at the time 'I don't believe it. It's inconceivable'. And it was. To me, Dennis was invincible, immortal, and I was completely unable to accept the fact that he had gone, for a long time to come

Tuesday 1 April 1941

School. In the evening went round to Christine's. She showed me some of Dennis' letters to her. There was one about telepathy and thought transmission. He said how he'd tried it with Bill and Vivian and how he'd made a promise that if ever he was crashing to his death he'd try and communicate by thought with Bill. He said that still stood. I thought it was very cheering. *(Because Bill had received no intimation that anything was wrong.)*

Also - by queer coincidence - Chris was looking into a drawer and took out a letter from Dennis that was not with the pile, and on looking at the date it was 1st April 1940!! Incidentally it was the first time he addressed her as "My Darling Chris."

Wednesday 2 April 1941

School. When I got back Mother said that Chris had passed her massage exams.

Chris rang up and asked me to celebrate with her. We went to the Forum to see one of the Dr Kildare films. Got back at 7.30 approx. and had some sandwiches, raspberries and cream and coffee.

Stayed and talked about the holidays and where to spend them - Stratford etc. and then at about 10.15 I went home - as usual Chris came 1/2 way.

When I rang the front door bell I shouted "Mind the light", dashed into the hall and shut the front door - and there, behind the front door stood Raymond - grinning all over his face. He said "Mind the light!" and went into the lounge.

I took my coat off and Ray stayed for a while longer (he had been to see Mother) and then he went. He kissed Mother goodbye in the kitchen and me in the porch - which was the better? Guess!

Thursday 3 April 1941

Mother received a depressing cable from Malta and an airmail letter from Den. *(Presumably this was the cable of 27th March from Squadron Leader Lambert and Den's letter dated 20/2/41. I therefore include them here.)* So did Chris, Kathleen and Aunty Nita.

27th March

Officers' Mess
R.A.F
Ta Kali
Malta

Dear Mrs Knight,
    By now you will no doubt have heard from the Air Ministry of the loss of your son on the 22nd March. He was carrying out an interception patrol over the sea between Malta and Sicily and failed to return after an engagement with enemy fighters. I do not wish to raise false hopes but there is the very slight chance that he has been picked up by the enemy and although we have listened to the enemy wireless broadcasts in the hope of hearing any news, we have so far been disappointed. As you probably realise we are rather cut off from outside communications and I would recommend you to get in touch with the Air Ministry and Red Cross Society who may be able to obtain news.

In the meantime your son's effects are being dealt with and they will be returned to you as soon as possible. Your son was with us for only a very short time but his keenness and courage set a very high example to the rest of the Squadron at a time when we were hard pressed. Please accept the deepest sympathy in your great loss, both on my behalf and on behalf of the Officers and Men of the Squadron. If there is anything further I can do to help, please do not hesitate to communicate with me.
    Yours sincerely
    P L Lambert
    S/Ldr

20/2/41   See last address

        <u>Cabled</u>.

Dear Mother, Dad and Pat,

    I got your telegram today, thanks very much; however so far I have not received any letters. I am not surprised at this however as even Air Mail takes about a month, and quite frequently letters are held up at Middle East Command for some weeks before they reach us. Consequently it is better to address letters to the addresses I cable to you.

    I don't know whether this letter will arrive too early or too late but anyway Here's wishing Dad a very happy birthday and many of them.

    I had a couple of days leave in Cairo recently and naturally visited the pyramids. I took some photographs but unfortunately it was beginning to get dark and the results were not too successful. There was a shop nearby that sold souvenirs and what were reputed to be relics from the tombs and the proprietor claimed to have known Uncle Tommy.

    The chief thing that struck me about Cairo was that everything was ridiculously expensive.

    We also went to Port Said a few days ago but weren't particularly struck with the place. It seemed that the chief feature of Port Said was the variety and intensity of the smells.

    We have done quite a bit of sailing recently and although I do not yet consider myself to be a master yachtsman I think that I have learned a good deal. Kelly, by the way, has won several first prizes at the Southend Sailing Club and Jessop had his own boat. The sailing here costs us a shilling each per afternoon and I think the fun is well worth the money.

    We have also done some cycling, but as we frequently leave the road to cycle down sand-hills it doesn't do the bikes any good.

    Last time we went out we had gone about six miles when Kelly got a puncture. Luckily he had no difficulty in getting a lift back with his bike on a R.A.F. lorry and so arrived at the mess long before us and also a good deal less tired.

    I cycled into town this morning and got myself a suitcase as I think they become an officer somewhat more than do cardboard packing cases. I also bought myself a pipe and a couple of combs which I naturally left at the telegraph office. I shall have to call in for them this evening when we go to the pictures.

We are hoping to go sailing again this afternoon but I expect we shall come back to the camp for tea as otherwise the day will be too expensive.

Yesterday afternoon we sailed across to Arabia and landed there, there was nothing at all to see but we wanted to be able to say that we had set foot in Arabia. Afterwards I had quite a good lesson from Kelly in sailing up to mooring posts and jibing; and I am now fairly convinced that I could manage a small boat by myself.

With all love
Dennis.

(The photo of Dennis sailing was sent home later with the very few possessions that were allowed to be shipped because of the dangers to our Merchant Fleet.)

It was only decades later that I realised that Dennis, having sailed all the way round Africa to Suez in order to avoid the dangerous Straits of Gibraltar, probably flew his Hurricane from Egypt to Malta, replacing pilot and aircraft at the same time.

Friday 4 April 1941

School. Had our gym competition. Went back to the form room and found we had to go to dinner in our gas-masks!

King Edward's School,
Birmingham 15

4th April, 1941

Dear Mrs Knight

Your information concerning Dennis has brought the greatest distress to me and to those of my Colleagues who knew him: his constant cheerfulness and courtesy as a boy in the School has caused him to remain in the minds of his former Masters here to an unusual degree, and in his passing we feel a deep personal loss. Perhaps I feel it more than some since Dennis and I had such frequent contact and grew to really understand each other. I know you are right about his readiness to sacrifice himself for England, - this feeling was so strong in him that I have always feared he would make that sacrifice: and now it seems he has made it.

May his example stimulate those of us who are left; and may it be a great comfort to you and his Father in your tribulation.

Yours very sincerely
A S Langley

"So much done for so many by so few."

Wednesday 9 April 1941

In the afternoon Chris and I had tea together, went for a walk and came to my house. Dad answered the door and said "Raymond's here!" He was helping Aunty D. do a puzzle. The warning went and Chris and Raymond went.

The raid was fairly bad, so we lay downstairs. Round 1.00 it got very bad so we decided to go to the shelter. I said I would go upstairs and get my jumper and socks. I'd got 2/3 of the way up when there was a loud whistling-shrieking-whizzing noise. I turned round and tried to run downstairs, but my feet caught each other, and the result was that I half-rolled, half-staggered downstairs. (By the way the noise was a bomb.)

Anyway I went up to the shelter without either, and once we were in the dugout it got real hot.

Several times whizzers came so close that I closed my eyes, hugged myself and thought "Here it comes! This is the end!"

This sort of thing cannot be described but I *can* say it was simply terrible. Fire pumps kept leaving the fire station near us, and searchlights searched the sky, and ack ack shook the shelter (when we did fire) and planes came so low they sounded a danger minus the bombs. Once I thought a plane was going to crash on the shelter, but it crashed in Bearwood.

Anyway, somehow, I did get some sleep.

Thursday 10 April 1941

In the afternoon Chris and I went to town, as we had booked to go to the ballet that evening. The bus only went as far as the Prince of Wales. We got out and waited outside the Prince to see if there was a ballet. But no - the front was all that remained, a H.E. had gone smack through the middle and destroyed all else.

Wandered round town. Destruction everywhere. The newly painted Theatre Royal had had a bomb opposite, and was thick with dust. Dust everywhere. Firemen everywhere, hose pipes, ambulances, rescue squads, police, ruins, smouldering ruins, water, dust, glass, an enormous quantity of glass, smells of escaping gas, and one fire still roaring away where a gas main had been hit.

What a hell for anyone in it last night. What hell for those toiling, sweating to clear up the ruins, mangled bodies, water, charred debris, glass, dust - oh God!

Saturday 12 April 1941

Went to town with Chris in the morning - got some sandals - very nice. The damage is simply terrible, although it is being cleared up.

In the afternoon Vivian came and then Bob. We went into the garden, and after a while Bill came. After a long time Chris came. I took a photo and then Bill took one.

We stayed in the garden until tea time. After tea we saw Bob on the bus. A blonde getting off looked as though she wished she hadn't (or had!!) when she saw him get on.

Next day Mother received a letter from F/Lt Dick, Den's instructor at Desford.

April 12th   No. 7 E.F.T.S RAF
                                                      Desford
                                                      Leicestershire.

Dear Mrs Knight,
    I must apologise for failing to answer your letter ere this, but I have been away in Cornwall on sick-leave and only received it on my return. Your news has come as a great shock to me for, where <u>you</u> have lost a son, I have lost the <u>**FINEST PUPIL**</u> I have ever trained. Dennis and I were not only Instructor and Pupil but we were also very firm friends. One of my last remarks to him was "Now, son, a D.F.C. first then get the D.S.O. after that"! And he said "I'll try and get them for <u>you</u> sir". I believe, and <u>still do</u> with all my heart, that had our lad survived he <u>WOULD</u> have brought much honour upon us all. He had that terrific keenness to get to grips with the plane and whatever knowledge I had to impart, he was all attention. I considered him one of the most naturally born pilots I have ever known. Added to his skill was a charm and cheerfulness which made for happiness amongst his associates. My four boys on that course were all good lads and my wife remarked that she considered them the nicest lads I had ever brought to my house. Our last party together was when Langrish, Jones and Dennis got their wings. We met in the Grand (they had come up to see me from their A.T.S) and we <u>had</u> a party.
    When the time came to return to duty, Dennis and I put Jones, Langrish in the back of the car to sleep it off! But Dennis was upright on his feet, and had taken his glass as you would have wished it. And I said Goodbye to these lads and their departure left an empty feeling. All grand boys but he was, somehow, to me, just so much more ahead and above the others. I am enclosing his last letter to me. Please keep it for I would like you to have it. Terrible as this loss is to you and Mr Knight and, if I may humbly say so, myself, I would have you remember "NEVER WAS SO MUCH OWED BY SO MANY TO SO FEW". Dennis was and <u>IS</u> one of these few and I know <u>he</u> would not have had it otherwise. A boy in years, but I say in all sincerity "THERE GOES A MAN!" You must be very

proud of him and I only pray that before this horrible business is over, I may meet up with the man who caused his death.

It is very kind indeed of you to wish to meet me and I shall certainly look forward to that meeting. I am flying every day from 9.15 till 8 pm (sometimes 6 pm), and the question of a holiday or even a few days off duty is pretty remote. Might I suggest that you come to Leicester one night when we could dine together and have a talk? Any night would be suitable now that my little wife has returned to New Zealand, every night is free - and very empty. To you and Mr Knight I offer my deepest sympathy and only wish I could lighten your burden for you.

    Believe me,
    Yours very sincerely,
    John Stewart Dick F/lt.

                           P/O D. F. Knight
                           5 Crosbie Road
                           Harborne
                           Birmingham17.

Dear Mr Dick,
    After these many months of weary labouring, I have at last been thrust out upon the world as a somewhat bewildered Hurricane pilot.

    Still in dazed excitement of becoming 'operational' at last, I volunteered for the East - and my application was accepted.

    So while you will be sitting in front of your fire this Christmas eating your ration of Christmas pudding substitute, I shall in all probability be far too overcome with the heat to worry about Xmas or any other damn thing.

    Anyway here's wishing all the very best to the Maestro this Christmas

    Yours very sincerely
    Dennis F Knight.

Sunday 20 April 1941

Hitler's birthday, he is 51. Although it may sound heartless I hope it is his last - if not his last, his last as dictator of Germany.

In the afternoon I went round to Christine's. It was a lovely day with occasional April showers.

I had bought a record of 'Begin the Beguine' and that evening put it on while we were having supper. When it finished I turned it over and played the other side, 'Heaven Can Wait'.

I suddenly saw, out of the corner of my eye, two great tears rolling slowly down Dad's cheeks and, with a shock, I realized the significance of the words.

I quickly said, "Shall I turn it off?" and he nodded gratefully.

Tuesday 22 April 1941

Mother and I went to town. Met grandma and had dinner in town. Stayed on in town and bought some pyjamas for me, two housecoats for mother (I tried a frilly one on and I think I have never looked so pretty!). We saw the damage near the Bull Ring. It is pretty awful! A few more raids like the last and there will be no shopping centre at all.

We got back round about 3, and in the evening I tried on my summer dresses while mother wore one of her housecoats.

I put on my dance dress and danced with Dad to some records. After 10.00 Raymond rang up. He said he had been round to Christine's. I told him about my 'engagement' to Vivian, so we 'broke ours off'.

These 'engagements' were, of course, just in fun, but Vivian and I kept it going for quite a long time.

Wednesday 23 April 1941

After tea I read "Private Worlds" then Dad asked me to go to Baughan's to get two books. When I got there there was a notice SHUT on the door. I walked away. But Mr B tapped on the door and let me in. He said that they shut early now <u>because they have nothing to sell</u>!! He had kept 2 packets of cigarettes for Dad - very nice of him.

Neville House

Birmingham 2

27th April 1941

My Dear Gladys & Fred

    I think you know the unbounded admiration I have for Dennis, from the time when he was a little fellow and showed such determination in delivering his Christmas message as the first grandchild, right through his school days to the start of his career. He has always shown the same brilliant ability and self confidence - an inflexible devotion to his job - and I am deeply proud to be his Godfather and a brother of his mother.

    I feel that Dennis' life should be an inspiration to others, and whilst I pray that he will yet come back to you, I would with all humility ask you to accept the enclosed £500* which I have saved, and with it found a "Dennis Knight Scholarship" fund at K.E.H.S. or elsewhere to perpetuate his shining life and name, as an example to all who come after him that they, like I, may realise in some part the undying debt we and all future generations owe to Dennis and those like him; the keen enlightened upright youth, the keystone of our progress, who, from their very purity of thought and purpose, are prepared and even eager to accept the supreme sacrifice in furtherance of their ideal.

    It is indeed their finest hour, and Dennis, inspired by all finest thoughts, unsmirched by any sordid worldliness, has, ere he is to this world a man, already led a life full of good work, honesty of purpose, and achievement such as is an example to all and the prize of few.

    Please do accept this token of respect to one whom I so very much admire.

    Very sincerely yours,
    George

*I believe that this would be about £20,000 in today's money.

Telephone: Holborn 3434
Q.J.Any communications on the
subject of this letter should
be addressed to:-

AIR MINSTRY, Dept.
LONDON, W.C.2.

THE SECRETARY,

and the following number
quoted:-
P.357922/41/P.4.Cas.

Sir,

  I am directed to refer to a letter from this Department dated the 26th March, 1941, and to inform you that it is regretted that no further news has been received of your son, Pilot Officer Dennis Frederick Knight, since he was reported missing and believed to have lost his life on the 22nd March, 1941.

  The aircraft is reported to have come down in the sea off Malta at approximately 2 p.m. on the 22nd March, as a result of enemy action.

  As you have already been informed, in the absence of definite news of your son it will be necessary, after a lapse of not less than six months from the date of the occurrence, to presume his death for official purposes. When such action is contemplated a further letter will be addressed to you.

  I am to add an expression of the Department's profound sympathy with you in your bereavement.

  I am, Sir,
  Your obedient Servant,
  J. G. Shrewe

  for Director of Personal Services.

F.W. Knight, Esq.,
5, Crosbie Road,
Harborne,
Birmingham, 17.

Monday 28 April 1941 - Den's birthday, age 20

At 12.15 Aunty Nita rang up and asked me to go to tea in town if she could get the car.

At about 3.30 she arrived with Dick. The 3 of us went to town, and she bought me a light blue angora jumper for my birthday present.

Monday 5 May 1941

Had a bath. Went to town with mother and had dinner at Pattison's. Mr Stuart Morris (Ann's father and leader of the Peace Pledge Union - also the owner of a vile temper) was there. If I had been a waitress I should have refused to serve him.

Bought some sandals and some red socks, and green ones.

In the afternoon went to the village - no lacto calamine - no foreign tomatoes (English ones 6/6 lb and over!), no face powder (except one box of green!), no face cream.

In the evening I went with Mary Dutton to a lecture at Station rd school on gas and its symptoms and treatment. It was very good indeed.

Wednesday 7 May 1941

School.

At night I had both the windows open to get a nice lot of fresh air, but I awoke in the middle of the night to smell an awful smell, which I discovered was caused by the smoke screen - I shut my window quick!

Saturday 10 May 1941

Had a bath. Had dinner. Did some prep and then read "The Surgeons' Log". At about 4.30 I went round to Mrs T's to tea.

Went to look at a house in Wentworth rd that Mrs T would like to take. Called at my house to ask mother to go and see it. She was in Den's room taking his things out of a case she wanted to use. She was crying. Why not?

The warning went in the night, but the raid was over London.

Sunday 11 May 1941

Did some gardening. Had roast lamb, mint sauce, kale, roast and mashed, buttered potatoes and thick brown gravy, then had tinned pears and rice pudding - who said there was a war on? After dinner I did some more gardening, as it was a lovely day. Put some metal things in the box for the war effort. Mother wanted me to take the pig-food up to the pig bin, but I wouldn't.*

Last night's raid was on London where casualties and damage were rather large, but we got 33 planes down!

* (Every street had its 'pig-bin' where all the householders put their collected vegetable peelings, plate scraps and so on, in order to provide feed for pigs.)

Monday 12 May 1941

School. Went to the poison gas lecture. Very good.

Sunday 18 May 1941

In the early afternoon, did some work, and then went round to Christine's to tea. Had home made raspberry buns, scones and some cream cake (not real cream, of course) then Chris and I went to the Paramount.
P.S.   Went in the 3/-s!! Were paid for by Mother, Dad and Grandma.

19 May 1941 - My Birthday, Age 15

Raining. Had a chiffon scarf from Mrs Taylor.
A tin of toffees, scarf, 3 vests from Mother.
10/- from gran (which bought the sandals) and 5/- she gave me today.
10/- from grandma
2/6 from Aunty Marjorie
2/6 from "   Kathleen
Postcard from Jo
Greetings Telegram from Raymond.

School Cert orals on at school!

Thursday 29 May 1941

School. I am going to Joan's to tea tomorrow.
Cycled home with Joan, had some lemonade at a tea shop in Harborne.
The news isn't so good - we seem to do nothing but retreat (according to plan!)

Sunday 1 June 1941

A glorious day! Real June weather, the sun hot and bright, so warm that I put a summer dress on, so did Chris who came round just after dinner. We went in the car to Middleton Woods, where we had a picnic. Chris and I went into the woods and picked bluebells and rhododendrons. After taking some snaps we went in the car to a large lake with reeds fringing it, and tall silver birches in the foreground, while on either side there are fir trees. Chris and I went through the silver birches to the part where the fir trees grew. They had been cutting them down, and it formed a wide path about 18 feet wide or more.

Tuesday 10 June 1941 - Christine's birthday, age 20. In the evening I went to a sort of tea party (only me invited) at her house. She was very pleased with the presents.

Sunday 6 July 1941

In the afternoon Chris and I went to Bill's. Went swimming at the Greswolde.
Vivian turned up and after tea we went for a walk.
At night (about 2am) I heard an awful crash and woke up to hear a crackling noise.
Next day I found that it was 1 of our planes returning from Germany. No-one knows much about it, but it is thought that it was damaged, and the pilot tried to make a forced landing on the golf course and hit a balloon cable.

Tuesday 8 July 1941

History and German exams. I awoke at about 2 to hear planes overhead - a lot of them. I called to mother if she thought they were ours on the way to Germany.

She laughed and told me the warning had gone.

We went into the shelter but came out after about an hour and got into bed - about 1/2 hour afterwards the all clear went.

Saturday 12 July 1941

Very stormy.

N.B. Had cherries for tea at <u>4/-</u> per lb!!

From 10.00 pm onwards there was a home-guard '<u>do</u>' - a mock invasion. Firemen went off on motor bikes and H.Gs marched along singing. The tank traps were up, but I didn't hear much.

Cleaned out the garage before Chris came.

Sunday 13 July 1941

<u>Very</u> Stormy.

On June 20th Germany attacked its former ally, Russia.

The papers were full of news of the conflict. Some of the Russian names seemed quite *extraordinary to English eyes, and the Telegraph (I think) sported the following poem:-*

From   Omsk to Minsk a thousand miles,
        From Plonsk to Plinsk is furder,
        From Plinsk to Plonsk you can't go wronksk,
        Though all the way it's murder.

        There are no trams from Tomsk to Omsk.
        No taxis up to Plopski.
        The trains are bad from Leningrad,
        And petrol not a dropski.

The road to Moscow goes through Umsk.
Through Dumpsk and Umpskidumpski,
And all the way from Omsk to Plonsk
You're marching on your tumski.

So Heil to Omsk and Tomsk and Plonsk,
And Heil to Plinsk and Plonski.
From Plinsk to Plonsk you can't go wronksk,
So now we shan't be longski.

Sunday 20 July 1941

Washed my hair. Chris came round. Then Raymond on 10 days embarkation leave. After dinner I read and finished "The Light That Failed" which put me in a depressed state of mind. After tea we went to Wishaw, called for Gran and Uncle Tom on the way. Uncle T looks awfully ill. Uncle Frank gave us some new potatoes out of the garden.

Wednesday 23 July 1941

School. We had Ministry of Information films. They were very good.

Friday 25 July 1941

Broke up. The boys came into our school, and the rowdier gang climbed onto the roof.

Saturday 26 July 1941

Did my hair up for the first time.

Monday 4 August 1941

Did a little housework in the morning. A lot of our bombers came over very low and did mock dive bombing attacks on Harborne. Some fighters "attacked" the bombers, and the sky was one mass of low flying, zooming, diving, roaring fighters and bombers. In the afternoon I went round to Christine's, had tea and then went to town to the pictures. At the Paramount there was a very long queue, so went to the Forum where there was another even longer queue. So went to the Gaumont where there were 2 long long queues. However we parked ourselves in the shorter of the two, and after waiting 1/2 an hour during which time it decided to rain, we got in and saw "Western Union" and "Target for Tonight." The latter was excellent.

Saturday 9 August 1941

Got the things out of the dugout. Most of them were all green with mould. I set myself to clean the shoes. After dinner I went down to the library, and then to the Paramount where I met Bill and Brian. Chris then came up and we went in the 3/- to see "Nice Girl" and "Target for Tonight." Afterwards we all came back to my house for dinner. Mother and Dad were upstairs, and Chris was sitting on the arm of Brian's chair holding a doorstop while he tickled her spine and squeezed her waist. Therefore Bill was left to make advances to me - which he did.

Wednesday 13 August 1941

In the evening Chris and I met Brian and Bill at Selly Oak. Went to Brian's house for the evening. Vivian turned up very late. Played Monopoly. Everyone was out except Brian and I and we had a fight for it. He won.

Chris and I had arranged to stay with some relatives of hers in Streatham for a few days.

Saturday 23 August 1941

Had breakfast early. Called for Chris and caught the breakfast train. Got hungry, so opened a box Mrs Taylor had packed and took out a bar of choc. The box contained sausage rolls, a cake, another bar of choc and some rations. Outside Euston our end of the train was in the tunnel, while the front was in the station. Gathered everything off the seats and marched down the train.

There were heaps of airmen going East - an awful lot of officers. Caught the tube to the Strand. On the tube Chris remembered the parcel - too late!

Sunday 24 August 1941

Got up rather late. Chris and I went for a walk up Palace Rd and to Streatham. Saw a police phone box. Were inspecting it from outside when policeman came out. Chris and I tried to look unconcerned, and he asked if we wanted anything. I explained that we hadn't seen one before so he asked us in and showed us the log book, the siren lever etc, and told us how the system worked.

After dinner we took a bus to Hyde Park Corner and got a boat out on the Serpentine. There were an awful lot of army, navy and airforce officers and men listening to the band, etc.

Monday 25 August 1941

Chris and I went over Vauxhall bridge, and saw Westminster Abbey, Westminster Bridge, Houses of Parliament, and walked along the Embankment. Crossed over and came to the road with the Cenotaph in it. Saw no. 10 Downing Street which was guarded by 2 policemen and 2 soldiers. Then went to see "Fantasia" at the Marble Arch.

Tuesday 26 August 1941

Went to St Paul's via Fleet Street. There is some very bad damage round there. Went to The Haymarket.

Thursday 28 August 1941

After breakfast Chris and I packed and tidied up the room etc., then said goodbye. It was quite a nice day and sunny, although a little windy. We took our cases to Euston and left them there. Then we got on the Underground at Euston and got off at the Strand. We had lunch in the

Brasserie at the Strand Corner House. After lunch we went boating and 2 Polish airmen tried to 'get off' with us, but we were 'not amused'. Then 4 sailors did their best to annoy us and splashed me and made us furious. We left the Serpentine 10 mins before our time. And caught the train home.

Friday 29 August 1941

In the morning the weather was pretty nasty. After dinner I met Chris (who was very late as usual) and we went to town to the library, *(to look for music scores for Chris – mostly Chopin. Many evenings I would sit listening to her playing.)* then we went to Scotcher's and listened to 4 records.

Then we went back to her house for tea. Mother was there - her head awfully bad - why can't they do something for it? Came home at about 6. She went to the Doctor's. The pain was terrible, it was obvious, and her left temple at times would swell like a half-egg.

Saturday 30 August 1941

In the afternoon Chris and I went to the Forum to see "Boom Town". Had tea at Taylors. They were coming to our house for the evening but Mother's head was too bad.

After tea Chris and I caught a bus to Bartley Green. It was after 8 when we got there. We walked around the reservoir. While we did so the red clouds disappeared, and dusk fell and dark came, and the stars and the moon came out.

We sat and talked by the reservoir, and then came home.

Sunday 31 August 1941

Rang up Chris and asked her to come for a run. In the afternoon she came round and we went to the back of Clent. Had a picnic there. Came home and I got supper. The eggs were preserved and the first 2 were bad so mother came and helped me.

Monday 1 September 1941

Mother's head was so bad that she went up to Doctor Winfield to get some M&B 693. She went to bed and I kept house.

The constant pain in Mother's head, at times was obviously more than she could bear.

At these times her left temple would swell like a great egg, but she said that the seat of the pain felt to be in the very centre of her head.

No-one, including the doctors, knew what to do. There were, of course, no antibiotics then.

Her concerned sisters bought her Cologne ice, the doctors prescribed a sort of mask that she wore over her nose and mouth, containing some coal-tar substance that burned her skin, but was completely useless in its effect.

It was thought that sea air might help, so she went to stay with Grandma's cousin, Dora Allen, at Clacton-on-Sea.

There is a fragment of a letter to her from my father which discloses his distress, and attempts to philosophise:-

" .... I wonder sometimes if it's best for people to love each other as we do, for 'tis hell when we are parted, still it is worth it again whenever we are reunited and the good times we have and shall have together, much more than make up for the times we are not.   Still I wonder how people feel who never have these upsets in their lives, I suppose they take everything for granted and they have no high spots as we do...."

Mother returned, with no change in her condition.

Each night I prayed, "Please let Mother's head get better", but it didn't.

Eventually, after months stretched into years, she went into hospital to have a Turbinectomy, which involves removing the nasal septum. It was hoped that the infected area might then be able to clear.

The operation is performed with the patient awake, and Mother kept asking the surgeon to 'go further back'; but he said he couldn't operate any further back as he was right up near the brain.

What in fact she was suffering from was an abscess in the ethmoid bone, one of the bones forming the anterior part of the brain case. The only other patient her surgeon had had with this condition died from it.

Following the operation she was, perhaps, in more pain than ever, and went to Chipping Camden to recuperate in the guest-house where Gran was staying at the time.

Like a wounded animal, Mother went alone into the orchard where, accompanied by the most excruciating pain she had yet had to endure, the abscess finally burst and started to drain away.

The pain, however, went on for many, many years after the infection had eventually subsided, and it was not until she reached old age that the pain finally faded away.

Tuesday 2 September 1941

Mother in bed. Dr W. came to see her. Kept house.

Saturday 6 September 1941

In the afternoon went to the fete. Chris and I helped Grandma raffle the doll.

(Grandma made dolls to be raffled in aid of the Red Cross, making in all over £1000, and, at the end of the war, receiving a letter of thanks from the British Red Cross Society.)

Sunday 14 September 1941

In the afternoon went round to Bill's. Went for a walk. Bill is going soon.

Saturday 4 October 1941

In the morning went to town. Met Colin. He said Bill had gone on Friday.

Monday 6 October 1941

School. Esmé is leaving school tomorrow and B'ham on Thur.
(Her family had decided to move back to Whitley Bay to be nearer to where her father was operating from, on minesweepers.)

Monday 13 October 1941

Mother had had her antrums washed out, but it was not they that were wrong, so she is going to have an X-ray.

By late 1941 Bill had joined the Fleet Air Arm, and Brian the R.A.F., and soon letters began to flow between Bill and me.

Sat. 25th Oct. 1941
                                                  H.M.S.St.Vincent,
                                                            c/o G.P.O.
                                                                LONDON

Dear Pat,
    I have managed to find a few spare moments in which to write you a short note, the main purpose of which is to request that you will take pity upon the lowest form of animal life in the Royal Navy and write him one of your interesting letters.

    I won't bore you with a description of life here, I will only say that it's one long rush, and one hell of a good time, and Oh Boy do I feel tiddly in my smart little sailor suit.

    I do all my own washing and sewing and one day should make a really super husband, you will really have to reconsider your selection of Vivian as the "Perfect Husband".

    Be a pal Pat and tell me all the news. Please give my love to your parents and to Chris.

    That's all for now. Looking forward to hearing from you very, very soon. Do you think Chris would be good enough to write to me?

    Yours to a cinder,
    <u>Bill</u>.
    Q.A.

2nd November

H.M.S. St. Vincent,
c/o G.P.O.
LONDON.

Dear Pat,

It was most kind of you to write so soon after receiving my address from Brian, and I was delighted to receive two letters, instead of one, in the same envelope.

By the by I still stick to my guns, the Navy is the finest Service in the world. I felt a bit of a hypocrite at the old Q.A. meetings defending and praising the Navy so loudly, whilst still wearing civvie togs. But proof of the pudding is in the eating and I don't think I have ever been so happy in civvie life as I am everyday here, and I haven't made a single girl friend here or been out in the company of females, luscious or otherwise.

Thank your parents for their good wishes. I do hope I shall see you all soon.

Remember me to Chris, Brian and Vivian and ask Vivian to write me as I may not have time to write to him for a few days.

Hope you are swotting hard and in good spirits.

Finally, I hope you will write again say in a fortnight's time to encourage me before the ordeal of the passing out exams.

Lashings of Love,
Cheeriohski,
Bill
Q.A. + N.A. (and B.F.)

Monday 17 November 1941

Had a letter from Kelvin. He asked me to go and stay with him after Christmas. I think I shall go.

Wrote to Bill.

Wednesday 10 December 1941

*School. Played netball. When I got home I discovered that the battleship Prince of Wales and the battle-cruiser Repulse have been sunk.

*On the 8.00 news we heard that America had declared war against Germany and Italy.

Tuesday 16 December 1941 - Mother's birthday, aged 43

    Broke up. Went to the village and got a temporary job at Shaw's, the chemists. Got Mother a large bunch of chrysanths. In the evening Chris came round with another large bunch of chrsyanths - the same colour!

    Her mother gave a small, framed illuminated manuscript that depicted the Air Force wings and motto at the top, with, beneath, the words:

"Sound, sound the clarion, fill the fife.
To all this sensuous world proclaim:
One crowded hour of glorious life
Is worth an age without a name."

Wednesday 17 December 1941

    Started work at Shaw's - it was quite fun. I dusted shelves, weighed powders, counted pills, measured out cough mixture (11 bottles) and had quite a good time.

Monday 22 December 1941

    Went to work at Shaws.

    Mother rang up the L.M.S. and G.W.R. to find the times of the trains. Then she rang up Kelvin's mother. She was out and Kelvin answered. I spoke to him. He sounds <u>awfully</u> nice - oh Boy! And he has found me some skates and ooohhh!!!

    Mother thinks he sounds marvellous too - oh h h h h!

So on Sat 27 December I got up very early and caught the 8.40 train to London, where Kelvin met me.

I stayed with him and his family until Thursday Jan. 8th. We spent most of our time skating and going to the cinema; also an ice-cream parlour, where Kelvin and another fellow kept putting pennies in a record playing machine and playing things like Rumboogie, Bounce Me Daddy with a Solid Four, and things like that.

I had a lovely time, but K. seems to want a bit more than kissing, and I didn't want any of that!

On the train back to B'ham there were some soldiers singing.

1942

Aged 15 ½

List of Illustrations

Page

332 KES girls working at Bennetts farm

339 Bill in Officer's uniform

348 The Picture Post photograph of Bill

355 Danny in West Point uniform

Saturday 10 January 1942

In the afternoon I went skating with Bill and 'Beaver'. *(Beaver, whose name was Bill Warner, had wanted to grow a beard, and, being in the Fleet Air Arm, had to obtain permission from his C.O. However, with the permission came the stipulation that he kept it for at least twelve months. Unfortunately, the beard only grew a fraction of an inch and then refused to grow any more, and as he was stuck with it for a while he thus gained his nickname.)* After tea at the Mecca Bill and I went to the Theatre Royal with Chris and Brian, Bobby and Vivian. Afterwards, when we went to the Imperial a Dago and a Czech were having words, and some Czech officers were standing round grinning, 4 Canadian airmen chucked the Dago out in the end. The bar was shut so we went to the Woodman which was full of smoke and people and empty of glasses - people were drinking out of jugs!

Sunday 18 January 1942

The ice was thick enough to stand on on the pond. I broke it, but an hour later it had frozen again.
In the afternoon Chris and I went to meet Bill and a friend of his. When we got to the Gaumont we found there were 5 of them altogether, all of them Fleet Air Arm! Saw "The Common Touch". It is an excellent film, there are 2 lovely pieces of music in it. I want to buy them, only I don't know what they are called. (I found later that one is Tchaikovsky's piano concerto.)

Tuesday 20 January 1942

The snow was frightfully deep. Dad had to walk all the way to the works and back. When I went to school, at Selly Oak there were plenty of trams going the other way, but none our way so we all had to walk. It was very funny - all those people walking down Lordswood road - it was like refugees fleeing before the Nazi invasion.

Saturday 7 February 1942

In the evening, after supper with two of his friends at a little Czech restaurant, Bill and I went to the Golden Cross where we met Viv, his nurse

Anne, Brian, Chris and Brian's parents.

Bill, Viv and Anne went home. Brian saw Chris and me home.

Monday 9 February 1942

School. In the evening met Bill, Brian and Chris and a sailor called Eric at the Midland and had a super meal.

Afterwards we went to the Hope & Anchor and met Viv.

We stayed there until about 10.10. When we decided to go, Bill asked me to help him put his coat on, but when I held his big square sailor's collar down for him he murmured "Come closer!" So I left him, took Vivian's proffered arm and followed Brian and Chris out.

Vivian saw me home and stayed quite a while, eating, drinking, and talking about mice and laboratories.

Sunday 15 February 1942

Went out in the car. Chris came. Went to the Crab Hill, Henley *(in Arden)*. There was a thick, pinkish fog at home, but it was warm and sunny out there. Had a lovely meal. Roast beef, roast potatoes, leeks with white sauce, rhubarb pie and custard. Also drinks.

The weather was foul on the return journey. Worked in the evening. Listened to the Prime Minister's speech.

Singapore has fallen.

Sunday 1 March 1942

Got up reasonably early. About 12.00, heard rifle shots. I went to the landing window and looked out. The H.G. were having a practice street-fight in our road and Wentworth road. They were advancing down our road. They were all in the front gardens; then they started coming into the back gardens and they peered into the lounge. It was all very amusing!

I did some work in the afternoon. Chris came round at 4.30 and we went for a walk after tea. We walked through Hillyfields and across the golf course. On the top of the hill about 7' above the ground was a ceiling of wire netting. In a field at the bottom of the hill were about 70 guns, tents and trenches etc all round the edges of the field. There were 7 soldiers being exercised.

Walked to Bartley Green - caught the bus back.

Sunday 8 March 1942

Chris came round in the afternoon and we had an early tea and then caught the bus to Clent. It was quite a nice day though a bit windy. On the top it was terrifically windy, we had to walk backwards so as to face the wind and keep our hair out of our eyes.

Up there all cares dropped off like a cloak. The wind and the natural unaffected beauty of it made us feel wonderfully light hearted. We laughed an awful lot about everything. Twilight began to approach so we came down. As we descended the heavy hand of depression began to descend again, but at first only lightly.

We had to wait for ages for a bus, but at last one came. We felt very tired, but pleasantly so.

Chris didn't come in as she had to get back to the hospital.

(I have no other other diary entries around this time of going to Clent with Chris, but on one occasion [which may indeed have been this one] as we came down from the hill, we were 'picked up' by a young man.

He was small and dark haired and told us his name was Gerald, he was a medical student. He seemed very keen to get to know Chris, and they must have exchanged phone numbers, although Chris later said, on the bus home, that she wasn't in the least interested in him.

However, in spite of this, she did meet him, and continued to do so.)

Friday 13 March 1942

Dad's birthday. Gran and I had a lovely meal ready for him and Mother. Ham, lettuce, watercress, cress, thick whip and salad cream, followed by chocolate blancmange and lemon milk jelly - oh boy! M-hm!

I had such a lot of trouble with my sinuses that Dr Winfield thought a change of air might help, so it was decided that I should go to Bournemouth with Kathleen.

Thursday 2 April 1942

Went to town with Mother. After meeting Aunty Edith and Kathleen at Pattisons for lunch, K. and I caught the train to Bournemouth.

We went 1st class.

There was also an elderly lady - elderly man and a Maori Pilot Officer, going back to the Royal Bath hotel.

I spent most of my time in the corridor because of my sinus trouble. We shared food. The P/O gave K a bar of Cadbury's (New Zealand) honeycomb choc., and the old lady gave us chocolate biscuits. The man was the only person with nothing to hand round.

When we got there (8.15 approx) the man and the P/O carried our luggage for us. The man went and the P/O tried to make a date.

K. like a fool told him the name of our hotel.

The sirens went that evening.

Friday 3 April 1942

Soldiers in hotel next door woke us by parading (sea opposite).

After breakfast - when we discovered a sailor with a D.S.O. was at our hotel - we set out for Bournemouth. Previously I had looked out of the window and seen the Maori wandering up and down. He appeared to have gone, tho'. But when we got to a corner there he was - waiting. He looked blacker than before.

He asked if he could show us Bournemouth. K. said no thanks we were going shopping. He said couldn't he come too? She said no, she didn't think so. He said "Oh that sort of shopping!"

He then said could he see us some other time - we said 'no' we had friends with whom we were spending all our time - finis.

The warning went while we were in Bournemouth. It was sunny and warm and the almond blossom was out. We had coffee at the Pavilion. Bournemouth was crowded with airmen, mostly officers. Boscombe was crowded with soldiers.

In the afternoon went to Christchurch. I was pretty awful *(my sinuses)*. We had tea there. There were 4 Canadians on the bus going down. They wore a lot of rings. I don't like them - they're fresh.

Went to a concert at the Pavilion.

5 Crosbie Road
Friday

My dear Pat
    This is the cheque to pay your main hotel expenses. You had better give it to the proprietor straight away, so as to give him time to cash it before you leave. I tried to get through to you this morning as we heard on the wireless there had been a considerable raid on the south coast, and as the sirens were going when you 'phoned last night we just wondered! However we got through to the hotel without delay, so know you are all right. Dad is waiting to post this on way to works. Hope you will have a good time.
        Love to you both
        In great haste
        Mother

Tuesday 28 April 1942

    Started school. Aunty Freda gave me Fighter Pilot as it was Den's birthday.

Saturday 16 May 1942

    In the afternoon I decided I'd cycle to Frankley and do some art. So changed into my shorts - open neck shirt - sandals and set out. I got lost at Frankley, found my bearings and cycled down a long hill singing Chatanuga Chu Chu at the top of my voice with the breeze blowing my shorts and hair and shirt. After a while I got lost again, but carried on.
    I became aware I was high up in wooded hills. I came to a B road with a few cottages. An old man sat in a trap. I asked him where I was and what time it was. "3 mls from Bromsgrove!" Gosh!
    He went in to see the time, looked at me and said, "You look hot. Would you like a drink?" I had some water and spoke to his wife. Her son was on the Royal Oak and has got the O.B.E. I congratulated her then left and had tea at Bromsgrove - Phew! Did I cause a commotion!
    Vivian was here when I got back.

Tuesday 19 May 1942 My birthday. Age 16.

    10/- from Aunty Marjory.
    6/6   "   " Freda.
    10/- "   " Dorothy.
    10/- " Gran.
    10/- " Grandma.
    Vienna Blood from the gang.
    7/6 from Chris.
    The whole of Tchaikovsky's Concerto in B Flat Minor from Mother and Dad.

Sunday 24 May 1942

    Showers. Vivian called for me and we cycled to Chipping Sodbury. We examined the church and as we left it began to pour with rain, so we sheltered under some lilac bushes, heavy with perfume in the rain. We left there about 5.15, had tea and started homewards; but we got lost and 20 to 8 found us back at Chipping Sodbury!

Bill was posted to Canada to continue his flying training. At first, things didn't quite go according to plan.

Saturday 30 May 1942   31. S.F.T.S.
                                                                       KINGSTON,
                                                                       ONTARIO.

Dear Pat,
    This is the third letter I have started to write you. The first one was interrupted by unexpected leave on account of snow and a consequential trip to taste the delights of Toronto, and the second was interrupted by a very anxious four day period in which it was touch and go whether I should be suspended from flying and sent home to try my hand at being a real sailor.

What happened was that I foolishly ate a large bar of sticky toffee, on top of a hurried lunch of strong curry soup, stew and dumplings and I forget the sweet, and an orange and was taken up to do loops and spins. As a result I spattered the cockpit and my instructor with little bits of orange (I don't know what happened to the stew) impelled with a backward velocity of some 140 m.p.h. I had my head out of the window, but not quite enough out apparently. Anyhow I was sent to the M.O. and on looking at my report he found I had had mal d'air at this place on one or two occasions. There followed a conference between the Medical officers and Chief Instructor and the next day I was given the order of the boot.

However I appealed against this decision. As a result I was taken up and looped, spun, half-rolled and steep turned with an anxious instructor in the rear cockpit waiting for the full blast of a very hearty breakfast. However resolutely chewing gum I determined not to be sick, was not, and so am being allowed to carry on for the present. However if I'm seedy again I shall doubtless be sent home well and truly sacked.

How are Mr and Mrs Knight and Grandmother, I do hope they are all in good health. Please remember me to them all and convey my best wishes.

I am enjoying my stay here in Canada immensely and shall be terribly disappointed if I can't finish my training to become a pilot. It truly is a land of milk and honey in comparison with rationed Britain. Oranges, apples, chocolate of all kinds (including Cadbury's Dairy Milk) are obtainable in our Canteen and in the shops, and the camp meals are excellent. For example the normal breakfast is porridge and milk (and what porridge), bacon and eggs, (or beans, or tomatoes) and as much bread, butter and marmalade and honey as you wish. Once a week we have half a grapefruit chucked in as well. So breakfast is a splendid incentive to get up and be washed early in the morning.

At the moment I believe that silk stockings are available and if I remain here I should like to buy a few pairs for your Mother and yourself if you would care to have them. But I must frankly admit that I know absolutely nothing about sizes, shades, thicknesses, brands and so on so if you are interested please write per Air Mail giving as much information as you think necessary. Then if (a) I haven't been chucked out, b) stockings are unrationed, c) I have some money left, d) I have room in my kitbags, I will do my level best to satisfy requirements. Incidentally cosmetics seem plentiful, are you interested? Which reminds me to add that I hope you have not taken to the sinful habit of wearing lipstick.

Well Pat I have two examinations to sit tomorrow and frankly know nothing, having neglected to swot (the old, old story) so I'm sure you will excuse me if I finish now and get down to the grind.

I'm looking forward to hearing from you, so do please write giving me the latest news of your doings, boy friends, position at school and so forth. Have you seen Colin at all? And please don't forget to save that photograph of yourself for me.

Keep fit, and be reasonably good,
Cheerio,
Bill

Saturday 6 June 1942

Went to town to get some brown corduroy shorts. It was terribly hot and I wore my greeny blue linen skirt and my greeny blue chiffon (?) blouse and sandals. I couldn't get the shorts and came home.

Went to Christine's to tea, felt lousy. So Chris and I went back to my house to take my temp., it was 100.1.

We sat in the lounge and talked and read books and then I went to bed early - Hellish head, glands in my neck swollen and ached, earache, pains in my arms and little shooting pains round my waist.

Monday 8 June 1942

School. I went to the Doctor's in the evening. He says all I can do is go to bed for 5 days and take M&B 760. I'll have to wait 'till after SC. (School Certificate.)

Wednesday 10 June 1942

Christine's 21st birthday. Mother and Dad and I arrived at the White Horse at about 7.30. Her brother and his wife and her uncle and aunt, Gerald, Mr and Mrs T and Chris were there. Brian was still to come. Chris looked awfully pretty in a black taffeta short dress with white lace collar and cuffs and 3 white carnations pinned on her bosom. I had on my navy taffeta with the coloured pin stripes, my sheer stockings and navy evening sandals. Brian turned up at 8.20 - he had been waiting at the White Swan!

We had soup, roast chicken, roast potatoes, cauliflower and white sauce - fruit salad and ice cream.

We drank Sauterne. Afterwards Chris blew her candles out on her cake and set her hair on fire!

Dad proposed a toast to Chris.

Chris "   "   " absent friends - she proposed it to Mother for Dennis and Mother had to leave.

Mr T proposed one to the King.

Then we went back to Ravenhurst Rd. Gerald has proposed to Chris.

When we got back Chris changed into a present - a deep cerise crushed velvet housecoat with a pale blue satin lining. She looked terribly pretty. She played her new piano - it is beautiful, low and smooth and dark. Chris came home with us, she had put on a nightie under her gown.

When she got back here (12.30) she rang up Mrs T. But collapsed on the bed in tears - I'm sure she was in love with Dennis.

Saturday 13 June 1942

Got up at 12.00. Played records. Gosh! I'd like to buy up all the Operas, Ballets and Symphonies ever written.

I wish I'd not grown up with a war on. I don't know whether it's growing up or the war, but I don't seem to get the enjoyment out of each day as I used. I suppose a child's imagination makes everything covered in a golden mist, and very wonderful, exciting and mysterious - or is it that the war has taken that element from normal life? I often wish I could remain my age and yet <u>feel</u> as I used. Not caring how I look, or what people think, and wander around on wild Cornish coasts, barefoot, swimming naked with my hair loose, climbing cliffs and trees with bare feet, lying half naked with the sun beating down, salt on my lips and not a care in my head. I want adventure at every turn but not danger at every turn. Maybe it'll come again.

Kingston

2nd *(sic. Presumably*   Ontario
22nd) June 1942

Dear Pat

    I was delighted to receive your letter a few days ago. Confound the people who returned it to you with the label 'lecture' attached, they could just as easily have deleted whatever they thought objectionable. However lets all be blunderingly British, there's a war on.

    I passed the Wings Exam somehow with fairly good marks so it only remains for you to dash triumphantly through S.C. to complete the scholastic picture. Believe me if I can pass S.C. then you have absolutely no excuse for failing to romp thro' it; unless of course you have been concentrating too much on cycling trips with Viv. (Lawdy; aint I catty). Incidentally that cycling get-up of yours which shocked the good people of Bromsgrove (Bucolic Clods) sounds terribly attractive. I hope my bike is in reasonable working order when I return, I want to see the dazzling oomph girl in action. Will you oblige?

    As an advanced swing fan I was very disgusted by your spelling of Chattanooga Choo Choo, though the thought of the two of us pedalling thro' quiet Worcestershire lanes to the rhythm of a 'Jersey Bounce' or a 'Chat Choo Choo' putting the aforementioned bucolic swine to flight appeals a heck of a lot to my holiday spirit. Though I must say your efforts at " gettin' in the groove" (a fatal thing to do on a bike) or "goin' to town" (seems more appropriate) with "Shoe Fly", "C.C.C" and "In the Mood" were in very strict contrast with your highbrow record sessions. Perhaps you believe in a tune to fit the mood, I do, otherwise there is a danger of one becoming a musical snob; either totally addicted to Swing (usually unbalanced adolescent type) or else to the Classics (blue stocking Upper Sixth K.E.S.). What a magnificent present that piano concerto was. Though you may not believe it I am looking forward to listening to it. Though to make things even you must visit No. 16 and enjoy a red hot jam session (unrationed). By the way I hope the censor knows what a jam session is or I shall get this letter back with a polite but firm admonitory label attached regarding shipping space and all that.

    Unfortunately the censor has cut two or three lines out of your letter with his sensitive scissors, and on the back of this slashed sheet I read the following startling news. Quote. "Oh - Chris has just had her 21st.

Brian was there and a medical student. Apparently Mrs. T. thinks they're going to get married." Unquote.

Fancy old Brian marrying the medical student, positively indecent I call it. Or hold on a minute, perhaps you mean that Chris and Brian are getting hitched. Then again it may be I'm to understand that the medico is the intended spouse. As you see I'm all mixed up.

I was very interested to hear of your future plans, *(My chosen career was, of course, nursing, but as I was only 16, I was too young to start training. I would, I hoped, have my School Certificate, didn't need a Higher School Certificate for nursing and was fed up with school anyway. So I decided to go to Art School until I was 17½, when I could start my training at the Birmingham Children's Hospital.)* though I hope the Art School is not still infested with spotty, long haired intellectuals, communists and amateur Bohemians. You know the type I mean, anaemic looking young 'men' (?) with dark blue shirts and scarlet ties, suede shoes and blatantly striped trousers.

You made no mention of the enlarged photograph of your charming self which I have been promised. I sincerely hope you are attending to this urgent matter, and that you will be able to hand it over when I reach B'rum. If not, the Tchaikovsky is definitely off.

Please give my love to Vivian when you next see him, and tell him I will write to him when I can snap out of my present lethargy.

I'm terribly "cheesed off" at the moment. I have squandered all my cash on a camera and two cap badges ($50 all told) and I'm beginning to wonder if I shall be able to buy anything to bring home, bit of a come-down to return home without anything after my wild promises, I mean a sailor can usually be relied upon for a parrot at least.

Gee I'd better be thinking of the weight of this letter. Damn it I can't finish properly in the space left on this sheet, I'd better carry on and post Sea Mail. Do you mind?

I was surprised to hear that Raymond was in Toronto at the same time that I was there; I thought he had arrived home about the time I left. I expect he was at the distribution centre there awaiting a draft home, lucky chap.

Gosh I'm looking forward to a spot of leave in Birmingham. I do hope you will be at home and on holiday when I arrive.

Assuming you are at home and enjoying your leisure I trust you will be sweet enough to give me plenty of your time. I shall expect you to play tennis, come swimming, rowing, listen to Swing records, have a few snaps taken with my camera, not to forget cycling and the "flicks" if its wet and windy. Knowing your unbounded energy I have half a hope that I may rely on your cooperation in this Marathon of Sport. You ought to absolutely tan the hide off me at tennis, I have played once in the last year; you have been stalling this oft mooted game of tennis for years on the flabby excuse that you weren't good enough. This really won't hold water any longer young Lady. It occurs to me that I might even be able to tempt you out on a golf course. Now don't get me wrong sister. What I mean is of course that I might tempt you to a game of golf and not the other thing. Oh dear what a nasty modern mind I have.

Jeepers Creepers, its good news that after S.C. is past and conquered you are going to write frequently and at some considerable length. I do hope that your promises with regard to writing letters are 100% better than mine, otherwise I shall be living the life of an uninformed hermit.

Please give my love to your Mother and Father, I do hope they are both enjoying good health and are quite recovered from past ailments.

Don't bother to answer this as I hope to be on the way home before a reply could reach here.

Cheerio.

Don't do anything I wouldn't do (which of course places absolutely no limitations upon your conduct).

Love <u>Bill</u>

Friday 7 August 1942

Mother and I went with Dad to the Optician's and then to Kunzles Union Street and had tea. A young flight-lieutenant with a D.F.C. came in with a girl - presumably his sister. After tea Mother spoke to him. He got his D.F.C. flying a Spitfire back on 1 engine. He was terribly nervy. Mother and I feel terribly sorry for him - I can't get him out of my mind.

After going to the West End to see "We were dancing" I came home on a bus before Mother and Dad. Colin was on it.

He's being posted abroad.

Once again I was unwell and in bed. This was particularly annoying because I was due to cycle down to Pershore on Monday 17th to the K.E.S. fruit-picking camp at Bennetts Farm with Joan, Jean and Pat.

Sunday 16 August 1942

Stayed in bed. Got up at about 3.30 and sat in the garden - Lovely day, warm and sunny.

Just before I went to bed I looked at rambler's guides to Tenby, Aberdovey, Cromer, Torquay, Newquay, Minehead etc. Oh, those were the days, when one lived in the present, not the past or future. I did enjoy myself then.

Monday 17 August 1942

Joan came round at about 9.00. She's meeting Jean and Pat at Northfield - lucky devils! I shall have to cycle down alone. My legs ache a bit, so I shan't be able to go until Wednesday or after.

It started off by being a lovely day, but it's clouded over a little.

I've been looking at letters I received since September '39. I felt very different in those days. I (naturally) felt younger - but not only a matter of years - it was more centuries. Mine was a more young soul from the beginning of time, but 3 years of war have aged it - I can't say I feel as happy and gay as I used - but I suppose it's only natural.

I cycled down alone to Bennetts Farm. It is a large fruit farm, with acres of orchards and its own cannery. The son of the owner of the farm is a dental student, and he has some dental and medical student friends staying on the farm with him during the summer vac.

Most of the girls are sleeping in one of the orchards in bell-tents, but some of us, including Nan, Joan, Jean, Pat and me, are sleeping in a different orchard, all together in a marquee. We feel very superior! We called it the 'Virgins' Retreat', and put up a sign, but one of the mistresses made us take it down! There is a toilet at the side of the field right up by the hedge. It is just an Elsan in a sort of canvas shelter, and one day I was in there when the students started shooting rabbits, and shot was peppering the canvas sides. I was too embarrassed to come out, and sat there in fear and trembling.

One night there was a tremendous storm. When it started I thought it was an air-raid; and I lay there thinking that it wouldn't be a bad way to go, with all my friends, all together, if it weren't for the grief Mother and Dad would suffer. Anyway, it wasn't a raid, and soon we had brilliant lightning - so bright you could see every leaf on the trees, and I thought I saw an owl suddenly illuminated.

Then the rain came down like stair rods, and we had to get out of our sleeping bags and let the brailing down, to keep the rain out. (We slept with it rolled up every night.)

K.E.S. GIRLS ON "HOLIDAY"

Fifty girls from King Edward's High School, Birmingham, accompanied by teachers, are spending their holiday under canvas at Lower Wick, near Worcester, where they are helping to pick and can thousands of pounds of plums. Below: Bringing the harvest from the orchards. Bottom: At the cannery.

Sometimes we would pick the plums, and sometimes work in the cannery, filling the tins with plums. That was when we came into contact with most of the students, which was quite nice!

In the canning factory; Jean Harvey left, Pat in middle, and Pat Evans, (Pat-of-the-gnat-bitten-undercarriage) on the right.

Once we were sent to pick cooking apples up tall ladders. I have never seen such enormous apples. You could only pick one at a time, and they almost needed two hands to hold them.

There were Italian P.O.Ws working on the farm as well, and we talked to them sometimes. They asked us if we were forced to work on the farm, and we said, No, we were doing it because we wanted to.

One day, out of the blue, I received a telegram from Mother:-

= BILL HOME PHONE ME BETWEEN FOUR AND SIX OCLOCK TODAY = MOTHER

She then wrote to me:-

Aug: 23rd   5 Crosbie Road

My dear Pat

      I did not post your gas mask yesterday as I thought it unwise that it should be left in the post during the week end probably under a great weight of other parcels. Dad and I have had a very nice quiet day, just lazing around reading and going for a walk this afternoon. The Taylors came for the evening yesterday, but Christine didn't turn up as she had several things to do, including washing her hair. Poor old Bill seemed very despondent when he found you were away for the whole of his leave. I hope you will be able to see him, he was really quite depressed. He 'phoned through to his mother as soon as he landed in England, only to find his mother was away for the night. He arrived home to find his father away in Bristol, and then the same night 'phoned you, only to find you away. Then he wanted a photograph of you, which I couldn't find, so altogether it wasn't the best of homecomings.

      I spent the whole of yesterday at a Rummage Sale at St Paul's church rooms. Miss Jagger and I had the shoe stall, and hats. We collected £8. Altogether I think it will be around £50 that this road will have collected through the sale. We aimed at £25 so are very well pleased, especially as it was in aid of St Dunstans.

You will be pleased to hear Dad and I are going to try and book for Prince Igor, we are going to make a real Brighter Birmingham holiday of this week. We have certainly enjoyed today very much. Don't forget, ring us up just whenever you like, and reverse the charges, we like you to, So don't forget.

Hope everything is still O.K. and your <u>bed</u>* to your liking.
With much love
Mother

*(*Although we were to be provided with palliases on which to put them, we had to take our own sleeping bags. If you didn't have one, you had to make one.*

Mother made mine out of some old red hospital blankets. It was incredibly heavy, but once I had managed to get it to the school, all our sleeping bags were transported down to Bennetts Farm.)

Bill arranged to come down to Pershore to see me.

Thursday 27 August 1942

Pat Evans let me have her afternoon off, and just before lunch I was attempting to make myself look glamorous in the hopeless dusk of the marquee when Nan discovered Bill for me up at the farm - I wasn't expecting him 'till after lunch but I went up to him and quickly showed him the farm yard. While we were standing in the hall wondering what he'd better do, Mrs B invited him into the parlour and gave him some food - was I embarrassed! He is now a Sub Lieutenant in the Fleet Air Arm although he hasn't yet got his officer's uniform.

No.9,A.F.U.. R.A.F.,
Errol,
Perthshire,
Scotland.

Dear Pat

Your father 'phoned Friday morning and said that he had heard unofficially that you had passed your School Certificate. I was naturally delighted to hear this and could scarcely keep myself from 'phoning the good news to you at lunch-time: but as your parents were 'phoning later in the day and you had asked me not to 'phone again I thought it best to leave it.

I do hope the full official confirmation has come through and that you have attained five credits. Please write as soon as you can and let me know.

Did you get back in time for prayers Thursday night? Thanks to one bus driver who wouldn't stop to pick me up I nearly missed the 9.20 train, but the next bus made up for the other's lack of consideration. The conductor told me to stay on at the terminus as the bus was then going into the depot and had to pass near Shrub Hill Station. So I was dropped off about 400 yds from the station, ran all the way and found the train in. What luck!

Well Pat it was great having the afternoon and evening with you in spite of transport difficulties, the neat, dirty minded mistresses, and curious bare-backed yokels.

Your mother and father went out on a picnic all day Friday and so unfortunately I was unable to slip over to see them and leave your stockings. I suggest personally that you 'phone my Mother and slip over one day and pick up your own and a pair for Mrs. Knight. I am sorry to have to put you to this trouble Pat but somehow the idea of silk stockings going thro' the post sends uneasy shudders up my spine.

I did not have time to visit Lewiss's re your photograph so have to beg that you will see to this as soon as possible <u>or else</u> ...

I shall be in this bleak and barren spot three weeks so get weaving with your cheery letters for lonely and despondent bachelor sailors.

By jingo it's cold tonight. What they would refer to as "Braw" I presume

My Superfine (this <u>is</u> the correct name for the cloth) uniform was ready on Friday and I now strut around like a cocky little bus conductor returning salutes left, right and centre. What a bore.

How is the plum production, I hope you are getting warmer and drier weather for it than we are for our flying. Though the country is very beautiful here and its great fun stooging round heather clad hills and weaving up valleys and through gaps in the mountains.

Has the "Virgins' Retreat" suffered any more male intrusion since my inquisitive nose first poked through the brailing. I hope you are not being too friendly towards the Medicos. That big cheeky bloke on the bike who commented on our shy unlinking of arms is far too good looking to be let loose amidst a Fifth Form of K.E.S. maidens (?). As far as he's concerned and any other menaces for that matter I hope that your two prudes do their very best to cramp the style of aforesaid Lotharios-would-be.

Can't think of any more now except to beg you to:-

(a) write at once, I'm lonely and far from home and letters take some time to get here
(b) get Lewiss's to work on a really superb photo all for me.
(c) look after yourself.

Lots of Love,
Bill

P.S.   Please thank Pat-of-the-gnat-bitten-undercarriage for substituting on Thursday in the Canning shed or Torture Chamber. It was good of her to thus make our little Malvern Excursion possible. I know what, give her a long-range (though very brotherly) kiss for me.

Cheeroh. Bill

The medical students invited several of us to a midnight feast, but only Nan and Jean accepted .....

Sunday 6 September 1942

I woke up at 6 (Breakfast not until 9) and heard a rustling noise. I turned round and saw Jean fully dressed, packing. I turned the other way and saw Nan also fully dressed and packing. I said "What the dickens are you two up to?" Apparently they'd had the picnic in the bathroom as the rooms downstairs were occupied; someone had come in and found them, and they were being sent home.

8/9/42

Officers Mess,
No. 9. A.F.U., R.A.F.,
Errol
Perth.

To a Lady of <u>Distinction</u>
(what a <u>credit</u> to her Papa and Mamma)

My Dear Sweet Wench,
 Hey! You can't do this sort of thing. 5 Credits and A DISTINCTION, it's positively indecent. Do you realise I only got 5 credits and NO distinction in my S.C. No longer can I play the part of the superior male 'cos if I do all you've got to do is to fling "DISTINCTION" in my face. Anyhow, well done, I'm so glad the unofficial result your Mother 'phoned thro' has developed into such a good result. You will now rest on your laurels for a bit I suppose.
 Thanks for writing so soon after my letter, it's good to hear from you, though I was perturbed to see that you made no mention of that there fotygraf.
 What about the press photos you've had taken amidst the plums. Can you get me a copy of one of these as well? Please try.
 May I repeat my request for a curl from your fair head. I know you think it's a "mushy" idea, but I'm quite serious about it. Perhaps you could look upon it as a mere male idiosyncrasy (gosh I wonder about that spelling), which it would be best to humour, and then shrugging your

shoulders with an indulgent smile, carelessly pick up the scissors; and snip, the job is done.

Life here is quiet and comfortable. We fly Masters (fast monoplane trainers something like a Hurricane) and the famed torpedo carrying Swordfish, slow but sure.

Bill Warner, Peter Ball and I went to Edinburgh Sunday night and spent Monday there. It's a great city and the people seem very kind and hospitable.

Hell, you were strong willed about not mixing socially with the medical profession at Lower Wick. Do you know I must admit quite frankly that if a bunch of female medicos invited me to their tent at the midnight hour I think I'd have gone, though only out of curiosity of course - perhaps. So there's one up to you again, you seem to be beating me at everything. I suppose next summer you will be beating the very life out of me at Tennis.

I must endeavour to polish my dancing up a bit, I'd love to take you to a dance, would you come?

Please give my love to all at home. I hope to see more of you all during my next leave. Though heaven knows when that will be.

Don't forget the curls and photo(s).
Oodles of Lerve.
Bill.

PS   Thanks for kissing the flea-bitten, Pat - in a brotherly fashion of course. Cheerio.

By Thurs 10th September, the rest of us had also gone home. However, I had a shock when packing up to leave.

Not long after we'd arrived at camp, my school hymn book went missing. I hunted high and low, but couldn't find it.

When I rolled up my sleeping bag and raised the palliase to stack it with the others, there was my hymn book. However, I didn't bother to retrieve it, for a field mouse had not only pinched it, but torn it into shreds and made itself a cosy nest under my palliase!

Much as I like field mice, I was grateful I hadn't known I was sharing my bed with one.

Thursday 10 September 1942

After dinner the twins Peter and David, aged 12, called for me and we went to Clent. They're funny kids. David said "Are you in love with anyone?" I said "No." Peter said "Why David, are you thinking of proposing to her?" I said there was someone in love with me. David said "Has he proposed?" I said no, I was only 16. He said "Will he when you're older?" I said he might. He said "Will you accept him?" I said "No." He said "Why?"!

24/9/42

Royal Naval Air Station,
Crail,
Fife.

Dear Pat

I will beat you to it by enclosing a photo of myself. It's a shocking snap, but the only one I have, so it will have to do for the present until I have a studio portrait taken.

As you see I have changed my address since last I wrote, so if you intend writing to me - I shall be very 'snooty' if you don't - please use the above address. Oh: I should add "Officers' Mess" just to make sure of no delay in sorting this end.

We are very comfortable here; our first R.N. station since our joining course at Gosport. We inhabit "cabins" - "rooms" to a landlubber like yourself - two to a cabin containing 2 beds, 2 easy chairs, 1 writing table, 2 wardrobes, 3 chests of drawers, 1 h & c washbasin, 1 mirror,

339

polished linoleum floor, 1 mat, 1 shelf, 2 bed tables, shelf for toothbrushes and toilet requisites, 2 rollers for towels, 1 bell push, 2 windows with appropriate black-out blinds, 1 radiator (not working as yet, curse it) and 1 WREN batwoman. I might hasten to add that the last named is not a permanent feature of the cabin but makes fleeting appearances; one at 0715 hours to "up black-out", wake two sleepy and tousled subs., and clean their muddy shoes; and the other at black-out time just to black out and pull back bedspreads. After this she is not seen again until 0715 the next morning - more's the pity. These batwomen change about every 2 days and range from "pretty", through "passable" to pure (or mebbe impure) "punk". However variety is the spice of life.

The food is really excellent - we had jugged hare for dinner today, to quote an example - and we have a fine mess to eat it in.

I should have mentioned that I share a room with Bill Warner, though unfortunately we are in different watches and he flies one day whilst I'm at lectures, then the next day positions are reversed; also he gets a different afternoon off.

The flying training is interesting but is going to be much more difficult than my previous training so if I "make it" I shall be pleased but surprised, if I fail I shall still fly for a living (in all probability) but shall be relegated to 2nd line stuff - "stooge flying" as it is known in the service - you know, ferrying, target towing etc.

I am waiting anxiously to hear all about your recent adventures.

My regards to your folks and now to bath and bed.

Lots of Love from Bill.

Sunday 27 September 1942

In the afternoon Joan and I went to Bill's house to fetch my stockings - oh boy! They're great.

Tuesday 29 September 1942

Have been looking thro' the Autumn part of my 1941 diary. It seems strange that this is my life. Before the war I never dreamed it possible for my life to work out like it is. As I have said before, at night time I sometimes wish I were a child again. Not because I dislike my age - far from it - I think it is a wonderful age to be in normal times - but to relive those pre-war days. All those that one loved and liked were always around. One could do as one pleased - no disillusionment - those were the days. I often imagined what it would be like when I became 16. Not like this .

Friday 2 October 1942

I have played Tchaikovsky's 5th Symphony this evening. I think it is the most beautiful piece of music I know. Mother, Grandma and I agree it is infinitely sad. It makes me think of infinite space and clouds floating in it - somewhere just on the border of heaven and earth - something half of this life and half of the next.

I had started at Art School on Tuesday September 15, and made friends with a girl called Pam. I found the senior students very 'arty'.
I was so accustomed to being with young men five years older than me, and not of my own age, that it was perfectly natural to me to seek out the company of the older male students (who were nevertheless younger than I was used to consorting with) - this was understandably resented by the older female students, and after a fortnight I comment in my diary, 'Peter G. and the 2nd year girls are even more snooty'.

Wednesday 7 October 1942

At lunch time Pam and I had lunch with Bandy's crowd (the architecture students). Gave him the painting book with a purple and a pink ribbon round it. He licked his finger and dipped it in Horsy's tea and wiped it over the picture and luvly colors came!

We also had dinner with their lot. Afterwards Duncan was annoyed and I had to put him right, told him about 'platonic friendship'. But I'm afraid he wants more than that.

Eden (the model) was a blasted nuisance. Wouldn't keep still for 5 minutes together.

Had tea with Duncan's crowd. The 2nd year students were foul to Pam, Duncan and me.

Sunday 18 October 1942

In the afternoon Joan, Bandy, Pam, Duncan and Vivian came round and we all went to Clent. It was rather a nice day, and we had quite fun. Bandy was rather morose but it turned out later that he thought Vivian and I were engaged!

Duncan confided in Vivian that he was disappointed in me because my principles were too strict, and altogether we had a very nice time!

I received a letter from Vivian:-

Northfield

26.10.42

Dear Pat,

I enclose the official invitation for your A-Secretaryship. I should be glad to receive a <u>written</u> reply as soon as possible.

May I suggest that once again you accompany me to the flicks, next Saturday, this time not the "bobs" *(ie 1/- seats)* at the Warley? Seven flicks of a 'phone dial (the right ones) will get me, to hear your hoped for acceptance.

If it is not inconvenient for you or your parents I should like to collect my records one day this week to dodge the weekend bus-crush [try saying that quickly].

All the best.
<u>Vivian</u>

THE QUINTIPLE ALLIANCE

Chairman's Residence:-
Northfield.

26.10.42

Dear Madam,

At a meeting of three of the officers of this alliance, a pre-war Quorum, and later by signed assents, it was agreed by Regulation E8, assented to by Mr Brian Morgan, Mr W. Bagge and the undersigned, that you; Miss H.P. Knight, Hostess to the Alliance, should be invited to accept the position of 'Acting Secretary'; owing to the prolonged absence of the Secretary, Mr D.F. Knight. I believe that he would have wished you to accept this position.

I should be glad to receive your answer as soon as possible.

The position is reviewable under Regn E7, at the Cessation of Hostilities, and carries with it all the rights of an officer, so long as the position is held.

Hoping to receive your reply at an early date,
I remain
Yours Sincerely
Vivian Morgan
[Chairman]

Miss H.P. Knight

                                             3 & 5 CROSBIE ROAD
                                             HARBORNE

Dear Mr Chairman,
   I wish to thank you and the two other members of the Quintuple Alliance concerned for the honor of requesting that I become Acting Secretary of the Quintuple Alliance.
   I very much regret that I possess no qualities equal to those of the Secretary, Mr D.F. Knight, but I shall do my utmost to follow in his steps.
   Thank you once more for your kindness in turning to me.
   Yours Sincerely
   H. Pat Knight,
   (Hostess)

Friday 30 October 1942

   Went to the concert with Bandy in the evening. Had 1/2 the Art School behind us.
   It was the Bournemouth Philharmonic and Mark Hamburg.

   I, and many other Art students, went to the Town Hall concerts twice a week. We were all fairly short of cash, and so went in the cheapest seats behind the orchestra. (The 'balance' was a little strange, the percussion being between us and the other instruments!)
   As time went by, and we realized what the older, more experienced students were doing, we followed their example, going outside 'for a breath of air' during the interval and reappearing in the expensive seats we had noted as unoccupied during the first half of the concert!

Saturday 31 October 1942

In the afternoon Vivian came round and we went to the Royalty to see "The Man who came to dinner."

Viv had his pocket picked in town. His wallet containing £7:10 was lifted. Mother rang up grandma who sent him £1. And Mother and Dad left a cheque for the rest on the table for when we came back from the flics.

I got myself a job helping out at a Day Nursery (for the children of women doing war work) in the evenings.

Tuesday 3 November 1942

Went to Art School. I went to the Day Nursery in the evening. Liked it very much. Bathed one or two babies. Fed 7 at once! Put them to bed.

Wednesday 4 November 1942

I met Vivian outside the Paramount and we saw "Salute John Citizen." He has had his hair cut for the R.A.F. and it doesn't suit him a bit.

Thursday 5 November 1942

Vivian went to Cardington. He is now in the R.A.F.

Sunday 8 November 1942

Washed up etc. In the afternoon Chris and I went for a walk.

In the evening I wrote to the Matron at the Birmingham Children's Hospital and posted it. As I heard the letter drop in the box I felt as though it was the sealing of my fate.

Letters now began to arrive from Vivian. As Acting Secretary of the Q.A. I was requested from time to time to help the boys keep in touch with each other and to pass on any news I might have of them.

Cardington
<u>9.11.42</u>

Dear Pat,

    Just a note to let you know I haven't forgotten you. We are not allowed to receive letters here so please don't write. You can bet that when I can receive them I shall ask you to write so get out your exercisers and limber up for a long letter. I'll write again soon anyway

    Did you see the 'Warsaw Concerto' on Sunday? It reminded me very much of that weekend when we played it at your house and also of Dennis. You know it's strange how it should remind me of him when it was composed so long after he went.

    My love to the Art School.

<u>Vivian</u>

26 Squad 17 Flight
F Squadron
2 Wing 11 R.C
RAF SKEGNESS
LINCOLNSHIRE.

Sat. <u>14.11.42</u>

Dear Pat,

    Above I've put my new address and so by now I live <u>only</u> for a reply from you (I know, I can hear your cynical laugh). When you do write please put the address <u>exactly</u> as written. I'm in civvy billets exactly as that boy used to be at Taylors, but we are not allowed to have any mail except to the above address. The people are quite OK and so far we've done very little except listen to lectures and drill, the latter in the streets. This morning however we were vaccinated and inoculated and were given Sat afternoon and Sunday to recover. It's now 5.30 and my arm is rather sore. We had 3 chaps in our squad of 30 men alone, who passed out while waiting [I was not one of them].

Life at Cardington was not too good, we seemed to spend our time queuing up for things and have managed to collect a whole pile of stuff.

We were confined to camp until we entrained for here last Thursday, but I went to the Cinema and saw "Icecapades" and to a camp dance on the Monday till 12.0. Other nights we had to be in hut at 9.30 pm.

Food was rough but not too bad, the methods of serving and eating, 10 to a table, decidedly substandard.

Here in Skegness we have several NAAFIs, and we go up there most nights.

I think the majority of your art students (male or female) would benefit considerably from a week at Cardington.

There's nothing else to say so please write back soon, not like the way you do to Bill.

"Your ever devoted fiancé"
Vivian

15th November 1942. Bristol.

Dear Pat,

Please forgive me for being such a long time in answering your last letter, please don't copy me in this disgraceful habit.

In another month I should with any luck be granted the privilege of a week's leave and my mouth waters at the thought of it. I shall then have time to visit both Bristol and Birmingham and earnestly hope you will be home then, and that you will allow me to monopolise you for a day or two.

I am very sorry to have to tell you that poor Bill Warner was killed on Thursday last a few hours before he was due to go on leave. He was flying his very last flight of the course at Crail, which adds to the terrible poignancy of it all. He was seen to stall from a climbing turn above the sea at about 90 ft. and dived in. The 'plane floated half-submerged for a minute or so but sank before a boat could reach the spot.

He shared a cabin with me at Crail and we were to have continued this happy partnership at Arbroath but for this futile tragedy.

A Picture Post cameraman took photos of our mob a few weeks back and they should be featured about Christmas time, so keep an occasional eye on P.P. Thanks for getting Vivian to write his party piece. These new friends of yours seem to be just the affected pseudo-normal creatures that I had rather feared. However it is something that you can see this. Fancy a guy having no sense of humour. Perhaps you've tried the wrong technique on him. Get Vivian to recite "There was a young lady of Gloster" and sundry others from the filthy depths of his inexhaustible repertoire.

I wish I'd joined up a year before I actually did. I might then be in on this N. Africa shambles, as it is it looks as though all the fun will be over before our mob get into action.

Although in the words of a current American song we shall still have to "Slap the dirty little Jap".

In one month I hope to be seeing you.

My love to your Mother and Father. Looking forward to hearing from you.

Buckets of Love,
Cheerio
Bill.

Bill is on the right

Sunday 22 November 1942

In the morning went for a walk with the twins, Peter and David. There was a very heavy frost. We went to have a look at the guns at Bartley Green - (California). They rolled in the frost in their suits and then we found a tree that the soldiers had been erecting scaling ladders against and also a rope hung down. We naturally climbed and swung about.

Arbroath.

7/12/42.

Hallo Pat here I am again,

Just a hurried note to ask you not to try and get a ticket plus partner for the dance as they are postponing this confounded trip and if in the end they don't cancel it I may not arrive until late on Saturday.

On the other hand if they cancel the whole issue I should arrive in Brum Friday morning.

If this happens and it will not be convenient for me to stay Friday at your house drop me a p.c. by return. If it will be O.K. don't bother to write. My visit to Brum will be short and in that time I have one or 2 people to say hallo to, so while you are out with the foursome on Saturday I would like to visit said folk if your Mother gives permission as Executive Commander of No 5.

If I reach Brum Friday I should like to take you into town during the afternoon (or morning) so will you make that a date if not already booked-up.

I will let you know by p.c. when I'm coming. Sorry to be such a nuisance.

Love to Everyone,
Cheerio
<u>Bill</u>.

P.S. I hope the gramophone is in working order.

Wednesday 9 December 1942

In the afternoon went to King Edwards to receive my S.C*. I was positively terrified, and when I sat down again I had to put my feet on the chair in front of me to stop them shaking.
School Certificate

RAF Skegness
9.12.42

Dear Pat.

Many thanks for your belated letter. As you say they are not too frequent and I'm afraid that for once I cannot allow your sweet personality to override my personal feelings on the matter of your excuse. Naturally I want a letter from you straight away, they are the only bright spots in my bleak existence, each day I watch the post eagerly and most days - no letter from Pat - my spirits fall, I fall out of step when marching and fall into a very chasm of despair - (my theme song is "Falling for you"). Naturally however falling into my usual sweet temper when receiving a letter from you I have already forgiven you.

Your second para. re Brian has been read and noted - I shall as Chairman have to send Brian one of my modern feminine underwear curt notes - very brief.

Turning the page your next paragraph filled me with utter dismay. To think that while I am stuck up here you will be under the baleful influence of that beer drinking boy Bill. My heart's in my boots. After such pure love as I have tried so very hard to show you, you spurn me and turn to HIM of all people. Maledictions on the mouldy man.

Your next paras on your fickle filanderings in the usual female manner have reduced me to facial foamings and utter unbounded heartbreak - still I bet you enjoyed yourself.

Yes, you <u>must</u> be really careful next weekend with Bill - or him with you. And you must after he has been at Sea introduce him to the Art School - he'll be all at sea then.

Then to see you sign yourself 'your fickle fiancée' and to deny the bitter word, well - you must send me a photo of yourself as a combined

Xmas and Birthday present for 1942-99, so that I can practice black magic and stick pins in it when you are especially fickle. Still I would like one - as one of my special friends.

While Bill is at your place perhaps I could 'phone you some evening between say 8.45 and 9.15, say on Sunday. Please write and let me know if it will be OK.

It's now 1.35 and I'm due on parade at 2.00 pm and as you can see by the brown at the top of the page this is my last sheet of paper.

Don't forget all my points, please write soon and <u>MIND</u>, BE CAREFUL.

Your HEARTBROKEN* Fiancé
<u>Vivian</u>

* Yes really. * Really???!!!!!

<u>P.S</u> Please excuse pencil

Thursday 10 December 1942

Was doing fig. comp. *(at Art School)* when Wilf breezed in and said there was someone to see me downstairs. Knowing W. I took it with a spadeful of salt, and was not a bit surprised when 1/2 way downstairs he said "Actually there's no-one to see you really". Damn the little devil! I got hold of him by the scruff of his neck and practically booted him all the way down. Then he said there was a phone call. Then he said perhaps there wasn't and so on. In the end I borrowed 2d from Bandy and phoned home - Then I had it! Bill had come on leave unexpectedly!

He turned up at tea time; and I summoned up as much self-control as I could find and escorted him into the canteen. - Gosh! did he create a sensation? I managed to get Phil and John to sit with us and Pam, but Bandy gave us a very icy shoulder.

Joyce's heart beat a little faster I imagine when she 'happened' to meet us 5 times in less than 10 mins!

In the evening we went to The Paramount to see "My Gal Sal".

Friday 11 December 1942

Bill and I went to the Midland to see Micky. Tom was there and "Bluey" and Wilf *(NOT 'Art School' Wilf!)* turned up later. We all went into the American Bar and I had a shandy - but he gave me a <u>pint</u>! I got thru it in the end, but only just.

Saturday 12 December 1942

In the morning Bill went visiting friends while I made some pastry.

After dinner we dashed off to Bournbrook to see Wilf get married. Bill and I then started walking to his house for the reception, but the party had stopped somewhere to have photos taken and we got there about 15 mins too early when only the maid was there. So we had to mess around till they turned up plus about 2 doz. Fleet Air Arm boys! A young New Zealander tried to "get off" with me much to Bill's amusement. We tried to go but people kept supplying us with chairs, food, sherry etc. but in the end we made it.

In the evening we went to a dance at Moseley with Mick and Sheila and Audrey. Of course in the refreshment interval Bill <u>would</u> have to trip down a step and spill his tea over the dance-floor! A young man with a head like a bull came with some flour and sprinkled it on the patch and scraped it around with his feet, every now and then throwing back his head and glaring 1st at a couple near him, then at us.

Mick, Bill and I went home in a taxi.

Sunday 13 December 1942

Stayed in bed owing to husky throat and temperature. In the afternoon Bill sat with me tho' I'd rather he hadn't.

Monday 14 December 1942

My temp. was 99.4 and I felt lousy but Mother said as it was Bill's last day I had better make an effort - who said that mothers know best? I felt rotten and was delighted when he went (looking very handsome, I must admit) so I could go to bed.

My temp. had soared by then to 101.8. so no wonder!

Dr Winfield came.

Wednesday 16 December 1942

Dr Winfield came.

A telegram came for Bill telling him to rejoin his ship on 27th but we don't know his address and he was supposed to answer the tel. immediately.

Thursday 17 December 1942

Wrote my diary. Thought a lot of classic day dreams as usual, but as usual they are all either too heavy or too vague to put down here.

RAF Skegness

<u>19.12.42</u>

Dear Pat,

I am still waiting to hear from you and hereby tender my apologies for not being able to phone on Sunday but there was a delay on the line. Thanks also for the telegram which was delivered to me on parade by the sergeant who hoped "it wasn't twins". By the way I'll accept the kisses on my first leave.

I enclose a small gift for Xmas accompanied by lashings of love and oodles of osculations. I'd wanted to get a Record token but nobody stocks them in this god-forsaken hole and only one person stocks book tokens.

Yesterday we had our second inoculation and hence today my arm is very stiff and so I feel "not too hot".

Our training continues as usual and we hope to leave this place on 31st Dec or 7 Jan, but continue to write here please. We get 3 days off at Xmas until 2359 hrs and if wanted a pass up to 20 miles, not that it's any good to us as even Boston is 23 miles.

There's little other news so with Best Wishes for Xmas and the new year to you, your parents and your grandmother.

    Yours with
    Basins of Benedictions
    <u>Vivian</u>

P.S   Don't make a pig of yourself at Xmas.

Skegness

19.12.42
Afternoon

Dear Pat,

    I have just collected your letter when we reported. We were then dismissed as we all said we felt bad. However a lot of us are going to the YMCA for a cuppa tea.

    Sorry to hear you were in bed and I couldn't visit you in all your glory. Nevertheless, light of my life, believe me I suffer with you (due to "inoc") [Latest Bulletin - very stiff and sore.]

    Bad luck Bill being called back on 27th of all days - still he has at least had the pleasure of seeing you. <u>Note</u> since when has your bed had such funny shaped feet or are they your own?

    Hoping to hear soon that you are better. My salaams to your mother.

    Ladles of Love
    <u>Vivian</u>

Wednesday 23 December 1942

    Doctor W. came. Said I could go out. He also gave me a severe talking to and informed me that if I wasn't more careful at the age of 45 I should be a heart case.

    Mother and I went to town and called in at the Hospitality Bureau to see if there were any soldiers wanting a home for Christmas. I wore my dark blue culottes with fringed hem, check shirt and neckerchief. The woman in charge said we could have Pilot Officers, and they turned up at tea time. The one was a Canadian, 'Stew' (pronounced Stu), dark, blue eyes, a bit taller than me. The other was a Californian, fair, over 6 ft., very good looking - his name- 'Danny'.

    Dad was awfully surprised when he came home.

    I washed my hair.

Thursday - Christmas Eve 1942

Danny, Stew and I went to town where we met Pam.

Danny, who sat by me on the bus, just couldn't believe the Birmingham accents he heard were 'normal' for Birmingham! He has a very attractive habit of pushing his cap up from his forehead - and a mischievous grin. He's 25, but doesn't seem like it.

After lunch I came home while they went to the pictures. In the evening they and Dad swapped tales. Danny had been in the army in the Philippines and they attacked a native fortress and found it deserted. So they presumed the natives had got scared. They returned to their camp and found it burned to the ground! Danny had joined the army to get into West Point where he went later, but left after a while because he hated, and disapproved of, the 'Hazing' that went on all the time; a sort of constant sadistic disciplining (at its best). He had subsequently joined the Canadian Air Force.

At about 10.30 we heard carols being sung outside the front door. Dad got up to give them 6d but refused one Stew offered him and wasted some time looking for one. In the end he took one of mine off the mantelpiece. When he opened the door he found it was some of the neighbours including Mr Vernon who was dressed as Father Xmas. Dad gave him the 6d.

They all came in and "Father Xmas" started stroking my cheeks and tickling me under the chin, much to the intense amusement of the two twerps! He then started to put the 6d in my breast pocket saying he didn't want it. Was I embarrassed!

Friday - Christmas Day 1942

The church bells rang. We went out into the garden, but Danny shivered and hugged himself, saying, "Brisk, isn't it!" He found the English winter terribly cold.

In the morning Danny (the collar of his long R.A.F. greatcoat turned up against the winter's chill), Stew and I walked to the King's Head where we had a drink. It was very nice there. People were singing and there was holly and mistletoe all over the place. Then we walked back and called in at the Old House at Home. That was quite nice too. Had a super dinner when we got home.*

In the afternoon we sat and talked. Later in the afternoon we went to the Warley to see The Fleet's In. Called at the pub opp. walked to the Court Oak and called in there. It was crammed with people singing and dancing - came out pretty quickly.

Walked home between Danny and Stew. My stony heart seems to be melting slightly in the warmth of California!

*Had turkey (!), Christmas pudding etc., and an iced cake for tea. The result of collections for a year

Saturday 26 - Boxing Day 1942

In the morning David *(the twin)* came round. He amused Stew and Danny very much. Saw him home. Had pork for dinner.

Didn't know what to do in the afternoon. So consulted and re-consulted the Birmingham Mail. In the end we had tea and went to town to the News Theatre. Afterwards we went to the Hope & Anchor which was practically deserted. Then we went across to the Town Hall to the dance. Had a few quick-steps with Stew. Then went out and had a smoke with Danny before going back in and having a couple of waltzes with him.

We came out and went to the Hope & Anchor. They'd just sold out. So we went to The Woodman - it was awful! Crammed full of tight people.

Sunday 27 December 1942

Got up late. Didn't do anything particular in the morning. In the afternoon we wasted up to tea time wondering what to do and ringing up various girls to see if they'd come. In the end Joan came. Went to The Royalty to see Come Live With Me. Single seats only. Stew wanted to take them which amused Danny very much. Got seats together and went in. Danny and I were together. So were Stew and Joan, but miles away!

Afterwards Stew went to see Joan home and Danny and I were supposed to wait for him in The Duke of York. We thought we'd have a long wait so decided to go for a walk first, so we walked across to St. Peter's church and started to walk over the Hillyfields along the path from the churchyard, when we suddenly stopped and he took me in his arms and kissed me! I had never before felt like I did then, sort of warm and happy and belonging. And then, at that moment, big flakes of snow began to fall. It was wonderful! I'll never forget it.

Monday 28 December 1942

In the morning Danny and Stew decided to meet Singleton another P.O.. They said they'd be back about tea-time. They were back long before, and asked mother and me if we'd like to play cards. They taught us a game called "Hearts".

After tea we got out the poor old newspaper and consulted the amusements. Then I rang up Chris and persuaded her to come to The Warley with us to see "The Young Mr Pitt".

We all came home and then later on saw Chris home. Chris and Stew walked in front, Danny and I behind. We had to keep moving to avoid suspicion from those in front, but somehow we managed a 'goodnight' walking along.

Her parents asked us in and gave the twerps some drinks. Then we came home.

Tuesday 29 December 1942

After breakfast I went into the lounge. Danny was there. He kissed me and said he'd wanted to say a lot of things the night before but hadn't had the chance.

Stew came down with his luggage and Danny fetched his, and we set out. On the bus Danny gave me his Observer's wing - to remember my 'brother'. The train came in early and I said goodbye to Stew and then differently to Danny. But the train didn't go so Danny said 'goodbye' again and got in, but it still didn't go, so he came and stood in the door till the whistle blew and then the guard came to slam the door but he couldn't - because Danny and I were saying goodbye for the third time!

The train moved out and I went to The Kardomah and had some coffee. I then wandered round bookshops and got asked out to coffee by a university student who wanted a dictionary. I naturally didn't go, and bought a book for 10/6 I didn't want.

RAF Skegness
<u>31.12.42</u>

Dear Pat

Many thanks for your very newsy letter. I'm glad to hear you had a merry Xmas and only hope that the coming year will be as jolly. So you have been trying your wiles on someone from the New World, not satisfied with the many Englishmen you have prostrate at your feet - maybe.

As for the book token - 'nuff said.

We are leaving here most likely next Wed or Thursday and then if my course hasn't started well I shall be home for maybe 48 hrs. Anyway continue to write here until you hear from me. We have really finished our course here and are wasting our time now. Furthermore snow has fallen on the last two nights and so the roads are pretty messy.

By the way haven't I told you we're in private billets. Please don't waste sympathy on me, thinking I'm in a camp. The Christmas we had was very jolly - ten people here, two ducks and all the usual liquid and solid fare, so we did pretty well.

Sorry to hear that you are still fickle - I shall have to look into this when I get any leave.

Your faithful [maybe] fiancé
<u>Vivian</u>

I could fill this space with kisses and hence not waste paper - but I won't - <u>see</u>!

1943

Aged 16 ½

List of Illustrations

Page

397   Airgraph-actual size

416   Ray

Friday 8 January 1943

In the afternoon I went to the panto with the Art School. Sat between Phil and Bandy. Phil was taken up with his girlfriend. Bandy was feeling ill and I was thinking with disgust on the personnel of the School. Pretty poor panto - no silk stockings - no beauty - Afrique with a bad cold - fairies etc got stuck 1/2 way up stage on trapdoor etc.

In the evening went to The Warley with Mother and Dad. Saw Holiday Inn, quite good.

Saturday 9 January 1943

In the evening Vivian rang up to say he had 36 hrs leave and he was coming round.

Monday 11 January 1943

Started back at Art School. Went to see Dr Winfield in the morning. Said he thought it was my tonsils. Did a very good character drawing in the afternoon. In the evening went to see "Bambi" with Chris - very good. Wrote to Danny.

R.A.F. Farnborough,
Hants

<u>11.1.43</u>

Dear Pat

I got back about 11.00 pm on Sunday having caught the 5 pm from New St. We had a rotten journey, being packed like sardines and stopping at frequent intervals.

Since then we've done nothing except sit and smoke and listen to lectures this afternoon.

Please thank your mother very much for the lovely supper and thank yourself for the photo. You look almost beautiful and it certainly beats the 25 WAAFs. (I'll send too a P.O. for 6¾d to have your hats made bigger).

Weather here is lovely today, a bit better than Birmingham had to offer.

I greatly enjoyed my visit and hope to repeat it very soon.

I was told today by the sock-darning WAAF that she's been posted again - this time to Chester so I shall have to darn my own.

The course here which has just finished have all been posted overseas so that looks bright - considering that the maximum leave any of them have had since joining up is 36 hours.

We've a lovely fire in the billet so tonight I'm going to toast myself in front of it.

Here's hoping you're doing the same and not gallivanting about with some student or other.

Your Photographical to-be fiancé
<u>Vivian</u>

Thursday 14 January 1943

Lovely day. In the dinner hour Pam and I walked thru' the cathedral churchyard. We didn't want to go back to the Art School but wanted to go for a walk. We didn't, however. In the evening Vivian rang up to say he's on leave again! He then came round.

Friday 15 January 1943

In the morning Bill rang up to say he's on leave!

He arrived in time for dinner. Then Bill went to get hold of Viv. Came back and had tea and Vivian came later. Bill, Viv and I went to The Paramount to see "We'll Smile Again".

Viv missed the last bus so stayed the night too.

Saturday 16 January 1943

Mrs Bonehill was very amazed when she arrived and saw a Sub Lieut. and an airman sitting down with me to breakfast! Especially as not so long ago she arrived to find it was two P/Os!!!

Bill went to town to see his boss while I varnished my nails. Viv and I went to town and met Bill and went to Pattisons for dinner. Then we went to the Hope & Anchor and then to The Grand.

We got a bus to Swanshurst Lane and went to see the Hills where we had some hectic games of table tennis.

We went on to the Matthews where we had a very warm welcome from Mr and Mrs who told us - Barrie is home on leave too! He turned up in a very little while for he was visiting like us so his mother phoned him. Helped Mrs M get tea.

Afterwards we all went to see Smyths. Bob is thought to be near Madagascar. His mother showed us photos. He looks very fit and strong and apparently is having a good time with 1 or 2 Wrens!

Then we all went to a pub for a "snifter" that Bill had been hankering after for a long time. We decided to go to The Billesley. I got on the bus 1st, then Barrie who said he'd pay and as he was paying it was his privilege to sit by me.

Everyone stared in the Billesley at the army, and navy, the air force and me. When we came out Bill insisted on catching a bus but we walked.

Joan (Matthews) had arrived when we got back. She is going in the W.R.A.F. as is Betty Smyth. It turned out that Barrie, Viv and Teddy Bear are all within 2 miles of each other and B. and V. have arranged a meeting at The Queen's, Farnborough.

RAF FARNBOROUGH
21.1.43

Miss Knight,
Being once again at Farnboro' I take up my quill to indite a reply to your epistle of Sunday and Thursday - oh hell to it let's write properly.

Anyway I got back OK after being to School for a word with Langley - who by the way inquired after you - sorry I mean your parents - he's no sugar daddy.

Returning to your letter - I note you won't pour out your love for me. Why not, is it
   (a) Non existent
   (b) Too much to put on paper
(I fear the former is the one.)

Your remarks re my New Year's Eve 'tightness' are treated with the contempt they deserve.

Re your brown and g. dress, I've already commented but being a safe distance from you I could comment again but will refrain and only ask you a question which worries me considerably - does it assist you in your music? - I of course refer to swing music.

By the way a spelling lesson. Keep the following spelling please TEMPERAMENT - NOT TEMPREMENT!!!! and you an OE *(Old Edwardian)* tho admittedly a female one!

By the way in your last para. you drivel a lot about hearing or seeing that I'm unfaithful - how could you? And you sign yourself 'yours suspiciously'. Well -.

Anyway may I point out the following to you.
1. Be very careful.
2. .... of Yanks and Cannucks (Canadians)
   (I shall have to communicate with S/Lt WB).
3. Don't go climbing any more trees at night or if you do:-
   [a] Be careful who's your escort -
   [b] If wearing skirts be careful that there's no moon

Anyway with all that uncle-ish advice you should manage to survive as a pure innocent example of English womanhood (tho' --) until I can once again act as your guardian angel.

Lashings of Love
Vivian *

*   Note how <u>I</u> sign myself you stuck up little twerpess

RAF Farnboro'
<u>27.1.43</u>

Dear Pat,
Above is a mistake so I'll start again
Dear [Lovingly of course] Superior Being,

With reference to your <u>charming</u> letter of 25th, you note in your second para that you dislike my remarks re your spelling. I should like to point out two which come after this monstrous remark of yours.

<u>NOTE</u>   TUSSLE [<u>Not</u> tussel] and DELICACIES [not delicersies]

Yours Spellbound
<u>Vivian</u>

366

Now here's continuation of my first start. In future I should prefer less formal letters. After all haven't I known you since -- well I suppose I oughtn't to mention legs.

I promised some time ago to lend you a coupon to get a larger hat - it seems by your remarks about the extraordinary superiority of your brain -- well you TWERPESS.

Furthermore I'm glad to see you are at last honest about your cooking. You realise that you only "throw together a cup of hot chocolate" instead of treating it with the respect you should AND the care -

Evidently you are in a bad way for male escorts if you are reduced to a twin - and the worse half too. Anyway cheer up - I hope to be home 6 Feb. Please reserve that evening for me.

Last night I went to a gramophone recital. This was given in the Toc H at F--ro!

On Saturday I saw 'One of our Aircraft is missing' again and on Sunday 'The Lady Vanishes'.

Here's my timetable for this week so you can see how hard I work:-

6.30 Reveille   7.0 am Breakfast
7.50 On Parade 8.0-10.10 Class
We're doing negative making now. *(Viv was doing a photographic course in the R.A.F.)*
10.10-10.30 Break for tea and buns.
10.30-12.10 More Work.
12.10-1.10 Dinner
1.10-5.15 Work (3 days a week we stop at 4.15 and do
1 hrs. Field craft, games or PT).
5.15 Tea.
Then we're free till lights out at 10.15 tho' we can stay out till 11.30 except 1 in 4 when we're duty watch and C.C. (Confined to Camp) as I am tonight.

For all this I am paid precisely 3/- p. diem. Anyway the RAF motto 'per ardua ad astra' is true of this course, the heights (astra) is 1/6 extra p.d. "Trade pay".

Well it is now 9 pip emma. I <u>NEED</u> a cup of tea, at the NAAFI - there's a 6d hop on tonight which I shall ignore and creep into my hard bed.

Yours <u>very</u> faithfully <u>and</u> adoringly*

<u>Vivian</u>

*   Yes really!!!!!!!!?!!!?!!?!!

Please excuse smudges due to bad blotting paper.

Friday 29 January 1943

I had a letter from Vivian. Haven't had a letter from Danny yet. I have felt in a pretty murderous mood all the past week, and my language has shocked even myself. I think the lazy life at the Art School is getting me down. A heavy, lazy blanket seems to descend on my physical self, and I moon around while all the time my brain is active and seems to keep saying "You must do so and so". I seem to be all think and no do.

I think the Art School is good as a break, for it gives one time to think at the age when one needs time to think. Sometimes I'm so pleased with myself I'm sure I'm unbearable and, other times, I loathe myself so I wonder how on earth people stand me.

At the moment I loathe myself. I feel petty - Yes, that's just the word to describe how I feel. What'll I do?

The solution as far as I can see is this:- a) Danny must write <u>quick</u>, b) I must do home work - consisting of, I think:-
Art, sociology, philosophy, religion, history, possibly a little French or German and anatomy, physiology, science etc.

I think all young people around my age ought to make a short study of the first 5 in the above list.

Sunday 31 January 1943

I am sure I shall get no peace of mind till Danny writes again. The funny thing is I have no illusion about my feelings for him. I know all I feel is a definite attraction - but I <u>wish</u> he'd write. I feel terribly depressed because I have been very bored for the past fortnight and a letter from him would be like a tonic. I may say I have no illusions about him, but maybe I have - the wrong kind - that's what haunts me so - makes me dream and - yes! spoils my sleep. Maybe some unwitty wits would describe these as symptoms of - well of a different disease. What do I mean? Love?

R.N. AIR STATION,
ARBROATH,
ANGUS.

5/2/43.

Hallo Pat,

How's life. I hope you are not so "cheesed" with it as you were last time you wrote.

That was a clever racket you worked in order to get Beethoven's 5th, but I really think its success was due to the fact that you have really first class parents. Indeed I bet you wouldn't have been so awfully wicked if you had known that their hearts were not going to melt on your return with the expensive discs and sadly depleted school fees.

I have made a new comrade here called Sam Hodgkiss. A tip top bloke from Bolton. He was one of the first to join the R.A.F.V.R. before the war and did some of his flying at Castle Bromwich. He remembers Den delivering a brand new aircraft to their station near Manchester. He remembers the occasion well since it was the first all yellow trainer they'd ever seen and he was able to describe Dennis fairly accurately.

I received a letter from Viv today. He says he may be seeing you this week-end and promises to pass on my salaams to all at Nos 3 & 5. If he turns up and he doesn't, please be very rude to him.

Have you seen "Holiday Inn"? Don't miss Coward's epic "In Which We Serve."

That's all for now. Please write again as soon as you possibly can. Convey my kind regards to Mother and Father and Grandma. I hope you are all in the very best of health, and cheer up Pat it won't be long before you are doing what you have set your heart on.

    Best of luck,
    Cheerio,
    Lots of Love,
    <u>Bill</u>.

P.S. Once again WRITE SOON, in fact WRITE <u>NOW</u>. - or else .... and I ain't kiddin' sister.

Tuesday 9 February 1943

Since I last wrote my diary Vivian has been on 36 hrs leave. Danny has written and so has Bill.

My state of mind is better than when I last wrote, tho' I'm desperately anxious to do something. I would like to join the W.A.A.F.S. if I wasn't going in for nursing. I feel so darn useless at the Art School. I'll be glad when May comes and I can leave, and then when August comes and I can really do something. I'm tired so I can't philosophize tonight tho' I'd like to.

RAF Farnboro'
16.2.43

Dear Pat.

Many thanks for your letter received today. This answer is being written in class, the instructors left us to swot up for our test tomorrow, and as we've been at it for a day and a half we're rather bored and quite a lot are trying either to wreck the cameras or to write letters. This paper has been borrowed off my partner, for the latter purpose. Unfortunately the Instructors walk in on occasions and then - hey presto, the letters disappear. Like the old days at KES.

You term me a 'callous AC2' *(because he hadn't sent me a Valentine!)* but when I remark about your envelopes you say you're being patriotic. Well the reason why I didn't send you one is the same - paper saving, tho' of course I sent one in spirit if not in paper. And by the way no dirty cracks please about not writing on both sides of this paper; it's an impossibility with this quality paper.

I'm glad to hear that Bill has started to correct your spelling mistakes.

When I see you next, the real reason for my visit will be to hear B's 5th Symphony so don't break it before I've heard it please. .....

Thursday we had a good ENSA show in camp. Very good ventriloquist and two dancers who were excellent "swing" fans - just like 'Auntie Pat' does it.

On Sunday afternoon 3 of us went for a nice long walk thru some quite respectable country. Do you remember our picnic out at Chaddesley Corbett. Oh! happy days.

If you're specially worried about the Valentine, one of the chaps in my room had one sent him. I'll borrow it and send it if you like, but you'll have to return it!

I guess that's all now <u>except</u>, you forgot your usual ending. Are we no longer engaged?

Bags of Blandishments.
Vivian

(your "fiancé"!!)

Wednesday 17 February 1943

I've had the strangest adventure today that I ever hope to have. Pam and I were walking down Needless Alley when a soldier passed us and then came back and caught us up. He said 'I hope you won't think me rude if I congratulate you on your long hair! It really is the most beautiful head of hair I have ever seen!'

I'd nearly decided not to continue this, but on looking back thru' my diary I feel this should be a complete account of the development of mind of an adolescent thru' experience.

So tho' I deeply regret this incident and heartily wish it had never happened - yet I feel it may play an important part in the building of character.

Anyway, to continue:-

Pam and I had been fooling around all afternoon and so were feeling quite barmy and so it didn't seem as strange as it was. He then said "I suppose I couldn't see it down could I?"

Well, I wasn't sure what he meant, and thought perhaps he was a photographer or an artist in civvy street, so I said "Yes". He then asked me if I could take it down there! I said "No not possibly" and so we walked to find a hairdresser's. (He said he'd pay for me to have it shampooed.)

Then Pam, like a twerp, said she was late and hopped it, leaving me to the tender mercies of the soldier. Well, being Wednesday the hairdressers were shut, and after a fruitless search I said I'd better be running along. He asked me to have one more try, and I did, and it happened to be the restaurant next to Smiths. It was deserted and we went up to the ladies' room.

It was only then, when I took the pins out of my hair, that I realized what I was doing. Fifteen minutes previous to that I'd felt in a dare-devil crazy mood, and nothing would have surprised me as can be seen. But now, alone in an empty café with a polite but rather strange soldier who was crazy about my hair, the fun seemed to ooze away leaving me feeling rather scared and lonely.

He made me turn my back to him and sit on a chair while he gazed at my hair. I was facing a large mirror, so I could keep my eye on him. He started stroking it from the back of my neck, and I thought with a horrible shiver down my spine, of the stories of young girls strangled by strange soldiers in deserted places.

I swung round to pick up my coat and do my hair up again, and caught him in the act of pressing a strand of hair to his lips!

I was simply revolted, but then I did the first sensible thing that afternoon.

I asked the strange soldier to open the window onto the street and look at the clock outside, telling him I was afraid of being late for class.

This was true, but my main motive was to break his fixation on my hair and bring him back into the real world, but it was also so that if I needed to scream for help, people outside would hear me.

I did my hair quicker than I've ever done it before. My hands were shaking so I could hardly plait it, and I hoped he wouldn't notice them.

Then I rushed him down the stairs into the sunny, crowded street where I offered up a prayer of thanks to be safely back in the midst of busy normal life again. He went to catch his train and I went to college.

But that incident and the realization of my foolishness were to cause me many a sleepless night after. But I can look on it as valuable experience and realize I'm not so superbly level-headed as I thought - which is a useful thing to know!

Tuesday 23 February 1943

I was in the metal-work room in the afternoon when Wilf came in and said a P/O had been in to see me. Well, I'd been expecting Danny since his last letter had hinted at a leave on the next poss. opportunity so I asked Wilf to describe him. Well, the description was sufficient to make me realize he was only fooling and then he said it was a 'phone call from Mother. I couldn't get much out of him, so borrowed some money and 'phoned Mother.

Grandma answered and said there was a P/O there. I crossed my fingers and asked if it was Danny, but it wasn't. He was another from the hospitality bureau. I promised to go home straight-away and wished dismally that it had been Danny.

I went home.

Grandma answered the door and said Mother and the P/O were out together. At that moment the front door opened and in they walked.

I looked at the P/O whose name was Dick and quickly compared him with Danny. But comparisons were odious. Danny remained no 1. on the list.

Dick and I talked a bit, and all the time I was weighing him up. All that I'd definitely decided by tea-time was that he was physically my ideal. Tall, fair, good-looking – rather snub features, green eyes, nice teeth, broad shoulders, age 22 – but mentally I hadn't quite figured him out. We went to The Paramount to see "The Pied Piper", which was very good, and he struck me as being a bit fresh.

But that was as far as my deductions went.

FARNBORO'
24.2.43

Dear Pat,

Many thanks for your letter, or rather packet and for the fags. It was a great surprise but very nice and I <u>do</u> thank you.

So you have been in a state of depression lately. That sounds bad and I shall have to see what I can do about it when I come home on March 6th - the date you guessed right.

Joan and you have been reduced to climbing the Lickeys have you. Anne and I used to do a lot of that when she was on night-duty last spring.

You mention Bill and funnily enough I had a letter from him this afternoon. He seems pretty cheesed off and envies me being able to get to Brum. He's so badly cheesed off that he desires a good, solid peaceful job, a <u>wife</u> and a home of his own. Watch out Pat or you'll be Shanghai-ed - or as that's in Japanese hands should we use some other term.

Please remember when you're taking the Canadian skating that his country needs him and so don't let him break his neck.

Anne is coming home this weekend and I'd hoped to wangle a weekend but my luck was out.

Our course is progressing steadily. We are now on the third part which is Film Processing. The one we finished last week was on air-cameras and in the exam I managed to get 73%.

My birthday passed very quietly but I'm saving them all up for a celebration after the war. Gosh <u>that</u> will be a binge with all the things I have to celebrate.

I've not heard from Brian yet

I'm afraid this is a very scrappy letter with very little in it but perhaps you'll excuse that. By the way don't go making fatuous arrangements for Mar. 6th as I don't want to have to go round all the pubs and low cafés looking for you when I get to B'ham.

Keep Smiling,
"Yours adoringly"
<u>Vivian</u>

Thursday 25 February 1943

Went to the Art School. Came home to tea. In the evening Dick and I went skating. By that time I thought my weighing up operations were completed, and I decided that if he tried to kiss me - which I thought quite probable - I wouldn't let him - a) because Danny still rated no 1., b) because I thought he was a bit cock-sure and it would do him good.

He skated very well, with perfect ease and very fast. He reminded me rather of Dennis because, besides having rather the same looks, he had that rather "snooty" look Den sometimes used to have. He took me round quite a bit, but he went so fast he just about wore me out 1/2 way thru'!

I then began to wonder just how much I did like him, and when on the porch he kissed me good night, my resolution was forgotten!

Friday 26 February 1943

Had breakfast at a fairly early hour. Dick had his at about 11.00. We had dinner at 12.00! and then dashed to catch the train to Stratford. We just caught it by the skin of our teeth.

We had to change at Hatton - a quiet little station with 2 cats playing on the tracks. The connection was a diesel engine - rather fun!

The weather was grand. When we got to Stratford we went down to the river to get a boat, but apparently it's out of season. So we walked back to the Shakespeare Gallery and had a lovely tea at 2.30! They gave us a large glass bowl of apricot jam, a pile of hot, buttered toast and tea.

Then we walked down to, and along, the river. At the end of the tow-path was a low stile, and we sat there for quite a while. It was then that I realized my deductions about him being fresh were correct.

We walked back to a tea shop opp. the S. Gallery, and had another tea there at 6.00! It wasn't as nice as the 1st tho! We then walked to the station and wandered around wasting time till the train came at 7.30.

When we got into B'ham we went to The Hope & Anchor and then home. After we'd got off the bus we went for a bit of a walk and then to our house. And were we hungry?!

Saturday 27 February 1943

I wore my black skirt, pink angora jumper etc. Went to the station with Dick. Wilf was behind us on the bus whistling "The Yanks Are Coming"! I didn't know till he got off.

On the platform I knew I had fallen for Dick - I realize it was only infatuation for his looks and his outward qualities - his charm, his athletic ability, his humour - those things tho' I knew that really he was not nearly as deep or as good as - say Vivian.

Unfortunately Dick had taken Danny's place - how difficult it must be to really fall in love!

Sunday 28 February 1943

In the afternoon Joan and I went - or attempted to go - to The Paramount. We just couldn't get in. So caught the 1st bus that came along - a 9. and got off at the 1st cinema - The Danilo - It was closed!

So we walked thru' Quinton while I poured out my tangled thoughts to her (about Dick and Danny), it really seemed a big problem to me.

She wasn't really any help, but it was soothing to get it all off my chest. Came back to 5 Crosbie and found Danny had come up for the afternoon with 'Bud' Fisher! That was awful for Dick had only gone the day before and I just didn't know where I was.

I think Danny sensed something, for when we were on the bus going to town he asked me what Dick was like. Then, when we found he'd missed the last bus and the train wasn't for an hour and we had a chance to talk he said a lot of things which gave me the impression that he felt something in the air.

(I think he had realized how much difference there was in age between us, and perhaps tried to make me see it, too.)

He said, "I'm not innocent, you know."

Of course, I was, very, but Christine had obviously sensed that Danny and I were pretty fond of each other, and had said to me - only a few days before – "Someone of Danny's age will have 'had his moments'."

So, rather stupidly I explained that I realized that he was not 'innocent', as Christine had told me!

'Bud' and Joan seemed to get on pretty fast - and all the time I was trying to forget Dick and bring Danny back to no.1.

Went to The Hope & Anchor and had some very flat beer - at least they did - we had a very flat shandy. When we came out we turned right to go down the steps by the fountain. Danny and I were in front. 'Bud' and Joan just behind. I called out to Joan "Where are the steps" (it was pitch black). She replied "Oh, quite a bit further on." So Danny and I strode forward and promptly fell down the 1st flight of steps. We all yelped with laughter, and 'Bud' and Joan decided they'd better go first and then Bud immediately fell down the next flight!

Saw them struggling to get on a very crowded train and left them. I went round to Joan's and had some coffee. Caught the last bus home.

Tuesday 2 March 1943

Art School. Went home and found Stew had come on leave.

Wednesday 3 March 1943

Art School. In the afternoon Stew and I went skating. He wasn't as good as Dick tho' I imagine he plays very good ice-hockey. There were a lot of American soldiers there. They asked me to teach them to skate so I said I'd come with a Canadian and they'd better learn from him. Just then Stew went past and I beckoned him over - they didn't seem so keen on learning then!

In the evening Mother, Dad, Stew and I went to The Warley and saw 'Coastal Command' and 'Are Husbands Necessary?' Everything in C.C. was "bloody fine"!

Thursday 4 March 1943

Saw Stew off. Went to the Art School.

Farnboro'
4.3.43

Dear Pat,

Many thanks for your short letter and here's an even shorter reply. You certainly seem to be making a collection of RAFfish officers.

I shall be very glad to meet Danny and thank you for the priority.

I shall probably arrive chez-K. at about 5.30 or 6.30 or 7.30 pm, depending on which train I catch. Sorry not to be any more certain.

You haven't broken Mr Beethoven yet? I <u>should</u> like to hear it.

Yesterday we had another oral test. Not too bad. Went a nice long 10 mile tramp on Sunday. Lovely country and weather.

Last night saw 'Gt Mr Handel' and 'Bluebeard's 8th Wife.' Both very enjoyable. Picked up some good tips on cinema cuddling from ATS girl and a CANADIAN in the row in front. This is being written in class so please excuse hurry and writing.

Cheer-ho old girl,
Yours fiancéically
<u>Vivian</u>

Friday 5 March 1943

Went to the Art School. Came home and found that Danny was coming tonight instead of tomorrow.

He arrived very late.

Saturday 6 March 1943

Danny told me that he'd written me a long letter and put in the snaps we'd taken on his previous leave, and then he'd torn up the letter, forgetting the snaps were in it! I wonder what he'd said that he'd decided not to say after all?

We went to Bearwood in the morning. In the afternoon went to town. Queued up for 45 mins outside The Gaumont and then decided that if we went in then we might be late for when Vivian arrived so wandered around looking for a cable-office. We went to The Kardomah and had tea and then came home.

Viv didn't turn up till about 8.30 so we could have gone to the flics. Danny went for a walk when Viv arrived and then Viv and I went round the square to pick up an appetite for supper. Danny and Viv got on very well together. I think it was then that Bill phoned up to have a chat with me and Vivian. As Danny was there we put him on the phone for a chat with Bill as well.

Danny had quite a conversation with Bill, and then put the phone down with a puzzled expression.

"Is that some kind of English greeting?", he asked. "Pips! That means goodbye?"!

(We had been talking to Bill on a 'Trunk' call - ie long distance - and at the end of three minutes the 'pips' would sound. Bill obviously felt by this time that his phone call had cost him quite enough and decided to bring it to an end - not realising that Danny wouldn't have any idea of what he was talking about.)

Saw Viv to the bus-stop. He said he liked Danny very much, and later, in a letter said he'd like to have had him initiated into the Q.A.

Sunday 7 March 1943

In the morning the Home Guard had part of their exercise in our front garden and up and down our road. Dad arrived about 3.00 absolutely exhausted. He didn't hear when one spoke to him and his face was drawn and grey. Danny watched him with a very sympathetic look.

We went to get some cigarettes and outside he said "I think it's a bloody shame that your father has to go on H-G duty when he's working a 7-day week."

We went to Bartley Green and sat on a gate by the reservoir and talked. His grandparents had been German, but had emigrated to California. He has a sister who lives in Gentry Avenue, Hollywood. She's married to a documentary film editor. Danny and his sister are obviously very fond of each other. She's older than him. He talked a lot about California and Mexico and I think he was rather homesick. He said "I sometimes wonder if I shall ever see it all again."

We came back and had tea and then I went into town to see him off. The bus was absolutely packed but he got on all right.

I forgot the buses don't go into town at night any more and waited outside Smiths for about 30 mins. Then I remembered and dashed to the Town Hall. It was getting dark and I hate being in town alone in the blackout. Caught the bus O.K.

Saturday 13 March 1943

Dad's birthday. In the evening Chris and I went to Bartley Green. As usual talked about many things ranging from Dick, Danny and Gerald to Masefield and Beethoven.

My mind, which has been in a whirl ever since Dick arrived seems to be settling down somewhat. I'm glad Dick never wrote - it's far better like that than this 'unfinished business' sort of thing.

Heaven knows how I'll ever know when I'm in love or what he'll be like. Anyway I'm not quite 17 so I guess there's plenty of time to find out!

Sunday 14 March 1943

Chris and I decided to go to Clent in the afternoon so packed up tea and set out. We waited at the bus-stop for nearly 30 mins and the bus came - full up! Learned that the next bus wasn't till 30 mins later so caught a 9 into town and went to Snow Hill station.

Found that the next train was the 4.15 to Worcester so got a couple of tickets at 5/6 each.

There wasn't much time before the train pulled out, so in spite of the fact that Chris had other things she wanted to do we got in the train, only to find to her dismay that it wasn't a corridor train!

Anyway I consoled her with the fact that Worcester wasn't very far.

- Well, ...

That darned train went to Worcester all right, but not before it had called in at Handsworth, Smethwick, Oldbury, Old Hill, Kidderminster, Stourbridge, Droitwich and a few dozen other places.

Poor Chris was nearly bursting when the train pulled into Worcester - it had taken two hours!!

Just had time to wait in The Gaumont café for 30 mins and then find all we could have was a cup of tea, walk down to the river, ask the time of the train back and dash back to the station and catch it!

Luckily it was a corridor! We had to stand all the way and we ate our sandwiches just outside the you-know-what. Lovely day!

Anyway it was a reasonably fast train back.

1648831 etc
Farnboro'
14.3.43

Dear Pat,

You open your letter; for which of course, I thank you; with a condemnation of my previous one's shortness, but as you say, due to your abundant generosity towards your fellow MEN, I won't bite on that, you reply with 4 1/2 pages of letter and 3 P.Ss. Your excuse of course gives you material for almost a page and so of course you're really cheating! Just like a woman!

The niceness of your seeing me is only surpassed by the niceness of my seeing you again!

I really did like Danny - and if the QA were in a position to do so, I should really like to have him initiated as I expect Den, Bill and all the rest would.

I saw some of the folks our way returning from that exercise so by the look of them I can guess your father was pretty tired. Thank you for making my visit Priority 1 and not going to the Gaumont.

Hey! and why end up your letter as 'Your <u>Futile</u> fiancée'? Don't put airs on!

Well life has gone on much as usual here except that printing has driven us all nearly crazy and the language in the dark rooms has been something 'orrible.

The only flick I've seen was last night, and was Keep 'Em flying with Abbot & Costello - not bad. On Thursday we had an Ensa concert, a Variety Show that was quite good. One of the acts was a song about stirrup pumps sung by "Starving Verandah". You can guess in what style. *(Carmen Miranda - a very 'over the top' Latin American singer who would dress in extravagant Spanish dress with great confections of fruit as headresses.)*

From next Wednesday for a week I'm confined to camp being a Fire Picket (or Picquet). We've had some quite good fun practising with our 1/2 ton, 30 h.p. Trailer Pump.

Yesterday, I once again won our Billet Room Football Pool (8/-); my team - Chelsea, getting top score in the South League with 5 goals. I won it a fortnight ago with Reading.

Weather here's glorious - too good to be stuck in darkness all day.

I've just had my dinner and am writing this over a coffee in the NAAFI.

Did you hear the Forces Programme of songs about 12.10 to-day? They played 'Home Town' and more than half the blokes there were whistling or beating time with their K, F, or Ss - it sounded very jolly.

I was woken at 0730 this morning by Bill (Critchley) tickling my toes and thought for a minute that it was P.T and then realising that it was Sunday lay back with a sigh of contentment. This afternoon he and I are going to take a nice long walk and as its lovely weather we shall probably enjoy it.

I've not heard from Bill lately so I expect he's forgotten again.

I've just realised that it will be your Easter Holiday when I come home for my next 7 days. May I therefore look forward to another picnic bike ride with you? Couldn't we once again visit Chaddesley Corbett?

Well I guess that's all for now old sweetheart.

Yours devotedly

(Theme Song, Music and soft lights for 'My Devotion')

<u>Vivian</u>

Vivian enclosed the following note for Mother and both my grandmothers, as, presumably, I had written to him reprimanding him and telling him that they were upset by his calling me 'Twerpess'.

To   Mrs F.W. Knight,
        Mrs Knight (Senior)
        (and not to forget) Mrs Dawes:-

I wish to explain the non-nastiness of the word "twerp". May I remind you that in no circumstances would I use any word to, or to describe, your most charming daughter, or grand-daughter as the case may be, that had the slightest taint of the aforesaid "nastiness".

>Yours very respectfully and obediently
>Vivian M

OK Pat?

Monday 15 March 1943

>Lovely day. My sinuses didn't feel too good so stayed away from Art School.
>In the afternoon got on Salome *(my bike)* and cycled to Frankley. Sat on the railway bridge for about 30 mins. Then cycled on and on and got completely lost. Found myself within a circle of hills. Then I suddenly came upon the row of cottages I came to last year when I cycled to Bromsgrove.
>There were four little boys playing by the side of the road. I slowed down and asked them what they were playing at, they answered "buses". (They had a tiny red and green tricycle they were having turns on.) I stopped and got off. They were four healthy little animals - different from the three slum children I made friends with a few weeks back. They were about 5 years old, the youngest about 3 or 4.
>They soon wanted a ride on my bike so the brave one, John, climbed onto the saddle. He hung on while I pushed the bike slowly along. Then the others wanted turns, so one by one they climbed onto the pedals

(they tried, but couldn't, make the saddle) and I went round and round, up and down a little bit of the road just past the cottages.

Then I started to lift them onto the saddle.

(A young man tacked himself on at this point and I couldn't shake him off. I hinted broadly but it was useless. He said "Don't you get tired?"

I said "No, but that question could apply to you, you know."

He laughed and said "Do you mean my following you around?" I nodded and he laughed again and said "I could never get tired of that." In the end, as I couldn't shake him off I had to cycle home with him).

When I got a bit tired I laid my bike on the grass verge and sat down. Roy and John immediately wanted to pump my tyres. Then they all started turning the wheels and the pedals, putting the brakes on and off etc, and I think a good time was had by all.

After a short tussle with John while the other children resumed playing with the trike and messing around with my bike, I gave them rides again. A yellow line painted on the road was the bus stop. Most of the time John 2 would ride the trike behind while the other two "helped" me push one of them on Salome. Then, as I neared the yellow line they'd all dash to it and yell "Me next, me next."

And all the time this bloke sat on his bike and watched - however, most of the time I forgot he was there.

Then an old woman came out with a coat and muffler for John. She said she was John 2's grandmother and his father hadn't seen him since he was 6 weeks - or was it months? - old.

Then a thought struck me and I said "Didn't your son win a medal?" She beamed and said "Yes."

So I realized she was the woman who gave me the glass of water last year!

Came home, only took me just over 30 mins.

1648831 etc

<u>21.3.43</u>

Dear Pat,

Please excuse this letter but it will have to be short. You see I'm in a fearfully bindinsh part of the course with stacks of notes to write up and 'gen' on and having already got writers cramp badly -- There I knew a nice young lady (?) like yourself would excuse me.

Glad my note has done some good. By the way I hope to be up again on Saturday, so please don't vanish before then. At present (from last Wed to next) I'm confined to camp as I'm on fire picket.

With that fact and also that I believe it's the anniversary of Den's accident tomorrow I feel pretty miserable. I feel like punching a F/sgt's nose or something else daft.

So you pick up Munition Workers, eh? *(the young man on the bike)*. Gosh!!!! Re your suggestion of a longer bike ride - I'm your man to anywhere. If it's to be an Embarkation Leave at the end of this then I shall want to do quite a lot. Anyway it'll be 14 days so there'll be quite a lot of time.

I've read 'Knight without Armour' but prefer J.H's "Lost Horizon" and "Mr Chips". Ever tried those?

What a life. Feeling runs high here at the moment about dubbined shoes. We've had to put dubbin on them tho' so far I've not done my best pair.

Sorry old girl but the only other things I have to say are:-

(1)   Went a nice long walk last Sunday of about 7 miles. Very sunny weather and the only thing wrong was that we had two giggly ATS girls behind us most of the way.

There are two things you must not do in my presence if you're not to get a dirty look.

(a) Giggle.

(b) Say "salvage" - I'll explain that later, it's a relic of the Printing Class

(2)   Saw "Under the Red Robe".

Very good with Anna Lee and Conrad Veidt. Story by Stanley Weymen. Ever read it?

Tea is calling and my arm's nearly dropped off.

Yours painfully

<u>Vivian</u>

<u>PS</u>   Am I looking forward to next weekend or am I?

Farnboro'
1.4.43

Dear Pat,
I'm so sorry I haven't written before but as this letter will probably be very foolish, I thought I'd better write on this day of days.

The reason I haven't written before has two parts - (a) I'd unfortunately had very little time and (b) there's no news.

We had another exam on Tuesday, this time on our plumber's job - the Trailer. It was not too happy a do and we haven't had the marks. Now we're back on photographing subjects and printing. The 1st printing class as I probably told you, I loathe, but the instructors in this class are jolly decent. Consequently I'm quite happy having had about 50 prints accepted today. The Flight came and stood over me to set me on the right path and this helped me considerably. He's very helpful and a jolly decent chap.

As usual troops are not allowed to travel this Easter between 21st and 29th and so we don't know whether we shall be home for Easter or not.

However assuming that everything is OK, will you please decide where you want to go on our cycle trip. Would you ask your mother if I could please stay with you for a night and then we can go to a show after the run. All my arrangements so far are on the assumption that it's seven days I get and not an overseas posting - touch wood.

I saw "Big Shot" with Humphrey Bogart last night. Very gangsterish. Tonight we have a concert and dance in Camp to celebrate RAF's 25 Birthday. As I've missed tonight's post and it's about time I went to this show - I'll close for the present --

Saturday.

I'm sorry I haven't sent this before but of course out of your great kindness towards your fellow <u>MEN</u> you'll excuse me! It was very nice seeing you last Saturday and I wish I could again today. However 3 weeks today and I shall be on leave - whoopee.

Weather lovely here again.

The concert on Thursday wasn't too bad tho' one of the comedians was very blue indeed.

I'm confined to camp over the weekend but I thought I'd finish this off today and then you ought to get it on Monday and then of <u>course</u> you'll answer very quickly and I shall have another epistle in your sweet hand soon.

    Well it's time to go on parade so please excuse.
Wallops of wellwishes
<u>Vivian</u>

<u>12.4.43</u>

Dear Pat,

    Many thanks for your delayed tho' very welcome letter which arrived this morning. Sorry you couldn't get tickets for the 'Messiah'. I should have loved to have seen it, especially in <u>your</u> company. However we must see something else. By the way the BIG news came thru last Wednesday. I was told that I had been 'selected' for overseas duty and at the end of 14 days leave, starting 23 April and ending 6 May I have to report at No. 5. P.O.C. Blackpool - so I've 'had' it. You can bet that I want to make the most of my 14 days and so if the weather's good we'll have to make more than that one bike trip. I don't know where I'm going, somewhere on the face of this globe – tho' I wouldn't put it beyond them to send me to Mars. There are 12 of us going, and the party includes some of my best pals, tho Bill, my usual confederate has a home posting.

    Blimey you seem to be really galivanting these days - 6 flicks in 8 days <u>and</u> two RAF officers. *(The Hospitality Bureau had sent us two more officers on leave.)*

    Amongst the damage done by that high wind was that it blew in part of the wall of the NAFFI 'Quiet Room' which has only been open for a fortnight or so.

    The course is rising to a very crescendo and we have our last class test tomorrow. On Wed we start our Final Exam after which Bill and I are going to spend a weekend in London - most of Sunday at Kew Gardens, as Bill is like myself a wild rockgarden enthusiast.

    We had an ENSA variety concert last Thursday which was quite good and this Thurs we have two plays by the Pilgrim Players.

    By the way in the future when you are writing DO NOT post letters here after 20 April 1943. Any after that date should be addressed to Northfield.

You can guess that all I'm looking forward to now is that 14 days. My head's still going round after 8 hours of gearwheels and things today so please excuse me.

Your frantically feverish fiancé
<u>Vivian</u>

Sunday 18 April 1943

Since I last wrote my diary two more Canadians have been and gone - Dick, very tall, fair and conceited, and Barny, not very tall, dark and quite a decent bloke.

Today is quite nice - at the moment it is only 12.25, and the weather may improve. It is quite warm, with a blue sky, but rather too many clouds which keep covering the sun.

David (the twin) is coming round this afternoon, and Danny may turn up. I shall have to stay in in case he does - I had to yesterday. It has been lovely weather for the past 3 or 4 days - really quite summery. About 10 days ago we had a terrific gale - it was described as 'of hurricane force' on the radio.

The garden is looking very pretty, all the blossom is out, and forget-me-nots, aubretia, rock rhododendrons, marigolds, Siberian wallflowers, daffodils, narcissi, grape hyacinths, saxiphrage are all in full bloom - apple blossom, bluebells and azaleas are all beginning to come out.

Well, dinner is ready and it's pork!

David came round in the afternoon. While I was getting tea the front door bell rang, and when I answered it, there was Danny with his navigator! He's a nice fellow, tall, dark hair, blue eyes - quiet, rather tenor type of voice - refined type - he doesn't drink or smoke very much.

He is accompanying Danny here next week. Went to see them off - the bus was in. Danny found he had no cigarettes, and George had none either, so Danny asked what time the bus went. A man there said 7.30. The time then was 7.05. So George said he'd hold a couple of seats while Danny went to get some cigarettes. We wandered around all over the place and at last got some. The time was 7.15.

Hared back to the bus stop, and found the bus had gone! The <u>last</u> bus went at 7.30 - anyway Danny caught that, but he had to stand.

BARBIZON PLAZA HOTEL
101 west 58th street ... central park south ... new york

RNVR
18th April 1943

Hallo Pat, darling,

How's life? Everything under control I hope.

I was so sorry I was unable to slip up to Harborne to say goodbye to you all. The whole thing came like a bolt out of the blue and left me gasping. The only people I did manage to say goodbye to were my grandparents in St. Albans.

Be a dear and write to me at H.M.S. Goshawk, c/o G.P.O. London as soon as you can and then your letter will probably be waiting in the rack when I arrive on this ship.

At the moment I'm living like a millionaire in New York's skyscraper hotel - at Admiralty expense.

Gosh you'd enjoy this amazing city Pat, with its beautiful shops, choc-a-bloc with lovely dresses, stockings, handbags, hats and scores of things to captivate the female eye. And the restaurants, why every fourth shop seems to be a restaurant, big or small. All clean places serving a wide variety of food from halibut steak to roast turkey. The streets and avenues simply teem with gaily coloured taxies - as you probably know the Avenues run from north to south and the streets cross the avenues at right angles and are numbered consecutively from No. 1 Street to about No. 250 St. So if one has an elementary knowledge of co-ordinate geometry finding one's way from A to B is all too easy.

I shall be glad to move on though and get down - or rather up - to some work for a change; it's over a month since I flew last.

Every room in this hotel has its own radio set on which one can get 3 stations only. But the programmes stink. All sponsored stuff and even the news is brought to us by the courtesy of Carters Little Liver Pills, or Hudsons Wonder Bread. The B.B.C. has the whole issue beaten to a "frazzle".

A city of plenty is New York and it's damnable being here without money - we could only take £10 out of G.B. However I expect to come back to U.S.A. before returning home and hope I will have enough cash then to buy a few stockings for you and Mrs Knight. Would lipstick be of any use to you? Just write a big YES in your letter if so, since as you know by bitter experience, the censor doesn't like solicited gifts.

Well Pat let me know all the local news. How is Vivian, have you seen him lately? When I write to him I will write c/o you - Q.A. secretary - as he may have moved from his Farnborough address by the time a letter could reach him from here.

I have placed your polyfoto on the desk and so every time I'm stuck for material I gaze at you for inspiration. I do hope the polyfoto people have finished the one which was originally for me. And thus enabled you to replace the one your Mother gave me.

Please give my love to Mother and Father and tell them how sorry I am that I was unable to come up and say cheerio to you all. However when I do get back I shall make a point of spending part of my leave in Brum. I do hope there will be room for 1 well behaved (?) "Subby" in Harborne's homely hotel - 3 & 5 Crosbie Rd.

That's all. I will write again from H.M.S. Goshawk in answer to the letter(s?) from you which will be awaiting me there, no doubt, (or else ....) Please be reasonably good.

Look after your sweet self.
Love - oodles of it,
from Bill.

Farnboro'
19.4.43

Dear Pat,

Many thanks for your letter of Sat and may I repeat your opening, "whoopee, the Messiah's coming back". I'd love to come.

I've spent last weekend in London with my pal Bill, staying at the Union Jack club. On Sat night we saw "Arsenic and Old Lace" at the Strand and we spent most of yesterday at Kew Gardens. It was lovely with beds of tulips and pansies and double cherries in flower and the rock garden - the weather was boiling hot and altogether it was a wonderful weekend. I'm writing this during school time. I've just had my oral exam and am now completely finished - boy it's a wonderful feeling.

My leave starts on 21st and so I may ring you up about 9.30 on Wed. It lasts until 6 May and then yo-ho-ho for the boat. I hope this weather continues for my leave - oh! bags of joy.

Yours very happily and lazily
Vivian

"That which is to be loved long must be loved with Reason rather than with Passion." Dr Johnson.

Monday 3 May 1943

I have much to write up in my diary. Tonight I have just seen Vivian off from his embarkation leave - he still has 2 more days, but he's not coming round here again. We had been to see the Messiah - Joan came too. It was lovely - I have marked the bits I liked in the programme.

Danny came on leave on Tuesday night. The first part of his leave, which he'd spent in London, had been pretty rotten.

We didn't really do much, only went to one show, but it was fun. There is something about Danny that I have never come across before, something that attracts me while I don't quite know why. When he's around, why, the sun is shining, but when he isn't it pours with rain - that's what I mean.

Another thing I like is that he has principles and that's the 1st time I've discovered such things in a man - excepting, perhaps, Vivian. We talked a bit about religion. He's a Lutheran, because of his German background. He's interested in philosophy of Oriental religions - Yogi etc.. I have lent him Monkey (by Wu Ch'eng-en).

Thursday 6 May 1943

It's a lovely evening - very cold, but a pretty sky. Blue, with one pale orange streaky cloud stretched across it.

I'm sitting at the desk in my room. When I'm alone in my room in the twilight I usually start to philosophise and moon on the days of my youth - my childhood, that is. There is some definite quality present in the early stage of life that is lost gradually with adolescence, Is it innocence? Probably mainly, but there is something else. Something that makes the little things seem important. Pleasant or unpleasant.

I know I shall never again feel as I did at first sight of the sea - climbing up the Valley of the Ravens chewing a banana - putting pennies in the machines on the pier - oh, some of the loveliest sensations I have lost! I have different ones now to make up for the loss, but somehow they're not as simple and ecstatic - silly, isn't it?

And yet Wordsworth expresses exactly what I feel in his "Intimations of Immortality from Recollections of early Childhood".

57 Squad.
No 1. Wing
No 5 P.O.C.
Blackpool
<u>LANCS</u>
<u>7.5.43</u>

My dear Pat,

Just a few lines to let you know my address tho' how long I shall be here I haven't the foggiest notion. Life's quite OK here and the civvy billet I'm in is very nice. The landlady comes from Bristol.

Please thank your parents - and of course yourself, for the marvellous time you gave me on leave.

Eight of our gang from F-- are billeted on the same house and the other 4 are next door but one. We sleep two or three to a room and are very comfortable. The meals too are good.

Tell your mother that the plant she gave me looked OK when I left.

I have just discovered that one of the chaps at F-- is a fellow rock garden enthusiast. It seems funny that you can know a chap for 3 months and not discover a thing like that in that time.

I'm afraid there's little else to write about as so little happens, only to say that if I'm still here on 20th I hope to see the Swan Lake Ballet by the Sadler's Wells folk.

Benedictions and Best Wishes
Yours almost nautically
<u>Vivian</u>

Wednesday 19 May 1943   My birthday, age 17

Vivian and Bill both wrote, saying that they had arrived at their different destinations, but, at first, I had no idea where they were.

Vivian, his training as a photographic technician completed, was now following the British Army across North Africa, and, eventually, up the length of Italy.

Bill was still continuing his lengthy training as a Fleet Air Arm pilot, and his first letter confused me completely. Referring to 'Pukha Sahib', 'Empire Builder', and an Indian market woman, I understandably, but wrongly, assumed that he was in India.

> H.M.S. Goshawk
> c/o G.P0.
> LONDON.
> 25/5/43

Hallo Pat,

Have arrived at far flung Empire outpost and am already becoming quite the little Pukka Sahib. So far have not gone down with malaria, dysentery or anything exciting like that; in fact have not even had a mosquito bite yet (touching wood like mad) but there's plenty of time left yet. Am gradually getting used to the insect life here. I no longer stand petrified with fear when I see an immense cockroach scurrying about my wardrobe, and no longer gaze with awe at moths as big as bats that flit across the room at shoulder level, or at locusts several inches long (like mammoth grasshoppers) with beautiful red and blue wings. I did think things were going a little too far the other day though when a bally great and hairy tarantula spider nipped out of a bunch of bananas my pal was buying, though it was smartly stabbed to death by the Indian woman store keeper. A better woman than I am, Bung it in!

A party of us spent a Sunday afternoon surf bathing at a tropical paradise - palm fringed beach absoballylutely as per Goldwyn Mayer - but will describe this in my next letter which shall be a much longer one than this. If you write to me, which you must at least once a month, can you afford to write <u>Air mail</u> as Sea mail is very slow, erratic and unreliable altogether.

Well, how are you all at No. 5? Please give my love and best wishes to Mr. and Mrs. Knight, it will be great seeing you all again though much time will have to pass before I shall once again, suitcase in hand, get off the 3A bus at your corner, bound for the best Service men's hotel in Brum. Well Pat your Malvern adventure draweth near. *(I wrote to Bill and Vivian, telling them that my nursing training was to start at the Preliminary Training School which, along with the Convalescent Home, had been evacuated to Malvern.)* I expect you're thrilled with the prospect, as hanging fire at the Art School must be pretty boring. Shall be most interested to hear how you make out there, do hope you don't keep going under with 'flu. Please remember me to Viv if you see him and tell him I shall write to him in the next few days, apologise to him for me for not having written before and give him my address and tell him to get cracking (<u>Air Mail</u>!!), I want all the gen about his recent misdeeds.

It is dark now and the insect and animal symphony is going full swing, crickets, frogs, toads, dogs and Lord knows what else grinding and croaking and whistling and barking away like fury. Then soon after midnight cockerels will crow - I can't tell you what for, if they are greeting the dawn in the usual traditional way they are very premature: perhaps they are patriotic and are greeting the English sunrise. That's all for now, please don't forget my insistence on air mail. Hope you are not becoming too Arty under the 'fluence of the Art School; are keeping in good health and intend to write me a book length's letter straight away - Air Mail! Salaams from Empire builder.

Love, Bill

Sunday 30 May 1943

Each month draws on, and the year is steadily slipping away. Since leaving school I know I have altered a terrific lot, and the alteration has on the whole accelerated since Christmas. I know, too, that I shall go on altering for quite a while yet. My ideas keep changing, and I am beginning to have a broad outlook, for my opinion is constantly changing.

Tonight Joan and I went to church. King Peter's chaplain read the lesson. He is very nice - he has a fine face, and wears a clipped black beard.

Yesterday morning Joan and I sold Alexander Roses from 12-2.30. In the afternoon we went to the gymkhana. Oh, while I was selling roses Peter came up and put 1/- in my box tho' he already had bought a rose. After talking for a while he suddenly said "Is is true that you're engaged?"!

I said "Good heavens no! Who am I supposed to be engaged to?"

He replied "Oh, some R.A.F. bloke."

I asked him where he'd got the idea from, and he said Chuck and a few other blokes had said so!

Tony came up later and took me for a drink.

One man came up to me and said "I can't resist you!" and bought a rose.

Altogether it was quite fun.

In the evening Joan and I went rowing on the reservoir. A lot of our planes went over later, and so we weren't surprised today to hear there had been a very heavy raid over Germany. During the night there was a pretty severe electric storm. I wondered how our returning planes would make out.

<u>No 1</u>   RAF
                      <u>c/o APO 4340</u>

My dear Pat,

This will probably be the last letter you will get from me for some time. Nevertheless I should be glad if you would do as I've asked you before, to continue to write even if you don't hear from me.

On my last night in Blackpool our landlord played us some of his records and one of them, Tchaikovsky's Piano Concerto reminded me of you and things we've done very much. That tune will always remind me of you. You know it's strange, but practically every tune I know reminds me of someone or something - and yours is the Piano Concerto and Den's is either the 'Barber' or 'Extase'. *('The Barber of Seville by Rossini, and 'Extase' by Vidor.)*

Did I tell you that I saw the Sadlers Wells Ballet at the Winter Gardens? They did the 'Birds' 'Quest' and 'Façade' and it was lovely.
Nothing else now.
Best of luck
Vivian

Letter No 2　　　　　　　　　　　　　　　　　　Royal Air Force
　　　　　　　　　　　　　　　　　　　　　　　　c/o APO 4340

My dear Pat,
　　Just a few more lines written 'en voyage'. The voyage so far has been unexciting from the action point of view, but extremely interesting. The change of color of the sea from brown, pure green, dark green with light green and white wash from the boat and the white capped waves, the clean sea air and the magnificent sky have been really wonderful.
　　Life on the ship, as on all troop carriers is very cramped and at times tempers have been rather frayed but we've managed O.K. Informal sing songs have been very enjoyable and the officers and NCOs in charge of us seem very decent. Apart from boat drill, fatigues and P.T there's little to do except sunbathe, sleep and read. The latter I've done a lot of and have found one or two good books either in the ship's library or amongst the Penguins sold at the Canteen. Amongst them 'Corduroy' by Adrian Bell, being a sort of diary of a chap who is apprenticed to a farmer. It's very light and from the point of view of us chaps rather nostalgic as it describes English farming life very well.
　　So far I have not been seasick, which has rather surprised me as I expected I should be. Some of the chaps have been rather ill. I'm still with my particular bunch of pals and hope to be as long as possible.
　　We get a ration of 20 cigarettes and either sweets or chocolate every day. Cigarettes at 20 for 8d (Players) and 20 for 6d Woodbines, which is one consolation. The ship is 'dry' and there is no beer sold to the troops, which is a good thing as anybody slightly canned would be an awful nuisance. Nevertheless the sight of one of your father's bottles of M&B or Davenports would be very pleasant.
　　Another disease which has attacked some is homesickness. I suppose we all get it to some degree or other but the best thing is to put it

out of your mind as much as possible. I should think that a combination of that and seasickness and the after effects of being inoculated for those whose 'inocs' weren't up to date; must be pretty 'berloody'.

That's about all for now, except to ask you to continue to write - they'll catch up with me someday. My regards to your 'family'.

     Yours 'nautically'
     Vivian

Letter No 3

                                             R.A.F. c/o RPO 4340

                                             31. May 1943

My dear Pat,

     Here are just a few lines to let you and your parents know I've arrived safe and well. It's boiling hot here, especially at noontide, but early morning and late evening are very nice, but it is very cool at night. Food here is good and plentiful. Passion fruit and cherries and tomatoes are in season and on the menu, besides lettuce and onions and NEW potatoes. We are under canvas and the lads go for dips in the sea. I wrote to mother asking her to let you know I was O.K. When you answer this will you please use an 'air-letter'. I get one a week which I shall use to send home but will airgraph* you regularly.

     Any news will be greatly appreciated. Heard anything of Brian or Bill yet? In between announcements on the camp 'Tannoy' they play dance records which gives the place rather a feeling of a fun fair. They're playing "Beguine the Beguine" as I write!

     I have had no mail as yet but am greatly looking forward to some. We use French money here - 200F to the £. There seem bags of eggs here at 3F each. Change from home eh? No more room now. Give my regards to your parents.

     Yours "desertedly & heatedly"
     Vivian

Letters were written on special 'airgraph' forms; they were microfilmed before being transported overseas, and on arrival were then enlarged to a just readable 3¾" x 5" format.

TO:-
MRS PATRICIA KNIGHT,
5 CROSBIE RD,
HARBORNE,
BIRMINGHAM. 17.
ENGLAND

135187

RAF CENSOR 197

Sender's Address: 1648831 A.C. MORGAN V.W.C., A9643, R.A.F. % APO 4340.
31. MAY 1943

My dear Pat,
Here are just a few lines to let you & your parents know I've arrived safe and well. It's being hot here, especially at noontide, but early morning and late evening are very nice, but it is very cool at night. Food here is good and plentiful. Passion fruit and cherries and tomatoes are in season and on the menu, besides lettuce and onions and NEW potatoes. We are under canvas and the lads go for dips in the sea. I wrote to mother asking her to let you know I was O.K. When you answer this will you please use an "airletter". I get one a week which I shall use to send home but with airgraph you regularly. Any news will be greatly appreciated. Heard anything of Brian or Bill yet? In between announcements on the camp 'Tannoy' they play dance records which gives the place rather a feeling of a fun fair. They're playing "Begone the Beguine" as I write!
I have had no mail as yet but am greatly looking forward to some. We use French money here — 200 F to the £. There seem bags of eggs here at 3F each. Change from home eh? No more room now. Give my regards to your parents.
Yours "devotedly & heatedly"
Vivian   Letter NR 3.

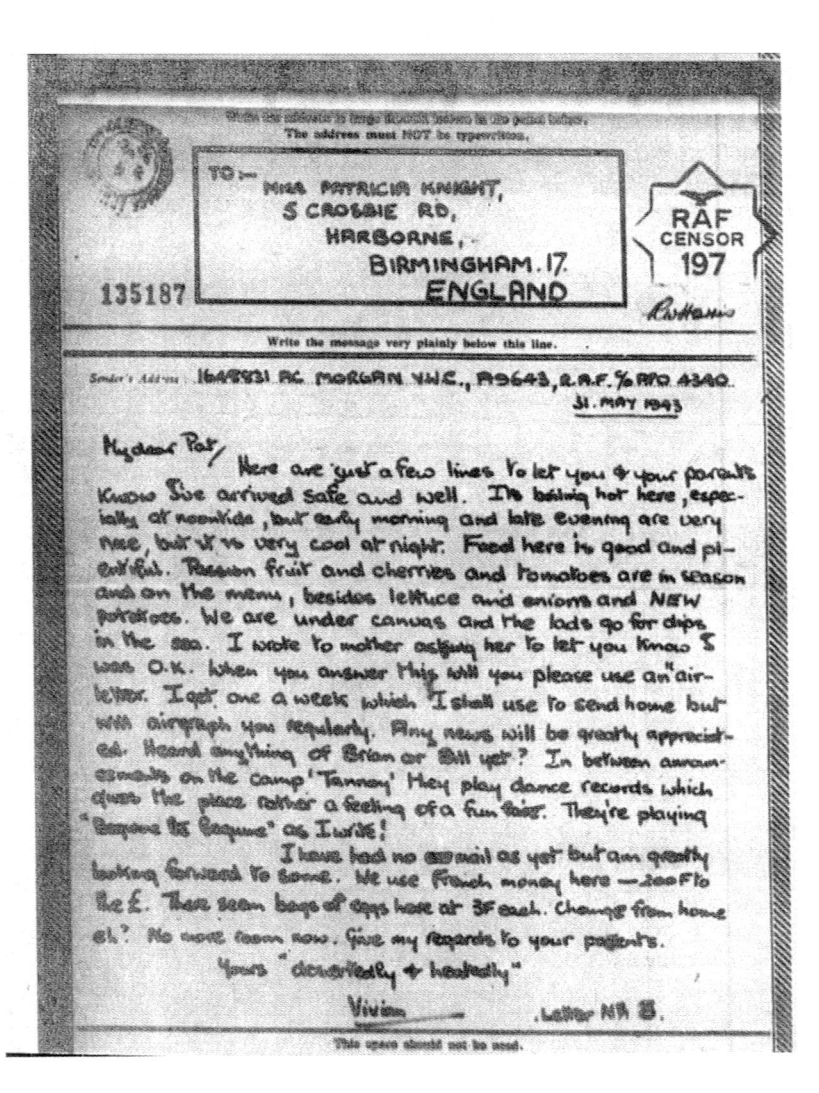

Airgraph actual size

8th/6/43

R.N.A.S.
Piarco
Trinidad
B.W.I.

Hallo Pat

Enjoying life? I hope there are some letters from your fair hand in the post somewhere. If not get cracking right away ..... or else -. I want to know all about you, how life has been treating you lately. What records have you bought, who the latest boy friend is, where you are going for a summer holiday before starting work at Malvern, any tit-bits of scandal, whether Chris and Gerald are married, separated, divorced or completely washed up, and so on and so on and so on - get the idea?

You would enjoy a stay here, mainly I think because everything is so very different from the type of surroundings we've been accustomed to all our lives - sorry makes us sound like old fogies. The natives are either Negroes, East Indians, or a mixture of both. They are of course imported stock, before their advent the Trinidanian natives were West Indians known as Carib. Whether or not there are any pure bred Caribs left I don't know but I don't think so, I suppose Carib blood has all been absorbed in with marriage with Negroes and Indians. They live mainly in primitive mud huts or ramshackle wooden shacks of all shapes and sizes, and all around their huts they plant banana trees, paw-paws, breadfruit, coconut palms, mangoes etc. And the Indians who usually live in the most primitive dwellings keep a cow in the back yard plus fowl and maybe an odd goat or so. This daily life seems to be a very happy go lucky affair, something after the style of Tortilla Flat, though now I come to think of it 'The Tuttles of Tahiti' with Charles Laughton is even more typical.

Have started to play tennis again for the first time in something like 3 years and am not too brilliant but hope to improve so that one of these fine days I can play off that long threatened match with you - no excuse accepted this time either. I also played in a cricket match the other day, but the cricket season unfortunately has nearly finished and can't expect to play again; worse luck.

Now that the novelty of living amongst hundreds of coloured folk and being surrounded by strange fauna and flora has worn off, and bananas, pineapples, grapefruit and rum (at 2 1/2d a tot) have become familiar and commonplace objects, I live only for the day when I shall leave here to more civilized (I hope) ports: as life is deadly dull and activities limited, besides which the war seems too far off and unreal. After all it's over 2 years ago since I applied to join the flying racket (Naval branch) and up to now have seen no action whatsoever. Would probably have seen more if I'd remained in the Home Guard, indeed I seem to spend most of my time running away to places thousands of miles from the nearest Hun, Jap or Wop, whilst you people at home have been dodging the odd bomb or so. Funny War isn't it.

Fortunately last night I discovered a new hobby which should keep me busy most days providing I can buy enough films, and this is photography from start to finish: by which I mean snapping, developing and printing my own pictures. The ultimate object being of course that I can come home and be a consummate bore. "I remember when I was in Trinidad in '43 - er pass me my photo album Vivian" – etc. Still joking aside, there are many interesting things and beautiful scenes to film here; and developing my own films is an accomplishment I've always wanted to learn, so - on with the Hobby.

Talking of Vivian, have you asked - nay, commanded rather - him to write to me. I will write to him through his home address. or better still thro' you in case his parents have moved.

How is the Crosbie Rd. Navy and Air Force Hostel progressing. Are the numbers so great that they still fight for admission in the road? Do your trans Atlantic friends still come to see you or have they been moved, or have you made new friends? Do include all gen of this sort in your letters.

Please convey my love and best wishes to Mr and Mrs Knight and Grandma. I have an idea that it is your birthday soon so will wish you all the very best on the "great day". Is it June 9th or 19th? *(It was, of course, May 19th.)*

      Will write again soon.
      Cheerio.
      Yours to a cinder (literally)
      Bill

Saturday 19 June 1943

Came back from Bath yesterday. It was wet and dull.

I had been to Melksham to visit Mr and Mrs Thatcher. It was lovely to see them again, but, as they were both working, I had quite a lot of time to myself, which I spent exploring Bath.

<u>Tuesday</u>. I went to Bath for the day. While I was waiting for the bus it began to rain, and I got my hair soaking wet. When I got to Bath I thought the first thing to do was dry my hair, so I went into The Parade Gardens and sat down.

My hair was very nearly dry when a small, just over middle-aged and very "retired cavalry officer hrmph!" type of man appeared just behind me. The deck chairs were all rather damp so he sat on a chair next but one to mine. I'd previously noticed a pool of water on the seat of that chair, so I moved my mac from the next one and suggested that he might find it a little dryer.

This started us talking, and we discussed music, composers, art, architecture etc. for nearly an hour.

He said he had been in the cavalry and showed me his horse (a snap!). He was now working at the Admiralty in Bath. He said he was sorry he had his nose to the grindstone or he would have liked to have shown me Bath. But was I glad! - he wanted to meet me for tea, but I managed to evade that quite tactfully.

As we were leaving the Parade Gardens he showed me a landscape he was going to paint - the river and the weir with a little of the bridge in the background.

After that I went to the Pump Room - where I wrote to Joan, and addressed a couple of letters to Vivian and Bill. Two soldiers came in, and one started to play the piano. He played very well, and I enjoyed it.

Then I went back to The Parade Gardens where there was now a band playing. Admission had now gone up to 6d so I leaned over the parapet and listened. An American soldier started talking to me, and then I went and had tea. There were quite a lot of American G.Is in Bath, many of them just sitting on the pavements (kerbstones to them, I suppose!)

<u>Thursday</u> was a lovely day. I cycled to Lacock where I met a W.A.A.F. We had tea together and then 2 hrs. later cycled back.

In late June Dad had his summer holidays, so we arranged to go to Llandudno (I had hoped Danny might manage to come too!)

Saturday 27 June 1943

Went to Llandudno. The taxi was late coming, so went on the bus. When we got to the station there was already an enormous crowd on the platform.

The train was due in at 8.20, but it didn't turn up till 9.40 - apparently there had been a train off the line between Coventry and Wolverhampton. Anyway, when it did pull in it was already packed. It looked absolutely hopeless. There was no corridor, and people were standing in the aisle between the seats. About 5 people got off, but the push and struggle was so terrific that they could hardly fight their way off the train.

We scooted down to the end of the train, and to our joy found a compartment with a free aisle. We leaped in, and shut the door. There were already 14 people in where it was only supposed to hold 12, so with us it made 17. Nearly 1/2 as many again!

Anyway the people in the compartment were very nice, and after we'd been on the journey for a while we began to take it in turns for sitting and standing.

I should think that, out of the enormous crowd waiting on the platform, only about 20 caught the train - I have never seen a train so full.

Going thru' the long tunnel was just absurd. Never has it seemed so long. The train just crawled along at just enough speed to make the difference between going at all, and stopping. One little boy in the compartment kept saying that we had stopped, and once he said "It's like being in an air-raid shelter" - we went over some points - "and that's bombs dropping".

Anyway, eventually we arrived at Llandudno. The weather had broken, and there wasn't a cloud in the sky.

We took our luggage to our hotel (which was in a lovely position; quite high, at the end of the Prom, and facing the whole of the bay - it was only just across the road to the end of the pier) and then went into the town and then back to the hotel, and had tea.

The lounge is quite big, and has a very nice verandah leading off it which faces directly over the bay.

After tea we went up The Great Orm.

I left Mother and Dad in the Happy Valley rock gardens, and climbed on up. I wandered over amongst some sheep barefoot (because the rock was slippery).

I looked inland, and saw the river Conway, Conway and the West Shore, and farther inland and a bit to the right of Conway, I could see misty mountain tops. It was lovely.

I transferred my gaze to the far end of the Orm, and saw two figures standing on the top. The sound of their voices carried easily across and sounded extremely 'Oxford'.

As I was picking my way I heard the voices again, and just as I got down a pile of rock two army lieutenants loomed up above me.

I carried on downwards, so did they, and then I discovered Mother and Dad lying under a rock by the path, reading. I sat down, and a little higher up so did the 2 lieuts. Anyway after a while we came on down and left them.

After dinner - which was very nice - we went up to the Happy Valley and watched a variety show from outside the enclosure - it's cheaper that way!

Sunday 28 June 1943

In the morning we went on the beach, and I bathed. There were a lot of jelly fish around. I swam along the shore to the diving tower, sat on it and got dry. The tide was going out, so I waded back!

After tea Mother and Dad decided they'd like to go to West Shore, but I thought I'd rather go up the Orm again. I climbed up and wandered around a bit.

I saw a grey ship far out in the bay. There were a lot of fishing boats around. Two of them were racing hell for leather toward the shore. I could hear a voice call out "Will you come alongside please", and one of the boats rowed to the ship's side.

I tried to take a snap of 2 lambs, and as I did so I heard the two voices I'd heard yesterday, and turning round I saw the officers. We started discussing the boats, and then we sat down and covered a good many subjects - art mainly. Then we walked - or rather scrambled - down the Orm and went back to the hotel. Outside we introduced ourselves. The elder was Arthur, and the younger David. Arthur invited me to dinner, and after David and I had hung around in the lounge for a while, while Arthur made a phone call and we waited for Mother and Dad - we went and had a meal.

The rest of the week was spent lying around on the beach, swimming, dashing off to Conway, and climbing the Little Orm.

H.Q.N.A.P.R.W. R.A.F.
B.N.A.F.
28.6.43

Letter No 5

My dear Pat,

    It seems as if once again I'd forgotten you and so please again accept my apologies. Yesterday was a red letter day as I received first mail which included one from you written on the 14 May. You can bet I was pleased. So you're now a 'second year veteran' eh, tho I suppose by the time you get this you'll be thinking of packing up to go to Malvern. You've certainly chosen a nice place to do your 'pro' training. When does Chris get married, where? Please give them my best wishes. Thanks also for the 'gen' on the D.K. Memorial Medals. It's a very good idea and is given for the right sort of effort. It means that there will be some permanent memorial to him. My other letters were from Anne and Bill Critchley & I haven't as yet heard from home. Still it looks as tho' mail is coming thru and we ought to get a more regular supply. Last Friday we had a film show in the open air in the camp. We are more comfortable in the tents now & have constructed beds & other "furniture" - our trade is now "photo-carpenters". My respects to your folks & best wishes to yourself (note the absence of <u>any</u> respect for you)

    Vivian

    Danny came on weekend leave. We had cold meat and salad and, as we were all about to sit down, he spotted a glass dish of home pickled walnuts, and with delight cried, "Gee, ahlives!" in his soft Californian accent and popped one into his mouth! Poor Danny!

    He and I went to the Hope & Anchor after trying to get in to the pictures. We had queued for ages. We were sitting drinking, me a shandy and Danny a beer, when he leaned forward with a grin and whispered for me to look at the table behind me. I turned, trying not to look too obvious, and at the table behind me were two American soldiers, deep in conversation. However, all the time one was surreptitiously pouring his beer down the other one's leg! He was completely unaware of what was being done to him!

R.A.F. B.N.A.F.
Letter No 6   6.7.43

Dear Pat,
    I have received another of your letters since last writing, it was the one dated 3rd of June in which you tell of your 'adventures' on the Reservoir. Mounting my little soap-box - as soon as my back is turned and you've got rid of your uncles to places like North Africa and New York (incidentally Bill's a lucky blighter isn't he?) you throw all restraint to the four winds and beef harmless blokes with boating oars. Having spent the last 5 or 6 years of my life trying to bring you up in the paths of righteousness, it comes as a hard knock to hear of such things. Sorry that despite your request for a long letter all you get is an airgraph but in the fullness of time I will attend to the other matter. The weather here is also lousy - far too hot. Somebody told me the other day that it was over 90 in the shade & this morning at 8 o'clock it was 77F - so only Lord knows what it will be at noon. If it wasn't for the breeze that blows most days it would be unbearable. Up to your usual beguiling efforts with flag days eh - I assume that the 'RAF bloke' spoken of is my own innocent self. I can see I shall have to change my letter endings before my name gets bandied about even more. I do remember the Gymkhana last year & believe I had the pleasure(?) of escorting you.
    Saw 'Priority Players' in the camp last week, but that & the fact that I received my first letters from mother on Sunday - are the only bits of excitement to report.
    Yours uncle-ishly - Vivian

Trinidad B.W.I.
7th July 1943

Hallo Pat
    Many thanks for your Air Mail letter posted June 12th in Melksham which took exactly 14 days to reach here. The other letter you say you have written has not turned up so far. I was, naturally, very surprised to learn that Viv had gone to the battle front so soon. Some people get all the luck. Your remark about my being in India was just a gag

I guess. Though if you held this mistaken idea the above address will correct your impression. You really are awfully vague Pat. You didn't mention whether you had left the Art School for good and all and were on a summer vac already; nor did you say one word about Malvern, whether you were still going there (and when) and if you were looking forward to same.

I'm afraid I've little to report about my 'goings on'. Day succeeds monotonous day in quick succession and all I do is eat, sleep, fly, read, and play innumerable games of snooker. Apart from these (in) - activities my sole hobby seems to consist of drinking large quantities of "coke", and anxiously scanning the letter rack for welcome mail. Still if things pan out as they should we have completed 1/3 of our stay here so may actually see some action before the new year is very much advanced. Please write again soon giving all the gen. Let me know if you've seen any decent "flicks" lately so that I can mark them down when and if they arrive on the camp. As soon as I have something interesting to report will write you a real letter in an envelope – won't that be nice. My love to your parents and Grandma if she is still with you. Don't go spilling any more tea down your "smashing" frock. Mebbe cocktails are more in your line. As for smoking - why even I have now given up this childish habit. Cheerio.

Lots of love. <u>Bill</u>

I had to be immunised against smallpox before going to the Children's Hospital.

My vaccination took quite badly and the glands under my arm came up, and for a while I had my arm in a sling.

As a 'last fling', before starting work, I went with some of my school friends to Stratford for the day. We hired a punt and got caught in the rain and tried to take cover under the punt cushions, which wasn't very effective. Later, by the river bank, we came across some apparatus for an army assault course, climbing up the rope nets and trying to scale the 'walls', which was pretty tricky with my arm in a sling!

R.A.F.   B.N.A.F.

20.7.43

Letter No 8

My dear Pat,

    Many thanks for your airgraph rec'd yesterday and your airletter received today. The airletter has come here very well, the best I have had yet. I was very sorry to hear that your vacc. had taken so badly, I know how ill they can make you feel, and I <u>do</u> hope that by now you are fully recovered, and gadding about as giddily as usual (despite the fact that you say you are living a "quiet" life). Glad you enjoyed yourself at Llandudno - in the usual Pat manner I suppose? Thank you also for Bill's address, I'll write to him one day. Next time you write to him (as I hope you are) please send him my address as my letter will probably take years to get there. I thought Barry would go in for something like the Commandos and am not terribly surprised. It certainly seems a long time since we were at his place - little did we think then that we should get spread out so much. Give my best wishes to Joan for her S.C* and I hope that you have every success at the Hospital. Keep on writing air letters please, they're much better.

    My regards to your parents, Good Hunting (or nursing)
    Vivian

*   *(Joan had failed her School Certificate and had to stay on at school to take it again.)*

Monday 26 July 1943

    Only a fortnight to go, and I'll be a nurse - 2 weeks today.

    I feel thrilled and yet a bit scared - it seems such a huge step to take – it'll be so different.

Tuesday 27 July 1943

    I've just glanced thru' my diary. I'm a terrific introvert* and yet I'm sort of impersonal. I sort of step out of myself, note my feelings and what I've been doing, and then write it down as tho' I were writing about a character I'd made up. Even now I seem to be looking over my shoulder watching what I write. Or rather, what my hand writes. I'm just watching to see what is being written.

I want to write a book - lots of books. I have the ideas for them, and skeletons of the plots, and I think I have the ability. But I definitely lack the self-confidence I need. Every time I write a few lines I think – "Oh, what's the use. I can't put it over." And yet I think I could do it.

I'm tired, I'm going to bed.

*   *(The word I meant was 'introspectionist')*

                                                                     R.A.F.   B.N.A.F.

Letter No. 9   28.7.43

My dear Pat,

A week having gone, I'm off again - have <u>you</u> written again yet, or are you once again slacking? On Saturday we had a RAF concert party give us a very fine show, considering there were only 8 of them - sketches, songs & instrumentalists - all of which I greatly enjoyed. I had a letter the other day from one of the boys, who came out with us, who was posted to Malta. He seems to like the place very much - I would rather like to go there, even if it was only 'cos Den was there. Weather's more unsettled lately & last week we had a short heavy shower which freshened the air up a lot. How are Danny & Stew getting on, as you never mention them?

All the very best.
Vivian

Monday 2 August 1943

A week today! I'm beginning to get things together, and get really excited.

Gran turns up today - grandma promised to be back before I go, but she won't. I wish Danny would come before I go, but I suppose I can't have everything. Still, I wish.

R.A.F. B.N.A.F.

Letter No. 10   3.8.43

My dear Pat,
   Very many thanks indeed for your Air Mail Letter of June 15. It was very nice of you to spend so much on it, but I am sorry to say that there is no air mail service to here except the 6d air letters and so it came by sea and only arrived today. A ten page letter was very nice and as usual, pretty crazy. Bill has certainly moved around hasn't he? I have written to him in Trinidad, tho Lord only knows when he'll get it. You seem to have enjoyed yourself in the Bath district. It was the 8th letter I have had from you, which makes you 2= in the "League of People who Write To Me" - mother is top. Sorry to hear about your arm hurting so much and hope it's really better now. Your latest adventure was in the usual Pat manner tho I'm beginning to believe that Joan helps alot - anyway don't go and do what Chris did at Clent*! Has she got married yet & how has Joan got on in the S.C? I don't know if I've answered all your queries about N. Africa, but if not let me know & I'll tell what I can. Hoping to hear again soon.
   All the very best - Vivian

(Chris of course met Gerald, to whom she was imminently to get married, at Clent.)

Sunday 8 August 1943

   Danny managed to come on leave after all. It was just for the day, but it was wonderful to see him.
   He and Dad went off to the Old House at Home to get some beer and were gone quite a time. When they came back and I asked them why they'd been so long, Danny teased me and said he and Dad had been picked up by two girls.
   Apparently he had bought Dad a drink at the bar and two girls started talking to them. Danny had kidded them that Dad was his Wing Commander, and when they doubted it he got Dad to show them his 'Wing Commander' lighter that Danny had given him – and they fell for it!
   The time went far too quickly, and after he had gone I felt there was so much we hadn't said. Perhaps next time.

Next day I left for the Preliminary Training School at Malvern. to start my training as a nurse)

The Preliminary Training School (P.T.S.) consists of the school itself, where we have lectures, do practical training and sleep in rooms of two, three or more student nurses. I am very lucky to be sharing with a girl called Betty, who I like very much. Her boyfriend, Freddie, who was in the R.A.F., was shot down a little while before she came here. He had given her a little rag doll which she treasures.

We can make ourselves hot drinks and cook eggs and things at the P.T.S. There is a kitchen where we practise invalid cookery, and there is a basement where the milk etc. is kept.

We eat our main meals up the road at the Nurses' Home. This is where the nurses working at the evacuated convalescent part of the B.C.H. live and eat.

Wednesday   5 Crosbie Road

My dear Pat

I was so glad to have your letter this morning. How nice it is that you like the girl you are sharing your room with so much, tell her we shall be delighted to see her during the week end. I shall probably put a bed up in your room, unless she would like the little front room, but I expect you would rather be together.

I am just about to write to Danny, but first I must find my own pen. I simply can't write with this.

We are looking forward ever so much to seeing you on Sat: - you and Betty, and shall be most awfully interested to hear just all about everything. I do hope you both will be happy and like your work. I am enclosing £1.10, for your books, and hope you got the ration book safely. I posted it directly I got home after seeing you off on Monday.

Until Sat.
Yours with love from all
Mother

Monday

5 Crosbie Road,

Aug: 16th 43

My dear Pat

    I hope you and Betty were able to get back easily and comfortably yesterday. I have done the little washing you left and when it is ironed and mended will post it on to you, probably Wed or Thursday. By the way I have fished out your school shoes and am having them repaired. They are <u>quite</u> the most comfortable shoes in Town I should think. If you will let me have your last new ones I will have them stretched and wear and wear and wear them and see if I can make them more comfortable, or if you like you can sell them at £2.5/- or whatever the price we gave for them. By the way talking about money, Dad and I have been discussing how much we think you ought to have a week, and we both agree on 10/- BUT, out of that you will have to save for your journeys home and teas out, etc: but I should have as many in the home as you can and so economise. And I will send you things from time to time, as much jam, marmalade, golden syrup etc as you like for I can always save those. Another thing Pat, is I don't think you ought to come home each week, both from the expense and the studying point of view, for you certainly don't want the other girls to get ahead of you. In fact I want you to get ahead of them, and of course 6/- a week would be terribly expensive just for fares, much as I love to see you, and I am sure you could have a decent week end with all the other girls and you could certainly get in some studying. After all it isn't very long before you are back in Birmingham. There were no letters for anyone this morning but unless I hear from you I will forward any that may come on to you.

    We were so pleased to see Betty, she is such a very nice girl, and very attractive too, don't you think. Let her know that we should always be very pleased to see her when she wants to come to B'ham. I must go, first to catch the post, and then to do my ironing.

    With all my love
    Mother

Monday 5 Crosbie Road,

My dear Pat
  Thank you very much for your letter and the chocolate but please don't send your rations again, eat them yourself. I had put some chocolate ready to send to you - some Kunzle ones, so I shall enclose them with your laundry which by the way arrived just in time to go in with the washing this morning. Don't ever mind sending it home. I don't mind doing it a scrap.
  Yes, Danny is bringing George so try and get Betty to come as well, you could all have a good time, do make her come, it would be so very much nicer, and she is so sweet. I really do hope she will come. I will probably send you a wire as soon as I know Danny really is getting his leave, but he has had so many disappointments lately.
  I am wondering whether you are coming home this week-end, will you let me know as soon as possible, if not I will make you a big cake and send it, but if you are coming I shall keep it for whilst you are here and you can take its remains back with you. When you write do tell me from whom the Air Mail was and how they are, and also how you think you are going to like your nursing profession. You seem to be settling down to a spot of studying.
  This is an awful scrawl but it is nearly 11 o'clock and I am ready for bed.
  I must go and pack up your laundry, Hoping to see you at the week-end.
    Lots of love
    Mother.

                                                  RNVR
                                                  Trinidad
                                                  B.W.I.
                                                  17/8/43

Pat darling,
  (Coo, what a forward young man to be sure). It's ages since I've written to you, I've been meaning to pen you a few lines for weeks now and yesterday the receipt of a long and amusing letter from you dated 26th

May (sea mail must be brought over on turtles) made me feel so guilty that I'm completely booted out of my slothful wickedness and writing to you feverishly like a madman.

I've now had 4 letters from you for which I'm very grateful and do hope you will keep on with the good work as suggested in your Airgraph letter, in spite of my poor response which I shall endeavour to improve. It's awfully discouraging writing letter after letter to someone who doesn't deign to reply, and takes a lot of good humoured patience. I'm anxious now to hear how hospital life suits you.

You know Pat I must have joined the wrong racket: there's old Viv and Brian both in or at least near the battle zone and Barry a paratrooper whilst I laze around in tropic sunshine and alas look like doing so for several months to come. However they also serve .... etc.

Well it's tomorrow (18/8/43) and yesterday evening I received an Air Letter dated 28th July in your fair hand which was written part in Brum, part in Bridgnorth.

To fight off boredom here I go to the flicks quite a lot, read a fairish bit, play poker, snooker and tennis, drink and sleep. Have seen some really first class films lately including 'Casablanca', 'Gone with the Wind' and 'Now Voyager'. Last night I was really enjoying Humphrey Bogart in 'It all came True' when the confounded electricity system failed and we had to abandon the film and go to bed in the dark, suspecting cockroaches, tarantulas and other fear producing insects in every dark corner.

The other day I was awakened from my afternoon siesta to find my next door neighbour holding a frog the size of a puppy dog (honestly! I'm not kidding) with another one on its back, a couple of inches from my nose - whow! did I move fast.

I hope you are getting some summer weather now, pity I can't lend you a couple of weeks of our weather; it is extremely pleasant being able to walk about in just shirt and shorts from 5 a.m to bed-time, quaffing large quantities of iced coca-cola, grapefruit juice etc etc.

As you remark things are certainly looking up though it's pretty galling to the operational pilots out here not to be 'in' on the Med. offensive or any other fighting for that matter. However enough of the old moan.

Well, adorable one, that's all this time, thanks a million for your letters; keep up the good work and let me know how you are enjoying your new job.

Please remember me to Mr. and Mrs. Knight, I hope you are all very fit.
Will write again soon.
Cheerio.
Lots of Love,
Bill

Letter No 12   R.A.F.
(You didn't number yours)   B.N.A.F
                                                                          19.8.43

My dear Pat,
Many thanks for your airletter of the 11th and apologies for not writing for so long, actually I was waiting for another letter from you before so doing. So at last you've started nursing. Should I address you as 'Nurse' now and bend gracefully from the waist (keeping the stomach well tucked in) or may I still call you Pat? I see that the sister has great sense and started off in the right way, and evidently they realise what a soft life you've been leading lately and have made you do some work - I wish I'd been there to watch! The wind seems to cause you a lot of trouble still, now it's your cap instead of your shorts. You seem to like your room mate OK, from your description she seems very nice – you'd better watch Bill the next time he comes to Malvern.

Locking you up at 8.30 hardly seems necessary and I know that up at Nottingham Anne was allowed out till 10.0, tho at the Woodlands she was not supposed to come out after 8.30 except on evenings off - tho nevertheless she used to come out and didn't tell me she wasn't supposed to until after she'd left there. She, by the way, is enjoying life still, has been on night duty since soon after I was on leave and goes yachting on the Trent with friends she met at TocH. Your time off on Sat and Sun will enable you to get home, won't it? I guess you'll enjoy that. By the way, when is Chris's marriage coming off?

One fact that may interest you that the security officer said we could write, was that I have visited Tunis. You see we're not allowed to say where we are, which is why you've never had any names before. Tunis is not a bad town, nothing much to buy except souvenirs, which seems to be what 90% of the shops live on. They sell 'controlled silver' rings, brooches etc. But having seen how the silver has come off a ring a pal of mine bought, I'm rather suspicious - and anyway they want 150-250 Fr for them and most of the stuff's not very well made.

There are a number of cinemas, showing English speaking films with French subtitling; an ENSA theatre and a NAFFI, YMCA etc.

There's not a terrible lot happened since I last wrote. I've seen one or two films every week. One of the boys is teaching me to swim. In a dry country like this perhaps bags of water is good for you, but it tastes foul!

I've had an AG from Teddy Gray who is in the M.E.F. Before joining them in Egypt he was at Durban, Bombay and Baghdad. His journey almost equals Bill's, from whom I've not heard. I wonder if he's still jealous of me or thinks that now I'm out of harms way?

Still very hot here and no rain and the flies seem to be an even worse pest that before – I've got umpteen flying and crawling all over me.

I've managed to borrow some books lately and have read 'Three men on the Bummel' and '3 men in a boat' by J K Jerome and also 'Steamboatmen' by Cuncliffe-Hyne. Please remember me to the 'Family' when next you see them. How did Joan do in S.C?

All the <u>very</u> best
<u>Vivian</u>

(The war brought people together as never before. The 'lady who lived at the top of the road' who had spoken to Mother of her admiration for Dennis and for Mother's and my cheerful mien, had remained friendly with Mother. So it was not particularly surprising when she suggested to Mother one day that her son Raymond, who was 25 and a Bomb Aimer in the R.A.F., should meet me; the idea being that when he came on leave he would have someone to go out with, with no strings attached.

And so, on his next leave, we were introduced and we went out together.)

Sat: 5 Crosbie Rd.

My dear Pat

Here are the promised shoes, they are American and so size 6 which it seems is equal to size 5 in an English shoe. I do so hope they will fit and be comfortable, but if not please send them back <u>without delay</u>, and tell me <u>where they are wrong</u>. I am sending you 10/-, and will refund the money for your telephone calls, probably send you 2/6 book of stamps or something like that. I am enclosing your Air graph mail, also a letter from Danny. Poor old Danny he does seem a bit 'browned off'. I will write to him again this week-end and will make some cakes for you and him, - only a few because of the fat and sugar. Raymond has just been in to see me, he is to go on Pathfinders, he also seemed a bit browned off, but only a bit. He wanted to know how you were getting along.

Christine and Gerald's invitation arrived yesterday. The wedding is to be on Sept. 15th at eleven o'clock, and is to take place at St Augustine's.

Just fancy some of the girls making off for home so soon. I wonder if you and Betty will see it right through. From your letter this morning it sounded as if you certainly had <u>quite</u> enough to do.

I am sending you one of Powels cakes to be going on with,
Lots of love, Mother

                                                               RAF Station
                                                               Upwood
                                                               Hunts.
25/8/43

Dear Pat

Tonight we are flying at 2 a.m, and as that means sitting up until zero hour I decided to write letters, and now having written to everybody I should write to I still have bags of time on my hands - hence the letter, hope you won't be too annoyed.

After leaving home I returned to Syerston to find that as I had surmised we were posted - but I was later shaken to find that we had been selected for the Pathfinder Force, it's supposed to be rather a compliment - but I'm afraid that we don't appreciate it - instead of having only twelve trips to finish I now have another twenty seven to do - besides which we shall henceforth be first over the target - all by ourselves - not a pleasant outlook - that of course may account for the shaky hands - which in turn account for the peculiarities in my writing.

As usual we took two or three days to leave Syerston - handing in various pieces of equipment and paying for losses - mostly the latter in my case.

On arrival at Upwood, we found that it was or is a training establishment - most annoying of course - we considered ourselves experienced - but P.F.F. have to prove their worth before embarking on ops.

Upwood is an irritating spot - like all training camps, we have to rise too early and make beds, sweep floors, clean buttons and boots, and generally deport ourselves like airmen - whereas on operational stations we usually look and live like tramps.

Oh! I nearly forgot - we had five days leave too! Life seems to be all leaves nowadays - the only trouble being what to do on them - this time I did absolutely nothing - just lounged about and got depressed and irritable, I think I was pleased to come back again - I think I nearly wore the carpets out with my constant wandering round the house in search of adventure - quite fruitless of course.

In about three or four days we shall be leaving here and joining our squadron at Wyton - our pilot tells us that he is due for seven days leave - I wonder if we too shall get it - and if so whether I can manage to wrest seven days amusement from B'ham - I doubt it very much.

Tell me, that is of course supposing that you decide to answer this epistle, how do you like your nursing and is the discipline as bad as you expected - do you really have to be in by eight o'clock etc.

Poor old Bruce *(their springer spaniel)* is ill again - the old trouble - he has strained his back and of course he can't walk - I do hope he'll recover - I don't quite know what we would do without him.

My flight engineer has just arrived in the billet - quite tight - all girlish giggles and staggering - how he'll fly tonight I don't know - probably be horribly airsick, and I sit down below and in front of him - most annoying.

Well it's almost supper time, so bye, bye.

Sincerely,

Ray

Danny and George came on leave to Harborne, and it was arranged that they would catch the train to Malvern when Betty and I were off duty and we'd all go out together. Betty, of course, hadn't met George.

We were looking forward to it so much, and rushed to finish our chores in time to get to the station to meet them.

The train came in, and my heart beat faster at the thought of seeing Danny again, and all the things I wanted to say to him.

But no tall familiar figures in R.C.A.F. uniform got off the train, and my heart sank.

We rushed to the nearest phone to find out what had happened:-

Sept 1st '43
Wednesday. 5 Crosbie Road,

My dear Pat

I am sending your laundry back tomorrow. I haven't yet had time to iron it, with Danny and George here. Oh, they were disappointed about yesterday. Danny said it was the one black spot of his leave. The taxi man wanted skinning alive, he was late coming, charged them 7/6, said their watch was fast, and just wouldn't hurry, with the result that they missed the train by about 2 mins. Danny kept on breaking out with it all evening, and George too was very upset. Danny kept saying how empty the house was without you, but all the same I am quite sure they really enjoyed their leave, and are hoping to come again in two or three weeks time, and then they say they will trust to no taxi, but will use the good old bus.

Danny thinks it is fine, the way you are sticking it at Malvern, he said you seemed much older when he saw you on Sunday. He really is a most lovable soul, and so is George too. I just loved having them, and am looking forward to them coming again. You will be pleased to hear we all took snaps of each other with George's camera and he is going to get them developed this week. I hope they will be good. I must end now, and write to them, they seemed quite depressed going back.

By the way it is Gran's birthday tomorrow Sept. 2nd. Can you phone or write to her. Please give my love to Betty and I hope you both are getting along alright.

Much love
Mother.

Sept 7th.   5 Crosbie Road,

My dear Pat

I am writing this amidst brick-ends, dust, and mortar, but I want to send you your pocket money for last week and this coming Friday, to last for next week, £1.0.0. to boot. At the moment it is very difficult to leave the house. The men keep either wanting cups of tea, or to know what to do, about something or other - the house is really indescribable but quite exciting. Though it looks as if with luck we may be straight by Christmas.

By the way DON'T forget to send Christine either a telegram or letter in time for next Wed. morning, and shall I give her the little silver tray from you, it is really very sweet. Write straight away and let me know and send a little note - here that I can put in with it. I have already given her the nightdress and she is <u>delighted</u>. For goodness sake DON'T forget, she would never get over it, and try and send a telegram, fix it Tuesday and ask them to deliver it about 11 o'clock Wednesday or 11.30.

  I want to catch the 4.30 post and only just have time hence the hurry.
> Hope everything is going well.
> All my love
> Mother

P.S.
Raymond was here yesterday asking about you. I am sure he wants you to write, he seemed rather depressed, and his mother said how much good you did him when you went out with him.

<u>Letter No 13</u>   <u>R.A.F.</u>
                                   <u>B.N.A.F</u>
                                     <u>4.9.43</u>

My dear Pat,
  Many thanks for your letter of the 22nd which, like most of the letters I've received lately, has taken longer than the usual time. Thank you for the compliment about writing regularly, tho this time I've done it, as I haven't written since 19th. You talk about having forgotten what you should have numbered it - if you take the numbers from and including the one addressed to the P.D.C, it should have been No 8; but if only from when you started to number them, then it's No 3.
  Something must have happened to Miss Knight if she decides to stay a weekend and do some work (?) - or hadn't she any dates at home? Knowing you I can bet there was some fun on that top floor, especially if you were in one of your mad moods. Your Sunday breakfast certainly sounded damn good and reminds me of the one Anne wrote and said she'd cooked for the Matron - grapefruit, bacon and egg, toast and marmalade and coffee! Anne, by the way still seems pretty happy, and has been acting as relief nurse lately. I had a letter from her on Wed which had taken 16 days. She, in it, cursed me for not writing and <u>I</u> did the same to her last week. Anne has a final 'e' to her name, by the way. Danny is still safe and

sound then - I wondered when he'd get his F/O *(he had been promoted)*. And you're still up to your old tricks are you, trying to get Betty and the Navigator 'tied up'.

My friends have come back from Malta and had some interesting things to tell me about the place. Another of our friends, whom we left behind when we landed, has joined us after touring over half N. Africa. Out of the 11 of us from the School who came here together, 8 of us are on this unit.

Brian has turned up in India after being at Durban, Bombay and Calcutta. He says he's in quite a nice spot but is bothered by hyenas, jackals, mosquitoes and crickets. He wrote an AG to my home which mother copied out in her last letter. I've written to him and also to Barrie to find out where he is now. Looks as tho they're getting on with the job in a hurry, with the invasion of Italy so soon after that of Sicily.

I could just do with one of our trips to Clent or to Chaddesley Corbett now - or an evening's excitement with the gramophone. May I invite you to another trip to 'C.C.' when it's all over? I saw in the weekly post that Loughland, who was in our form at K.E., has just got the D.F.C. How is the garden at home now, and anyway how are your 'family'? You haven't mentioned them lately - and what about the 'Arty Folk'? There's plenty for you to write about now, so let's have a nice tightly packed airletter <u>soon</u> - don't waste any paper!

Salaams Salome and all the <u>very</u> best
Vivian

Many weeks have gone by since I last wrote in my diary.

Life at the P.T.S. had gone on as usual, and then, one otherwise normal day, as the day progressed, a deep sense of depression descended on me. I tried to shake it off and concentrate on my work, but the feeling just got stronger.

Then I began to have a sort of 'daydream':- I was in the Nurses' Home, where I was told that there was a phone message for me. I knew it was something awful, and followed the messenger with a deep sense of dread. I was shown into a small room where all the furniture was shrouded in dustsheets, but, in the corner of the room, black and uncovered, was a telephone. I picked it up and was told something terrible.

It was an absolutely overpowering feeling. I just couldn't get rid of it, try as I would.

Eventually we finished work and went over to the Nurses' Home for supper. When I entered the Home absolute cold dread clutched my heart, and I waited for the 'messenger'. However, nothing happened, and we sat down to eat. Every time one of the maids approached the table I expected her to be the messenger, but they merely came to remove a plate or bring some vegetables.

I could scarcely believe it when we had finished the meal and nothing had happened.

We got up and walked out of the dining room and down the hall to the front door. Every step of the way my back tingled as I waited for a tap on it and a summons to the phone. We went through the black-out curtain into the blacked-out lobby, and I thought, "See, it's nothing; just your imagination". I was just about to open the front door when, behind me, a voice called urgently, "Nurse Knight! Nurse Knight!"

I froze. I knew exactly what was about to happen.

There were two slight differences from my 'daydream'. There had been a phone call from Mother, and I was to phone back, and my vision of the shrouded room had been in mirror-image. Otherwise, everything was exactly as I had visualized.

I picked up the phone and dialled. I knew I was going to be told something terrible.

I was.

Danny had been shot down.

Outside, I didn't want Betty's words of comfort, although I was grateful for her understanding. I just wanted to be alone, and back at the P.T.S. I locked myself in the bathroom and lay in the comforting warmth of the steaming water - tears and water all one.

Mother sent me the letter she had received from F/Sgt Oldman, which had borne the awful news about Danny.

                                            1320221 F/Sgt Oldman J.K.
                                            Sgts. Mess, R.A.F
                                            Middleton-St-George
                                            Co. Durham

11-9-43

Dear Mr and Mrs Knight,
    I am writing you these few lines on behalf of 'Danny' who gave us your name and address in the event of his non-return from a flight. Unfortunately he went off last Monday and did not to return to us here and I am very sorry to break the news to you in this manner. If it is any consolation to you I feel confident that 'Danny' got out of his aircraft safely and is in all probability trudging the long miles back home again. He is a good friend to me and I'm hoping it will not be very long before hearing some news of him and seeing him once more. He had got his plan of campaign thoroughly worked out in the event of an emergency and am certain in my own mind that he was able to apply it. There is very little else I can add except that if you should wish to communicate with me over him on any matter please do so.
    Sincerely yours
    James K. Oldman

Sept 14th.   5 Crosbie Rd,

My dear Pat
    I am sending you the strawberries*, try and eat them and enjoy them as Danny would like you to do. Dad thinks his and George's chances of landing in safety are quite good, and Danny told Dad in <u>very very</u> strict confidence of the great number of air crews who turn up again months and months after having been given up for lost, and then of course there is the great possibility of them being prisoners of war, and out of danger for the duration.

I am not sending you any more clothes unless you especially ask for anything as you will be back in B'ham so very soon now and can then pick up anything you want.

Don't worry about things too terribly much, but hope and HOPE. All my love

Mother

Don't mention to anyone about so many air crews turning up again as it must not get to the knowledge of the Germans and so many lives are involved.

*I think perhaps Danny had left some money and asked Mother to send me strawberries.

                                                    RNVR
                                                    Trinidad B.W.I.
                                                    12/9/43.

Dear Pat,

Received your letter dated 12th Aug. 2 weeks ago so guess it's high time I wrote to you again. I wrote last on Aug 19th according to my mail records. I see you scold me for not putting enough meat in my letters, but really Pat life here is such a long straight rut that I can't help being dull. At the moment I'm in more of a rut than usual. My partner in crime ('The Bat') and myself are at present confined to camp for an indefinite period and have had our wine bills stopped through a little incident that occurred 3 weeks ago when we celebrated the passing of the first four months here rather too well. To round the evening off we burst into song which was not appreciated by one or two senior officers then in bed. Such a charming olde English folk song too about a fair young wench called Tiger Lily from Piccadilly.

However as there is little or nothing to go out of the camp for (all the pictures featured in town come on to the station cinema after their town run) except to deposit laundry, things aren't quite so bad as they would be if we were virtual prisoners in a station in more civilized countries.

Anyhow we are a lot better off than 3 of our comrades who are confined by reason of sickness, one has sciatica* and can hardly walk or sleep, another has eczema rashes on both legs and round his throat which is not helped at all by the sticky climate and the third has as yet undiagnosed chest pains.

I guess if you were a nurse out here Pat, the sick bay would be filled to overflowing.

Films I have enjoyed recently were:- Shaw's "Major Barbara" (saw this in Brum ages ago), "Keeper of the Flame", "Mr Kipps" and tonight I shall see Mickey Rooney in "The Human Comedy". Also went to a piano concert given by Trinidad's virtuoso.

Witnessed a fire walking feat just before our incarceration but will save description of this to my next letter. Keep on writing to me when you get a chance, look like being here for a heck of a time yet so send me a noughts and Xs game next time, being a lady you can put your first nought in as before. Don't forget to note the room temp. today. Cheerio Nursie,
Bill.

* (this is Bluey best man at the wedding we went to, ginger haired chap. Remember?)

Officers Mess,
RAF Wyton,
Hunts.
15/9/43

Dear Pat

I had quite decided that you were not going to answer my letter - and then my rear gunner came out of hospital and said that all his letters to Upwood had been returned stamped 'unclaimed' and that his Mother had been snowed under with enquiries as to whether he was still alive - and I began to wonder if Upwood had returned your letters too - however it arrived the same day - and I had one worry less - which is something these days. You certainly do take a hell of a time to answer a letter - but of course your study does come first - I wish I could put mine first - normally I put mine off until the day before the exam - incidentally I have one hanging over my head now - so I'll be burning the midnight oil tonight!

It's an odd thing but I always feel desperately lonely in the country - all sort of chilly down the spine - there are always a lot of people in the

Mess - (nothing else to do here!) - and we have billiards, darts and table tennis, a decent radio and films on the camp - and still there is something sort of quiet and unexciting about it - except when there are ops on!

By the way <u>must</u> you call me Raymond - I <u>hate</u> it - only my mother calls me that - because I suppose she still thinks I'm a little boy!

You people work too hard - would you like one of my time tables? I suppose not but here it is:-

       7.45   Cup of tea (in bed!)
       8.30   Breakfast
       9.15   1st Parade
      10.00   Flying
      12.30   Lunch
       2.00   2nd Parade

Then either flying or off for day! Or for keen people (like me!!!) bags of study in astro navigation or bombing etc: much easier than yours I think!

Today you are visiting the sewage farm - I do hope you have enjoyed it - such a charming way of spending an afternoon.

I am glad I'm not a nurse - how does one manage on 12/6 per week - I found it impossible on 15/- per day - also not paying for keep or anything!

I am looking forward to your 'longer and more interesting letter', do you stay in B'ham when you go there? I hope so, then I can come and drag you out when I'm on leave - if I ever get any more after the amount I've recently had!

Well I guess that's all for now – I've got to play schoolboys again and do some swotting.

    So Cheerio,
    Sincerely Yours,
    Ray

P.S.   Like my drawings? Of course I'll do better when I'm a big boy.
       R.

(I had written to Ray, and, finding I had left a large area of blank paper at the end, suggested he used it to draw on. He did, and enclosed the end sheet of my letter with his artistic efforts with his next letter.)

"My room-mate, Betty, and I are almost alone here this weekend, as most of the girls have gone home. There is one other girl and Sister left here, but they are both out most of the time.

I didn't finish this all in one go, because we went swimming, in the middle of this. It was very cold, but very nice. Unfortunately my swimming cap has no strap, and of course it's absolutely impossible to get new caps now, so I can't do any diving now. But it was fun anyway.

When we got back here we discovered that Sister had sprained her ankle. I don't know what is going to happen now.

As you can see, I've finished off this letter on some other paper. It seems a pity to waste this - I think you'd better draw on it!"

(from Ray) thank you, I have!

Wyton
24.9.43.

Dear Pat

To begin with I'm beastly cold - it's a cold day but of course we are not allowed any heat until October 1st so I guess one just has to be cold - or do violent physical jerks or something, and that wouldn't do in this Mess - everybody is so sedate - my room mate (also new here) says it reminds him of a girls school, but I wouldn't know much about that.

It's going to rain in a few minutes - that is very pleasant - it means that I shall be free for the evening and able to go to the pictures - I only have to cycle 5 1/2 miles for that pleasure - and so the question of the moment is either to get my nice new uniform wet and see a flick or keep it dry and be miserable in the mess, I am afraid it's going to get wet.

I think the fair idea is excellent - but I am rather afraid the earlier blackout will have stopped them by my next leave, which won't be for some time I'm afraid - after all that leave that I just had I suppose I'll have to do quite a bit of work before I get any more.

(We did, in fact, manage to go to a fair when he came home on leave. It was terrific fun and we went in a sort of racing-car thing that went round and round while also going up and down.

It went terribly fast, and I was in serious danger of flying out, but Ray hung onto me and we enjoyed it so much we had several rides on it.)

My nerves are considerably better since I have been back on the job again - I think the shock of the skipper's death had a lot to do with them - they are quite OK again now however - except that I still get quite fiendish nightmares - which usually end by my either jumping or falling out of bed – it's rather amusing to find yourself sitting on the floor when you wake up - although at times it can be quite painful!

Well the bar is open now, and I can never concentrate with the bar open, so I shall finish this tomorrow - if I am not too stiff after my cycling!

Hello Pat, it is now 10 p.m. - I am in bed - and as you would probably say, I should have taken more water with it - can you tell by my writing?

Well I didn't go to the pictures after all - it rained like - like - well it rained anyway and I decided that discretion was the better part of valour etc. So we stayed in the mess and I produced my coveted table tennis ball and played with my room mate, we played 12 games and he beat me 7-5 - which he insisted was because I drank beer and he didn't - we finally left the table because a wing commander and three squadron leaders insisted on playing - they were rather annoyed when we agreed that they were entitled to use the table and went away taking the ball with us - I felt rather ashamed about it - but there are only three in the mess, and it must be preserved until a future stock arrives.

I am glad you dropped in to see Mother while you were in Harborne - she gets pretty lonely with nobody around - although I shall never live at home again now.

25.9.43
Hello Pat,
Owing to a lack of paper last night I had to end rather suddenly - just as well because I can now answer the letter I received today.

Why don't you stop worrying about that examination you are bound to pass - unless you worry yourself into a flat spin - then you will forget everything - just take it in your stride - they do say that girls can't have brains <u>and</u> beauty - but of course there are exceptions.

Of course if when you are writing letters in an 'institution' (lovely word! always makes me think of a mental home) it inspires people to borrow jam, tea and cocoa, you will obviously have to stop - how does one obtain such things nowadays anyway?

I am purchasing a bicycle - a nice quiet mount - Raleigh sports model - actually I hate the things, they make one appear so energetic, but it's the only means of getting about and I hate running around borrowing one all the time.

  Well for me too duty calls though I admit I'd rather stay here and write.

  Cheerio,
  Sincerely,
  Ray.

Letter No. 15

              R.A.F. B.N.A.F.
              <u>25.9.43</u>

My dear Pat,

  Many thanks for your letter of the 14th received today. I'm awfully sorry to hear that Danny is missing. I'm not very good at writing this sort of thing but it must have come as a terrible shock to you and your parents, especially as you've already lost Den. There <u>is</u> a chance tho, that he is P.O.W. as he might have come down over land and may have managed to get away, and the fact that there is no news is nothing to go by, as word usually takes quite a long time to get thru. As you say, next time you write you may have some good news of him - I <u>do</u> hope you do. This is the quickest way I have of answering your letter and doesn't leave me much room. Still I've practically no news and haven't heard from Bill as yet. Please tell your mother how sorry I am.

  All the very best - Vivian

                Crosbie Rd,

My dear Pat

  I am just sending you these undies in case you are in dire need of them. The rest of your laundry will follow as soon as I can find a moment to iron.

  Dad is still on holiday and hates me to be busy, and is now waiting for me to go out with him. The wedding was a great success and Christine made a very sweet little bride, she really looked awfully pretty. Your telegram turned up O.K. a bit belated but with others also a bit belated.

We still haven't heard any more news of Danny and George, but of course it is <u>far</u> too early, probably three months ahead would be as early as possible, and we must just wait and HOPE.

Lots of love
Mother.

R.A.F, B.N.A.F.
11.10.43

<u>No 17</u>

My dear Pat,

I am wondering if you have had any more news of Danny and I <u>do</u> hope he's OK after all.

I haven't heard from you lately, but I have a reputation to keep up & so here I am. Last week I saw Spencer Tracy in 'Dr Jekyl & Mr Hyde' which I greatly enjoyed. We are having quite a lot of P.T now which personally I quite enjoy but it's pretty cool in the water & I haven't been bathing so much lately. I had a letter from Bill on Sat, he appears to be having a wizard time. I also heard from Wishy's mother, but she didn't give his address. We had the third of our Gramophone Concerts last night: Brahm's No 5 Hungarian Dance, aria from 'Snow Maiden' & the Tchaikovsky Piano Concerto (Memories!!) & Wolf's Italian Serenade. I greatly enjoyed it. No other news now, so what about you having a shot?

All the <u>very</u> best - Vivian

One evening, when we were sitting in the dining room at the nurses' home waiting to be served, Betty started to cry quietly. I, of course, thought, "Oh my God, she's lost someone else". So I gently asked her what was the matter.

"I've got nits in my hair!" she sobbed, "and so, probably, have you."

I just laughed with relief, and, after her initial annoyance at what seemed to be my callousness, she saw the funny side too.

Apparently she reasoned she had picked them up off the train on our last journey to Birmingham; so, later, back at the P.T.S., she and I inspected my long hair, and there they were. At least, we thought, we have been trained in what to do. However, when we told Sister, she prescribed a proprietary soap, instead of the carbolic solution we had trained with! Anyway, we were soon able to clear the problem up.

Monday 21

My dear Pat,
Thanks for your letter, and your washing arrived safely but I shall not return it as you will be in B'ham so soon. I am sending you the £1 and a very small amount of jam as you will be there such a short while now. How is the hair going? I hope all the trouble with both you and Betty is a thing of the past, but you will have to always keep a good look out.

I really have absolutely no news, I had some films sent from Darlington but they are the wrong ones, so I am returning them as neither Danny or George are on them, and F/Sgt Oldman is going to do his very best to trace them. He says it is still very very early days to get any news of them yet.

With BEST of wishes for a successful result in your exam, also to Betty and in fact All of you.

Much love, Mother

Saturday 23 October 1943

Many weeks have gone by since I last wrote in my diary. I have been at the B.C.H. 3 weeks now and am in my 3rd month of nursing.

There is still no news of Danny and George. There is still hope - and that's all one can do - hope and pray. They are grand boys, and I'm really fond of Danny.

I have a 10-2 and I'm at home. I must go back soon. I miss home a lot and try and get back here whenever I can.

We had transferred to the hospital in Ladywood road in Birmingham, and the salary had just been increased from £16 to £32 a year.

The Nurses' Home was round the corner from the hospital. At night, in order to ascertain that the nurses were not taking men into their rooms, we had to return to the house via the main entrance to the hospital in Ladywood road. Alone in the black-out this route was rather daunting, and on one occasion, returning from my off-duty time at home, I asked a policeman returning to the police station nearby if I could walk with him. When I told Ray about this, he remarked that, knowing the ex-police that he did in the R.A.F., this was maybe a false security!

A most peculiar rule applied in the Nurses' Home, where we had lifts and stairs. Junior Probationers were on the top floor, but nevertheless, nurses were not allowed to use the lifts. They were exclusively for use by the sparse band of cleaners! (And, presumably, Sisters.)

When we were allocated our wards, I crossed my fingers and hoped that I would not be starting as a junior probationer on a surgical ward, as I felt that would, for me, be going in at the deep end. So, which ward was I allocated to? Yes, the surgical ward!

I was shattered to find that several of the babies and toddlers were being nursed in prams due to the shortage of beds. And when I was sent to blanket bath the children, instead of the shining chrome and glass trolley and modern equipment I had been trained on at the P.T.S., I was shown a battered tin tray, a chipped enamel bowl, and a bucket which I had to kick along the ward floor, in which to put the soiled laundry.

As we were on two months' trial, we only had to provide our own black shoes and stockings as we had been issued with uniforms on loan. These consisted of white short sleeved tunic dresses, large starched white squares which we had to fold into a flowing nurse's headdress, and, incredibly, a black and white striped cotton petticoat, long and voluminous. This was compulsory wear; we were told that it was in order not to reveal anything when leaning over, making beds etc! It is worth remembering that it was a <u>children's</u> hospital!

We were also issued with long white elasticated sleeves, which, for some reason, we had to wear when serving the children's meals from the big dinner trolley on the ward. It seems ridiculous when the more senior nurses had bare arms!

And we also were issued with threadbare cloaks, which were pretty inefficient against the early morning chill, when we were awoken at 6.00 by a peremptory knock on the door, and, "Six o'clock, nurse!", and then filed down to chapel for prayers, to sing the lovely hymn 'Morning has broken', before making our way over to breakfast.

Uniforms were only to be worn in the hospital precincts. Even though our off-duty was only four hours, in that time we had to change out of uniform into 'civvies' and then back again on our return.

There was a strict pecking order in the dining room.
Senior staff were served first, with junior probationers very definitely last. At breakfast, boiled eggs arrived en masse in a large kitchen bowl, and by the time they reached our end of the table they were often in a somewhat sorry state. However this didn't really make much difference, for, by this time the senior nurses had finished their breakfast, and, rising, uttered, "For what we have received, may the Lord make us truly thankful", and we all then filed out, with, if we were lucky, maybe a couple of mouthfuls of egg and toast, and a quick swig of tea!

The vast majority of cases on Ward 1 had hare lip and cleft palate repairs which, particularly when executed by the Registrar, were incredibly well done, and, in many cases, were invisible when healed. The other common repair was for a condition I hadn't previously known about, which is hypospadius. This is a condition where the urethra fails to exit at the tip of the penis, and appears, instead, elsewhere along its length.

One little boy was refusing to pee because it was so painful after his surgery. Matters were getting rather serious when Staff bribed him with the promise that, as soon as he had pee-ed, she would let him play with a little toy sewing machine we had among the toys on the ward. The bribe overcame the thoughts of the pain, and he bravely performed, and, of course, was duly rewarded!

Certain cases were considered of special interest, and a notice was posted on the notice board to inform nurses throughout the hospital. We had one such case on our ward. She was a twelve year old girl named Pam who had fallen onto the fire and suffered terrible burns. It was a miracle she survived, but she had a very long way to go. She was burned from her neck to her knees and in these areas had no skin remaining, resembling nothing so much as rotting meat. The only method of treatment that proved at all beneficial was to enclose her in a sort of plastic bag, and periodically irrigate this awful suppurating flesh with a diluted Milton solution. When this was being done her screams could be heard outside the ward.

One evening, towards the end of my shift, I was called into the side ward, where these sort of procedures were carried out, to watch her having a saline drip introduced. This needed to be done frequently, as she lost a lot of fluid due to her massive skin loss.

Presumably she had asked the Registrar if it would hurt. He made an incision in her ankle and was fishing around for a suitable vein, which in view of the amount of trauma caused by so many previous transfusions, wasn't all that easy. She suddenly said, "I can feel a bit of a tickle now, doctor". It brought me back with a shock from watching an interesting, if somewhat gory, procedure, to my little patient. The blood roared in my ears, the room went black, and as if from a long way off, a disembodied voice said, "Are you all right, nurse? Sit down for a minute." I felt so ashamed!

Pam was such a good, uncomplaining little soul, and I was horrified when, one day she called me over from the other side of the ward and told me that the nurse who was my mentor refused to give her a bedpan. This was clearly because of the fearful stench of pus which assailed one when delving into the 'bag' in which she lay. The callousness appalled me, and I quickly gave her the bedpan myself. Another miserable problem that she had to contend with was flies entering the bag, and from time to time I had to try to get them out for her.

My other 'mentor' was quite difficult to assess. She occasionally gave me strange, philosophical dissertations on the significance of caring and compassion. Other times she would bring back a patient from theatre almost at a run, banging and bashing the trolley on furniture and doors.

On one occasion I was in the sluice room, washing the dozens of nappies of the babies and toddlers on the ward, when she came in and told me not to wash them by hand, but to put them into the bedpan sterilizer; this being quicker and easier. So I did. When I took them out, toward the end of my shift, they were in an absolutely disgusting state, and I had to wash them all again by hand, only this time the job was much more difficult. I was furious because she had obviously done this to 'haze' me, as Danny would call it.

Yet, one evening I was down at the far end of the ward, having been delegated by the Staff Nurse to polish the floor with a 'bumper', an extremely heavy sort of large mop. (We had virtually no lay staff for cleaning the wards as they'd all been called up.) I found it terribly hard work, but I didn't realize it showed so much, and was surprised when this same nurse appeared and said, "Here, let me do that; you look exhausted!"

I was on the ward one day, the Staff Nurse busy at the top end of the ward, when the phone rang, so I answered it, "Ward 1."

"This is theatre. Is the First Aid Chest on the ward?" a voice enquired.

I had no idea. I couldn't think why they would want one, anyway. However, I said I would find out, and went to Staff and relayed the query. She was as puzzled as I was, and went to the phone. After a short conversation she came back convulsed with laughter.

"They didn't want the First Aid Chest", she chuckled. "They wanted the First H.S." (the Senior House Surgeon!)

Another bit of confusion took place with one of my small patients concerning my name, Nurse Knight. This particular little boy would persist in calling me Night Nurse, and one day, obviously perplexed, he called me over and said, "Night Nurse, why do you work in the day-time? Don't you sleep?!"

The ward was divided into two or three sections by glass screens, and his section was at the far end.

One dark wintry evening, near the end of my shift, I was alone with the children in this section. Suddenly, we were startled by a knocking on the outside door of a little vestibule right at the end of the ward. I hesitated. It was such an unexpected and unusual occurrence, I wasn't sure what to do.

The knocking came again; more urgently.

I said to the little boy I was attending to that I'd better go and see what it was. His eyes round with alarm he said, "If you don't come back, I'll call for help!"

I must admit I felt rather grateful for his support as I disappeared through the black-out door into the pitch black vestibule and unlocked and opened the back door.

Outside, the night was moonless and dark, and I could just make out the silhouette of a small, thin man in a trilby.

"Is this the fever ward?" he enquired.

I told him that it was, in fact, the surgical ward, and that he shouldn't be in that part of the hospital at all, and directed him to the main entrance. The whole time I was really quite frightened, because he just shouldn't have been there, and I was wondering if he was truly a genuine parent or some character with criminal intent.

Anyway, he disappeared again into the dark, and I thankfully closed and locked the door once more and returned to the ward, where my relieved little protector said, "I was going to call for help if you hadn't come back soon!"

I loved working with the children, bathing and feeding them caring for them, making their beds. But the necessary aggressive procedures to cure them I was finding extremely hard to take. I was dreading the day when I would be told to give an injection. The thought of plunging a needle into that tender flesh appalled me. I began to dream every night of the grimmer aspects of my work on the ward.

Then I began to suffer from backache, and feel tired all the time, and one day, when Ray came on leave, he picked me up in the car from the corner nearby (no men were allowed anywhere near the Nurses' Home!) and drove me home. The plan had been to call in and then go off together for a couple of hours. However, when I got home I just dissolved into tears, and couldn't stop. He was so sweet and understanding, and, although it was his precious leave, he said he would go, and come back again later to take me back to the hospital.

I just sat on the floor and cried and cried, and couldn't stop. I began to wonder if my dream of nursing wasn't working out right, and that perhaps I couldn't really go on with it.

My situation was obviously quite apparent to Sister, who, on my return to the ward, asked me to have a word with her in her office. I suppose I was a bit vague, but then I felt pretty vague about it all, and, thinking about the dreaded injections that must be by now imminent, I muttered something about not feeling 'competent'. She thought I said "confident", and replied that that would come with time, so I repeated the word competent and she was obviously somewhat at a loss as to what to say at that. However, having told her of my severely aching back, she said she would arrange for me to see a doctor.

So, next day, I had my physical problems investigated and, after some discussion of my other problems, he told me that he was recommending that I had two weeks' leave.

And so I packed my bag and came home and Ray and I spent the rest of his leave together – mostly at his house or mine.

I then tried to sort out my thoughts. Deep down I think I knew what I had to do, but nursing had been my main goal in life for so long, it was very hard to come to terms with the thought that I would abandon it. I wrote to Ray, asking for his 'candid opinion'.

R.A.F.
Wyton

My Dear Pat

Well here I am with nothing to do at 11 a.m. - mind you I <u>have</u> been doing a spot of work - I've been on parade and then out to my aircraft and cleaned my guns - and did they need it - nobody had touched them while I was on leave and of course they were rusty - so having now removed the oil from my paws I am free till after lunch.

Of course it's too early to go into the mess - the Waafs will all be rushing around with dusters and things - so I am braving the wrath of my batman and sitting in my room - he doesn't like anybody in the rooms till after lunch - must have some secret process of cleaning.

I had a beastly journey back - it rained all the way - the train of course was packed and arrived at Peterboro' an hour late - thus I missed my only connection - however there were about a couple of dozen of us all in the same boat and we managed to prevail on the station master to persuade a through train to London to drop us off at Huntingdon - all I had to to then was walk the five miles to camp in the rain - I arrived there a drip in all senses of the word - wet - tired - hungry and thirsty - although I did have a dry scone and a pint of what tasted like vinegar but was sold as beer at Peterboro.

Yesterday it was decided that a little night vision training would do me the world of good so I sat in a dark room all morning peering at a screen and trying to see little aeroplanes (I was assured that there were some there - but I couldn't see 'em!)

In the afternoon I was informed that having improved my eyesight the time had now arrived when I should develop some physical fitness - or do some muscle building - I said I ate an apple a day to keep the doctor away - but nothing would satisfy the big noises - except that I should run round the perimeter track - a mere four miles - so with other unfortunates I did - and of course it rained.

Well for the rest of the day I lay on my bed and endeavoured to forget the affair - crawling down to the mess at intervals for meals and was asleep by 9 pm - quite a record.

This afternoon I am doing some practice bombing from 16,000 ft - I warned them to evacuate villages near the range but as usual they ignored me so if you hear of a raid near Peterboro' that will probably be me - missing the target by a mile or so.

Gosh I wish I was back at home again – I've been frozen since I left - of course we have no heat yet and the fresh air fiends <u>will</u> open the windows.

Well its night now _ shall probably be writing this for the duration - the bombing did not come off - due to some technical failure of the aircraft - so I spent the afternoon reading in the mess.

This evening I licked my pilot at snooker - I believe he only played because he can't pay his mess bills and wants me to make him a loan. After that I had my half pint of beer - I have rationed myself to a pint a day - and so to bed.

Well 'night nurse' another day is half way through and I still haven't finished this - today we have done very little - a lecture lasted all morning and I have at last succeeded in doing my bombing this afternoon - results as yet unknown.

Tonight we have a so-called dance in the mess - and we have the choice of starving or going - Sherwood and I are going to drop in about halfway through for something to eat - but it will be the usual drunken brawl with officers' wives and the town low types present so I don't suppose we shall stay long - I must try and remember my beer rationing!

Thanks for the letter little one, but I see you have done it again - the name is <u>Ray</u>!!! not Raymond. By the time you get this you will be fed up to the teeth with your beds, bathings etc. again.

So you would like my '<u>Candid</u>' opinion of the business eh? I can't imagine why - but here you are.

In the first place you didn't want to stay at Art School or at home - you felt that you wanted to <u>do</u> something - right?

Well you have plenty of choice - there are the services - awful thought - leave them till last! The attraction to nursing I presume was your liking for children - but <u>not</u> for the dirty work. The great point is of course that if you don't feel that you can carry on - leave while you can - but be careful that you don't eventually get called up and bunged into a factory - or become a bus conductress or something grim like that.

If I were you I would do something that allows you time to live at home - then you will have more spare time when I come on leave. Anyway it's your problem and you seem to know pretty well what you want so I imagine you will solve it quite satisfactorily.

I saw the Bob Hope show in Nottingham - very good wasn't it - but I prefer him with Bing I think.

Yes I do like Boogie rhythym (y trouble!) but Father doesn't and usually switches it off.

People <u>have</u> been known to have seen pink elephants with purple snakes - but not red devils dancing death dances in the mists - or have you been improving your already great acquaintance with Birmingham's pubs?

Well that's enough drivel for now I guess - I shall now make myself pretty for the dance.

Sincerely yours,
Ray

R.A.F. Wyton

23/10/43

My Dear Patricia,

So glad you enjoyed your fried egg and tomatoes - doesn't make my mouth water at all these days - steak - potatoes - bacon - tomatoes and egg - is our regular pre-ops tea.

I'm terribly sorry I aroused your wrath - and now get down on my metaphorical knees and humbly apologize - or do I? I didn't mean 'dirty' work but dirty work - get me? Any heavy work in the RAF is dirty work (any work in the RAF is a miracle!) and of course I meant bed making and bathing etc - and now having had regard for your extreme youth and considerable beauty and apologized I guess I needn't look out when I come on leave - <u>when</u> I come!

I <u>am</u> sorry however that you are still so tired - I think the infant teaching idea is excellent my infant - would be much less tiring but perhaps a little more exasperating.

I have only been out of camp once since coming off leave - I cycled down to Hunts with Sherwood to purchase an electric stove - makes a lot of difference to the room - until we are caught with it!

Apart from that I have been to three picture shows on camp - all old films that I had already seen – I'm also still going strongly on my ration of a pint of beer per day - but I suppose I'll break down one of these days and the result will be awful.

Had one real thrill since coming back – I'm still dithering - we had a new wireless operator - ours was sick - well it turned out that he didn't know how to fuse certain flares - but we didn't find that out until he'd done the wrong thing and made the darn things live so I had to become a one man disposal squad - I hooked on an emergency oxygen bottle and stumbled down to the darn things and sure enough they were just about rife for a big bang - I had to open the door and throw them out and the second one went off just after I'd dropped it - with a blinding flash and threw the old kite over on its side and me half way up the fuselage which was lucky as I might have been thrown out through the door without a parachute! However I escaped with a few bruises and a couple of scratches - but ran out of oxygen on the way back and passed out - however the navigator saw me go down and came and plugged a fresh bottle on so all was well - apart from five attacks by fighters and some deadly weather the trip after that was as usual quiet and uninspiring.

Well, I guess that's about all for now – I'm going for a cycle ride with Sherwood tonight - the fresh air will probably do us good.

And now I suppose I should write to mother and tell her that sonny boy is still kicking and finish with the old phrase "nothing exciting ever happens here".

So Cheerio Florence (Florrie for short of course), mind you don't get the bath water too hot for the dear children.
Sincerely Yours
Ray

R.A.F,
B.N.A.F.
31.10.43

<u>No 18</u>

My dear Pat,
Many thanks for your airletters of 8th & 19th Oct. You will probably be interested to hear that I am now 'Somewhere in Italy'. I am sorry to hear you've been ill & hope that you are better now. Next time you see the Matthews, will you please ask them to get Barry to let me have his address & give them my new one. Teddy Gray is also in Italy & I hope

I may hit up against him somewhere. Bags of fruit here & we're having good food. The money is funny as there are British Military Authority notes, U.S dollar bills, Italian lire notes (400L =£1) & Allied printed lire. Pity the poor Italians with 4 kinds of money. Bags of greenery about which is very pleasant after the N. African dryness. I will write again soon but let's hear from you soon. Anne sent me a cutting announcing Chris' wedding so I must write & give my blessing.

All the very best – Vivian

Wyton
Sunday

My Dear Pat,

I applied for a 48 hour pass this week end - but was told that I couldn't be spared and palmed off with a 24 hour pass - from 10 this morning to 10 tomorrow morning - now what use is that? There are only three possible places to go to on a 24 - London, Peterboro', Cambridge - the last two are most uninteresting and I couldn't possibly get back from London by 10 so that's out too!

So I'm being miserable and staying in camp and not doing anything that could be considered work.

Life here has been very dull lately - one long round of gun cleaning and general maintenance and of course bags of lectures calculated to brown off even the most studious types - I was one of the first to be browned off (naturally!)

Two of my crew are in hospital - one with a broken hypodermic needle somewhere in his arm (what a doctor!), and one with a ruptured ear drum - remember what I told you about flying with colds? I don't think he will <u>ever</u> fly again - maybe he's lucky at that.

My skipper and engineer have been giving new aircraft their initial tests and since a navigator is necessary on all flights, I've been going along with them - my navigator said he wasn't keen - and of course wherever I go the mid-upper gunner also goes - so Tommy has been going too - and it's been quite fun.

And talking of leave - I believe I shall be coming home again on the 16th - they don't say what month - but I guess it's November - that means that the next leave after that should be the 30th Dec but that of course is impossible - I haven't been home for Xmas or New Year since the beginning of the war - would be fun though!

And now the bar is open and I shall proceed to have my pint although as it's a day off I think I shall slip tonight and mildly celebrate.

Well it's Tuesday now and the clans are gathering for P.T. - not little Raymond though – I'm sitting by my stove - playing hooky as usual - I don't like P.T.

I ran out of notepaper there so I'm using Sherwood's now -
I'll have to ask if he minds when he gets back from leave - by which time it will all be used I suppose.

And for now I guess that's about all - I fancy you owe me a letter - am I right? But of course you are so busy with the dear little children - and I suppose your poor little back still aches - however if some day you should feel really strong the address is still Wyton - but I shall be home on the 16th and that doesn't really give you much time, does it?

My regards to your people.
Sincerely,
Ray

Thursday 11 November 1943

I have left the hospital and I'm now looking around for a job - I hope to take up infant teaching.

Raymond is probably coming on leave on the 16th. It'll be nice to go out on the spree again. Posted 'Spirit of Man' *(a book of poems)* to Vivian yesterday. I hope it doesn't go to the bottom.

I miss the boys a lot - Vivian and Danny especially. However I must get a job and throw myself into it till the old times come again.

On Monday night Joan and I went to The Royal to see 'Cavelleria Rusticana' and 'I Pagliacci'. They were both great, especially the latter.

We are having the house re-done - all the walls are being distempered and we have had the kitchen turned into a dining room.

Tomorrow Mother and I are going to town. We shall go to the hospitality bureau to see if we can have two airmen here for Christmas.

Nov 11th! How I wish today could be a repeat of 25 years ago - how I wish we could have news of Danny - but it's 2 months now and time's getting on. Oh how I miss him and Dennis - and Vivian, The Rock, The Faithful Hound isn't here - he who was always around.

Royal Air Force
Wyton,
12-11-43

My Dear <u>Patricia</u>,

So! we are back on the Raymond stuff again, wait till I get home, if I have the energy I will deal with you.

The party was quite as grim as I expected - queueing (yes! that's quite correct (I hope) five deep at the bar - so I didn't have a drink!! I <u>did</u> try to fraternize with a Waaf - but she continually trod on my toe dancing our first and only dance - after a very short stay I decided that it was too hot and deadly and that I didn't want to stay anyway so I dashed off back to the mess - my pilot got absolutely blotto - I don't know how he managed it - but then these Canadians don't need a lot to do it.

Incidentally I haven't had a drink since then either although I have been considerably tempted - Sherwood started by saying that I couldn't completely stop if I wanted to - so I'm just showing him that I can.

The thought of your new boyfriend made me really jealous until I turned over the page - of course I can't compete with good looks - nature did me wrong in that line - however in the few days left at my disposal I will endeavour to achieve some scars - should be quite easy around here - anyway if the worst comes to pass I have a bottle - so I'll only need a smoke bomb – what's that anyway?

I have also been trying to stand on my head - but after nearly breaking my neck a couple of times I've given that up - I do however know a good trick with a new laid egg - is that any good? And confidentially I do think he's a little young for you (or is he??!)

Before I had left the hospital, we had had an admission of a twelve year old boy with bad facial scars, who had come in to have the scars cut and re-stitched with lots of tiny sutures, to reduce the scarring. He was, in fact, quite a good looking boy. The surgeon did an absolutely beautiful job, and it was clear that his good looks were going to be restored.

Imagine, then, my dismay when, only a day or two after, on going into the side ward he was sharing with the other children, I was greeted with the sight of him standing on his head to impress me! I got him to right himself very smartly, and when, after he was discharged some few weeks later I was invited by his mother to have tea with them both in town, it was obvious he had come to no harm. The thing, in fact, that impressed me most, was that, out of bed, he was nowhere near as tall as he had seemed when in bed!

(I had written and related the story to Ray.)

I am glad that you finally gave up the nursing racket - when I used to think of your poor back I'd get all morbid! And I am sorry that you are lonely - it must be awful having to stay at home! Anyway try not to be too depressed next week won't you.

Well even I can't write any more of this sort of drivel so for now beautiful, farewell, all things being equal etc I should start my nine days on Monday - I am spending the first night in town and shall then set forth for home and a valiant attempt to relieve your depression.

    Yours,
    Ray

                                        RNVR
19/11/43   R.N.A.S.
                                    Trinidad.B.W.I.

Hallo Sweetheart

How are tricks? It must be just over a month since I wrote you last so is high time I penned you some more rubbish from my tropical retreat. Though if this is a retreat I'm all for advancing myself. Your letter dated rather vaguely as Oct. (is this a subtle hint that you are only going to write one a month) arrived a few days ago, for which many thanks. I can't over-stress the joy and delight which letters from home bring to me here. So please, please, please keep up the good work.

Barry Matthews is an acting captain you say, my hat the army is the service for promotion. An army captain is one step higher up the ladder than a mere naval 'subby'. However considering the rather up and down nature of his work I don't begrudge him his success at all; in fact I take my hat off to him. Huh! Catch me jumping out of an aircraft on the end of an overgrown brolly - no future at all in any fun and games of this sort. Anyhow please convey my congratulations to him if you chance to meet him on leave. Congrats also to Christine. I suppose the next bombshell you'll throw across will be the news of your engagement to Gerald's pal the R.S.O., or at any rate some handsome young surgeon. It's been done before, and it will happen again - Nurse marries boss - you know the sort of thing.

Well you say you are working very hard and wonder whether you'll be able to take it. Don't you enjoy the work, or do they insist upon too much menial tasks and not give you enough real nursing to make the job interesting? I suppose the proportion of medical work entrusted to you increases with each week you are there. Or am I just talking thro' my hat! Do let me know when you have time to lay that thermometer down for a few minutes. Love to the family and a big kiss for you.

Cheerio, Bill

Saturday <u>27th!!!</u>

ROYAL AIR FORCE
WYTON,

My Dear Pat

Don't you have any calendars at home - or any other means of knowing the date - or are you just too idle too look - I thought all little girls kept Diaries anyway - and made nice little entries such as "Clarence looked at me this morning - happy day!" - but then I suppose you would have so many entries about people jumping into water tanks - and of course such things as letting one's hair down - been doing it lately, little one?

And don't allude to me as 'you'. I prefer even Raymond - you'll be calling me 'thing' next.

Glad I managed to relieve your depression - I certainly <u>did</u> enjoy my leave – it's a hell of a time to the next though!

Had quite an amusing journey up - at first I had a carriage to myself - but an officer and his wife and baby got in - one of the climbing type of child - I was trying to sleep and after she (her name was Patricia - now there's a thing!) had torn the cover off my book - she decided I made good climbing and did! all over me - sticky fingers and all!

I got rid of them at Coventry and settled down again - then two Yanks and their girl friends got in - and argued as to whether they could or not (1st class). I was doing an imitation sleep - the girls said I should object if I woke up - so I woke up - one of the Yanks said was it OK and I said Yes and proceeded to drink their whiskey and smoke their cigarettes while they occupied the corners and spooned - they left at Rugby and a parson and an old maid got in - I think the smell of whiskey rather annoyed them but after 3/4 bottle I went to sleep and didn't wake up till I got to P'boro'.

The whole crew met at Huntingdon and did a little celebrating and I toddled back to camp quite enthusiastically and threw Sherwood out of bed - he was <u>not</u> amused!

Well that's about all - other not so amusing incidents have occurred but security says we can't write about them - maybe I'll tell you sometime.

I'm in my room at the moment – it's devilish cold - you would be hissing beautifully *(when Ray had come on leave it was bitterly cold, and when we were out in the blackout - coming back from a pub, or the cinema or whatever - I would draw in my breath with a hiss because it was so cold)* - when I finish this I'm going back to the mess to try and get a little warmer.

Sherwood is <u>in</u> bed - he's got 'flu and feels pretty grim - I'm trying hard to catch it - but I don't suppose I'll have any luck!

Well don't work <u>too</u> hard - although I don't need to tell you that do I? And if you <u>do</u> get time before Xmas let me know how school goes!

I got my Spam medal today - looks quite pretty.
Sincerely yours
Ray(mond!)

Here you are,   R.N.V.R.
finger well out this time   Trinidad B.W.I.
                                                                                   1/12/43

Hallo Darling.

Your letter dated 11th Nov. arrived on the 29th. for which many thanks. I'm sorry you haven't heard from me for some time, the reason is that there has been a hold up in the transmission of mail from here to the U.K. but I believe things have improved very recently. Anyhow I wrote to you last on the 18th Nov.

I was very glad to hear that you had the courage to face up to the fact that nursing wasn't your vocation and had also the good sense to immediately leave and start looking for some other form of work. Many people are foolish enough to stick to their chosen job, although they hate every moment of it, thro' sheer obstinate pride or thro' fear of others thinking they are quitters. Whereas in reality their friends would be only too willing to applaud and appreciate their looking for a more congenial channel in which they could make better use of their talents and energy. I haven't put this very well but I expect you can see what I'm trying to say. Anyway, best of luck in whatever you decide to take up. I hope you don't have to muck about too long searching for a job.

How do you like the "Darling" approach. Getting quite fresh in my old age, aren't I?

As for myself things here have take a sudden and decided turn for the better, and instead of the restless, bored, completely depressed individual you would have met a week ago you would now find a much happier guy completely prepared to spend another 6 months out here. The reason for this transformation is two-fold:-

(a) I've managed to transfer to another squadron, flying much, much better types of aircraft.

(b) With four other fellows I've bought a 14ft. sailing dinghy, a 'real trimmer' as the N.Z. boys say. She was built by two N.Z. pilots here. It took 'em best part of a year: one has already left for U.K. and the other is returning to N.Z. shortly. It's a grand little boat - sorry I mean <u>SHE</u> is a grand little boat, and I will send you a photo of her when we get her off the slipway and fully rigged again. Just at the moment she's undergoing minor modifications and also is being painted - wonderful colour scheme. Red inside the cockpit, grey floor-boards, duck-egg blue deck, green piping and cream sides.

Philip's address by the way is:- H.M. S/M "Tactician", c/o G.P.O. London. I expect you know that his brother is engaged. Heck I feel like a miserable old bachelor with all these folk getting themselves spliced.

My love to your Mother and Father. Hope the distemper still looks new when I can actually walk into 3 & 5 once again. Enjoy life Pat and keep me posted of your progress.

Lots of Love, Bill.

Wyton,
1/12/43

Dear Blondie,

How <u>did</u> you manage it? Maybe you've taken 'Digit removum' as your motto these days, anyway it <u>is</u> nice to get a letter these days - takes your mind off other things.

So you've been out into the wicked world again eh? Now there's a thing eh, I hope you haven't been letting your hair down.

Don't you think this new job will be a little too much for you? <u>Please</u> don't overwork. I should hate to come on leave and find you all haggard or wan or whatnot - and as the Posters say "mind your back!"

No thanks Helen I don't need any socks - the last pair knitted for me by a sweet young thing fitted perfectly - over my flying boots - but Bruce could do with some woolly boots for winter - I'm afraid I don't know his size though.

Oh! by the way as you have the bigger children mixed with the tinies you had better be careful not to get mixed up with them or some well meaning teacher will be putting you to bed or something.

No, Patricia I have no little book wherein I enter my shafts of wit - rather a pity I suppose - definitely a loss to posterity - and as for a soul to lay bare - my dear! - how can a bomb aimer have a soul! No we are all heartless brutes who revel in the unwholesome joys of mass murder (or do we?)

I'm afraid we are not allowed to mention ops – it's really a great secret – you'll have to wait till I come on leave and then of course we can find something more interesting to talk about!

Trouble with you girls is that you're always wanting to <u>do</u> something - don't you realize that by just being you and looking pretty when people come on leave is good for morale - what would we do without you?

Did I say I considered you respectable - now there's a thing eh? And you always letting your hair down for strange soldiers too!

I said I had my 'Spam' medal - that's RAF for 1939 Star - sorry you were troubled – it's nothing to get excited about anyway - but it <u>does</u> look pretty.

I'm sorry about my writing but I normally write your letters either before or after ops and - my shattered nerves! *(Ray's nerves were, in fact, absolutely shredded by his nightly sorties over Germany, and he was desperately in need of a long-delayed break.)*

I gave Sherwood your - (er - er) - love and he insists on writing a postscript - I guessed he might be funny so I said he could only if I censored it – I've only just read it - the man is obviously nuts – he's laughing his head off now and hugging a photograph of his wife.

Well I guess that's about all for now - there really isn't a lot to write about these days unless one touches on subjects which are verboten (German!!!)

So Cheerio,
Yours,
Ray

See over!!!

P.S. Ray told me that you sent me your love which I appreciate very much, however you know what Ray is like and it has made him insanely jealous of me. In fact it is almost impossible for me to live in the same room. I can't reply in suitable terms in the postscript as Ray is going to censor it first, so I hope you can read between the lines.
Ferdie.

The Nursery School where I worked as a low-paid, untrained junior teacher, was in a slum area in Smethwick. The children were mainly four-year olds, but there were a few three-year olds amongst them. Their activities were, basically, constructive play, and I enjoyed the work, although I was conscious I was not using my educated capacity. However, it was interesting, and I began to learn about lives very different from my own.

In particular, there was a little girl called Rosie, who had only one dress.

One day she wore it normally, then back to front, then inside out, then inside out and back to front. There being no clean surface left, she would stay away while her mother washed it.

I asked the headmistress why, if the family's poverty was so acute, they couldn't be given assistance. She replied that, on the occasions they had been given assistance, the father pawned the items and spent the money on drink.

Once I knew this, I found Rosie much easier to deal with, for she had appeared as a very spoiled child, obstinate and difficult, whereas she was, in fact, very deprived. So I never <u>told</u> her to do anything, instead suggesting, "Shall we go and wash your hands?" and she would comply quite happily.

I learned quite a lot about child psychology. At dinner time one day, I was serving out fish with vegetables. One little boy said, "I don't like fish, teach". So I said, "Oh, this isn't fish, it's cod", and he happily ate it all up and asked for a second helping!

Wyton
7-12-43

My Dear (a) (b) or (c),

I don't quite get this a,b,c, stuff but if you prefer it, its OK by me! Personally I like Blondie.

With regard to the small child who called you a - er - whatsit - I have heard that "out of the mouths of babes and sucklings etc". I should imagine he <u>must</u> be a sweet child - I bet he doesn't stand any nonsense from the 'gentle sex' when he grows up!

(Ray is referring to a blue eyed, blond haired four year old who, when the children were lying on their cots for the afternoon rest, refused to do so himself.

When told to at least keep still and quiet, he sat there, glowering from under his eyebrows, chanting, "Bloody sod, bloody sod!"

In the end, the situation being quite unresolvable, the headmistress collected him and took him up into her room.

As she left with him, one of the little girls, round eyed with excited apprehension, asked, "Is she going to put him in a cupboard?!")

I don't think you have much idea of dealing with kids - fancy standing them in corners - with their hands on their heads I suppose - get your blue stockings on teacher!

Well Toots (oh doctor!) I suppose one should let you celebrate your first pay packet - so if I survive that long I'll let you treat me - Shandy please!

I do <u>not</u> consider it low for you to go into a pub either escorted or unescorted - so long as you have the sense to know just what you are doing and drinking - the only objection to your going in alone would be that any unescorted (or escorted for that matter if she's pretty enough!) female is 'target for tonight' for any of the boys who happen to be hunting.

Hallo Sugar - I had to finish there for dinner - and now having had a deadly dinner of veg. soup - pork pie (no pork!) and peach flan - the latter would have been better named leather flan - two crafty pints of beer and a couple of games of snooker - I am back in my cold and lonely little room and ready for bed at 9.20 - at least I'm not <u>ready</u> for bed but there is nothing else to do - I can't even argue with Sherwood - he's on leave this week so I am afraid I can't send your p.s. to him, his wife might not like it - or shall I send it? And get you involved in a scandal - teach you to only write what you mean in future!

Naturally I read the p.s.- thanks for the kiss, are you sure I don't have to jump in a water tank or something for it?

By the way I have just discoved - seem to have missed an er somewhere there - that the tune we whistle in the ops bus when going out to the kites for take off is your 'Pedro the Fisherman' - I rather like it.

Remember that news we saw so often with Woolton speaking and the 'Grecian' picture in the background - I saw it again yesterday!!!

Well that's about all I guess - I wish I could write some more - because theres nothing else to do except go to bed - and if I do that tomorrow gets here too quickly!

So Long Helen,
Yours,
Ray

R.A.F.
B.N.A.F.
<u>8.12.43</u>

My dear Pat,

I am writing this in answer to your AL of Nov 19, for which I shall have already thanked you by the time you get this. However I want to give you the programmes of the two Symphony concerts I've been to and there's not room on an AG for them. The first was on Sun. 2 Dec *(here he includes the two lengthy programmes).*

The next concert (next Sunday) is to include Tchaikovsky's Piano Concerto No 1 and even tho I heard it at one of our gramophone concerts in NA, I shall be glad to hear it again.

That's not the only entertainment we get as we can go to flicks every other night as well as shows in Town. So you can see we are by no means cut off from civilisation.

It seems amazing that Chris has been married now for 3½ months. It certainly came as a surprise to me - especially as it happened and I didn't know for so long afterwards - failed again in your duty as Acting Secretary Miss K!!

I haven't written to Brian since I heard as I am waiting to hear from him in answer to the letter I wrote nearly 3 months ago. I have written and offered my congratulations to Christine, addressing it to Ravenhurst Rd. Where are they living now? Do your 'family' still go over to the Taylors now on Sat or has that been given up? Despite your regular letters (when they are regular) it's surprising how little news about such things you pass on. Come on wake up!

Today I have at last managed to unearth some green oranges - at least they're mandarins - tangerine things. You'll know what they're like as there's some for you as I promised. I had a bit of fun getting them I was walking towards another village when a young fellow (Italian) on a bike rode up behind me and started talking. He knew a little English as he had been a Prisoner of War (so he said) and we walked along together. I told him I wanted green oranges and so he told me he knew where I could get some. Arriving in the village we went to a fruit stall, but they hadn't any. So then he took me right thru the village and up back alleys, calling at a café for a Marsala on the way and arrived at an orchard. Then ensued a hectic half hour (it seemed like one anyway!) whilst he explained to the owner what I wanted. This wasn't made any easier by his children (7 in number) talking at the same time. In the end the whole family took me to the orchard and started to pick these green mandarins. In the end I'd got 14 kilos of mandarins and 4 of what I think are limes. After much handshaking, "grazis" and "buon sera's" I started off with my two bags of fruit and my two "henchmen" (the 2nd one joined us in the orchard).

They accompanied me to the edge of the village, shook hands half a dozen times (that's not exaggerating!) and I set off hoping to get a lift. I <u>did</u> in 3 farm carts and a ladies carriage. The occupant of the latter spoke

French and took me about a mile and then asked me in for a cup of coffee. I accepted and was introduced to husband, ma and pa and two children and after 3/4 hour departed. I eventually arrived home 4 hours after starting out and it's only about 3-4 miles to this village. I enjoyed myself immensely and the passers by were very tickled to see the "Inglezi" carrying his two sacklets between lifts!

I shudder to think what would have happened in those circs if the rest of the QA had been with me – we'd probably be in the local jail now.

Your mandarins shall be posted off in the next day or two Madam. Trusting they will meet your requirements,

I remain etc etc ....
That's all for now.
All the very best
Vivian

B.N.A.F.
10.12.43

My dear Pat,

Many thanks for your AL which arrived yesterday. Thanks, also, in advance, for the Christmas present - tho you leave me in suspense as to what you're sending. Glad to see that for your escorts you're still patronizing the RAF! By now you will have had some time at the nursery school and will know how you like it. I must say though, that they don't pay you much. Still I expect there will be enough to do to keep you and your mind occupied. I have already written a letter to you in answer to your's - a sea letter. This probably accounts for not having much to say, but I knew I should get told off if you had to wait that long.

All the very best – Vivian

Wyton
15/12/43

My Dear Pat,
There, how's that - no Salome's, Blondies or anythings to cut you to the quick.

My dear child don't ever say anything about <u>my</u> writing again - that terrific description of your dress - I can't make any sense out of it - first you say its <u>not</u> white lace - that tells me a lot - what is it? - and then you go on to say there is enough material in the skirt to provide curtains for a bungalow - well a) I thought it was a dress not a skirt, b) who wants to use a dress as curtains and c) where's the bungalow? And then you say it's more than a circular skirt - I've never seen one! And you can hold the hem up to about shoulder level each side - well I guess you could do that with most skirts - but its not very lady-like now is it - you don't intend to dance like that I hope? Anyway I still haven't the faintest clue what it looks like - but I guess I can wait and see - and we certainly <u>will</u> do some dancing.

Well now we get to the subject of your conceit - you wanted me to tell you why before and I spared your feelings - but now, well here you are!

And having got to the next page I've changed my mind - after all why should I hurt your poor little feelings - when I tease you that's different because you know darned well I don't mean it - but you don't <u>have</u> to fish for compliments do you? Still if you want them so badly here you are little one - sort of make up for my lapse.

You say that even if I don't like you somebody does - did I ever say I didn't like you? - do you think I wander around kissing people I don't like?

And I <u>do</u> like your hair - but I don't like the style - or the snood - because you look much sweeter without it darling.

True I said you didn't know how to use make up - but I didn't mean it - I'm sorry - satisfied? And to go on - re your face I find it exceedingly attractive and I can think of no complaints with regard to your figure and with regard to your last question - that's a leading question so I don't have to answer it - ask me next leave and maybe I will!

Now with regard to my next leave - all things being equal I shall get away to Brum on the 30th -- <u>now</u>! Can you find the gen on any decent dances around at that time, and you will be able to appear in all your glamour and then I suppose everybody will fall in love with you and you will be really conceited then! However I positively refuse to jump in any static water tanks!

Well that's about all for now I guess - by the way I <u>never</u> let my hair down - not for strangers anyway!

Ferdie insists on writing a p.s. again - blast the man - however his wife has sent me a couple of kisses - to make up for the ones you sent him - send him some more if you like - as long as <u>I</u> can collect them for him.

Well I guess I'll warm my hands a little now - they are almost as cold as yours usually are - by the way you <u>do</u> kiss nicely.

Sincerely yours,
Ray

Dear Blondie

I asked Ray how I should address this postscript to you and he thought it would be best as above. Ray didn't keep the note you wrote to me but tore it up in a fit of jealousy so I'm afraid I'm in ignorance as to whether you returned my overtures. I also think that he took an unfair advantage of me in going on his 48 hour pass, for the personal touch outweighs the letter, and then I know what a flanneller Ray is!

Still perhaps you can reserve one corner of your heart for me and I can return your love.

I can't say more as you know what Ray is? He is going to read this afterwards.

Cheerio
Ferdie

Blast the man! I'm <u>not</u> a flanneller - am I?
R

Betty, my old room-mate from the Children's Hospital, had been out with me before going home on leave.

I went to see her off at New Street station; it was about 10.30 pm, with no moon. It was absolute pitch-blackness, and I had to walk to Broad Street to catch the bus.

As I left the station I was conscious of American soldiers all around, though I couldn't see them. (I learned later that they had been confined to barracks for some time, and this was their first time out since.)

Suddenly I was grabbed by a shadowy form, with his shadowy companion by his side.

I told myself that there must be M.Ps about, and that if I screamed they would come running, but I thought that first I would try cold, dispassionate reasoning.

I therefore informed him as coldly as I could that I was about to catch a bus, and that I would miss it if he didn't let me got at once.

He grumbled and groped and argued a little, and then his companion said, "Aw, let her go, Bud!"

Then he released me, and I walked away, as calmly and coolly as I could, to run the gauntlet of the pack of sex-starved G.Is that I sensed were all around me in the inky blackness, and finally reached the comparative security of the bus stop and its waiting queue. When I wrote to Ray I told him about it.

also approx 10.15 pm!!   Wyton

22-12-43

My Dear Pat,

I'm slipping, I normally answer your letters on the day they are received but yesterday being a very busy little boy I didn't get time - and I've nearly left it too late today.

Firstly thank you for the tokens - we shall certainly have to have a selection session during leave - theres a new Bing number – "If I had my way" - why didn't you fill them in though? – I'll do it for you and you can see what I put when I come home - you *do* blush nicely!

With regard to your dress I *do* think you are mean - just think how tantalising it is to have to sit here miles and miles away and not even be able to imagine what your glamorous creation is like.

Really you do have fun in the black out don't you - I think you need a nurse or guardian or something.

Well here's a thing now - I certainly don't want to jump into a water tank - much too cold at this time of year - so I suppose I have no alternative but to apologise. Anyway I've decided not to tell you why you are conceited because I rather like it and if I told you you might change. And <u>do</u> go on thinking that I'm really <u>so</u> nice because I am aren't I?

Pity about the Midland Red dance on my Birthday - because I definitely won't be home for that! And furthermore little one - I'm afraid we shan't be able to dance the New Year in - you see I have to go on playing soldiers for a bit longer - in other words I've had my *!!!? leave postponed until the seventh of Jan which means that granted an abnormal stroke of luck I'll get away on the sixth - sorry! - however I'm sure we can still dance when I <u>do</u> come - unless you've worn your dress out by then!

Well our Christmas here is beautifully organised for us - one could almost do it by numbers! On Xmas Eve we have an Ensa concert - we then invite the bods back to the mess and carol sing also gargle with the odd pint or so I suppose.

On Xmas day we go to church in the morning – I'm <u>so</u> excited about it! - in the afternoon we play football - after having served the airmen's lunch - in the evening we have a race meeting - played with cards and dice and a tote and the odd pint or so!

I don't think there is anything on on Boxing morning except the odd hangover - but we have a picture show in the afternoon and our Xmas dinner at night followed by a thrilling dance attended by all the officers - two Waafs - the odd officers' wives - not very tasty or sweet! - and a few popsies from the nearest village - grim huntresses of the 'weaker' sex.

All this of course is dependant on old Butch Harris *(Air Marshall Arthur Harris, known as "Butcher" Harris, Chief of Bomber Command)* not wanting us to prang the European fortress every five minutes or so - I personally expect he will - the spoil sport! Oh we also have a dance on New Years Eve - but they can - (no I'd better not say that - might shock you!)

Anyway I think you had better save a chunk of mistletoe for the sixth - although I suppose it really isn't essential - the mistletoe I mean!

Emmy the engineer decided to finish ops at 30 and we gave him a farewell party last night - we all got well and truly plastered and almost wept over each other - lucky little man has gone home for 14 days leave and then goes on rest for six months - which usually turns out to be a year - I think maybe the rest of us who are pressing on should see the doctor about our heads - we had also dispensed with the services of our tame navigator - got quite a good one now too! Also our rear gunner has finished flying - he burst his ear drums - so only three of the original crew are left - Tommy, Ellwood and myself.

Well I really appear to be burning the midnight oil tonight - however I think that's about all - you see nobody ever even tries to get fresh with me in the blackout so I haven't much to write about.

I don't suppose you will get this till after the Xmas rush so I hope you had a good time and didn't make your little self sick or anything, and also happy new year - and think of me on New Years Eve wishing I was there to wish it to you.

Love,
Ray ((D.L.Y.H.D.D.)*

*which being translated from the original Zulu means, "Don't let your hair down darling"!

(Ray, and his two fellow crew members, could also have finished their 'tour' of 30 ops, but decided that they ought to carry on.
It was very brave of Ray. He found the raids a terrible strain, he suffered continual nightmares and his nerves were shattered. The light banter he enjoyed with me was his way of coping.)

At Christmas Mrs Watts gave me Ray's Christmas present to me - a gilt cigarette case and matching match case that I had seen and admired.

Wyton
26/12/43.

My Dear Pat,

This is I think the most peculiar and least interesting Xmas I have spent in the services - it might have started with a sing song on the 23rd, but the Butcher had other ideas and we flew the jolly old Xmas mail to that place instead - naturally the major part of the 24th was spent in peaceful (?) oblivion in bed.

However most of us managed to rally round around tea time and we started a party - I phoned home to cheer up the family - Mother was down at your place - and Father informed me that I sounded very miserable - I was - I normally manage a spell of homesickness around this time of the year.

After that we had a rather blue and very corny Ensa show and then a sing song - <u>very</u> blue in the mess - in the middle of which I got very fed up and phoned you and then went to bed.

Xmas day started badly - we nearly flew the mail again - however that blew over and we put in some hard work serving the erks dinners - getting back to the mess to find our own cold buffet finished except for some bread and butter and sausage meat! - what an Xmas feast!! In the afternoon a picture show – 'You were never Lovelier' - not bad - then a cup of tea and a bun - In the evening we had a race meeting - I had intended to attend but the sight of the opening parade finished me - an ancient and idiot Lt Col dressed in frock coat etc prancing round the dining room ringing a bell followed by a bevy of Waaficers in jodhpurs - so most of the other younger officers immediately breezed off out to the local - it was closed however the next one wasn't - and a five mile walk isn't really much - got back and into bed at 12 - what an Xmas!

Today - everyone seems to have a hangover - very few of us had breakfast – doesn't seem to be much work to be done – I've been in the billet most of the morning – it's almost lunch time now so I shall toddle along to the mess and have a pint before the rush starts - will continue later.

Hallo again, it is now 5.30 - we had a lunch time session and then I decided to have a nap - beer at lunch time always makes me sleepy - however P/O Pilgrim seeing me asleep got his clarinet and made such a hideous noise that sleep was impossible, so after a bit of a rough house we went and played snooker till tea time - the bar opens at six so I must run along again - we are having our Xmas dinner tonight and its going to be all officer and gentlemanish - one does all kinds of odd things that tradition has made ritual, but as most of the bods are just about on their knees and very much the worse for the large quantities of liquor that have been consumed I can imagine a large number of blacks being put up.

So now I shall go and say good evening to the C.O. and drink a pink gin - and then sneak out and have a beer - because I prefer it - I <u>do</u> hope nobody makes any boring speeches or I'm liable to break a noble record here and get quietly plastered like the majority of others.

And again hello, its now 11.4 1/2 and I'm back in the billet again - fed up to the teeth! Firstly the bar didn't open till 6.30 and so all the types were sitting around in the ante room twiddling their thumbs and waiting for the word go!

Eventually we started - I decided that as we might be in the dining room a long while it might not be wise to drink too much beer - I was right!

Dinner was a morbid affair although the meal was excellent and the station band tried hard - but the A.O.C. was present and everything had to be done according to the book and that's pretty dull - however there weren't many blacks - a few people got a little mixed over the port - but who gives a damn anyway. At 9 o'clock we managed to tear ourselves away and started a sing song in the lounge - but that blasted Lt. Col. appeared again and announced a dance - imagine! five Waaficers and three officers wives and 200 hungry men!

It was pretty deadly so we went into the kitchen and got hold of the waitresses - I managed a couple of quicksteps, a few beers and then as the necking process was starting and the bar too crowded - decided to go to bed - after all we *may* be flying the mail again tomorrow - and that's about all for now. I'm going to bed now to pray for fog tomorrow and then dream of thee! 'night.

Boxing Day now - so far rather unexciting - we had a normal working morning and afternoon, also a lecture by the C.O. on the nasty behaviour of a number of officers towards Waaf personnel – I'd hate to be a Waaf.

Tonight we have a film show - I suppose I shall go, there's nothing else to do - but I think it's going to be corny.

Thanks for the miserable little note of the 24th – you've got a cheek! Who kept me waiting for about three weeks for a reply - about a month ago?

Well that's all for now - and also makes it <u>your</u> turn to write - by the way young ladies don't usually use such vulgar expressions as 'digit removum' but I do know what it means. *(I had written to Ray telling him to "Pull your finger out, and write to me". I was unaware of the significance of the phrase.)*

You have exactly nine clear days writing time left before I get home (fingers crossed!) so press on darling.

Love,
Ray

Royal Air Force
Wyton.
31-12/43

My Dear Pat,

I now have two letters to answer - you really are doing well these days. I was going to write day before yesterday but of course business comes before pleasure and so I couldn't - however I have no excuse for not writing yesterday- Freddie asked me to go out on a binge with him and in a weak moment I agreed - however I consider that I redeemed myself by phoning - how does it feel to get out of a nice warm bed to answer the phone?

The idea of a private New Year celebration when I come home seems OK - what do we do?

You don't seem very keen on Pantos – what's the matter - getting too old? Personally I'm still young enough to enjoy them - or maybe just the chorus I like!

So you made a beast of yourself at Christmas did you - and not being content with overeating you start serious drinking - better watch those gin and limes they aren't quite as tame as they might appear - three or four usually produce quite a romantic mood - with little girls I mean of course.

I say that's a good show, your having a WAAF billeted with you - I've no doubt we shall have fun - make sure she's glamorous won't you, and it's no use removing the mistletoe because I'll bring my own!!

Most RAF slang has at least two meanings – one for little girls and the others airmen for the use of – your little Waaf will probably enlighten you on that subject – I certainly don't intend to!

So you still want to be an artist eh? I thought you had changed your mind and were thinking of raising a family of at least fifteen, anyway you certainly seem to have an artistic nature, you say you like sitting in pubs talking – there's a thing now!! I'm beginning to think you're not nice to know - and I'm certain you'll lead me astray unless I'm very careful – I'm not thinking of being very careful of course!

I suppose I shall have to confess why I take you to the 'Hungry Man' - *(On Ray's previous leave we had gone to the 'Hungry Man' for a drink, but found it absolutely packed with drunk R.A.F. types squirting soda syphons all over the place. On the wall was pinned a pair of cami-knicks with 'Target for Tonight' written on a banner, pinned across them -*

460

actually the raffle prize for the war-effort. Anyway, we decided discretion was the better part of valour and moved on to a different pub.) - you see I have a secret passion for the barmaid - and of course I just can't keep away from the place – she's <u>so</u> slim isn't she?

I won't take you there again tho', I know a better place out at Beoley - twin barmaids - I once got seven days C.B. for borrowing an army car to go and see them - but that's rather a long story – I'm sure you'd like them better than ginger!

I can hear quite a lot of aerial activity at the moment and I've got a nasty feeling that instead of sitting here in the billet I should be flapping my wings - that means I'll get a large strip torn off when I'm eventually found - still I'm quite used to it by now.

Only five clear days to leave now - never have so few days taken so damn long to pass - still I suppose they will pass and I shall come home - and then its only for a measly seven days - still fifteen more trips and I'm all through – I'll get fourteen days then - but that's looking a long way ahead.

And that's about all Pat – I'm going to the mess dance tonight - probably get beautifully tight too - must think up some new year resolutions quickly - easy ones though!

Love,
Ray

1944

Aged 17 ½

List of Illustrations

Page

475   Mother presenting the first Knight Memorial Medal

486   Pat at Stratford on Avon

1944 New Year

On New Year's Eve I had a very long 'phone call from Ray. It must have lasted about 20 mins. I could hear a raucous Mess party going on in the background as we talked. Then, suddenly he said, "I love you." Before I could say anything, he said, "Tell me you love me."

The awful thing was that, although I was fond of him, I didn't love him. I was trying to think quickly, and said, "Not over the phone." But he pleaded with me to tell him that I loved him, and I thought what a terrible thing it would be if I told him I didn't, and then he were shot down; so I said, "I love you", reasoning that on his leave I could explain that my love was a fondness for him, but nothing more.

He had also phoned me the previous night (8 lots of pips) and Xmas Eve (2 lots). He gave me a wonderful Xmas present - cigarette case and match case.

Lately he has spent all of every leave with me - Now I know why, for it is now Jan 8th, and on Jan 3rd Ray was reported missing, and now his mother has told me he was very much in love with me. It seems to me now that everyone knew but me. I was so busy thinking of Danny all the time I didn't manage much time to be thinking about Ray. On his last leave I began to get around to it - but when you've had one person on your mind for a long time, it's hard to discover your feelings for another one. I know I was very fond of Ray, but I never dreamed of anything else.

It was strange, the night I learned Ray was missing.

Bandy invited me to go with him to see a film at the Warley Odeon. We caught the bus from town but the further into the journey we went, the more restless and depressed I felt.

In the end the feeling was so strong I could stand it no longer, and, trying to explain to Bandy, who didn't understand, I got off the bus, and caught another bus home.

As I walked down Crosbie road in the intense dark of the blackout I looked up at the sky, black, but blazing with stars, and a sort of refrain started going through my head: "There are millions of stars in heaven, but one has gone out tonight." It kept going through my head, over and over.

At last I reached home, and knocked on the door.

As Mother opened it in the total darkness of the blackout, I <u>knew</u> with absolute certainty, and without her saying a word, or even my being able to see her, I said, "Ray's gone down."

At the moment nothing is in sight for me – I'm going to The Slade after the war - but my job is not the sort of thing I can throw myself into and I need something to occupy my mind and stop myself incessantly thinking about Danny and Ray - Will they come back? Who? Which one means most to me? Did Danny love me as Ray did? - all the time, I can't help thinking about them - Dennis I've now accepted as gone from here and I know I'll meet him again - but the 2 boys – it's just a muddle.

Ray's mother thinks I was in love with him - that makes matters worse, too - I feel an imposter - I don't know what to think or do.

His sister, too, must think the same, and sent me a sympathetic note

London

Dear Pat,
There's so little one can say at a time like this but I felt I must just send you a brief note.

I always had a feeling Ray had a lucky star so do let's hope he will turn up again – somewhere.

I'll be coming home for a few days on Thursday and maybe we'll meet.

Yours – Joyce

And Ferdie, with whom I had shared so many flippant, nonsensical postscripts in letters to and from Ray, wrote to me:-

F/Lt Sherwood
RAF Station
Wyton

Dear Miss Knight,
No doubt you will have heard the tragic news that Ray was missing on the raid of Jan 2/3rd. I can't say how deeply sorry I am that this should have happened to Ray. He was in a highly experienced crew and it must have been pure mischance.

As you know he was a great friend of mine, especially so since we have lived together in the same room since he came to Wyton. However there is every chance that he and the rest of the crew are safe, probably by now being prisoners of war. It just remains to wait for the news to come through, although that may take sometime, as it has to come through neutral sources.

If I hear anything at any time concerning Ray I shall be only too pleased to write to you, for I know he thought a great deal about you.

Yours sincerely
Ferdie.

*

Meanwhile, letters continued to arrive as usual from Vivian and Bill.

No2.M.F.P.S, R.A.F, C.M.F.

<u>1.1.44</u>

My dear Pat,

I am sorry I haven't written to you for some time, but I haven't heard from you for a long time - indeed the last day I had any mail was 8 Dec! I have however received your book, *(the 'Spirit of Man', an anthology of extracts from poems and other writings, originally produced and edited by Robert Graves during the '14-'18 War)* for which I thank you very much. I have read part of it, and it's very enjoyable and includes some of my favourite bits. We had an extremely enjoyable Xmas, tho a bit of mail would have been welcome. However, we now have a new address and when mail starts coming thru using that address, it ought to be much quicker and more regular. You might remind Bill that he owes me a letter please. No news from this end, this time. Nothing of any importance has happened since I last wrote - and I'll give you more news when I next write.

All the <u>very</u> best.
Vivian

R.A.F.
C.M.F.

22.1.44

My dear Pat,

Many thanks for your A.L. of 10 Jan and I'm sorry that my last Aerograph was so newsless.

I was very sorry indeed to hear about Ray - especially because of the special circumstances you mention in the end of your letter. I heard of a friend of mine who had also not come back from that raid - the news came thru yesterday.

As you say fate does seem to have been very unkind to you, but once again there is a chance. It was even worse because he needn't have gone as his tour had finished. There's no need to be sorry about having to pass such news on - I like to hear all the news, even if it's bad.

Thank you for Philip's address, but I know it and I believe Bill got it from me - at least I wrote and told him. Bill's getting very lax - I'll give him 'a piece of my mind' when I next write. I shall be very glad to have Barrie's address - I've written to their house twice, without answer Could you get Bob Smythe's at the same time? Perhaps you could also let me have RKR's home address, and then I shall be able to get in touch with them.

I have often wondered what has happened to that Sgt Pilot who Den brought to that one meeting and also what has happened to Peggy and Betty. When you do go and see the Matthews please give them my regards and collect all the gen you can.

Life here goes on just as usual and I haven't any news of interest to tell you.

I have finished your book and found it very interesting and thank you again. It will be very nice to dip into at future dates.

I hope to be able to see Teddy Gray in the next few days as I believe I know where he is. All for now.

All the very best
Vivian

My Regards to your 'family'!

Feb I have joined a Women's Canteen where I prepare and serve meals with another girl on Thursday evenings, and I'm going out a lot with no particular friends - Jean, Pam etc. but it's not very satisfying. We're having some boys from the Hospitality Bureau again but……..Had 1½ doz mandarins from Viv, only 9 ½ were not bad.

R.A.F,C.M.F.
12.2.44

My dear Pat,

Thanks very much for your airletter with the addresses – I'll write to them both in the next day or two. I haven't seen Bob since he went to sea, and you know how long ago that is.

I should like to hear how Ray *(Raby)* is getting on, as Brian asked after all of them in his last letter. I haven't heard from Bill since I last told you - he needs another jolt. I haven't done anything in particular since I last wrote and so it's lucky your letter had something in it to reply to, or I'd have had nothing to say. You seem to be collecting canteens now - are you going to carry on with the YWCA as well?

All the <u>very</u> best,
Vivian

Still Feb .... 14th, Mon

Went to a concert tonight with Betty. The last item was 'From the New World Symphony'. Betty had to leave just before the finale - Thank God I'm not at that hospital! She goes on 2 weeks leave tomorrow. I only get 2 per annum but I don't mind - 5 days a week from 8.30 - 4.20 suits me O.K. I'm not complaining.

Had a photo of Ray yesterday – it's very nice. At the moment it's on my dressing table without a frame. Had a letter from Vivian -

Here comes the news – I'll end off.

As I had no photograph of Danny, I wrote to his sister, whose address he had given me. I sent her my photo, and when she replied, sending a photo of Danny in his West Point uniform, she commented, "I can see why he thought you were <u>pretty nice</u>."

This was, of course, the photograph I have placed at Christmas 1942, all of his other photos having been torn up or lost.

Thursday Feb 24th

On Sun I went to a Spiritualist service with Ray's mother. About 1/2 the people got messages. She and I both did! He said something about a cloud the size of a man's hand that is getting lighter - well, that might apply to anything.

The Sun. before that I took Bruce for a walk. We went to Bartley Green.

Oh, how I wish this year looked as full of promise as last year did - how I <u>lived </u>last year!

Sunday March - Strange that those should be my last words because since then things have happened. It's really all because of my sinuses (same old thing).

They've been getting worse ever since before Xmas, and Friday I went to see Dr W., he prescribed a spray and <u>Cod Liver Oil</u>(!) but it didn't seem to do much good and the following Wed. I stayed away from college.

On the Thursday morning Mother and I walked to Bearwood. On the way there we met Dennis Raby, who is now a F/Lt., with his mother, and he invited me out the following evening.

In the afternoon I took Bruce for a walk. Friday morning I decided my sinuses were no better and went to see Dr W. again, he said the only thing to do was to spend at least two weeks in the country! So it was decided I should go and stay in Oxford with Aunty Marjorie.

Later in the morning Mother and I went to town and with <u>great difficulty</u> bought 2 prs of shoes from the same shop.

<u>**Monday**</u> **March**

I caught the morning train to Oxford and was met by Margaret.

Tuesday

Went into Oxford in the afternoon with Margaret. Had tea. Went to the Ritz to see North Star - 2 Yanks sat next to us, and one started pawing me - I stood it as long as I could and then M. and I decided to go. As soon as we got up they did. So we went into the ladies - M went into one of the whatsits and came flying out and said "There's an American looking in thro' the window!" We emerged eventually to find the Yanks waiting in the foyer - so we doubled back - into 2 more - we retreated to the ladies again, and eventually came out with 2 hefty looking W.A.A.F.s!

We lost them outside, and it was just like walking into a pack of wolves. It was a moonlight night and M. and I both had white swagger coats on - 6 Yanks followed us for about 10 mins down some side street - then 2 tried to stop us on Magdalen bridge - when we had pushed them off (Margaret elbowed one in the midriff and said in a rough voice "Bugger off!") they stood back and one yelled at the top of his voice "I wanna dame! - Gimme a dame!!"

Wed In the afternoon I went into Oxford alone, and had tea at Fullers. Three students sat at my table, 2 males and one female - we got talking and after tea I adjourned to The Randolph with them. Then I more or less arranged to meet them for lunch the following day.

Thur M and I went to The Randolph in the morning and found the others in the bar - a fellow called Michael was there and three others, Tim, Mike and John - Margaret and I went to The Angel for lunch, by taxi! There Mike asked me to a dance at the Hollyoak on Sat. night.

I am writing all this just over a month later, and it is a little difficult to remember just how things happened - but I know I went to Mike's college (Pembroke) for tea and met two other undergraduates, Sandy and Dozey there.

Someone actually brings in tea on a tray to them! They poured me tea, and Sandy offered me the plate of 'sensuous cakes', as he always insisted on calling them.

I went to tea with them several times. On one occasion we didn't notice how time had passed, and they suddenly realized I was still there after visitors were supposed to be out of the College. So they rigged me up in a cap and gown, and smuggled me out!

Sometimes we would cycle to 'The Trout' for a drink, and one evening we got into conversation with some American army officers there. When it was closing time they said they would give us a lift in their Command car back into Oxford. We explained that we had cycled there and had bikes. They didn't consider that a problem, so we all crammed into the Command car with Sandy and Mike hanging onto the bikes on the outside and progressed like this back to Oxford!

Several of the boys were in the Sea Cadets and it was decided that one evening we would sail up the Isis in the College whaler, have a few drinks and a few sandwiches at a pub, and sail back. We were to meet in Mike's room, but when I got there no-one had yet arrived, and a note from Sandy, and another from Mike, awaited me.

PEMBROKE COLLEGE,
OXFORD.

If we are not back, please sit down and make yourself at home. If you are thirsty you know when the Kümmel is! Cheerio
    Love
    <u>Mike</u>.

Wee one,

Mike D on parade also but expects to be back about 4.45; Dozy is sure to come out of his exam early so may get here before you do; God knows where Henry is; I ought to be off parade by 4.15. I hope one of us is back before you. If none of us are some of us will be in very shortly - what hospitality! That is all very complex but it is logical. In the meantime there's a pipe on the mantle-piece, a load of tobacco by Venus. Whilst you puff pray God it will be fine.
    Sandy.

Gradually the boys came in, and we all went to see the 'Bosun' who was in charge of the cadets and the whaler, and who lived on the College barge.

When we arrived, and I was introduced, he insisted on us all having some Algerian wine. Unfortunately, he had no glasses, so we had to drink it out of thick, white teacups, which didn't do a lot for the wine, which needed all the help it could get, anyway!

That little ceremony out of the way, they made ready the whaler, and we all piled in, including the Bosun.

I had never sailed before, and I thought it just wonderful, swishing through the water quietly - apart from my rowdy companions! - until we came to our destination and eased in, mooring the boat.

How long we were in the pub I have no idea, but after a few drinks and some food, I decided that some of my companions were getting decidedly the worse for wear, and said so to Sandy, who agreed, and we began the difficult task of trying to extricate them and get them into the whaler. As the Bosun was as pie-eyed as the rest of them, he was no use to organize them, and, as soon as we got some out and went in to extricate the others, those first out went back in!

Eventually, somehow, we got everyone back into the whaler, where it was obvious that, their condition apart, the weather conditions were not suitable to sail back, and we would have to row back.

One of the undergraduates, Henry, was delegated to untie the mooring ropes, and we all grabbed an oar, and when he shouted 'O.K.' and jumped into the boat, we all heaved on our oars. Unfortunately, he had forgotten that there were two mooring ropes, and had only untied one, so when we pulled on our oars mightily, there was a sudden jar as the remaining rope went taut, and we all fell over backwards off our thwarts!

Anyway, we eventually got going, and somehow managed to row back to the College barge without mishap. Having secured the whaler and said our farewells to the Bosun, Sandy said he'd see me home and sent the others off on their way back to the College. Next day, when I once again went to tea with them, I was told of their journey back.

We had delegated Mike, as being the most sober, to lead them back, but we were misled. He was, if anything, the most drunk of the lot (apart from the Bosun!) but it had stupified him into the appearance of something nearer sobriety. He decided to take a short cut, and led them all over a wall and into a builders' yard where, following his lead, they all fell into a large hole. However, somehow they did all manage to get safely back eventually.

One night near the end of my stay in Oxford, I was in the kitchen with Aunt Marjorie, when we heard a sound like a swarm of bees. It got louder and louder, and became a sort of ceaseless humming roar. We ran outside to see what it was, and the sound was tremendous, and over our heads the sky was black with hundreds and hundreds of planes; they just kept coming, wave upon wave upon wave. As far as one could see, the whole sky was one mass of planes. It was incredible and awe-inspiring; one knew something special was happening, and felt terrific emotions: excitement, pride, apprehension for the flyers, and the tremendous power and might of the overhead armada.

Monday   5 Crosbie Road

My dear Pat,
 Grandma is still away but returns tomorrow. Nita' phoned this morning, I think she is wondering when you are going to stay with her. I hope you received your bicycle O.K. also the box containing your shoes, dance frock etc. I will phone one of the next evenings to see how you are, and whether Aunty Marjorie can put up with you for a bit longer.
 By the way Ray's mother is beginning to feel very anxious and worried about Ray as time is going on. I wish you would write to her or even phone her (not forgetting to pay Aunty M. for the call). She says you are the nearest she can get to Ray, and she absolutely needs you to bestow sympathy and love on. Don't be afraid to let her do it - it is the only way you can really be of help to her. I think she has more or less given up hope of Ray ever coming back, and really it was such a ghastly raid that I am afraid I haven't much hope either. She keeps asking whether I have heard from you. I know she is <u>expecting</u> either a letter or a phone call so, do get in touch with her, she says she is terribly lonely with you away.
 By the way it is Dad's 51st birthday today. I know you will hate to have overlooked it but never mind, it is so easy under the circumstances. He and I are going to the pictures tonight – isn't that a wonderful birthday treat?
 Please give my dearest love to Aunty Marjorie and to Margaret not forgetting Paul. Lots of love to yourself and I do hope you are better, from Mother. P.S. The first Dennis Knight medal is to be presented on Sat. next at 2.30.

Mother presenting the first Knight Memorial Medal

R.A.F.
C.M.F.
13.3.44

My dear Pat,

Many thanks for your AL of Mar 6th received yesterday - and about time too! You've been getting rather lax lately. Anyway I'm very glad that you've liked the parcels, and no return is necessary at all. They're merely a <u>very</u> small return for the kindness you and the rest of your family have always shown me.

I'm glad that the tangerines got home OK, because they're over now and so you won't be able to have any more. I thought the brooch rather cute and thought you'd like it.

Thanks for Ray R's address – I've now got everybody's, I think - thanks to your efforts. Still, as Acting Secretary it's your job!

I've just looked back in my diary to see how long it was since I heard from you - 11 Feb! Since then I've seen 4 films; two operas:- 'Madame Butterfly' and 'Pagliacci' and 1 ENSA stage show; slept many hours and - in case you should think I'm here for my health - worked many!

Mother is ill again - anaemia, blood pressure and her heart isn't too good. I'm rather worried and hope she gets better soon. We've also had some 'alarums and excursions' and lost, amongst people, two out of our tent and the C.O.

Anne has been ill too. She had streptococcal infection and had about a fortnight at home, but has returned to the hospital now.

No word from Bill lately. I'm going to write him a snooty letter and pass on a rude remark from Brian. I've had a second letter from him – he's cheesed.

That's about all the 'gen' I can think of at the moment. Let's hear from you next time with less interval than a month.

All the <u>very</u> best
<u>Vivian</u>

R.A.F.
C.M.F.
<u>4.4.44</u>

My dear Pat,

Many thanks for your long overdue AL of 28th March, but as usual you find a good excuse and your apologies sounded <u>most</u> 'umble.

I seem to have rather misled you - quite unintentionally, I assure you. I received news only today that Roy Sharp and the others were quite well, they were only posted to another unit. That's one of the disadvantages of using slang terms and I hope it didn't shake you too much.

I was sorry to hear that there was definite news of Ray - at least of that sort. It certainly looks as if he's had it.

Since last writing to you I have only seen three films.

For the last week or so we've had lovely weather with clear skies and quite warm. Tho there aren't many trees in leaf yet, there are some trees with flowers like Japanese cherries in bloom and broad beans are about 15" high and in flower!

I had a 'report' from Barbara *(his sister)* on the rock garden last week. She says that everything is well settled and growing well and that the sole death was a viola - all those plants your parents gave me are still alive and doing well.

Like you, I haven't heard from Bill as yet and not from Brian again. Tho his mother sent me Wishy's address some time ago, I haven't written yet. One of these days I'll sit down and use all those addresses you so kindly got for me.

You didn't mention your job in your last letter and so I assume the kids haven't driven you quite mad yet.

All the <u>very</u> best
<u>Vivian</u>

On my eighteenth birthday, Ray's mother came round with his birthday present to me, with this message:

"Hello, Many Happy Returns of your birthday.

The last time I spoke to Ray over the phone, he asked me to get these records for you, in case he was not around today.

I do hope dear they are what you wished for and that you will find a lot of pleasure in playing them.

The ring is not of much value, but very old, it is so difficult to find a nice present so will you accept this with my love.

You have been a great comfort to me Pat, and I hope you will always look upon me as one of your most sincere friends.

Once more, dear, Best Wishes from us all
E. Watts"

Sun. June - 1944

Tomorrow I start back at Art School again - I hope I can really make it a good thing.

(Although I enjoyed working at the Nursery School, I felt in need of a position with more authority, but I was told that this was impossible without having had specialist training. This would take about three years at Training College - away from the children.

I was once again in a dilemma, and sought advice at the Citizens Advice Bureau.

I explained that I wanted to be doing something useful during the war, but that after the war I knew now that I wanted to go back to Art School. So they advised me to go back now!)

Sat June 17th

I wish I could find time to write my diary regularly. Today 'Salute The Soldier' week starts. Just 10 days ago was D-day - ie. we invaded Normandy. Now we have established quite a large beachhead and it looks as tho' we're quite firmly fixed.

Yesterday we had news that the Germans have been sending pilotless planes over Southern England.

Mon June 19th

I heard that the Q.E. hospital was asking for women to go and sit with the soldiers back from France and relieve the nurses. I asked Mrs Vernon about it. She is going to find out from her sister - there is 1 ward full of wounded German prisoners and her sister says how nice they are. That started a violent discussion between Mother and Dad about so-called 'nice Germans'.

How I miss all the boys - specially Danny and Ray - I miss the fun and the long interesting conversations I had with Ray and I just miss Danny for himself. When shall I again feel that funny tight feeling around my heart when I meet a certain person's eyes, and that terribly emotional relaxed feeling when I'm in a certain person's arms? I know it sounds silly: but only one person has ever made me feel that way - and he was - Danny.

Tues 22nd Thur

Went to hear Barbirolli and the Hallé, at the Big Top with Phil. When we came home Mother said Colin had phoned and was coming round to see me Fri. morning. I flatly refused to stay in and see him so Mother had to confess - it was <u>Bill</u> turned up from Trinidad!!!

We spent his leave sitting in the garden, going out for drinks, seeing friends, and found time to write two crazy letters to Vivian.

When I saw Bill off on Sunday night, he asked me if I knew he'd been in love with me - I just didn't know what to say and then I asked him if he still was and he said "Yes". I told him I liked him a lot but was not in love with him and he didn't seem surprised. Then he said he thought he'd boobed in confessing like that, and was afraid it would spoil our friendship.

I went to bed in a whirl -

- Oh when we came back it was still broad daylight, and I dared Bill to climb up the ladder in front of the house - he did and as luck would have it Dad was in the 'little room' with the door open! Oh, boy! It was funny! Dad asked Bill if he wanted to come in!

Mon.- Bill came round at about 9.30 and we played records and had some tea - we went into town for coffee and then picked up his case and I saw him off. He may be back soon.

- I've missed out a lot of description I can see - Bill has gone thinner and very tanned – he's rather good-looking now. He's certainly improved - but what surprised me was when he kissed me goodnight he said "Now you'll know how inexperienced I am." - and he was. He says he hasn't bothered about women at all, but spent most of his spare time drinking and doing crazy things like chase 'The Bat' round the swimming pool in the moonlight.

I was 'fed up' with my long hair and decided to have it all cut off. Vivian was <u>not</u> pleased to hear about it.

R.A.F.
C.M.F.

23.6.44

My dear Patricia,

Considering our respective great ages (see: your last para) I suppose I ought to address you as Miss Knight, but in case you might think that a little unfriendly, I have dropped the more childish 'Pat' in favour of the more senior 'Patricia'.

As usual (note this) you have been lax in your reply - but as you say you are working hard (?) I shall have to forgive you, but there is one thing I cannot. This is the utter vandalism of destroying a life's work - to wit, the cutting off in all its glory of your hair - a pandering to a modern fashion. Apart from this it puts your photo out of date - in other words, despite whatever other people may think I most definitely do not approve. Consider yourself thoroughly told off. What does it look like anyway? In actuality I suppose the real reason is that owing to your hectic gaddings about, you have been unable to find time to arrange it and have taken the easiest path and cut if off - shame on you! Does Bill know yet - you might have consulted your 'joint guardians' before taking such a step!

Please congratulate Den R on his first kill, for me, will you, please? (*D.R. was flying the new, superior fighter - the Mosquito.*)

Your confession (I'm not laughing now) about Ray and Danny interested me. However, when Bill and I can get together, we'll find you someone who'll beat you twice a week!

I rather like the Dvorak Symphony myself and your other presents sounded interesting. I wanted to send you something myself, but couldn't find anything suitable. As a poor substitute tho, there's a box of almonds on the way. They are greatly improved by blanching.

Referring once again to your last paragraph - as you say, cycling used not to be as popular and yet don't forget that I could hardly take you onto main roads such as the Stratford Road in those shorts of yours. If, on Whit Monday, you were wearing them, then I can understand where all the cyclists were going!

There's no news this end, I'm afraid. I haven't heard from Bill since the letter I told you about.

An order has just come out saying that we can write about places we have visited S of a line from Naples to Bari and that we can say we've visited Rome. The latter is the best town I've visited overseas. Clean wide streets with the slums carefully hidden from the main streets, unlike Naples. St Peter's is huge, wonderful paintings and yet it didn't quite come up to expectations. At the entrance to the courtyard stands a Swiss Guard and a notice saying 'Vatican City - Neutral Territory'.

Naples Bay is lovely - wonderful blue sea and Vesuvius behind. The latter is well worth the energy of the climb. Naples itself isn't so hot - bit dirty, too many hawkers and high prices. Very fine opera house tho. Other places I've visited are Castellemare, Torre Annunziata, Herculaneum, Pompeii. Ruins there are wonderful and are very well preserved. Sorrento and Amalfi have English 'Colonies'. I have also visited Salerno. There's not much room in an Air Letter, but I thought you'd perhaps be interested to hear where I've been to.

That's all for now. Despite the hair cutting business, my best wishes to your family and to yourself.

All the <u>very</u> best
<u>Vivian</u>

30th June - Fri - My pen is downstairs and I can't be bothered to fetch it. We go to Stratford tomorrow. Can't say I'm all that thrilled - I feel rather - no very - depressed, dunno why.

Well, in fact, I had great fun at Stratford and a thoroughly enjoyable time after all.

BRISTOL
England.
5/7/44.

Dear Pat,

How's the holiday? I'm still at home as you can see. I wrote England in the heading before I could stop myself, one of these habits one acquires after much travel abroad. One becomes internationally minded my sweet little insular idiot.

Pause while I wait for you to realise how broadened is my mind by travel compared with your narrow outlook, thou jingoistic June flower.

If I do not hear from My Lords before Friday I shall in all probability toddle down to Brum once more, on that day. I had thought of whistling on down to Stratford from Brum to keep a fatherly eye on you and possibly lure you into one of those rowing boats for two that are for hire, on the off chance that you don't know the Navy policy of "Once aboard the lugger and--" yum, yum makes me paw the ground to think of it. They tell me some of the reaches of the river are very beautiful - and lonely.

Anyhow to finish up on a more serious note, I hope Old Viv has had - no not in the R.A.F. sense - should I say "has received" - our 2 letters and that his reply will be there on your return, though I suppose it will take longer for this to happen.

That's all for now. Am interested to know if the Knight family is considered sufficiently haute monde to drink in the Exclusive Club*. Think of me as you raise your glass of champagne to your luscious lips, my love, won't you.

Ta ta for now. <u>Bill</u>.

*A *private bar in the hotel*

To <u>A/Secty</u>   No 2. M.F.P. Squadron
This memorandum should be sent A.S.P.   R.A.F.
to the member for Bristol and the Flt.   C.M.F.
Air Arm. <u>Chairman</u>

Dear Pat and Bill,

I have addressed this to you, Pat, because by the time this letter reaches England, Bill will probably be at his station. Nevertheless this is really to both of you two ruffians - especially you, Pat, treating your old uncle so rudely.

Right, here goes. I've heard of some jammy blighters in my life, but William - you take the biscuit - I'm absolutely green with envy, when I look round our 'beautiful' Italy and then think of you in England. You announce your first letter as on an <u>auspicious</u> (only 2 s's please) occasion - personally by the tone of the letter, I should say suspicious (suspicion of alcohol) occasion. Talking about alcohol, we've just had our beer ration restored after 3 months and secondly as you <u>gloatingly</u> talk of one (note one) gin and orange - I'd like to shoot you down in flames by saying that when I visited Rome, I celebrated my entry into my first enemy capital with THREE (note - <u>three</u>) gin and oranges - and it wasn't bad gin too. I then spent an interesting two hours with a member of an enemy country - a Bulgarienne - spoke English (and in case your low, tropic-besotted mind – Bill's mind, Pat's isn't tropic-besotted) should think anything - she lives at a convent (Private note to Bill:- If you go to Rome ever, I'll give you her address. Blonde, 23, and about 5' 6" - tho not as nice as some blondes I know)

You say Bill was recognised by his dirty laugh?

Birds of a feather .....

I too, from the tone of her letters, have noticed the degeneration in the formerly pedestal position of A/Secretary and have been worried not a little by it. I look to you, Lt.B., to guide her in the paths of righteousness and good guidance - note righteousness not riotousness! I, too, will use my influence to see that when all the best blokes emigrate once more to England, that those who were former intimates of the aforementioned A/Sectry, do not find her in such a low state of degeneracy, that they no longer feel that they can meet her even as an equal - much less a human to a goddess. As examples of this degeneracy may I quote the following:-

(1)　That following the present trifling and stupid fashion for short hair she has shorn her hair.
(2)　She now finds that a mere L.A.C. is only worth one letter a month. (Hurry up and get your Rear-Admiralship, old man, or she'll drop you!)

I hope you will go into the question with her revered parents (my best wishes to them both - and my condolences to them for such a daughter) and tell them all the dark tale. Enough of Miss K, you sir, shall have a strip torn off, for not writing - continuation of this will lead to my keen displeasure.

Re the wolves, if she is interested in that kind of wolf (the S on Avon brand) - then I'm finished, she can go to the wolves (I mean, dogs).

Life proceeds comfortably at --, my summer residence in Italy. My doctor (the RAF) has recommended me to continue my stay here and so I shall be unable to show the Navy how the RAF can consume xxx* - even after 14 months away from it. (*Not kisses, they come at the end).

I believe I know where you will next be going Bill, may I wish you all the luck in the world, and a safe return to the xxx (beer or the other).

Buena sera, signor and signorina (not bad, eh?). Love and xxx (have either, whichever you want)

Your lonely exile

Vivian

Bill was posted to Arbroath in Scotland.

ARBROATH,
17/7/44

Hallo me darlint,

And how's the wolf hunting? Many thanks for the rather angry letter with Vivian's little effort enclosed. I hasten to assure that I disassociate myself entirely from his disparaging remarks about your coiffure, he is obviously still blundering around in the Victoria period where hair is concerned. After all, witness the green headdress with which he conceals his own ruddy, tousled locks, if that isn't a relic of the Victorian era I'll eat mine - hat not locks.

21/7/44

Four days later; due to the fact that when I haven't been on duty I've been taking advantage of the long evenings by essaying terrific cross country hikes with a New Zealander here who's a real bush ranger type.

But now the sun seems to have left us for a further period of days and I'm duty boy tonight so cannot get out. Yet, I was privileged to be one of the few people in this part of Scotland to see the sun beaming out of a cloudless expanse of blue today; how come? Well by climbing above the unbroken grey cloud layer I came upon this glorious blue world carpeted by the billowing white top of the layer. One of those few occasions when the airman is in a world all his own, shut off completely from all sight of land and sea, chasing up and down hills of white vapour and thro' valleys in the stuff with the sun shining on it all for his exclusive enjoyment.

It is a queer sensation when having taken a look at this deserted upper world you dive through a grey-white mist of cloud suddenly break through the bottom of it and without warning the green and yellow chequered landscape bursts into view beneath you.

Well Pat I'm sorry to inflict this prosaic padding upon you, but upon my life I can think of damn all else to write about except to write screeds and screeds of chiding nonsense as is my usual wont.

What a pity the 'Bat' didn't call on you. He knows one of the barmaids in the 'Hungry Man' very well, her name is Edna and apparently she's a terrific character. She serves in the Bar I believe. If you see her ask if she knows Bat, the New Zealand Subby, and his pal Mike also of the F.A.A. Tell her Bat sends his love. He spent an evening with her when he was in Brum a couple of weeks ago and when he walked into the Bar she pretended he was her long lost sailor husband. So she's bound to remember him.

What about 'line shoot' Phil* has he got his ship yet?

Thanks for enclosing Viv's letter which I return herewith for the benefit of your filing system. Will write again to the old codger some time. Will you send him my address when you write him next as it's about his turn to write me seeing as 'ow you and I wrote 2 smackeroos to him straight off. You'd better mention this to him as well.

Well really my Sweet that's all I have to say except to ask you to look after yourself and not to brood too much on your rather lonely existence.

My love to your Mother and Father. I do hope Mr Knight has fully recovered from the shock of my unexpected appearance!

Lots of Love,
Bill.

* A Merchant Navy officer I went out with for a short time. He sent me an excellent recipe of his mother's for chocolate cake made with dried eggs and other substitutes.

Once again, a Canadian F/O arrived, via the Hospitality Bureau, to spend his leave with us.

His name was Dave, and like virtually all Canadians I had met, was a good skater. He was also a skier, and had, on one occasion, crashed into a wall and smashed his jaw and lost all his teeth, which worried him terribly. He was excessively sensitive about smiling and kissing, and perhaps my sensitive and understanding attitude caused him such gratitude and relief, he proposed to me on the train as we rode back from a day trip to Stratford!

I told him he was making a mistake as we had so little in common, and, despondent, he accompanied me back home.

Next day, he told me that he had thought over what I said, and realized I was right. The funny thing was I knew I was right, but I still felt it a blow to my vanity that he concurred so easily!

As usual, I wrote to Vivian and told him of my latest adventures.

Pat at Stratford on Avon, with her newly cut hair, photographed by Dave

R.A.F.
C.M.F.
<u>6.8.44</u>

My dear Pat,

    Many thanks for your letter of 31st, tho I was just beginning to rub my hands with glee before writing a stinking letter about young women who cut their hair off.

    Assuming that you didn't know the Canadian before he spent his leave with you, he was a pretty fast worker - have you been having some nice moons lately? As your adopted brother-cum-uncle, would it be rude to enquire as to whom the other two gentlemen were?

    Three such proposals at your age are pretty stiff - one can't understand with all the best blokes exiled! You make me feel very old when I think that I can remember you as a black stockinged spindly legged schoolgirl. Do you remember that first Sat afternoon I came to see you?

    Tell Bill not to be a lazy, stinking shirker - he actually owes me two letters even if we count him as writing all of both those joint air letters. Trouble with those Navy men!

One of these days, not so far distant now maybe, we'll go one of our cycle rides – don't forget our date, you shall wear your shorts (as much an emblem of the QA as my hat) and we'll go somewhere near a river where I'll show you how to row at the greatest possible danger to everybody in the vicinity. I, too, would like one of those rides - but what's the use, it'll never be the same now you've cut your hair off!!

Why are you always doing things to annoy me, like the above and playing records I don't like? I suppose you won't like shandies when I come back – wouldn't mind a pint of Mr Ansell's beer at the moment. Please ask your father if he could save a bottle for my first post o/s visit - I shall probably need a reviver when I see you again. (That of course is a very clever compliment to you - or is it?!)

I feel in the mood at the moment for a really silly argument with somebody and shall probably get it when Jeff wakes up. He's as mad as a hatter!

I'm glad you enjoyed the almonds - they certainly took long enough to reach you. At the moment the fruit is pears -greenish, hard, juicy ones - 3 of us ate 3 kilos between us the other night in the flicks (we weren't ill, by the way). Seen quite a lot of films since I last wrote.

It's very warm out here and I do little except bathe - sun and water - sleep, quarrel, talk and read - AND work.

I shall be very glad to see these new polyphotos - to see the full damage done. So let's hope they don't take too long. I have the previous photo you gave me, with me - it lives in the same folder as Den's photo. Mother has been asking for a photo of myself and so I'll get one of the lads to take one and make some small return – that's if you want it?

I will enquire if my hat is still extant - I hope it is, I shan't be able to afford a new one after the war.

Having taken the trouble to send you an AL with all the hard work on the outside - I <u>expect</u> an answer 'on the double' - no cracks about "blessed is he who expecteth nothing"!!!

Your affectionate 'uncle-cum-brother'
<u>Vivian</u>

PS This ought to begin "Madam"   R.A.F.
or "Miss Knight" - 18!!!!!! (make it <u>3</u> ALs!)   C.M.F.

<u>24.8.44</u>

My dear Pat,

     Do you remember in one of your last letters saying there was never more than a fortnight between your letters to me? I think that this is a time when I can chortle and rub my hands with glee - <u>18</u> (note: <u>eighteen</u>) days this time!!!! I realise that this may be due to indisposition or being so busy acting as guide and companion - but really - your oldest friend and the bloke that rumour once had you were engaged to! I was reading thru some of your old letters today and came across the one in which you told me of this rumour. At one time I kept all letters I received, but have thrown a lot away and now you're one of the few people I still keep - consider yourself <u>greatly</u> honoured!

     Once upon a time you promised me some photos of your beautiful self - when do I get them? I have 4 photographs of myself - not very good, but if you can stand the sight of my face – you're most welcome to them.

     Reading thru your old letters was extremely pleasant and amongst things, reminded me that your last Birthday was the second that I have been unable to send you any remembrance. I greatly deplore this, but when I get the chance to obtain some, I think a pair of silk stockings would be acceptable wouldn't it? I believe your shoes are either 5 or 6 aren't they - ie 9" stocking (1/2 sizes are a bit difficult to get). Tho you may not receive them for some time – I'll send 'em as soon as I can and perhaps you'll excuse my lack of attention before.

     You haven't written me a decent letter for a long time. I suggest you take an evening off from your 'duties', buy at least TWO Air Letters and sit down and using very small, close writing write me a letter giving me all the gen about everything, about your family, people we both know, your latest excursions (if they're of the sort you can tell your adopted brother-cum-uncle) and make it really interesting – it's not much to do for one who knew you as a spindly legged schoolgirl before you became "orl luverly".

     I can see that I shall seriously have to exert my guarding influence when I come back – you've evidently got to the stage when a strong hand is needed (<u>18</u> [note eighteen] days and your hair cut off!) I shall have to speak to your father.

I should like to hear how Mrs K is these days - you know my opinion of her - and I greatly miss the evenings at 5 Crosbie and when we used to go strolls in the evening round the square – I'd give a lot to have the old (and further back than that) days again. I suppose we never shall, we're none of us getting any younger.

Look after yourself and all the <u>very</u> best

18 (note <u>eighteen</u> days)

Vivian

WARDROOM MESS,
R.N. AIR STATION,
CRAIL, FIFE.

10/9/44.

Dear Pat,

Will start off this <u>short</u> (please note) letter by thanking you for my excellent half day with you, which I think you'll agree proceeded very smoothly despite:-

(a) my late arrival
(b) the rain
(c) shortage of time
(d) the -- bike

With reference to (a) above, I do think that I gave you warning enough of the likelihood of this eventuality.

The way in which that near-empty No 3 bus so obligingly turned up on the tick, shook me considerable, it did. So much so that I found myself almost trying to escort you aboard plus aforementioned bicycle. Do hope you reached home safely, warmly and undrenchedly (new word) without any unpleasant black-out incidents.

Have racked my brains to think of any young girl or fellow I know still in Birmingham whose company you might enjoy but found I didn't know of anyone either suitable or unsuitable.

Well I started this off on the right foot by warning you that it would be but a small offering from my gifted pen. When you decide I deserve a letter please include Vivian's address therein as I must drop the old so and so one of my morale building letters.

Sorry I can't fix you up with a companion as I know how very lonely you must be. However it should not be long before all your old friends return once more.

Do write soon.
All my love,
Bill

Apart from all the 'boys' being elsewhere, Esmé was, of course, now in Northumberland, Joan was away in the Land Army, and Christine had now isolated herself from virtually all connection with me and 'the old life'.

R.A.F.
C.M.F.

<u>11.9.44</u>

My dear Pat (NOTE!),

Apart from the fact that there must have been about 26 days between your letters, you start off in a very argumentative fashion, picking me up in a clerical error and then talking of your "usual sweet affectionate self ".

You are leaving yourself open to some very rude remarks by telling me to never mind who the other bloke is - remarks which really I should have no compunction in making - considering your treatment of the green trilby.

And then - to crown all; you tell <u>me</u> to be good - well! In all the years you've known me, have you ever known me to be anything else - even alone in the moonlight with a certain young lady?

No news from Brian or Bill lately - jog Bill's memory please. Your letter has been a long time getting here, due to the fact that we've had no mail at all for 16 days, it had all gone astray.

We've been given permission to give the names of places visited in Italy, south of a line from Leghorn* to Ancona. I believe I sent you a list of those S of Naples so pin your flaps back for more:- Caserta - a large and ornate King's Palace and gardens; Capua, dirty and uninteresting - no romanticism from Romeo & Juliet; Littoria, Fondi, Anzio, Cisterna, Villetri, ROME (wizzo town, very interesting tho I prefer some of our cathedrals to St Peter's); Geosseto, Tarquinia (small walled town with catacombs), Follonica (nice stretch of sea for bathing), Volterra, Arezzo, Siena (interesting town; queer, clean twisty hilly streets and a fine 14th century Cathedral). Some of these visits have been sketchy, others longer and more frequent with chance for shopping and photographs.

In her letter, Mother mentioned that my brother Tony had visited Chaddesley Corbett. He walked there one day. I couldn't help remembering our picnic ride there. Happy days those, and like you I wish for the '42 period again – tho x'43 I was in this racket and it contained the time when I had to leave Blighty. Tom, our unit 'bookmaker' lays 5-1 on the war being over by the end of the year and can't get any takers. I hope he's right and that next summer we'll be able to go to C.C again - or will my presence be needed in the Far East?

Nothing much has happened here lately. Last night there was a dance in the village but as I was on duty I didn't go - not that I should have done in any case - you know my dislike of dances. Anyway, the signorinas turned up fully chaperoned and partnered and wouldn't dance much with the Allied soldiers - always the same.

I haven't got those stockings I promised you yet, will do so in the near future. let's be hearing from you (in less than 26 days)

All the <u>very</u> best
<u>Vivian</u>

(*Livorno)

R.A.F.
C.M.F.
<u>3 Oct 44</u>

" Sweetest Honeybunch" (What a hope!)

Bottom-most (of heart) thanks for your wonderful (??) epistle of the 22.9.44 which owing to its guilty conscience has only just managed to crawl here.

Referring to the "what you haven't got now" (quote) - might I refer to

(a) your glorious long hair piled up in such a Heath Robinsonish creation and

(b) your such sweet disposition, which never allowed you to treat me (and Bill) as you do now - buckets of tears to the fore.

 Impress on Bill the necessity for writing to me and tell him that not knowing my present address is no excuse - letters always follow you round.
 I rather thought that my list of places visited would rather muck up your idea of where I was – I've never been in the 'toe of Italy' - furthest S is Baltipaglia.
 So you don't think that you'll ever be able to cycle to C. Corbett again? How old do you think you are - 90? A young woman of your age should be fit for anything and so by the time I come back I expect you to be trained for it - cutting out smoking, drinking, late nights and vicious living and be ready on your toes. However as I probably shan't be back till round 1954 or so, you will have plenty of time, so don't worry!
 Glad to hear that the lights are on, tho now you must miss that nice large dark porch. I remember congratulating Den on having parents who tactfully thought of such things when choosing their porch. It just shows how you've changed since I last saw you - in those days you never thought of the possibilities of porches – not with me anyway (here I whisper: thank goodness). No doubt however on my return you will be too old for walks round squares or moonlight tree climbing - do you know it slips my memory for the moment why you did that time? Funny, I used to enjoy those strolls and also the short journey to the bus.
 Now (after this long interval) I expect a letter in less than 11 days.
Do I?
All the <u>very</u> best
<u>Viv</u>

 One evening before the blackout ended I had gone, as usual, to the Y.W.C.A. to serve suppers, and found myself on my own.
 Usually another girl and I shared the work and walked up to the bus stops together. When it was time to walk up Hill street to catch the bus

all on my own in the deep darkness I just got so alarmed at the thought that I phoned Dad and asked him to use some of his precious petrol to come and pick me up.

After that I decided that discretion was the better part of valour and left the Y.W.C.A., and applied to the Officers' Club, which was near the Hall of Memory, and near to my bus stop. Pam, who had been in the first year at the Art School with me, was working there as well, which was nice. I went in early each morning to serve breakfasts before going on to Art School, and also at weekends.

R.N. AIR STATION,
CRAIL, FIFE.
17.10.44.

Hiyah Blondie,

By the way how is work proceeding at the Officer's Club? I must say I fear the worst from this latest rash step of yours, thrusting your head into the lion's mouth without even so much as a word to your staunch guardians. It is obvious to me that even if you had made a token gesture of first asking our advice you would have ignored our negative answer. You wayward child, what ARE we to do with you? I have written to Viv of course and told him of your latest sad step on the downward path, and eagerly await the wisdom of his reply since it is too grave and ponderous a burden for my shoulders to bear alone.

As I pointed out to him, whilst commending your voluntary withdrawal from the Kardomah Coffee Cads Circle I cannot but feel that by serving purple veined Army officers with their morning quart of whisky you have merely taken a step from the frying pan into the old proverbial. Eh what?

Your humble admirer,
William C.B

R.A.F.
C.M.F.
23.10.44

My dear Pat,
	Many thanks for your AL of the 14th. Slight error there I think - the 14th was a Saturday, not Sun as you said. And anyway, why write it on a Sun and then not post it till too late for a Mon postmark? Think of the precious time lost!
	Evidently your 'house breaking' plans are the same as when I left, and it certainly sounds as if it will look very nice. *(We knocked the scullery through into the coal-house that we had built on before, and turned it into a large, sunny kitchen.)*
	You did <u>not</u> tell me you were back at the Art School, last I knew you were at the Nursery School - will you please tell me the full story? Again you didn't say anything about working at the officers' club. You certainly sound a busy young woman, <u>but</u> I still think you could write to me more often - a fortnight lapse again! I'm glad you realise you owe me two letters – you've no real excuse you know. All I can think is it's that you've become just unheedful - no reservoirs handy at the moment, so I'll have to find some other way - suicide is the only thing.
	I will send the stockings during this week and if they are silk, I'll collect my reward when I get back - I shan't forget it either!
	I've told you the films I've seen lately, I haven't read any decent (or for that matter, any indecent) books lately.
	I'm having 3 days leave at the end of this week 27-29th and hope to spend it at a town and thus get away from the unit for a space, the first time for a year - the whole time I've been in Italy. I intend seeing a play, film or two and also a Symphony concert or an opera and also finish off my Xmas shopping. It will be a welcome break as we've had nothing except our on and off duty since our last leave back in May.
	By the way, when do I get those photographs you promised me?
	Your letter for once was quite polite, tho your beginning was hardly the way to address an uncle, however depraved a niece you may be. I think that will be all for now, don't forget to write <u>in less than a fortnight</u>!
	All the <u>very</u> best, Pat
	<u>Vivian</u>

P.S	are any of the students I knew still at the A. School?

R.N.A.S.
Crail
Fife
6.11.44

My Own Sweet Helen,

How does that suit you? First and foremost do please excuse this writing paper which is a page cut from an exercise book. The reason? Well it's not because I'm indigent (ha ha, I'll wait while you refer to the Dictionary) but because the Wardroom Mess has temporarily exhausted it's stock of headed letter paper and I neglected to buy a pad when 'ashore' last Saturday.

On Friday 27th October who should walk in the mess but a very old New Zealand pal of mine named Ed Morrison with some other guys who used to be instructors here not so long ago. The result - a beeg party, and what a party. It was in the course of this monumental carousal that I conceived the brilliant notion of 'phoning you up. I vaguely remember exchanging florins for shillings until I had the correct change and after the pressing of the button 'A' I remember very little else except asking you for a photograph? Was I frightfully rude, did I say any naughty words, did I let you get a word in edgeways, did I propose immediate marriage or what? Do please let me know, that is if we're still on writing terms. Anyhow I apologise in advance for any possible blacks I may have put up. Nice and nearly put my perishin' 'oof in it, I nice and nearly did. What?

Glad to hear you're taking a firm line with the would-be wolves at the Pongo's Club - Navy slang for Army types. Don't weaken, my Sweet, they don't mean well in fact to crack my old chestnut, their intentions are strictly 'orrible.

I'm writing this in the cold light of the afternoon without alcoholic stimulants to champfer up the old imagination a bit so am finding it rather heavy going.

That's all for now Pat. My days of idleness have ceased to be and I'm flying like nobody's business now: have a 3 hour jaunt tonight I believe.

Give my love to your Mother and Father and of course extra special love for you.

Cheerio,

Your contrite admirer,

Bill

R.A.F. C.M.F.

9.11.44

Greetings Niece!

There's an 'e' in the middle of that word, so it's not meant as a descriptive adjective. Thanks very much for your letter of the 4th, received yesterday and answered, as usual, at the first opportunity.

No doubt I shall have some rude remarks in return for this bit of gen, but here it is. Tomorrow I go on 7 days leave plus a day making 8 days in all. I shall probably spend them away from camp in company with three or four of my pals - there will be no need for you to make remarks about 'being good', that I shall be, goes without saying.

I was glad to have the gen on your various occupations over the last few months and at last get you 'fixed' in my mind. You know, sometimes you're a dead loss as a correspondent, you often don't keep me up to date with your doings (those you dare tell your uncle) and I have to work it all out or ask you months later.

Thanks too for your 'gen' about the other art students - why is Bandy coming out of the Navy? Does Pam still look the same?

The fact that you hope to post the photographs this week definitely meets with my approval – I'll see what I think of the hirsute deed's effect on your appearance. I have both yours and Den's photos with me, Den as an erk and after he got his commission.

There is little news from Italy this week but here's what there is. The leave went off well, we slept in civvy billets and ate at a Services restaurant.

Your stockings are on their way at last - posted them on the 2nd. As they're coming in a registered envelope, you'll probably have to pay on them. Despite this, I hope you like them - they come with my best Xmas wishes. I don't think we shall have such a good Xmas this year as we did last year - really I think the best I've had in the Service. I've just celebrated my 2nd anniversary in the RAF.

10.11.44.

This is being finished a day later – didn't have time last night. We've heard quite a lot of Vera Lynn on the radio, don't like her much nor do many of the blokes. What's the opinion of you, a representative of the younger generation? However, I _do_ like what's playing now – 'Tales from the Vienna Woods' - brings back memories of you and our gramophone sessions.

I have been off duty today, and as our flight is off duty next Sat (18th) I actually get 9 days leave. Shall probably be bored stiff by the time it's over, there's not so much to do, at least not enough to last all that time in the way of shows and the weather makes travel not as pleasant as it would have been in summer.

I think that's all for the moment, don't forget to continue the good work of writing often to this 'lonely airman' will you?

All the <u>very</u> best Pat and in case I don't get another chance - Best Wishes for Xmas and the New Year to you and your family

Vivian

Christmas Day - Dec 25th 1944

Somehow tonight, more than I ever have before, I realize the mortality of men. We so want time to go quickly, and tomorrow to come, and yet if only we realized it - it is <u>life</u> slipping away - Life is going, rapidly.

H.Q. 336 Wing
R.A.F.
C.M.F.

My dear Pat,

Many thanks for your LONG OVERDUE letters of the 4th which reached me two days ago. Their long travel time was no doubt due to having to be redirected and for your future notice my new address is at the top. I'll not trouble to tell you off for not writing before, I'll just leave to your imagination as to what I'm thinking. As I told Bill, I'd given up hope for you and now am just sitting back watching you sink; down, down --!

I'm glad you liked the stockings and that I was able to bring a little sunshine into your life. Seriously tho, if you are pleased with them, I'm very glad - and only wish that conditions at home were such that all you girls could indulge to your hearts content in things of a like nature.

As far as I can see from my diary, no letters have passed between us since 9 Nov. and since then quite a lot has happened - including my arrival here, tho thankfully there are a number of my friends with me. I've seen several good shows including an ENSA company doing 'George & Margaret' and also Maurice Winnick and his band with the Dorchester Follies.

I had a letter from Bill (a sea letter) from Scotland, which reached me on 3 Dec. Written in his usual manner, completely genless and gormless. I've also had some more leave which was messed up by the weather. Also too, I've had opportunities to meet friends I've made in Italy previously including the Bulgarian wench I told you about.

The English-speaking invasion of Italy has certainly 'done her a lot of good' 'cos she's now raking in the shekels teaching English (and the piano) to Italians. Doing very well by her appearance compared with her on my last visit. Actually I was surprised that I was remembered, tho I oughtn't to be if a remark Den once made about my physiognomy is anything to go by – 'once seen, unfortunately, never forgotten!'

I was very interested to hear about your latest war work *(the Officers' Club)* - poor devils. As to your threats about 'seeing when you come home m' lad' concerning my opinion of you as a member of the younger generation - for some reason or other I think I'll refer to something else.

How on earth can you consider a statement like '3 to females, so there' with regard to your letters, likely to quieten down my rampant jealousy, I don't know. One rival out of 6 would be bad enough but when only 3 out of 5 are to females that still leaves <u>two</u> males!!?? Each week I scan the 'Engagements & Marriages' columns in the 'Weekly Post' - but perhaps you won't descend to such a lowly rag?

Enough of this ragging though, if there were more space I would e'en try to raise your lowly mind to a higher plane by discourse on such elevating subjects as Beveridge Reports, skyscrapers and even the stars but from your latest shillingsworth it is brought home to me once again, that the sweet innocent girl who accompanied me in my rustic peregrinations has gone and in her place --

    All the <u>very</u> best
    <u>Vivian</u>

PS   How's the family?
PPS   Today is "Innocents Day"!!

1945

Aged 18 ½

List of Illustrations

Page

523   Vivian

528   'Johnnie'

549   Stuart

550   Pat

'Dost thou love life? Then do not squander time, for that is the stuff life is made of.' B. Franklin.

20.1.45.
R.N.A.S.
Maydown
Londonderry
N. Ireland.

Dear Pat

Well and how are you doing me dharling goil? Bedad and begorah etc. I've been over here 3 weeks and am living like a fighting cock. This afternoon for example two of us tramped across the white fields to a nearby farm and returned with 18 eggs, so that we shall enjoy a boiled egg for our tea each day this week. Our 2 observers made a similar excursion also and returned with 2 dozen.

I live in a Nissen hut with the gang, 3 pilots and 3 observers. Our air gunners being humble petty officers live elsewhere, but we are all good comrades and meet down town over a cordial pint or two.

This is going to be a shocking letter Pat, I'm sitting round the hut fire with 5 other blokes, one reading all the juicy bits in the News of the World, 3 others toasting bread and pea-nut butter, the other trying to write (like me) and as a background to the general hub-bub the wireless is blaring out some modern music. One of the observers has just raised a laugh by filling up a white enamel sloppail with water which he optimistically hopes to boil an egg in, over the stove. However he has been disillusioned by the toasters, one of whom has produced a tobacco tin for the job. They now propose to put this tin right in the heart of the fire, no they've decided against that and are now filling the stove to the brim with coal.

Well Pat I really don't think I can compete with this madhouse any longer. Anyhow my main object in writing this letter was to start our correspondence cracking again. I am anxious to hear all about you, so do please write as soon as you can, and don't forget that polyfoto you promised. Next time I will try to find a quiet spot or else wait until all the gigolos in the hut are cutting a rug at the local Palais.

All my love,
Bill

H.Q.336 Wing
R.A.F.
C.M.F.

4.2.45

My dear Pat,

So you've remembered me again at long last? I received your AL of 21 Jan yesterday and still in the faint (extremely) hope that perhaps you'll follow suit, I answer toute suite! Don't talk to me about Baked Beans (especially Heinz) and chips - they, like pints of foaming draught beer, are things of my dreams.

I was glad to hear that none of the old favourite records had gone to salvage, ones like 'You're an education' and 'Begin the Beguine' and 'Tipi tipi tin'. I deplore your new love for jive, don't tell me you're a jitter-bug fiend as well. If so, then my derogatory remarks about the modern generation <u>must</u> apply to you!!? I'm glad to hear that you still enjoy classical music – there's a faint hope for you yet! I do <u>not</u> approve of Melancholy Baby or Harry James - so what!

What on earth do you mean by saying that you haven't a male friend in England since Dec '43? What about all these blokes you mention and the <u>3</u> who proposed. I know that not all of the three are still OK, but <u>who</u> was the 3rd, who you wouldn't tell me of?

Why you don't seem to have so many I don't know, don't forget I've been away sometime - by far too long. I know from my own experience tho, that one mentally sets up standards and perhaps most of those you meet don't come up to your standard?

I hadn't heard about the death of Bill's mother. If you have any more details perhaps you could let me have them - I haven't heard from him for some time. I'm very sorry to hear it, and I expect that he's very cut up over it.

Glad that you're cutting down smoking, you didn't much when I was in Blighty, but from what you say it sounds as if your consumption went up in the interim.

I've seen several flicks lately, and our Wing Drama Club also gave a play. I'm still pretty cheesed off with the joint, the weather hasn't been so hot up till the last few days and our mail has been terrible - I didn't have a single AL for 10 days.

My father had an attack of phlebitis, but has recovered, tho he finds long distances a bit of a strain especially his daily journey to Burton to his work.

I'm hoping to go on leave on 7 March when I intend (if poss) to go to a large town and have a bit busier life.

I know two lots of people there. I revisited the place in Dec and they remembered me and made me welcome so I'm hoping I shall be able to get organised in March.

To pass my evenings off, I've taken up French and Italian. I still remember a lot of the former that I learned at School and found it useful both in Italy and N/A* - but my Italian is the soldier type – I'm starting practically from scratch there. The Military authorities publish 'Language from Scratch' books which are quite useful - they deal with everyday things instead of 'pen of my aunt' stuff.

I can't think of much news these days, so little happens. Brian wrote to me about 3 weeks ago and wishes to be remembered to you.

Please could you remember me a bit sooner next time - and what about letting me know how your family is? In the meantime, please give your mother and father my respects.

All the <u>very</u> best
<u>Vivian</u>

(* North Africa)

H.Q. 336 Wing
<u>10.2.45</u>

My dear Pat,

Many thanks for your letter of 5th received today - I thought something terrible had happened when I received another letter from you so soon - tho I agree that it's about time you did something about it – you've been pretty shocking in the last 6 months and it would only have been your fault if I'd got my self involved with thousands of dusky signorinas - or would it?

I was surprised to hear that Bill was in N Ireland - good show, I've had news of several of my friends being killed or wounded lately and I don't want old Bill to go that way.

Of course I agree with your idea of posting me to Blighty - but I don't expect it will come off for a long time yet - besides I hear that the beer situation isn't too good at home now and it's no use me coming home when there's none of that about.

I'm glad that the weather is better these days, Mother wrote and told me that it was pretty deadly and that pipes were freezing up all over the place.

You sound most annoyed that the males at the Union Dance were mostly younger than yourself - surely you realise you're growing up now – you'll be 19 in May? Now when I was that age!

I've seen a couple of films lately, but both old. Tonight tho I've been to a show that I really enjoyed - the Anglo Polish Ballet, who are touring Italy at the moment. They were very good indeed and I really did enjoy it - besides which it was such a change from ENSA variety shows and films. The orchestra was Italian tho conducted by Dr Erik Chisholm, and like most Eyetye orchestras was very happy when the cymbals and drums were going full blast and hence made a good show of the 'Dance of the Tumblers' which they played in an interval.

Weather here for the last week up till last night, has been pretty good, but last night it rained and so there's bags of mud about again. I'm still hoping that it will have decided to keep fine for my leave, but another spoke has been put in my wheel in that I don't think I shall be able to get permission to visit the town I want to.

Did I ever tell you that I'd visited Florence - I expect I did, but I'll make sure so that you can't say I don't tell you all the news.

Last week I went sick with my leg (I know, it would be hard to go without it - so don't tell me) and had to have X-rays and a blood test. I don't know what actually is wrong but I've a tender patch by my knee and it hurts if I keep it in one position for a long time. The Doc. said it wasn't anything serious – don't tell me I've told you all this before, but then it's so disturbing to have you writing so soon again. Still, it would be a good idea if you remembered your ginger haired 'uncle' (it was uncle, wasn't it?) a little more often.

I can't think of much more news now, so little seems to happen here – I'm more cheesed than ever, if that interests you at all. Must be old age creeping on or something like that.

I shall look forward to a succession of letters from you in the near future (and probably shan't hear for about 3 months).

Still, all the <u>very</u> best, Pat,

Vivian

How are your mother and father - you never mention them - my compliments to them!

I am writing this in Feb., and it's difficult to remember things that did happen and in the right order. I had a letter from Bill – I'm not sure when - saying he was in Ireland, and then, just after I'd answered it, I had a phone call saying he was in Bristol and would it be O.K. if he came up for the day – I'd heard about a week previous that his mother had died suddenly.

Bill came up, and we spent the evening in town. The next morning I met him for coffee and saw him off on the mid-day train.

I'd so longed for the Guild Dance at the University - evening dress - and quite a do - and so when Ron told me it was on the following Sat, and he had a double ticket for himself and Jill, and another for me and whoever I wanted to bring I was really bucked - I thought it was such a pity Bill had gone back. And then I got around to thinking - who <u>was</u> I going to go with? The dance in 4 days and no-one to go with.

Sat Feb 10th

The day of the ball. I got all the work done at the club - Officers started coming in for lunch and I summed them up - No - no-one I wanted to share the ball with - hell!

I had some Americans at one of my tables - heavens! Would I have to end up asking one of them? I knew 2 of them would come if I asked - but I didn't want to.

One of the other waitresses said she'd ask a young Australian F/O at one of her tables. She brought up the subject very tactfully and we were introduced, (his name was Kevin), and he said he'd come.

At 3.00 we went home, had tea and I changed and Ron came and off we went. I wore my long blue taffeta dress with hair upswept. I went well with Kevin's Royal Blue uniform.

As usual, I wrote and told Vivian about it.

H.Q. 336 Wing
22.2.45

My dear Pat,

Many thanks for your AL of 14th which arrived yesterday. I was surprised to hear again so soon - you can't call that a rude remark because you <u>were</u> pretty lax in 1944 - I hope that you will improve during 1945? I haven't as yet received your photographs – didn't know that you'd sent them - when did you?

Not content with such people as Canadians and Yanks, you're now taking in Australia – doesn't Great Britain get a chance? I'm glad that the dance (sorry, Ball) was such an enjoyable one and that you enjoyed it.

So Bill is off again is he? You don't know where he's going to do you? When he writes, please let me know his whereabouts - and you might remind him, that once again he owes me a letter!

Who the <u>third</u> is I don't know - I could make guesses, but won't - in case I put my foot in it too badly. Whilst on that subject, I must tell you that at long last, the rot has set in amongst the original QA members. Phillip has broken the ice and I saw an announcement in the B. Weekly Post for Jan 5 that he's got engaged! I must write and congratulate him and also tear him off a few strips for letting this rot start.

I will send Brian your sisterly kiss. Brian by the way, wrote again a few days ago and his one bit of gen was that he's in Burma. If you ever get time, could you hunt up some news of some of the others - Barry and Bob? Barry owes me a letter (as usual) but I've always depended on you for news of Bob.

Weather on the whole is better here tho we've had one or two days of really cold breezes, but, thank the Lord, no more snow. We're ready for the next lot tho, as our stove is now fixed up and roars away like a hungry giant - you wouldn't realise how much more enjoyable life is with some heat.

I think that that is all the gen for the moment - your turn to get weaving on an answer.

All the <u>very</u> best,
Vivian

HQ 336 Wing
<u>11.3.45</u>

(My dear 'Profligate Niece'/My dear Pat,)

I definitely go a huge bundle on this 'system' of yours of keeping two series of ALs going - should mean that I hear more often from you.

I rather wondered if Bill had been the 'third one' but could hardly say so - in case I was wrong. I'm not surprised, I know he's at least liked you for a long time and I believe at one time wondered where I was in the game - I often wonder what he thinks these days. Remember the night at the 'Hope & Anchor' where I walked off with you and took you home? I know he was really mad at me then! So you've turned him down – I'm not going to make any comment because it's your own private matter (yes, I know it's strange I haven't cracked at you, but -).

I saw a film the other day called 'Home in Indiana'. Nothing spectacular tho it passed a few hours away, but I couldn't help noticing how like you the younger girl was. Perhaps the likeness isn't so great but she made me think of you. I'm particularly sorry that your photos have gone for a Burton because I should have liked to see how you've changed in the last two years. Doubtless I shall see one - I didn't recognise my own sister when she sent me a photo some time ago and as you're about the same age, you've probably changed as well.

Referring back again to the subject of your preferring Englishmen, I still have never met any girl in my travels to touch several girls I knew in England. I've met some nationalities too - apart from the native Italians and French here and in N Africa I've also met Poles, Americans, a Dane, an Armenian, two Spaniards, a Yugoslav (she was tough too - met her hitching along a road and thought she was a bloke until I got close to her), a

Hungarian and a Bulgarian. True I've not got to know them particularly well, but there were only three of them I took the faintest liking to. And yet I've felt much more 'at home' with the one or two English girls I've met out here for the same length of time. It's not really so strange tho, because each nationality usually prefers it's own and probably has a certain subconscious 'suspicion' of any other. I shall probably see the Bulgarian when I go on leave, she speaks perfect English and is quite a good companion if you keep her off her national politics. We had one glorious row when I told her off for being snobbish - trouble was that I don't know all the things she called me, some were in Italian and the others in Bulgarian, but they sounded pretty bad.

That's a strange paragraph – but we're (I mean you and I) hardly strangers - remember that first Saturday afternoon I met you?

I must say that Kevin is keen to phone or see you every day for 3 1/2 weeks! More than I've ever done - my best was 16 evenings in a row when I first met Anne and then I didn't see her for 8 or 9 months afterwards!

This has been a pretty good 3d worth and I only hope that you've been able to read the writing – it's pretty bad - one day I'll try and improve it. Maybe those photographs will turn up yet, you never know, I suppose they were addressed to my old unit? Let's hear from you as soon as possible and until my next letter -

Look after yourself and all the very best
Vivian

                                                814 Naval Air Squadron,
                                                        c/o G.P.O.
                                                           London.

11.3.45.

My dear Pat,

Just a few lines as I may be off shortly and I must plead with you to keep pumping out letters to the above address as fast as you can; so that I shan't be without mail for weeks and weeks which is bad for a 'fighting man's' (at long last) morale.

I can't say very much else, though I don't think I'm giving anything away by saying that I'm in a damn fine ship and perhaps before the end of the war I shall actually see some operational service. I haven't heard from you for a month and if you have written since about the 9th of Feb guess the letter will catch up with me in about 3 weeks time, so again must beg you to make me a No 1 priority on your mail list; bracket me with Viv, there's a dear.

I share a very comfortable cabin with my NZ pal, Ed Morrison with whom I've been reunited, and soon I hope to meet the 'Bat' and other Trinidad pals, so the future holds promise of much cordiality.

My love to your mother and father, and to you an extra specially oomphful kiss.

Write, my sweet, please write.
Your ever ardent admirer,
Bill.

HQ 336 Wing

22.3.45

My dear Pat,

Many thanks for your AL of 17th received yesterday. I haven't heard the tunes you mention, you see our radio has been hors-de-combat since Dec and so we're still some months behindhand. We've great hopes of having it back soon tho - we bought a new valve for it last week. Don't break them before I get back - and then as a special favour I'll let you play the Tchaikovsky No 1!

Thank you muchly for Bill's address - as usual he owes me a letter and by the way I'm still waiting for one from Wishy. I had one from Teddy Gray the other day, he's still OK and now works with a Psychiatric Unit. I'm hoping to go and see him one day. Letters don't seem to be getting home as quick as they get here - 3 days is quite a normal time lately and SL are only taking 3 weeks or a month - March 1st SLs arrived today. It looks as if I have definitely had those photos you sent me - have you any more you can spare? There was absolutely no necessity to 'rub in' your hirsute deed tho! What difference will your registration papers make? Will you be allowed to carry on with what you're doing now, or will you be directed to something else? If you have to, what's your choice?

Despite my several requests, you still don't say how your parents are. Surely you don't believe that I used to come to No 5 to see you do you - the attraction was your father's beer and your mother's cooking! Seriously tho, I should like to know how they are - they always seemed to make me very welcome and I had some enjoyable times there. Far cry, back to the QA days of pin sticking and Nelson's Eye – wasn't Christine annoyed when she went thru the mill! *(The Q.A. Initiation Ceremony: I forget most of it now, but 'Nelson's Eye' entailed the initiatee being led blindfold round a 'Nelson Museum', feeling the empty sleeve and his eye patch, and, lastly, his 'blind' eye, whereupon the victim's finger suddenly felt itself plunged into the squelchy socket - which in fact was a half orange!*

The part that especially annoyed Christine was the 'swearing in', when (still blindfolded) she had to 3 times lay her hand on the Bible and repeat the oath. The Bible was - naturally - replaced by a bowl of water for the final oath-taking, and she managed to unwittingly produce quite a major splashing of water.)

Tho you say you're at Bournville part of the day - you don't say what for exactly - to do with the College, no doubt. Note that I've taken your words to heart and no longer refer it to as the Art <u>School</u>.

That's about all, I think.

All the <u>very</u> best,

Vivian

P.S.   Barbara visited C. Corbett t'other week and it's still the same as ever!

814 Naval Air Squadron
c/o G.P.O.
LONDON.
<u>24.3.45</u>.

Me darlin girl,

Your letter arrived here today and was very gratefully received by me. I wish I could tell you where 'here' was but censorship forbids, however I can say that I'm no longer on board ship but have been put ashore for a spell with my pals.

I can see that to ensure having a regular output of your letters following me round the world I shall have to do my share and pour letters into No 5 Crosbie Rd like that cunning old rascal Vivian. Incidentally I'm not so very far from aforementioned gent but shall have no chance of meeting him.

Would you send me his address again in case it has changed since I last heard from him. Thanks old girl.

Actually I am very hard put to it to find anything to say as all the interesting things that have happened since I last saw you are censorable and all I'm left to burble about is the weather, the food and my health, all three of which are damn good.

Be a darling and write Air Mail as soon as you've received this. I believe you civvy types can write Air Mail for 1½d if you keep the weight down, anyway expect you know all about this.

Heaven alone knows when I shall be able to see you again, I fear it may not be for years, but you never know your luck in this outfit. I will now sit back and go to sleep until I hear from you again.

Cheerio.
<u>Bill</u>.

HQ 336 Wing
<u>31.3.45</u>

My dear Pat,
Many thanks for your AL of 23rd which arrived today. I'm sorry that my usual frank way of addressing you didn't meet with your approval, your generosity in overlooking my slip overwhelms me and I stand corrected - with tongue in cheek. Of course there are other ways you could address me - but having previously suffered at your hands (or rather tongue and/or pen) I'm pretty hardened.

So Strauss still has charms and he seems to remind us both of the same thing, practically any of his tunes remind me of 5 Crosbie with both of us sprawled in inelegant attitudes on the floor.

You're as bad as my sister moaning at your age - she, by the way is your senior by 1 month 11 days. Wait till you get to my decrepit age!

Which of the Forces would you prefer if you aren't allowed to carry on with your present job?

I must tell you about a queer dream I had some time ago in which you figured – don't be alarmed at it, by the way, it's quite sane compared with some I've had. I dreamt I was standing on the platform of a 3 bus coming up to the fork by Crosbie from the 'D of York' and you were holding onto the bar with both hands and the rest of you was flying thru the air parallel to the ground, as per the attached 'sketch'. I said "Put your feet on the deck" and you replied "I can't, I've got balloons on my feet" - and you had too, two great big ones!! Just then they burst and we got off the 'bus and you said "You'd better hold me down in case I grow any more balloons" - and then we were opposite the H.*(Hall)* of Memory, just getting onto a bus and you said "Billie missed us, wonder where he's got to". You'll no doubt recognise part of the dream, but I don't remember you having balloons on your feet that evening!

That's wasted a lot of space, but I've laughed at the dream several times since and I thought you ought to share the joke.

Space almost up, let's be hearing from you as soon as poss.
As always,
All the <u>very</u> best, Pat,
Vivian

HQ. 336 Wing
9.4.45

My dear Pat,

Many thanks for your AL of 3 April; which arrived yesterday. You may be surprised to receive this sort of answer, but I'm carrying out an experiment - and you're the 'guinea pig'. I should be glad if, when you answer this, you give me the date when it arrives, as I want to find out how long ordinary letters take to travel as compared with ALs.

Another thing too, it gives me more chance to 'spread myself' and so this is the 'suitable brotherly letter' you asked for!

I haven't heard from Bill and so didn't know he was 'near' me - I wonder how near? When you write to him, please remind him that I'm still alive and that it's his turn to write several times over.

I have told you, I'm sure, that my sister is in the WAAFS. She's wanted to join for a long time and did it all on her own bat, volunteered and was called up in Sept. of last year. She's enjoying herself very much and is in Lincolnshire at the moment training as a Radio Tel.Op.

I was glad to hear that your parents were OK, you so seldom mention them and quite frankly I've always liked them - apart from their cooking and beer, and they've always made me feel <u>very</u> welcome. Of course you don't <u>have</u> to write to me - but I'll be frank with you that <u>perhaps</u> all the attraction wasn't just the beer and cooking!

I see that you cover yourself by saying that you've changed since then. I wonder if you have all that much? From your letters you don't seem to have, except on occasions - here it comes, 'straight from the shoulder', under the guise of <u>brotherly advice</u>:- some of your letters sounded as tho they were written by a very artificial person, and I've been tempted to just sit down and write and tell you not to be a silly little fool. My brotherly love has forestalled me tho because I didn't think it was really you. I used to notice it when I was in England, with some folk you seemed rather silly and yet later on there'd be a flash of what I always thought was the real you - and strangely enough I used to rather like that person. You may think this rather queer, but out here I quite often think back over the 'old days' and sort of 'analyse' them. I'm blessed with a good memory and can think over and laugh over some of those days – don't rub it in that I've not been overseas 2 yrs yet, but those days sometimes seem very far off. Remember the time you showed me that hat of yours - actually I didn't like it but didn't want to hurt your feelings, the time I first saw that green and brown frock of yours, which I <u>did</u> like, but out of pure cussedness I wasn't complimentary - and I've liked Tchaikovsky's No 1 for a long time, but cussedness again. And yet you know I was chaffed on several occasions about going out with such a young girl and yet I didn't mind; at the risk of your head size going up, I'll admit that I used to enjoy your company and that was all that mattered. And yet I never even held your hand in the pictures - would Miss Knight have been terribly shocked if I had?

So you've changed since those days - I wonder? I rather hope not - at least tho you've probably grown older, I've a feeling that basically you're still the same. Right?

In another of your letters, you were going to start a lengthy discourse on how different you are these days - well, here's your opportunity, 12 pages this size don't weigh an ounce, and <u>that</u> should give you plenty of room. I'm ready so let's have your opinions on any mortal subject you like, I'll send you my answers – it's a poor substitute for our moonlight walks round the square, but the best possible at the moment.

I'd better close down, before you get too tired of this letter – let's have your answer as soon as poss.

All the <u>very</u> best, Pat,

<u>Viv</u>.

P.S.   Don't forget to let me know when this arrives, will you, please?

HQ 336 Wing
<u>3.5.45</u>

My dear Pat,

Very many thanks indeed for your Registered letter and the photographs which I received yesterday and as usual this is me answering same 'on the dot'. You once wrote and told me that I ought to feel honoured as you were answering one of my letters before those of other people that you'd received before mine. Well, I'm doing the same, I had a big bunch of mail t'other day including some from people who only write once in a blue moon and so far I've only answered 3 out of the 9 letters - consider yourself greatly honoured.

I was <u>very</u> glad to get those photos*, but I must say they gave me a shock. Not having seen you for two years, I had subconsciously expected you to look as you did then and so when I saw these latest photos, seeing how you had changed came as a surprise. It was silly really because I had a photo of my sister (who's a month older than you) and she'd changed and so I ought to have expected the same with you. I got out the photo you gave me when I was in England and compared it with the new ones. Well, there are certain similarities, but there's a lot of change as well.

I had a letter, in his usual style, from Bill amongst the batch I was talking about – he's one of the 'blue-mooners' and as yet I haven't been able to find time to answer it.

Funnily enough a couple of us were discussing how far off those days before the war seemed to us and one of the blokes said that he always felt as tho time had stood still since 1939 - the only unfortunate part was that his age wasn't standing still as well – he's 36 this year and still single, tho he's got an AT all 'lined up' I believe. I wonder if you would enjoy those prewar days again considering how you've changed - perhaps they wouldn't feel as enjoyable now.

Of course the trouble is regarding the sort of people one likes depends entirely on you, people you like I might dislike and we, being of different sex and living rather different sorts of lives probably judge people differently. Your letter got me thinking and I tried to crystallise my ways of judging people. You mention 'physical attractions' and my mind went over the folks I've met o/s, both blokes and girls, and I ticked them off to see how many of those I have had any real liking for were physically attractive. Then again different people's ideas of physical attractiveness are different. Personally I don't go much on physical attraction in either sex, usually subconsciously I decide pretty quickly whether they interest me or not tho how I do it I don't know. Don't run away with the idea tho, that if I saw a pretty girl I shouldn't look twice - to quote an old joke, my eyes aren't on their last legs yet!

Surely tho, we've all changed some way or other since the beginning of the war? Personally I know that now I can live quite peaceably with folks who'd have driven me crazy before – I've had to; and secondly I don't worry over things anywhere near what I used to at one time - and then it wasnt much.

I can quite understand you sometimes wishing that you had someone to, as you say, encourage and reassure you, I'm sure it would be a great help. As to your letter, I was very interested to read it, I sometimes hold 'soul searching sessions' with myself as 'Exhibit A' and moreover I quite often wonder what I shall do with myself when this racket is over and done with. Still, the end hasn't come yet and I wonder what conditions will be like - probably no one can gauge that yet.

The news since you wrote that letter has become even more 'bang on' with the surrender of the Germans in Italy. We've got a 'book' on the end of the European war - next date is May 6 held by Bart - wonder if he'll win? In any case it can't be long now and then I shall be very interested to see what happens to me then - stay in Europe or go East? In any case I've still got two years to do of my tour - unless they cut it down to three as they're talking of doing.

By the way, remember what happened two years ago today? We saw the 'Messiah' at the Town Hall and it was the last time I saw you.

And why should you be <u>surprised</u> if I had held your hand? After all, I'm like several million other blokes on this earth.

To quote your own words, that just about answers your letter. A funny thought has come to me, brought on by your remarks about the green and brown frock - I bet you don't wear those shorts you wore on our cycle ride to Chad. Corbett, these days?

Last week I saw 'Lady let's dance' with Belita which was enjoyable until they <u>had</u> to let the hero join up 'in the greatest show on earth' (loud hoots from the audience).

I'm sorry, but I <u>must</u> close now, it's almost time for tea and then work. Let's be hearing when you can spare the time. Thanks again for the photos, I'm looking forward to the next lot and when I have some, I'll send you some of myself in return, tho I'm afraid the model in <u>them</u> won't have much in the way of 'P.A.'

All the <u>very</u> best Pat,
<u>Vivian</u>

*the photos were those taken by Dave, in the boat at Stratford.

As the end of the war was finally imminent, I wrote to Vivian of my expectations of seeing him again soon.

HQ 336 Wing
<u>11.5.45</u>

My dear Pat,
You started your letter off - the one dated 7th which arrived today and for which I thank you, very optimistically and I'm afraid that I can't feel as optimistic - even tho since you wrote the Surrender has taken place. I can't see many of us getting home yet awhile, even those who are almost time expired and as far as I am concerned my theory, and it's only a theory mind; is that if I <u>should</u> get home in the next 6 months it will only be a month's leave prior to going way East. Practically everyone at home, from what other blokes have told me, seem to expect us home soon - I wish they were right, but even looking at it optimistically, I'm afraid we're not as hopeful.

Your question about what do I think about going abroad is one that's not easy to answer off hand, because there's reasons for and against. Against it are the separations from one's friends and family and the great discomfort of living - tho I can't shoot much of a line about the latter. For it, are the interest of the war - seeing with one's own eyes a few of the things and places in the newspapers and also seeing a new country and its people albeit not at their best. As regards Italy you'd be disappointed in one way in the conditions of living of a large part of the population and the dirt - tho as a tourist living at decent hotels you wouldn't see this so much.

Naples is best from the sea I think and of course there's Pompeii and the Sorrento peninsular - but the part of Italy I've seen and liked most is Rome and N of there to the Arno river. This includes Tarquinia and Grosseto area where there are Etruscan ruins, Siena which is a quaint town with a lovely cathedral, queer twisty hilly streets into the old town and pageants in the summer, Perugia, Assisi, Florence and Pisa and for my own liking a small seaside place just about 50 miles S of Leghorn called Follonica, where I spent a gloriously lazy 3 weeks last July, If you ever do get a chance to spend time in Italy, you'd enjoy it, but wait 10 years or so!

I don't know what the feminine counterpart of a misogynist is, but you seem to be becoming one! I'm very glad to see tho that you're realising that a decent bloke can be of different types and that where they're concerned too, 'all is not gold that glitters'! Why the self humbling tho - if you're still like the 1943 Pat you made the grade pretty well then.

Both the Waltz and Polonaise and the Bumble Bee are favourites of mine – don't break them before I get a chance to hear them please!

A library has opened on the unit and I read a lot - but like you I daydream a lot - the trouble here is to find enough to fill the time up. Another Services cinema has opened near here, so it now means we get about 4 different films a week but quite often I don't go unless it's a good film.

From your remarks about how you daydream it looks as tho you need cheering up thoroughly. Come on, cheer up and don't get morbid! I should hate to have a letter from Mrs K to say that Pat had faded away and disappeared - surely the old Pat chuckle hasn't disappeared - or don't you make unprovoked attacks on young men these days - like all those I suffered at your hands?

Just lately you've been writing some most provoking letters in that they provoke long answers. On the other hand, letter writing to certain people is a 'labour of love' as far as I'm concerned and so I fill some of my time up very pleasantly that way. On the other hand I have great difficulty in answering some letters – I've had one for nearly 3 weeks and <u>can't</u> get down to answering it.

It's boiling hot out here these days - the coolest place I know is our room which faces N and so tho it was freezing in winter, it's lovely and cool now. Outdoors tho, even in shorts and short sleeved shirt it's like an oven in the afternoon.

You may remember me telling you that when I had that kit stolen in March I lost your 'Spirit of Man'. You'll be pleased, as I was, to hear that I've found it - another bloke borrowed it unbeknown to me months ago and has just returned it.

This is the first letter I've written since I left England that I've been able to put in an ordinary envelope and to seal down. The reason is that since V day, there is no unit censorship and they're only liable to opening by Base Censor. That's about all for now, so here goes.

All the <u>very</u> best Pat,
<u>Vivian</u>

<u>May 13th 1945</u>

It is a very windy night, and it has been warm all day with showers, and now it's a restless melancholy evening. I'm sitting in bed - it must be 11.00 or after, but I feel I must write or bust.

I've been having one of those soul-searching sessions after which I feel an absolute slithering parasite sucking the life juices out of Mother Nature and giving nothing whatever. What can I give? Art is essentially a selfish calling.

HQ 336 Wing

<u>13.5.45</u>

My dear Pat,

This is not going to be a full size letter, merely a short note, but then - even I can't write a long letter even to such a charming young lady as yourself very often and it's only a couple of days since I wrote. Nevertheless, this letter (or note) deals with a very important matter - to wit, your birthday. I believe, if my ageing memory serves me right, that on 19 May 1926, there burst onto this earth a stupendous charmer or horror* (whichever one prefers), yourself. In honour (or otherwise) of this great fortune*/terrible misfortune I therefore send you my very best Birthday Greetings and wishes for that day and hope that this and all the succeeding days will be happy ones. I should like to have sent you a more concrete piece of evidence of my aforementioned best wishes and devotion (?), but circumstances (lack of suitable gifts in this part of Italy) will not allow me to do this, and so you'll have to take my word (and a written one at that) for the aforementioned best wishes and devotion (?).

Anyway old girl (and former sparring partner), have a good time, hitch the old face up to withstand another year of trials and troubles (former male and latter of the heart) and maybe by the time your next one rolls round I'll have had a chance to wish you well, personally - anyway I should very much like to.

Once again 'A very happy birthday' and all the very best.

Vivian

*   Delete words not applicable

R.N.V.R.
c/o G.P.O.
LONDON.
11/6/45.

Greetings from somewhere in the Indian Ocean, My Sweet,

And how are things with you in peacetime Birmingham? In especial how did that wretched exam come off?

I am stationed on shore for a bit in a place that reminds me for all the world of Trinidad, in a grass roofed hut infested with snakes, tree rats (that eat our soap and chocolate overnight), fire-flies, spiders, scorpions and scores of other delightful creations of nature, added to which the rainy season is on at the moment and everything, in particular clothes and bedding, become damp and remain permanently damp. However I'm quite accustomed to this tropical way of living after my year in the West Indies and at least I've a mosquito net over my bed which is more than I had there.

The most exciting place I've visited since leaving England (apart from a smashing leave in Taormina, Sicily) *(from where he had sent me a card)* was Alexandria which was a most extraordinary mixture of the old and the new. The centre of the town is very modern and apart from brown gentlemen walking about in fezzes might have been any European or American city with fine shops, cinemas, restaurants and bags of coloured taxis - rather like New York in this respect. We patronised a restaurant known as Pastroudis every afternoon, where we consumed hand picked fresh strawberries and real cream, followed by the most delicious iced and chocolate cakes I've ever seen. When I say the strawberries were hand picked I mean that any bad ones had been discarded. Then for dinner we patronised the Union Club where the fare was grilled steak with chips with 2 fried eggs, peas, and fried tomatoes with strawberries and cream as dessert.

The streets are full of beggars, touts and shoeshine boys and chaps selling everything from 'feelthy peectures' to walking sticks, and they certainly aren't kidding when they say 'feelthy'. The touts offer to take you to some unmentionable disgusting 'exibeeshes' (ie. exhibitions) which if you're really interested about I'll tell you all about in a quiet corner of the town hall at midnight - not that I went to any of these 'exibeeshes', of course!

The native districts of Alex smell to high heaven and are no places for a sailor to walk down alone at night. The usual trick being to lure a half drunk matelot down any of the thousands of dark alleyways, 'filling him in' and pinching his wallet and most of his clothes and parking his 'bod' in the gutter.

After a very enjoyable stay at this said port of Alex we passed thro' De Lesseps great Suez Canal which took twelve hours, passing Ismalia where I believe Dennis was stationed before being drafted to Malta. Incidentally I suppose I did tell you that I was at Malta for a couple of months?

Anyhow after leaving Suez we journeyed thro' one of the hottest and stickiest seas in the world known as the Red Sea. It was impossible to sleep in our cabins and sleeping on the flight deck was just about possible with the ship creating a relative wind of say 15 kts. Everyone's body was just oozing bucketfuls of water every minute and I should think a good 50 per cent of those on board had a sweat rash of some sort. The trouble with a carrier under 12 hours of blazing sunshine is that the deck being metal becomes too hot to touch and this heat striking downwards thro' the bulkheads which are excellent conductors meets the engine room heat from below and then you have your perfect sweat bath.

We called in at Aden but I was duty boy and unable to go ashore though those that did go found absolutely damn all of interest. Then we plodded thro' the Indian Ocean with its grey skies and rain storms which kept the deck cool and made life much more comfortable.

Well Pat I reckon I've shot as big a line as possible in one letter so will close down until you send me a big peacetime Britain line. Please keep writing, especially now that your exam is over and done with (I hope!!) and write <u>AIR</u> <u>MAIL</u> - very important.

My love to your mother and father and a great big oomphy kiss to you.
    Cheerio
    My fickle blonde.
    Write soon.
    Oozingly Yours, Bill.

    R.N.V.R.
    824 Naval Air Squadron
    c/o G.P.O. LONDON
    17/6/45

Dear Pat,

Your letter of the 29th May arrived here yesterday and was the first letter I've had since leaving Alexandria. Good show, keep it up, nobody every writes to me and it's bad for my morale.

I haven't much to tell you since I wrote a letter to you a few days ago and my main reason for writing is to point out that I've changed my unit from 814 to 8<u>2</u>4 squadron recently so please address all the hundreds and hundreds of letters that you will be writing to me in the next few weeks as per the heading. Oh! and please note my Sweet that you can drop the S from S/Lt.

The thought of your 3 months leave makes my mouth water. And as for your Lake District trip, well that simply makes me green with envy. I've never seen Lakeland and in fact when I return from this wretched Jap trouble I shall give myself a month or so to explore Great Britain by bicycle before settling down to the thought even of joining the Dole or Labour Exchange queue.

I feel I should know Esmé. Is she the blonde job I met once in New St on a bike?*

Good old Brum, trust them to arrange a typical Watch Committee VE day for you all. Even the Sicilians did better than this even if they didn't produce an illuminated omnibus.

I see you've been gadding about recently as per usual. Really my Pet if you fail the exam this time I shall have no sympathy for you for I shall judge you on the principle of work and pleasure not mixing and not on the saying that all work and no play makes Jill a dull girl. Not of course that you could ever be dull, Precious One, no, not for a single minute.

You ask me how I celebrated VE day and I must ask you to believe that it was spent in strict sobriety except for 1 glass of the local champagne which I had thrust upon me by a very drunken comrade who awoke me out of a deep sleep with bottle of the sparkling vintage in one hand and glass in t'other.

Quite seriously as we knew that we were on our way to another war at the time, the finale of the German effort didn't mean quite as much to us as it would have done if we had been actively engaged in killing off Germans at that time.

That must be all for now Pat. You have my permission to gad about as much as you wish during your 3 months vac, you lucky girl.

Cheerio. Yours enviously, Bill.

*   (*I had written to Bill, telling him that I had arranged to go Youth Hostelling in the Lake District with Esmé, in July.*)

HQ. 336 Wing
<u>26.6.45</u>

My dear Pat,

Many thanks for your letter of the 11th-cum-20th – you're a fine correspondent ain't you? Anyway I don't see why I should have to wait for any damned marine, he can't have known you longer than I have – I'll bet

<u>he's</u> never seen you in black woollen stockings and a skirt 3" above the knee - tho I bet he wouldn't mind the latter?!

You had <u>not</u> (as usual) told me about your change of course - the hours seem pretty long (keep you out of mischief!), but surely you've made a mistake – "9.0 till 6.30 3 nights per week" - do you get time-and-a-half for night work?

Glad you like the snaps *(these were the snaps he had promised to send me in his letter of 24/8/1944)* - they seem to be generally liked - I did smoke a pipe <u>very</u> occasionally in Blighty, but dropped it over side of the ship 'en voyage' and it's now at the bottom of the Atlantic - about Long. 10° maybe! And I do <u>not</u> smoke old socks - I manage to get enough from NAAFI without <u>that</u>!

I had a letter t'other day from Bill - I don't think I told you, did I? He doesn't seem too unhappy, moaning about the beer ration, but he's getting extra Jap Campaign money.

Very little news from this end, I'm still managing to keep my head up - temperatures hellish 102° in the shade today. That's the max. so far, but the middle nineties are quite normal.

Saw a film this evening, first for ages; but I felt like it tonight, despite the heat.

I am, DV and RAFV, going on leave on 4th July - Independence day in a double way! I have put a pass in to go to Milan, but I shouldn't be at all surprised if I'm not allowed to go – they're like that here, sometimes. If I can't go there, they won't let me go to Rome as the rest camp quota is so low and I've been once, so I don't know where I'd like to go.

I had a letter from my sister today – she's near Chichester and enjoying life, getting a lot of cycling and swimming in and drinking cider - wonder what the Watch Committee would say. There's nothing I'd love more now than a pint of cool Ansells (or M&B), but I'm torturing myself with the thought that tomorrow, I'll go and drink my beer ration - made in Italy - but iced!!

I've been trying to think of some brotherly advice to give you - be careful how you pose* tho' because even Marines can't stand too much, they're only flesh and ber-lood!

Enough of this idle chatter – I've a bed calling for my attention and tomorrow - I wonder what that will bring forth?

All the very best,
Vivian

* *(The students would take it in turns to pose for 'costume life' from time to time.)*

Tuesday 26 June 1945

I have started afresh, because something rather terrific has happened to me. As I write I can't help wondering what the future holds for me. Maybe it's as well I can't. If, 5 or 6 years ago I could have foreseen what was to happen between then and now I probably would have thought I would not be able to bear it, and if I'd had the courage, might have ensured that I'd have no future.

At the moment I'm in the unfortunate position of being in love with someone who is not in love with me. But to start at the beginning:-

Thur 14 June 1945

I went to the club. I was alone and did not have time for breakfast. When Mrs Collins came I took it easy - I was taking the morning off from College anyway as I had eyestrain.

At the counter table were 3 Aussies, and a Canadian F/O who looked very much like Danny came and sat down- after I had looked at the clock which said 9.28 - and told him he'd only just made it. After everyone had finished I sewed on a button for one of the Aussies, while being watched by him and the Canadian.

Then Mrs Collins and I had our breakfast while those 2 cleared the tables. Mrs C. said she wanted 12 yds of pale blue lace, and asked me if I'd buy it. I asked the F/O if he'd come too, and off we went.

After buying it - he put it in his tunic pocket as they had no bags - he asked me to have coffee and we went to the Satis where we stayed for about 1 1/2 hrs. He asked me to go skating in the afternoon, but I couldn't and eventually I arranged to meet him at 4.30 at College the following afternoon.

Friday 15 June 1945

I was rather apprehensive as to whether he'd turn up, and couldn't concentrate at all during the afternoon. I went out early and had a wash and started to put my face on during which time the 4.30 bell went and people started pouring into the cloakroom to go home. Two girls came rushing in and said to someone - very excitedly – "There's an Air Force Officer in the hall; is he your boyfriend?!" And I said "No, he's mine!" Then 2 more came flying in crying "There's the most smashing airman in the hall!"

Eventually I put the finishing touches, went out and - he was gone! I flew round in a panic and learned he'd left a few seconds previous. I flew out and wondered what the blazes to do, when I saw a tall calm figure walking down Edmund Street. It was he!

We had tea at the Satis. when he told me he was Swedish, his name, 'Johnnie', being RAF shortening of his surname. We went to the

Royal and luckily got 2 returned Dress Circle tickets for 'Duet for Two Hands'. John Mills was in the leading role. It was a marvelous play.

Afterwards we had dinner at the Imperial and ended up by being the only couple in the dining-room. From there we went to the Grotto downstairs in the Grand. I had begun to fall, but had only got to thinking he was terribly like Danny, and very nice.

In the Grand he held my hand, and suddenly asked me if I'd like to go to a Mess Dance at Perton aerodrome the following Fri. night. He said he'd phone later. He saw me to the bus and caught the 11.00 train.

I wondered very much if I <u>would</u> hear from him again, he seemed sincere, but I wasn't going to bank on it too much, however <u>Wed</u> night Johnnie phoned me and we made all the necessary arrangements. (I was to meet him in Wolverhampton, and then I would stay with Ted and Nita.)

Friday 22 June 1945 (Actually I'm now writing this on July 2nd - it seems more than 10 days since I met Johnnie that Friday. At the moment I have written to him and I'm waiting - and hoping - for a reply. I feel much more philosophical about the whole affair now. I've <u>almost</u> (?) reached the state where I can turn emotions on and off at will - bad thing!)

Anyway, Mother and I went to catch the bus and were 1/2 hr early. So to save standing around waiting I eventually persuaded her to come to W'hampton with me. She had to catch the next bus back again, but before she went we met Nita, Carroll and her small daughter "Teesha". *(Nita had an R.A.F. Officer and his family staying there.)*

Dead on 5.00 Johnnie turned up and we went to Long Common (where Ted and Nita lived) and had tea and I changed. Rip - Caroll's husband - was night flying and came down around 6.00. We were introduced, and when Rip learned we were going to Perton and had no transport he suggested - in all seriousness - that he dropped Johnnie and me by parachute over Perton! Johnnie said "How about it?". But I said "<u>No</u> thanks!"

Eventually Ted and Nita dropped us in W'hampton, and we went to the 'Star & Garter' where we met another Canadian – O'Brien - and his dumb blonde. They phoned for a taxi - and at 8.45 off we went. We arranged for the taxi to pick us up at 12.00.

The dance was wiz-o. It was an R.A.F. Mess, but they were mainly Canadians. I met someone I knew from the club. The buffet was also wiz-o. A salmon which Johnnie's friend Johnny brought down from Scotland, and masses and masses of food.

Towards the end we took our beers outside, and when empty deposited our glasses by the side of the path thru' the wood. It was then I got the mosquito bites that are now causing me to stay away from College and sit on the sofa with my feet up as my left ankle is so swollen!

At 12.00 the taxi came, and Johnnie and O'Brien and the dumb blonde and I all piled in. The idea was to drop me and then the d.b. and then take the other 2 back to Perton.

- Well, we directed the driver to Bobbington, and we thought that we could direct him from there. Well, after about 20 mins driving around in the teeming rain, without a clue, and with the driver getting steadily madder and madder, we realized we couldn't! At last in desperation the driver drove us to the gates of Bobbington 'drome and dropped us.

We got directions from the guard at the gate and started walking. We had only Johnnie's mac between us, and the rain was coming down in bucketsful. We walked for about 1/2 a mile and I recognised the road and knew it was only about 3 miles to Nita's - well, something went wrong with my calculations, and 2 1/2 hours later found us still walking!

Now and then the rain stopped, and occasionally the moon came out for a second, and then slid behind a cloud again.

At about 3 o'clock we hit a cluster of houses, and at the 1st one - a bungalow - we knocked on the door and asked where we were. Apparently it was an elderly lady alone in the house, and she would not open the front door. At that time the rain was coming down in sheets, and Johnnie had insisted that I wore his mac.

Anyway following on her directions shouted through the closed door we found our way home by 4.00 am. (Nita was still up, waiting for me to return. She was furious!) I fixed Johnnie a shake-down on the couch and eventually around 4.30 I fell asleep.

Saturday 23 June 1945

At 8.30 Dick and Peter, the collie, bounced into my room, and eventually, after I'd shoved them both out I got up. Ted and Dick went off - then Rip to Stourbridge. Johnnie had borrowed his razor and cut himself. He mowed the lawn - looked for, and found the nest where the hens were laying out (with 16 eggs in, too!) and then came for a walk with me, along the top of the bank. I was completely happy with him and hated to think of the time he wouldn't be there.

After lunch we - Ted, Nita, Dick, Johnnie and I - piled into the car and off we went. We dropped Johnnie near Perton aerodrome to pick up his stuff, and they dropped me in Tettenhall.

I waited for Johnnie in the Gaumont café. I was 1/2 an hr early, and had an awful apprehension he wouldn't turn up - well, he did, dead on time, and after a cup of tea we caught the bus in to B'ham.

We had tea at home and then went skating - it was great. Then went to The Grand for a drink. We went downstairs again. There was a party of Americans, and girls and a couple who went after a while. We didn't talk much, but listened to the Yanks and murmured a few inconsequential things.

Then Johnnie told me he'd volunteered for Japan.

Something hit me then, told me how much I'd miss him, and I nearly burst into tears. We tried to keep the conversation going and I recovered, only to feel like weeping again. I fluctuated, till at the last I very nearly broke down and Johnnie squeezed my hand and kissed my hair and made me feel worse than ever. I stood up and banged my fist against the pillar until I'd got control of myself again, and then we came home.

After supper we sat down to talk things over, and after a few minutes of what I believe is called a 'pregnant' silence Johnnie suddenly said, "I haven't been misleading you have I?"

I told him no, but by his saying that I knew it was no go. We talked until around midnight and then went to bed - when he shook my hand!!

Next day there seemed to be no morning. It seemed dinner time straight away after breakfast. After dinner Johnnie decided to press his tunic, and I endeavoured to clean off some Brasso he'd spilt on it. Then he decided to press his trousers, and came down in his mac carrying them over his arm. He did look so funny!

He phoned about the train time when we started out for a walk, and was told the last one before the 10.00 one was at 4 something.

We sat on the golf links for a 1/2 hr or so, and I felt so low and wanted to say so much that I lay in the sun looking at him and said nothing.

We walked back home, and he phoned again and found there was a later train, so we sat in the garden, had tea, and sat in the garden again, and then I went to the station with him.

He didn't want me to. I know he was afraid of a scene - he needn't have been. But I felt I must go. Maybe I'd be able to say something that would help matters. But I wasn't, and he said casually that if he was in B'ham he'd look me up in such a way that I knew he wouldn't be in B'ham.

I left the station soon after the train came in. By the time I got on my bus there were tears in my eyes. I purposely sat in the back-seat, but the bus was crowded and a man came and sat by me. As I kept making furtive dabs at my eyes I soon aroused his interest - but he made no attempt at conversation and merely offered me a light for my cigarette.

I felt I couldn't go home feeling as I did, so got off the bus and walked to the T's. I poured out my heart to Mrs T, and, slightly comforted, made my way home.

I came straight upstairs and had a good old weep and once more poured out my heart to Mother and Grandma.

About 3 days later I wrote to him. and about 2 weeks later I had more or less got over him.

Now, looking back I can feel amused about the whole affair. I realize it was infatuation - but while it lasted ....!!

Once more I am in bed with sinus trouble. It would be a chance to get so much done, but it makes my head feel so heavy.

It is a long time since I last wrote my diary, and I don't quite know first what to write about.

In July I went Youth Hostelling with Esmé in Cumberland. We had a grand time and plenty to eat. The country is lovely - wild and lonely - and I hope to go there again next year.

However, I've got ahead of myself.

I had written to Vivian, pouring out my heart to him about Johnnie, and he wrote back a sympathetic and understanding letter.

HQ. 336 Wing
1 July 1945

My dear Pat,

Your letter of the 25th has just arrived and so here goes for my answer. As you thought, I was certainly very shaken when I heard your news and <u>very</u> sorry to hear that he'd had to go - sorry for two reasons: firstly that if you <u>were</u> in love with him you've 'had it' and secondly that you will have no opportunity, in his company, to find out whether you were right or not. I know, your immediate thought now is – "What does he know about it, I <u>know</u> I'm right". Perhaps you are but if you don't mind me talking about it in a cold blooded way, I'd like to say this. You were attracted to him and found his company good and then out of the blue (that's very important) he tells you he's beetling off and you may not see him again. You, being the sort of person you are, may have been affected by this and thereupon did what you did. If you had time to know him longer, you might have found you were wrong and would have saved yourself a lot of sadness.

Still, you haven't had the time to do so or to try that and saying how you <u>might</u> have been able to find out doesn't help you much now.

Instead <u>if</u> (!!) he writes to you, don't greet his letters as a parched man would water, but try and take them calmly and if it's possible analyse your own feelings - just be friendly - <u>whatever</u> he says unless he's obviously trying to get rid of you, until you've had time to think it over thoroughly and <u>that</u> won't take just a week or so. In the mean time carry on as usual - that may sound hard to do, but just do it and <u>don't</u> for the love of Mike, go and make a fool of yourself over someone else - I once knew someone who did and she was only saved from making a real ber-loody mess by something happening to him. If he doesn't write to you at all forget him as quick as you can and don't write to him - it will probably mean he doesn't want to have anything more to do with you.

It's not easy for me to do the brotherly act for you – don't forget I've not met the bloke and I don't know the real ins and outs of it - I should never expect you to tell me everything (nobody would) and no doubt you find it hard to say all about it. For one thing, I'm not so very old myself - despite the fact that I feel "nigh on zeventy vive!" some days and my middle name doesn't happen to be 'Juan'.

I can understand exactly how you felt when he told you tho – I've felt something similar myself and my advice to you is something similar to what I did myself and I think it's been worth it. I think anyway, you've enough sense to see your way out of the wood and in any case you've someone at home who's advice I'm sure would be worth taking - your Mother. If she doesn't know the whole tale, tell her and let her advise you.

Despite my cracks, I've quite realised you've not gone around consciously collecting scalps just for the fun of it – you'd have had a very different set of letters from me if you did and by now wouldn't even send Airgraphs to me. I must say I take my hat off to him for his behaviour - he didn't seize the opportunity and play you for a sucker as some would do. I was quite interested to hear your story, if it did anything to ease matters, honoured to have you use my shoulder and you'll usually find it round the corner it you need it. And in case you have regretted telling me about it all now a few days have lapsed, don't worry, it won't go any further - OK? Oh! and another thing – don't go weeping too much - your eyes are much too nice to get all red and weepy!

If I can sum up all the above, take things easy, carry on as usual and see what your mother has to say. As I said, to carry on as usual may be hard at first but it's the sanest and best thing to do.

If there's anything else I can do, let me know - the shoulder's parked just round the corner and will be as helpful as possible -I only wish

I could do more, I don't like to see my 'sister' unhappy (or is she my niece?) - but that's something else you can blame onto Hitler and Hirohito.

I'm not laughing at you if that thought has come into your mind - I said I knew how you felt and thus can fully sympathise with you - life, no doubt, feels pretty hellish at the moment but you <u>will</u> get over at least the worst, if not all, of it in time.

Well, there you are for what it's worth, I'm not infallible and I'm not 'Aunt Jane' from 'Peg's Paper' – I've just tried to see your point and ease your troubles a bit, I hope I've succeeded a little anyway.

Nothing much from this end lately, just vegetating - trouble is, I have to watch out to see I don't take root. We're still hopeful that somebody will remember us and take us away from this hole before we become pillars of salt or summat else.

I'm going on leave on Wed 4th until the 12th. to Sorrento. Hope to get some bathing hours in and a trip to Capri and maybe feel a bit less like a corpse warmed up when I get back. Keep on writing, by the way, I like to find a nice pile waiting for me when I get back.

I won't waste any more of your time now, but let's hear how you get on.

All the <u>very</u> best Pat, and thanks for the honour of using my shoulder.

  Vivian

               HQ. 336 Wing
               <u>13.7.45</u>

My dear Pat,

Many thanks for your letter of 2nd which was brought down to Sorrento to me the day before I came back. True I had been pondering over your little problem and also over my answer to it, wondering whether perhaps I'd said the wrong things and that when you read it you might think I was making too much fuss over it. Still, soon I should be receiving your answer to it and till then I'm glad to hear that your "life is hanging by a thread".

Your last page about your mozzy bites left you open to a number of rude cracks - I seem to have got into the habit of noticing where I can make them - no doubt self defence! However two places this time – I'll make them as examples to you; firstly you say you'll not take your beer outside again - may I suggest – "you were lucky in only being bitten by mozzies", and again you say "luckily I wore an evening dress which covered my legs" - you can make your own mind up to the remark to go there!!

My leave - yes, quite enjoyable, very quiet and mainly spent bathing, sun bathing, boating and otherwise just lazing - a change from my April leave in Rome which was pretty busy. I went on a day trip to Capri - disappointing in that it's sickeningly commercialised - Yank Rest Camp there adds to that, and rather over-rated. The 'Blue Grotto' <u>is</u> rather wonderful and the whole place is much cleaner than the mainland. I've come back feeling much fitter and much browner and also much more cheesed off with this ghastly hole.

You've no doubt heard of the RAF leave scheme from here, 14 days in Blighty. However as I'm not time expired till 1947, I probably shan't get mine till next year - poor show that, because a married man who came out here up till 31.12.43 will get home this year as he's time-ex. in 1946, whereas I, who came out in May 43 will have to wait longer. Blast these married men – it's bad enough having to do 4 yrs o/s to their 3, without them getting this leave before us. <u>When</u> my leave looks a bit nearer, then I'll let you know - we must paint the town red or something.

I saw in the 'BWP' that Wishy has got married. Well, there's the first of the QA "been gorn and done it" - whos going to be next, a member, out member or our charming Hostess? I think we ought to "start a book" on the subject, 2 to 1 on Brian, evens on the Hostess, sort of thing.

At the moment I can think of little else to discuss - you may get on with your letters to other folk when you've answered this - you said "<u>two</u> of them were females" - oh yeah, but how may males to those <u>two</u> females?

All the <u>very</u> best Pat,
Vivian

HQ. 336 Wing
7.8.45

My dear Pat,
Many thanks for your letter that arrived yesterday - as you said you were writing, I thought I'd wait till your letter arrived before answering.

You know, "you are a one", the way you start a letter on 22nd and eventually post it on 1st! After two and a bit years, I'm beginning to get used to it tho.

I'm glad you enjoyed the hiking holiday and that it did you good - visions of you with that "open air look" and legs like young trees*. To hear of 15 or 16 miles/day walks makes me shudder - a walk to the Toc H puts me on my knees until a cup of tea revives me. Evidently the cave-woman stunt has got you bad - making your own furniture - I suppose you keep a bludgeon under your pillow o'nights?!! Still, you in skins, shouldn't be a bad sight, with addition of a little 'Eau de Cavewoman' behind the ears. Seriously tho, the open air has no doubt blown a few cobwebs away and you certainly seem a lot more cheerful than your last letter - you sounded as tho "suicide was the only way out"!!

Glad to hear you've got over your affair of the heart, but I disagree with your "I'm tired of uniforms" - so are we, but there's nowt we can do about it, but I don't think there are many who would disagree over it being nice for us all to be demobbed - they can give me my 'ticket' just as soon as poss.

Unfortunately my leave won't be coming off until next year sometime, and in any case if I leave Italy, the whole affair will be changed. I'll let you know when it's coming off. As you say, I may not like you when I do see you - after all, when I left you were a sweet (?) innocent (?) 16 year old and since then --? May I remind you, young lady that whatever age you feel, according to the old adage, "a woman is as old as she looks and a man as old as he feels" and so, no doubt, your sins will show! .....

I haven't any news of the boys lately - Brian, Bill, Wishy and Barry all owe me letters, but they're all dead losses as correspondents go. Wishy no doubt, is wrapped up in his missus - I heard that Barry was home on leave from Germany a couple of months ago, but of the rest, I haven't a clue.

No news from this end either, it's still hot, far too hot and a bit of cool would be OK. We're just jogging along, hoping and waiting for things to happen. I've seen quite a lot of films, the best was 'Dragonseed' but the rest were pretty trashy.

I am afraid I have more letters to get thru and so I'll ask you to excuse me. Let's have less of this "Be good" stuff – you're a nice one to talk!

All the very best, and watch your step,
Vivian

*   *For my Youth Hostelling trip with Esmé, I had bought myself a pair of coupon-free farm-workers' corduroy trousers, and a pair of army surplus officers' boots to hike around Lakeland.*

I caught the Birmingham-Carlisle train, where I met Esmé. We went by bus to Patterdale and got so wet in a downpour as we walked from the bus-stop to the Youth Hostel, that we were asked by other hostellers if we had just hiked over Helvelyn!

824 Naval Air Sqdn.
22/8/45

My dear Pat,

I seem to have had a spate of letters from you recently - at least 2 - tearing me off ginormic strips (all well deserved I must confess) for not having written more frequently and holding up Vivian as a shining example of the ideal correspondent.

Put it all down to the feeling of inertia induced by the tropical heat, and by the lack of anything to write about. If I was your fiancé, I could write reams and reams of passionate nonsense, but as I'm not, I can't, and so finding that I have to follow convention and send you news and at the same time finding I have no news to send you I'm in a devil of a hole which isn't made any shallower by rude messages from your fair hand.

How lucky you are to be in England now that Labour is there, dashing all over the country to dances, and the Lake district, and failing exams, right, left and centre and having your friends marrying, and divorcing and having babies and doing all sorts of exciting things. Think what a wealth of material you have to cram into your letters. But as for me - do you want a description of a practice dive bombing trip I did yesterday, or to hear that I made a good, bad or indifferent landing on Monday and had curried salmon and peas for lunch? No, of course you don't, any more than I want to sit sweating at my table churning out such mundane stuff.

Actually I have a flying line to shoot but will save it for my next letter.

However Pat despite the severe handicaps to frequent correspondence outlined above I shall and will write to you more and as soon as I receive your answer to this I will start. Cunning aren't I? All the best old girl, please write soon.

Lots of love, <u>Bill</u>.

Finally the war ended with the surrender of Japan.

I believed that, with the end of the war, all the boys who had survived would return home quite soon.

However, in this I was mistaken,

HQ 336 Wing
<u>28.8.45</u>

My dear Pat,

Many thanks for your VJ day letter received here a few days ago when I was on leave – don't faint, it was only spent on the Adriatic at Radi in a villa belonging to the Wing. Nothing much to do except bathe, sunbathe and generally slack around, cinema show twice a week and another night we had a 'hop' with a few of the local girls - but I enjoyed the leave very much because being near the sea it's a damn sight more pleasant than here at San Severo in the middle of a dusty plain.

I notice that this latest letter only took you two days to write - <u>a lot</u> better than your previous effort which seemed to have taken you about 3 weeks. Anyway I'll see what points there are to answer therein.

VJ day passed here very quietly - we had a day and a half's holiday, but there was little to do - free vino in the bar in the evening, but very few folk got even respectably 'canned'. I guess most of us were thinking that it wasn't much use celebrating anything whilst we're stuck out here and likely to be still for some time.

Once again you're off about me "watching my step" – I'm a mysoginist (spelling?) where women - especially Italian ones are concerned and so have no need for your advice - but you?!!! At the present moment we single men's morale is pretty low - at least in our bunch. The reason is the mess-up and unfairness of demobbing and the UK leave scheme. Here are one or two things we think are grim:-

(a) Despite the war in Europe having been over for nearly 8 months and the war with Japan over for 4, by the end of this year only up to Gp23 will be out at the maximum and yet;-- at the same time over 1 million so-called war- workers are to be released from factories and thus will be able to have the pick of post war jobs over those men in the Forces who haven't one to return to.

(b) A married man who came overseas in May 43 is due home in May 46 and goes on UK leave this year (they're actually going this week) whilst single men who came o/s at the same time are not due home until 1947 and will not get their leave for some time - at the same time as a married man who came out a year later - in other words single men have to do longer o/s to get their leave than married men - is this fair?

(c) It was stated some time ago that if one had done half one's tour one would not be sent to the Far East – now they say than anyone over Gp30 who has 12 months or more o/s to do, may be sent to the F. East.

(d) The 6 months reduction in our tour to 3y 6mths does not come into effect until Dec 1st and thus until that date people like myself have more than a year o/s to do and this gives them plenty of time to whip us to the F. East before Dec 1st.

In other words there's a grand 'carve up' on and definite 'finger trouble' somewhere or other over this business. In addition there are all these newspaper rumours about increased releases, and so perhaps you can understand why we are not exactly as "happy as sandboys".
Enough of this griping tho, I'm sure you're bored by it all.
All the very best.
Vivian

In late August I went to Torquay with Mother and Dad.

We nearly didn't go.

We had booked the holiday because it was our first peacetime holiday without Dennis, and we at first thought that a large hotel in a popular resort might be best, but it then turned out that none of us really wanted to go, but then Grandma got to hear about it and told Mother "You must go. Pat's future is at Torquay!"

And so we found ourselves at the Torbay hotel, Torquay, and, at first, it seemed to be the mistake we had anticipated. For the first few days I wandered around Torquay on my own

However, one day a new arrival appeared in the hotel.

Across the lounge, sitting with his father, was a very attractive dark haired young fellow. At the very moment our eyes met, a little boy in a kilt came down the stairs and I smiled at him. He in return scowled back at me and started walking sideways across the room, his eyes on me all the time. I laughed, and met the eyes of the other two, who were laughing too, and I decided that I would very much like to get to know the young man.

There was a dance at the hotel that night and the young man appeared and asked me to dance. His name turned out to be Stuart, he was a veterinary student, and a year older than me. We got on very well and I went to bed feeling the holiday might buck up a bit after all.

Next morning Stuart came over and asked me to go swimming with them, to which I readily agreed. The weather was hot and sunny, and the rest of the holiday we spent together, mostly on the beach and in the sea, where I discovered that he was a powerful swimmer, strong and fast.

With petrol rationed, if we wanted to explore around Torquay, we had to walk. One of our walks took us to Cockington village, where we arrived hot and thirsty - so thirsty that I astonished Stuart by asking for, and downing, a pint.

We went to see Henry V. But most evenings we danced at the hotel - he was a very good dancer - the band would play 'Sentimental Journey', and our feelings began to match the music.

We talked a lot, and, gradually, I learned more about him.

He told me that his mother had died when he was seventeen, and his father now had an elderly housekeeper. His brother was still abroad in the R.A.F. in a non-flying capacity. He, Stuart, seemed perhaps a little isolated and lonely in his home life. Having been to boarding school, he only had one friend in Salisbury, where he lived, and, incredibly, he turned out to be the medical student who Gran had been trying to get me to meet at her 'digs'!

It seemed as if both my grandmothers had been conniving to arrange that Stuart and I should meet somehow!

Towards the end of our holiday my period arrived with a crushing pain. Stuart was very sweet and escorted me to bed and ordered some tea and a hot water bottle for me, and, kissing me sympathetically, he managed to drop his cigarette, which rolled down my neck and gave me quite a nasty burn!

He went to the suite he shared with his father and fetched a dressing for my burn, but next day we went to the suite together so that he could put a fresh dressing on it for me. As he was applying the dressing the door opened and the chambermaid came in, apologised, then looked at Stuart and said, "Oh, I remember you; you came here at Christmas, but" - with a glance at me and the twin beds – "you came with your father then!!"

Our wonderful holiday finally ended when we went home to Birmingham; Stuart and I having promised to write to each other.

TORBAY HOTEL
TORQUAY
Monday

My dear Pat,

Well, here I am keeping to my promise to write - the first of the few - or perhaps - the many! I hope I didn't forget to say anything when you left - as I'm never any good at saying goodbyes. One moment you seemed here and then all too quickly you had gone. I miss you quite a bit - in fact a hell of a lot today Pat - especially as the so called 'band' is playing dance music at this moment. And by the way, you ought to feel honoured, as this is the first letter I'm writing tonight - <u>then</u> one to my brother - but as your conceit is so big - no doubt that was what you expected!

They are playing S. Journey - blast them - Pat dear - I like you - and miss you - I want to get away from here and get back home - as everything today has reminded me of you. You've given me such a fine holiday old girl, that I shall not forget, and to say thank you doesn't sound much - but it means a lot - same as – "I like you Pat".

I must close for the present - and don't forget me - please -
Look after yourself
yours
<u>Stuart</u>.

Sept 4th   5 Crosbie Road,

My Dear Stuart,
 I'm sitting here surrounded by work trying to get it all done, and I just can't seem to concentrate, - and you - you Rat - are the reason.
 I wrote you five pages last night, but they're so full of crossings out and incoherent ramblings that I've scrapped them.
 So in desperation I decided to start another letter to you and hope I can settle down when it's written.
 I hope you've missed me these last two days. Mother said you might hitch up here one weekend. I <u>do</u> hope you will. <u>Do</u> try and come up.
 I <u>do</u> want to thank you for being so sweet to me on Saturday. I've been persistently rude to you, but all the same I did appreciate the cups of tea etc. that you got me and candidly your gentleness surprised me beyond words - Thanks.
 Well, I guess I'll have another try to do some work, but I hope I don't have to wait till Xmas to see you.
 I'm really ending off now - Oh, I'm enclosing an application form for Y.H.A. – I'm making sure you come hostelling with me!
 'Bye Now
 <u>Pat</u>

P.S. I haven't said I miss you. Well I do. You occupy every 2nd thought I have. You're rather nice, really. That'll help your conceit considerably.

Salisbury.
6th.Thurs.

My dear Pat,
　　　　Thank you for your letter which came (duly expected) this bright and sunny morn. In fact - directly I heard the postman coming I was out of my bed and downstairs in a flash waiting for them to fall thro' the box. A thing that has never happened before - for <u>anyone's</u> letters thro' my whole and eventful life!! And what a letter! - ten and 1/2 sides for the first one - gee - it shook me - but I'd better tell you the news - such as it is - first.
...The chambermaid and I had a conversation before I left - quote -
CM: "When are you going to get married gentleman?"
Me:- (sotto voce and straight face!) "Oh! not just yet".
CM: (as she starts to walk away!) "Oh well, you have a nice partner for life".
Me: "Thank you! That's what I think as well." (Retires gracefully and disapp. Peals of maniacal laughter float back on the warm air! Unquote.) What a dozy wench she is - I didn't know I looked all <u>that</u> cow-eyed - or did I?
I start seeing practice tomorrow morn - so I'm spending today getting things mended etc - so I don't guarantee ever again to reply by return of post. But I do like you Pat - for all the names you call me!! You don't seem to realise that I can't seem to do much without thinking of you.
I probably <u>will</u> hitch up next term in my rags - but it will be fairly soon on - as I <u>must</u> get thro' the exam. I promise I will see you before I see you (as I hope) at Xmas. But do some work old girl - or your Father will write and tell me to "flake off and die" or something! I've got to start on the old grind-stone tomorrow and keep at it till Xmas - starting at one hour a day and working up to 15 h.p.d. with the help of caffeine to stimulate the old brain.
　　　　Cheerio for the present old girl
　　　　Yours
　　　　<u>Stuart</u>.
P.S.　Might leave off the 's' on the last word but one - one day. It's only put on with will power - now!

Have just seen this - what do you think of it?
<u>To those I love</u>:

If I should ever leave you, whom I love,
To go along the silent way, grieve not,
Nor speak to me with tears, but laugh and talk
Of me as if I were beside you, for,
Who knows but that I shall be oftentimes?
And when you hear a song I used to sing,
Or see a bird I loved - let not the thought
Of me be sad, for I am loving you
Just as I always have -
You were so good to me -
So many things I wanted still to do -
So many many things to say to you -
Remember that I did not fear -
It was - just leaving you I could not bear to face -
We cannot see beyond ..... But this I know:
I loved you so - 'twas heaven here with you!

<u>September</u> 9th   5, Crosbie Rd

My Dear Stuart,
    I find myself in the position of having 2 letters from you to answer. I'm afraid I don't feel particularly bright, and so this letter won't be a worthy effort in reply to your 2 pretty good ones. Especially the last one.
    Incidentally I liked that poem <u>very</u> much. Who wrote it? I shall stick it in one of my anthologies.
    I am honored - for 2 reasons: firstly that you wrote to me before writing to your brother and secondly that you actually arose from your slumbers to receive my letter.
    And I hope you are honored by the fact that right now I should be working, but I wanted to write to you first. Just how I'm going to get all my work done before term starts I don't know.
    You said you were spending the day getting things mended - can you cook too?!

I'm having a race against time. The post goes in 1/2 hr. I couldn't possibly write to you yesterday (and I did want to) 'cos I was working at the club till 3.00 - we had 50 dinners. It was murder! And in the afternoon a Lt. whom I met a year ago came here with a friend. They're both Bomb Happy if you know what that means, and I was horrified to see the change in the Lt. He was pretty bad when I knew him - last Oct. - but that's nothing to how he looks now. It's really left me pretty depressed ,'cos there must be thousands of boys who've been affected mentally by the war. But he looked almost - mad. Mother and Grandma were both awfully shocked when they saw him, but Dad couldn't see any change!

I'm afraid I don't feel light-hearted and flippant, which is the easiest mood to write in. Maybe I'd better end this and write again when the mood hits me once more – I've only got 20 mins to the post.

It's grand hearing from you. Do keep on pouring out letters my way. I wish you lived in Brum, but maybe it's just as well you don't - I can imagine how much work I'd do!

Well, once more do write often, and I'll try and recover from my lethargy (you've no idea how I'm forcing myself to think - not that this letter shows any signs of thought behind it, but still) and write to you again soon.

Be Good -
Yours
Pat.

I can't think it's only a week tomorrow since we left Torquay. It seems weeks and weeks ago. Do you know I can hardly remember what you look like! I know you had very nice blue eyes.

Oct 6th.   5, Crosbie Rd.

My Dear Stuart,

Once more I must offer you my very humble apologies for having been such an age in writing. This week the reason has been work, and last week I was ill - I think it was a slight touch of flu. I'm sitting in a window in the upstairs lounge at the officers' club waiting for the Savings Week Parade to come past. At the moment the Postmaster General or someone is speaking. I wish he'd stop tho'. I must get home and do some work.

We've got a super view from here - clear down the street where they're having the march past.

Well, it's now Sun. The parade came past at that point and I got too interested to write any more. It was quite good - tanks, bren gun carriers, soldiers, sailors, airmen, nurses and what-have-you. I managed to get a little work in and then went to a hop at 9.30. It didn't end till 11.45, so I got plenty of dancing in. Ron had gone on early, and I'd had to cycle alone thru' dark lanes with a faulty rear light, and holding a very faulty torch for a headlamp! My light gave out once or twice, and going across some fields I just missed 3 trees, and just when I was thinking the worst was over I passed a derelict barn which started groaning and creaking, and in my fright I let my light go out once more, and just missed a fence! I felt very relieved when I got into civilization once more.

The dance was a freshers' hop. I've never seen The Union so crammed in my life. We had to dance with my right arm and Ron's left down by our sides. There must have been 500 or more in The Union - that includes not only the dance-floor and the bar, but the corridors, stairs, balcony, lounges and roof! Not that I patronize any of the latter with Ron!

I'm looking forward to your coming up. There's just got to be a hop the weekend you come up. Don't fix the W.E. too definitely and I'll try and make sure that there will be a hop.

I do seem to recall a sort of pier thing at Torquay. I think I used to do a simply tremendous amount of sketching around there and the harbour.

Don't you know my ambition? I want to marry and raise a family of 3 or 4 or maybe 5. Tho' someone who read my palm said I'd only have 1. In which case I'll adopt t'other 4!

Ah! - we far exceeded our target for Savings Week - somewhere around 13 million - it was well above the target the day before the last final effort. (That's bad, I've repeated myself - please ignore).

The "graceful illustration in pen and wash" was for Valentine's day and depicted a couple sitting on a wall and a few others grouped around at the bottom of the wall - I think it one of the best things I've done. *(I had sent Stuart a cutting from the Birmingham Post which, under the heading 'Outstanding Works' contained a review of a student exhibition which had selected my work, with that of four others, as "beyond the plane of student work in both conception and technique".)*

Remember me to your papa if you ever write to him.

Yours

Pat

"X" Photo Section
R.A.F (AUSTRIA)
C.M.F.

7.10.45

My dear Pat,

Very many thanks for your letter of 24-27 Sept which reached me last night, having been posted on from San Severo. My new address will no doubt surprise you, but I've been expecting to come up here since July and was waiting for it to come off.

I left Foggia area on the 18 Sept, by truck and we came up "over the hills" into Austria to our present home, which is at Velden in the Wörtersee, roughly halfway between Villach and Klagenfurt. We slept and ate on the roadside on the way up and altogether I enjoyed it greatly but was very disappointed that I didn't get a chance to see Venice. Mestre, where we spent a night is only 5M from Venice, but the driver wanted to get here as soon as poss and so we didn't get a chance to ride in a gondola. The Wörtersee is a summer holiday resort and Velden consists mainly of hotels, one of which "The Hotel Bundschuk" is where we live. The Hotel consists of three buildings - one is occupied by the Austrian owners, and the other two are billets and workplace.

The country around is beautiful - hilly, and wooded with green fields - a change from dried up San Sev. On the lake there are yachts and rowing boats and we have access to the golf course and tennis courts, a NAAFI club on the other side of the lake (20 mins drive or by boat), an ENSA cinema - so altogether, it's rather enjoyable. It seems terribly cold tho - especially at night and half of us have colds due to the sudden change from hot San Severo.

The folks here are very different to the Italians (especially S. Italians!) I've not had a lot of contact with them, but those I have seem perfectly polite. As for 'fratting', lots of the blokes have Austrian girl friends, you see umpteen of them out together and there are always plenty of girls at the dances. There's absolutely nothing to buy in the shops - rationing is pretty severe here and yet just as in Blighty (when I was last there) everyone looks fairly normal. Food is pretty scarce I believe and prospects are not too bright for the winter. Actually, some of the things in the occupation rather tickle me - the troops don't walk around armed (except sentries) and yet the Civil Police - they look very smart in green uniforms - have revolvers (tho I don't think they've any ammo); the civilian telephones are used by the military and they have English speaking operators.

As for Ann<u>E</u>, I can't remember if I told you of her illness - she 'passed out' on New St Stn one night and was ill for a month and was pretty bad, but has recovered and is back at hospital and in her last letter seemed pretty perky and said she felt OK. She asked after you a short while ago and I told her that apart from being the champion scalp-hunter of the Midlands you seemed pretty OK - at least you were still as rude as ever and still had no respect for your elders - think of it, I shall be 25 in a few months, only comparatively a few years to the Old Age pension! - oh to be young and flighty and 19 1/2 again!!

Seriously, I have a terrible lot of letters to answer and I think it my bounden duty to at least knock off two or three as it's Sunday. I'll write again soon and let's be hearing from you again soon.

All the <u>very</u> best Pat,
<u>Vivian</u>

During the war The Royal Veterinary College had been evacuated, the first three years of the course to Sonning on Thames, and the fourth and fifth years to Streatley.

Now that the war was over, the new intake would once more train at the R.V.C. in Camden Town.

I received a letter from Stuart (who was in Sonning) describing conditions in the newly re-opened College.

Sonning.
14:<u>Oct</u>.

………..….Well as usual the college mucked things up and lectures started on the Tuesday - so we went up to town on the Mon. to the opening, and to see the college in Camden Town - that went off O.K. but I hear that the 1 & 2nd years are having a hell of a time up there – it's chaos - dust and dirt of six years everywhere even to the writing on the boards - no labs or lecture rooms to go to etc - in fact not much work has been done. Also there are 120 in 2nd year and 140 in 1st, that's about half the size of the whole college in pre-war days.

Thur 29th On coming home from College I was informed that Bill was on leave from the Far East and would be coming up on Tue! It was grand seeing him again. He's thinner and very tanned and really rather good looking.

R.A.F. (Austria)
1. Nov.45

My dear Pat,
    Many thanks for your letter of 16-22 Oct, which arrived yesterday - the gale you had in Blighty held up mail. Since I last wrote to you I've had another small move and am now with our detachment on Klagenfurt aerodrome. Quite nice here and I'm learning to do a part of my trade that I've never done before - and as usual something new is always interesting.

    Unless I get posted away from Europe - owing to my trade being overstaffed as the war's over, some _may_ go to the M. East - I ought to be home somewhere round Xmas. I'll let you know when it comes off and then I'll have a chance to see whether your fast life is beginning to show yet.

    I had a letter from Brian with yours, posted on from Brum. He was nearing the end of 14 days leave at Maymyo, 40 miles NE of Mandalay; where he was having a very good time but wasn't looking forward to his return to his unit at Toungoo, 200 miles N of Rangoon. He sounded pretty fed up there but says he hopes to get home on leave somewhere round next June. He's time expired somewhere round Jan 47 (if I remember rightly). I don't know what his Release Group is, but it's lower than mine which is 47. He seems to have 'got around' fairly well and mentions:- Bombay, Calcutta, Poona, Darjeeling, Lucknow, Delhi, Manngdaw, Imphal, Mandalay, Rangoon etc. - but describes them as all very similar in that they all – "stink"!

I wonder where Bill is at the moment and whether he's reached Japan or is around Singapore? Teddy Gray is still in Sicily - from where I had a letter last week. The rest of them I've no news of at all.

All the <u>very</u> best.
<u>Vivian</u>

Fri 2nd

After two months, and only two weeks acquaintance, I was going to see Stuart again:

I met Stuart's train, and we went to Barrows for lunch. We came home - and had a nice little reunion in his room. He's nice.

After tea we were going to a show but I didn't feel so good. Mother and Dad said they were going out and then grandma surprised us all by saying she was going to the flics. Never has the family been so tactful!

Anyway she eventually decided to work in her room and Stuart and I played records with just the lamp on and the firelight - very nice. The next evening we at last went to the long-planned Union dance.

<u>Nov 6th</u>   5 Crosbie Rd.

My Dear Stuart,

As usual I'm writing this during a rest in life class. Six of the boys are playing shove ha'penny or something on a table in the corner, they've done it every rest today and periodically send various possessions of mine flying - a bottle of ink - my gloves, portfolio - and of course, every now and then they knock my easel over. They're making one <u>hell</u> of a row and confidentially I think I prefer it when they sing in "harmony"(?).

You ought to see the room. The desks and easels are just littered all over the place. There are odd scraps of paper and pencil shavings on the floor. Students are reading or writing letters, and of course these dear boys are still gambling in the corner. Only there's nine of 'em now.

Well that's enough of that. The weekend was <u>pretty</u> <u>nice</u> - and I hope it's repeated in the near future. Of course I've done nothing but talk about you since…..

Sonning.
Sunday 11th.

Pat my dear,

I like the way you say you've written twice as much as I did - seeing that you took at <u>least</u> 2 days to write it I don't wonder at it!!

When we were having a lecture last week in anatomy – it was hell's involved (blood supply of the head) and he went at a deuce of a speed – and sounded like Yiddish for all that it conveyed to us – and at the end he (lecturer) said – "Now do you understand that Mr So and So?" and he said "Oh, yes Sir" and a loud whisper came from the back – "Bloody liar" – it really cheered us up no end.

      I've got your photo framed above my desk and in between a motto – "Work or fail" - you'd be surprised how often it brings me back to my books!! And I've been fighting tooth and nail for your virtue and my honour - all because the boys can see something in "Time alone will tell"!!! It doesn't seem a week ago that I was up there - I admit it took me two days to get over it and settle down - poor old Frank* - every time someone asks me how I got on - he says – "don't start him off again - or I won't be able to get him working again for some time."

      Well I must pack up now - write soon green eyes -
      Yours, <u>Stuart</u>.

*   *Stuart's room-mate and friend*

I had inscribed the photo with the above sentiment as I needed to be absolutely certain before I committed myself to what I think we both believed to be inevitable – the rest of our lives together.

I had once again grown my hair long, having decided I hated it short.

C.M.F (Austria)
16.11.45

My dear Pat,
 I have two letters to thank you for at the moment - the joint one from you and Bill and yours of 8 Nov. I was very surprised to hear from Bill in Blighty so soon again - how does he manage it? When Brian and I get home we'll tell him what it's like to spend 2 1/2 or more years away from those we love!!!.....

Vivian at last came home to England on leave and I wrote to Bill to tell him:-

11.12.45

Hallo Pat,
 So the great red-haired, green mildew hatted twerp *(i.e. Vivian!)* is in Brum. Well well this is auspicious. I wish the silly idiot had given me warning of his approach, or maybe he wanted you all for himself.
 The great news comes rather at a time when we're at sixes and sevens for the squadron is flying to a new airfield tomorrow - provided the weather is O.K of course - near Liverpool and we shall go on leave from there. But it is quite conceivable that said weather will "clamp" for anything up to a week this time of the year which would leave us stranded here in Scotland waiting for a good day. Hence I cannot promise to reach Brum before Viv leaves. However all being well expect me Wednesday morning. Anyhow will wire you when things are more definite. Must go eat.
 Love to you both.
 Bill

Stuart and I began making plans for Christmas, and his father decided they would stay at the Grand.

Dec. 16th.   5 Crosbie Rd

My Dear Stuart,
    First of all congratulations on passing your exam. *(Stuart had written to tell me that he had passed his exam and was now in the 4th year.)* You deserved to do so anyway considering the amount of work you did for it. I wish my exam was over - I very much doubt if I'll pass. I'm supposed to be working this weekend, but so far nothing has got done. Do you know we have a mere 2 weeks' holiday and they've already set us 2 lots of holiday work.
    I'm glad you've fixed up at The Grand. They have dances there and I imagine they should have a pretty good 'do' on New Year's Eve. Incidentally have you evening dress? I imagine it is bound to be formal. Poor Dad had his made over to fit Dennis so he now doesn't possess one.
    As for the color of my evening dress - well, I have 3, but the one I wore at the Medical Ball (which, incidentally, was pretty wiz-o) consists of a dark burgundy skirt* and a pale blue chiffon blouse - you know, the sort that doesn't leave much to the imagination! I like it the best of the 3. The other 2 are pastel shades of taffeta and don't give me the air of sophistication the other one does!
    Oh, I bought a super rucksack for 42/- t'other day. Steel frame, 3 pockets, 1 with a zip. Very large, but very easy to carry. <u>If</u> they still have any would you like me to order one for you? You'd have to reply <u>immediately</u> 'cos they're selling like hot cakes. If you could send a P.O. for 42/- as well it would help, 'cos I borrowed the money for mine off Mother and can't see my way to paying it back yet. But if you really wanted one urgently and sent me a telegram saying merely "Yes" I imagine I could get the money out of the bank.
    Anyway, they're probably all sold by now!
    Well, the post goes in a few minutes so I must end off now.
    Yours
    <u>Pat</u>

* *(I had made the burgundy skirt from a beautiful fine, soft wool voluminous nightdress of Gran's. I made a deep stiffened cummerbund waistline (I had a very small waist) and gathered the skirt onto it and then dyed it burgundy.)*

In the end Stuart and his father did not, in fact, stay at the Grand over Christmas, but with us.

Being able to spend over a week together enabled our relationship to deepen and grow and by the time Stuart had returned home, and we once more resumed our letters to each other, thoughts of engagement were in our minds, and not only ours, apparently, for I received a letter from Vivian telling me that he had become engaged to Anne, while on leave.

1946

Aged 19 ½

List of Illustrations

Page

566   Esme, Pat and Stuart tasting Esme's Instant Junket. (verdict: bright yellow and disgusting)

I wrote to Stuart to tell him:-

Jan 5th.

"…..Rumour, by the way, is fast flying round the family, and one aunt has already informed her son's fiancée that I'm engaged!
  Also Mother, Dad and Grandma have each given me 2/6 toward my bottom-drawer in case I should ever get engaged! So what with your £3 and my 7/6 we haven't a worry in the world.
  Incidentally, I get paid 1/6 per hour for posing - a bit more toward the old bottom-drawer!?!….."

And, on **Sunday 13 January 1946** I was able to report:-

  Received my Xmas present of over £40 worth of Savings Certificates from Gran.

I was concerned about money and frequently kept records of my expenditure in my diary:

Thursday

  College. Gledhill liked my water-color life effort. I like it now.
  In the lunch hour Peter, Roy, Colin, John and I went to buy art materials. The shop, which was in the basement of a bombed building, was shut, and no-one was around so we came back upstairs and John and Roy went out first and shut the door and it was a spring-lock! For about 10 mins we tried to find a way out – but the building is unsafe and the art materials shop is the only one there. Suddenly a light switched on and a small boy came upstairs from the basement! He let us out and across the road, Roy and John were standing looking very worried! Mind you, <u>we</u> were pretty worried!

	Bought some wizard Watmans rough water color paper	
		2/-
But Pam owes me for half =		1/-
	rubber	9
	tea and bun	2
	lunch	2/6
	paper	1½
	tea	6
	paint, drawing pins and brush	3/11
	bus fare	6
	Vera owes me	2/½
		9/3
	paint	2/8
	lunch, tea, bus fare, cup of tea	1/10

It wasn't only money that was short, either; the end of the war did little to ease the shortage of food.

Tuesday

Queued for over an hour for a rabbit.

Meanwhile, I had written to Bill to tell him of Vivian's engagement to Anne, and he wrote back:-

LONDON. S.W.11.
17.1.46.

My dear Pat,
    Fancy old Vivian taking the plunge. Poor chap must be crazy. I suppose his years of exile have turned his brain.
    Seriously though, jolly good luck to him. I wish I possessed his nerve.

Who is Stuart? Really Pat you can't expect me to keep track of all these admirers that I've never met. Is he a University student from Torquay, and is he more or less your 'steady' at the moment?

A R.N.A.S. observer named 'Belf' Brown wants me to meet him in Brum soon I believe, so I may be applying to your Mother for board residence in the 'Hotel'.

By the way I suppose I'd better describe my recent movements. We returned to the Liverpool district on Jan. 3rd after our fortnight's Christmas leave. My Lords then decided to break up the squadron and we flew the cabs to Cornwall and returned to Burscough, closed everything up and went on indefinite leave last Thursday. I hope this leave will last until I'm demobbed in March, or thereabouts.

I could stay on for another 4 years in the flying racket, but though flying appeals to me very much it isn't leading to a very permanent job so instead I shall have to start a new life as a civvy. I shudder to think of this humdrum existence looming ahead and am sorely tempted to continue with flying.

Damn funny if Viv and I both become School teachers - pity the rising generation. *(In fact, neither of them did. Bill went back to accountancy, and Vivian, after returning for a while to H.P. Sauce as first manager, moved with Anne to Naples, where he became technical manager in a food factory there.)*

Please thank your mother for her letter. I sent the tea from Ceylon last September and to tell you the truth it was so long in transit that I'd completely forgotten about it.

I must write and congratulate our bold lover, be a dear and send me his address, is he still in Austria? When does he expect leave again or will it be for good next time he steps on Blighty's cold shore?

That's all for now Pat. Please write again soon. My love to your Mother and Father and my very best love to you.

Cheerio.
<u>Bill</u>.

From time to time Stuart came and stayed the weekend, and I was then invited to stay at his home in Salisbury, and I wrote to Stuart:-

Feb 11th.   5, Crosbie Rd,

Hello Darling,

    It's 9.0 am. I've just got back from College to find the house empty - you know what I said about hating to be alone in a house at night!

    Anyway I've got the landing, hall, lounge and breakfast room lights on. And Romeo & Juliet is now playing - very loudly! I've got 2 pokers lying handy in the hearth - and when I came in I went all over the house switching on lights, flushing the doings and coughing etc. just to show any lurking prowlers outside that the house is occupied!

    But to be quite candid I really <u>am</u> scared these days. If "they" have no qualms over hanging a boy of 11 - they certainly wouldn't stop at a female of 20 (not quite!) more capable of looking after herself.

..... I've just realised with a bit of a shock that it's only 3 months to the exam.

    Only 8 weeks - only 16 more anatomy classes - only 8 more architecture lectures - only 24 more life classes - and only 8 more fig. comps., which come on <u>Fri</u>.

    However in spite of my apparent keenness and zest for work I'll probably end up at Salisbury on the 15th!

    I'll catch the 8.55 (means missing some of Fri afternoon - still.....) How shall I dress? Tweeds, slacks or glamour?!

    I suppose while in Salisbury I <u>ought</u> to sketch the Cathedral. I shall have to present them with something on Mon. morning in lieu of my architecture homework.....

    I went to see 'The Road to Utopia' with Ron on Thurs. It was rather funny, I had bought Mother some anemones, not expecting to go out in the evening, and when Ron left a message at College saying he wanted me to go I wondered what to do with them. I tried to sell them. Then I thought I couldn't leave them in my locker 'cos they'd wither and I was afraid they'd do likewise in the flics. Eventually I got a jam jar, 1/2 filled it with water, and carried them in that to the flics! As it happened we were too late to get in without getting into the most enormous queue so we took the flowers (in the jar!) home, and got back to the cinema and after 10 mins. queuing got in to see the whole of the last house. .....

Stuart and I kept up a constant stream of letters to each other, and, of course, the letters still flowed between Bill, Vivian and me.

Monday 25 February 1946

Had a letter from Vivian, who is all caution about getting engaged!

Vivian's letter of caution set me off on my emotional see-saw again, and I began to seek the opinions of any friends who would oblige. Should I marry Stuart? Was I making a mistake?

Probably from the moment I first met Stuart, I had known that he was the one person with whom I wanted to spend the rest of my life.

But, as time passed and I became more and more aware that I would eventually have to commit myself one way or the other, the more I shied away from commitment. I was terrified of making a mistake and began to be hyper critical of everything to do with Stuart.

My opinions and emotions fluctuated wildly, and caused Stuart to write to me in exasperation,

"....... Sometimes darling I don't think you've quite got out of your silly habit of turning your emotions on and off - the sooner you do - the better I'll be pleased. If you ever do get a 'cold spell' dear - for goodness sake don't forget me - I know I'm quite a long way off - but don't you believe me when I tell you I love you?......."

By the time Stuart came up for a weekend in early March I had convinced myself that I might be making a mistake.

We went to the News Theatre, and afterwards went to the Grand for a drink, where we had a long and earnest talk and I tried to explain how I felt.

My confused and tangled emotions wormed their way into my subconsciousness, and four days later I wrote in my diary:-

Tuesday 12 March 1946

It's rather cold sitting up in bed with the window open, so I don't think I'll write anything much. I dreamed I had a typewritten letter from Danny – from Wales. I couldn't understand why I hadn't heard from him for so long.

Wednesday 13 March 1946

I feel depressed, have done for some time. Lots of people at college do too. It may be approaching exams – lack of food – or perhaps I think about S. too much and worry whether he's for me or not.

I wrote to him, trying to explain my feelings:-

March 14th

…..D'you know, I'm most dissatisfied with my life at the moment. Funnily enough, in some ways I felt the most satisfied when I was at the hospital. I don't seem to get much kick out of life these days. It may be because the war is over and with peace time one expects everything to be as it was before the war but that's impossible. And then thinking on that it's awful to think that things <u>never can be</u> as they used to be.

It makes me think of those lines of Wordsworth's:-

Turn whereso'er I may
By night or day
The things which I have seen
I now can see no more.

And now I think I'll make some Horlicks and go to bed.
Lots of Love,
<u>Pat</u>.

Streatley.

March 17th.

Darling,
I don't know quite what to say in this, because you sound as tho' you were feeling very depressed when you wrote your letter - and I don't know whether at the moment you are still feeling that way or have got over the bout. I sometimes start getting dissatisfied, and like you dear - recall that things will <u>never be</u> the same - but my sweet we are both young, and a long time to live - and many things to do - at least I have - if I try to leave this

old place a bit better than when I came into the world. Maybe it's your work, amongst other things, that's getting you down - I could explain better to you my dear - than trying to write it down - but just plug away little one - you have a gift, to be used - that I suppose is your creative instinct, your painting etc - mine is just trying so to speak - to make new dogs from old! I wish again I lived near you sweet, as I might have been of some use, to snap you out of a few of those "brooding" moods you get into - but I hope by now my love that you have got out of it? (I like the Wordsworth.) .....

<u>March</u> 31st.   5, Crosbie Rd,

Darling,
    I feel very affectionate toward you tonight. I wonder why; perhaps I've been working too hard!

    I got up at 7.30 this morning, and by 9.0 I had got everyone's breakfast (in bed too) and washed it up. I did my room - stripped my bed and turned my mattress - did some washing and by 11.0 I was painting! After dinner I had a bath and went swimming, came home, got tea and then went up and worked until 1/2 hr ago – how's that for a full day?

    I have heard from Esmé that she and her cousin (male) are coming up to the Lakes for 3 or 4 nights. They couldn't get in at <u>any</u> of the hostels so are camping. We are to meet them on Fri. - either on top of Helvellyn during the day, or after supper at one of the hotels in Grasmere.

    I'm awfully glad they're coming - I like Esmé very much. .....

    Ron, by the way, has passed his exams and now starts work at hospitals.

    Peter, Roy, Colin, Jane and I went along the canal again - this time about 1/4 - 1/2 mile going towards Aston and the worst part of Brum. It got depressing and rather horrible just about where we turned back. I <u>hate</u> factories ..... - at least the sort you find in the heart of Brum. No wonder the people who work in those factories and live in those slums are ignorant and immoral and irresponsible*. I may take you along the canal one day on a bus, into the heart of horrible Brum and show you a thing or two!

    I remember Danny once saying he thought B'ham the nicest town in England. The reason was partly 'cos he liked our family so much, but also 'cos the only part he saw was Harborne and the city centre. I wonder how many people who spend short sojourns here or merely pass thru' realize what the greater part of Brum is really like. Why should children have the misfortune to be born into such an environment when other children - superior probably in no other way than that they have the advantage of a cultural background - are born into an environment such as yours and mine. ....

*   *(A group of youths had shouted an exceedingly vulgar epithet at Jane and me, and all of us were quite shocked.)*

Stuart replied to my letter.....

What on earth do you want to take me to the worst part of Brum for - to depress me? I could sense a bit of Socialism in that long harangue - but for once my love - I agree with you.

How is the painting going - a few more Sundays like last week and it ought to soon be finished!!

Once again there's nothing much to tell you about any cases little one - a calving today - but simple - one fore leg back - that's all – it's strange, but when it's a scorching hot day the cow is 'in' under a tin roof and we sweat like dogs - but if there's snow about or a thunderstorm on - then the damn thing is out on a down - miles from home - and we get wet through thataway. What a life - what made me decide to be a vet - I don't know!!

... I've been looking about for a car - but there's none at my price - still patience is a virtue - as you keep on telling me!!

(Austria)
<u>7.4.46</u>

My dear Pat,

Many thanks for your letter of 25 March which arrived a few days ago, so had taken 4 or 5 days, as (as usual) you didn't post it till 29th. - do you do that to Stu's letters or is it reserved for second (or lower) priority correspondents!? I suppose I ought to feel honoured to think that at one time I used to have priority - or ought my pride to feel hurt that I haven't priority now? So your exam is looming ahead - my best wishes in anticipation that you'll pass with flying colours. Lots of folk seem to be taking exams these days - Anne has her finals in June and I'm going to take Forces Prelim. also in June. Anne would have taken her finals last month if it hadn't been for that "black out" of hers, but she lost so much time getting over that, that she decided to postpone it until the next lot in June.

    I hope you enjoy your holiday in Cumberland - but <u>please</u>,- for the mental good of the Cumberlanders <u>and</u> Stuart, don't wear those shorts you cycled to C. Corbett with me in - they had a bad enough effect on me! Quite honestly I think you're doing the best thing in letting your little problem with Stu. settle itself and quite frankly he's gone up in my estimation by saying he's prepared to wait.

    Last week, I had 4 or 5 days on a job down in N. Italy - at Udine. I had only a couple of days work and the rest of the time off and had a pretty good time altogether. I did some shopping in Udine and was amazed at the tremendous variety and stocks of clothing in the shops - absolute heaven for a girl with loads of lire and of course there are no coupons to worry about. Bags of beer too and lots of eggs and I consumed plenty of both and also brought 18 eggs back here with me - they were only about 3 ¾d each!

    I had a letter from Brian last week – he's expecting to be repatted this month and as the o/s tour has now been cut to 3 yrs, I shall be coming home in June. Providing you haven't got yourself too inextricably tied up with S, you'll have to come out with Brian, Bill and self and visit a few of our old haunts like the 'Hope & Anchor' and 'The Golden X' - and maybe we could find some snow so that we can queue up outside the 'Oak' in it - remember?

    Lets be hearing from you some day
    All the <u>very</u> best,
    Vivian

So in April the long-planned Youth Hostelling trip with Stuart finally materialised.

We caught the train up to the Lake District, where we met Esmé and her cousin Alan, and once more I was tramping over the fells and bogs that enchanted me before.

In his company, my undulating feelings toward Stuart settled and deepened again as our natural companionship flourished.

And so the see-saw of my feelings rocked me unsteadily into the summer, and I told Stuart:-

" …… At times I like you so much and at times you annoy me so intensely. Poor Stuart, I do treat you unfairly!……."

And poor, long suffering Stuart wrote back:-

"……. You're a queer girl darling - it often amazes me that I still love you. But I always do - believe me……"

By June we had planned another trip - this time to the Forest of Dean .Stuart having phoned and told me he had at last bought a car, wrote:-

"…..I've been busy all day up to now - tacking some felt on the (wooden!) floor of the old bus and puttying up the holes in the dashboard - awaiting some varnish. I'll try and get her waterproof and painted up before Friday. Still it goes - no matter what the thing looks like.

It's a Singer 8. Canvas folding roof - and a dicky seat at the back - but I'm not taking people in that - the chassis won't stand up to it!! I'm going to get some stuff and re-do the inside – Rexene (?) I believe they call it - but only expect 4 wheels an engine - and a body of cardboard, 3 ply, and tin!! So I'm warning you. I'm going to call her "Ann Thrax" - as one main feature of the disease is sudden death!!!….."

Friday 7 June 1946

Stuart arrived in the evening in THE CAR. It's a glorious contraption.

Saturday 8 June 1946

We went to the garage for petrol - it shot up in the air like a fountain! We got off very late complete with food, cushions and heaven knows what else. It began to rain at Malvern. We drove to Aylburton. On the way we had boiled bacon, b & b, jam, cakes and tea for 2/- each. We parked the car in the backyard of a pub at Aylburton because you are supposed to go Youth Hostelling under your own steam, and not by car. The hostel was 3 1/2 miles from where it was marked on the map and we got lost, and walked in a circle round it. We kept hearing music and not seeing any habitation - eventually we arrived at 10.30. They were still letting off fireworks in the garden (for the Victory celebrations).

Sunday 9 June 1946

We had hoped to walk in the forest of Dean, but everywhere were notices saying "Danger, Poison Gas" etc. So we preferred to keep to the road.

The forest was one vast dump of W.D. stuff.

Monday 10 June 1946

We left the hostel in drizzle. As we went on it became a downpour. When we got to the car it was nearly awash. We tried to start it in vain; then discovered a flat tyre. After the landlord had towed us about 1/2 a mile it started and off we went, driving on the flat tyre, as we had no spare. About 1/2 a ml further on the back mudguard fell off! But at the next garage we got fixed up and went merrily on our way with rain pouring thru' the roof and where the side windows should be, and where the windscreens didn't meet.

We finally arrived in Cheltenham, and after going to the flics and having tea at the G'mont, we went to the hostel. It was a lovely evening. So we went for a walk over Cleve Hill, and watched the sun sinking down to the horizon. It was beautiful, quiet and romantic, and I began thinking, "I hope Stuart doesn't propose to me here, and now; I'm just not quite ready!"

In fact he didn't, but he later told me that he so nearly did.

Tuesday 11 June 1946

We left the hostel and went to my old billet in Welland Lodge Road to see the Joneses. David was away, but Mrs Jones and the 2 children were there. She was delighted to see me. She seemed to like Stuart and I noticed her looking at the 3rd finger of my left hand.

She asked us to stay for lunch so we went to the bathroom for a wash and as I was washing my hands Stuart – who was sitting on the edge of the bath – asked me to marry him.

Still hobbled by my reluctance to a commitment that for me would be forever, but at the same time realizing that this was what I wanted, I somehow managed to answer with a sort of non-committal affirmative. Quite a feat!

Later, as we walked down the main street in C'ham Stuart said, "You didn't really answer me properly. Are we engaged?" So, there in the middle of the main street I turned to him, embraced and kissed him, and – at last – said, "Yes! – I suppose so!"

MALTA EPILOGUE I & II

List of Illustrations

Page

573　Unveiling of the RAF Memorial, Malta 1954

577　Memorial Dedication Plaque

578　Names of those who fell in 1940 and 1941

MALTA EPILOGUE I

When the Royal Air Force Memorial on Malta was unveiled in 1954 I was unable to accompany Mother.

We had just gone through a bad patch. Within the space of three years I had had polio; my second baby was stillborn as a result of the polio; my father became desperately ill; I had my second living child, but developed a rare tumour in the groin while pregnant. By this time my father was dying, and I delayed the operation until after he died.

So it was obvious I could not go with Mother, and she was therefore accompanied by her dear sister Marjorie, and brother George and his wife Kay.

It must have been terribly poignant and difficult for Mother - especially without Dad. However, at the unveiling she found herself sitting in the front row of seats next to a high-ranking Air force officer. He was Air Marshal Sir Hugh Lloyd, and he began talking to her.

He was obviously deeply moved, and asked if there was anything he could do which would be helpful. He offered to place his car at her disposal if there was anywhere she wanted to visit. She replied that she wanted to go to Hal Far. He told her that this had been a bomber station, and that Dennis, being a Hurricane pilot, would have flown from Ta Kali. Nevertheless, Mother insisted that she felt she must go to Hal Far.

So, later, they set off for Hal Far, driving across the island through small villages and open countryside, when Mother suddenly stamped her foot on the floor of the car and shouted, "Stop! Stop the car!" An astonished Hugh Lloyd ordered the driver to stop, and Mother exclaimed, "This is what I came to Malta for! This is where Dennis last flew from!"

Then a look of amazed comprehension crossed Hugh Lloyd's face, and he said slowly, "This is remarkable. I remember now. This was Safi airstrip; when Ta Kali was too 'beat up' the fighters would take off from this field." He added, "It's not the first time this sort of thing has happened".

Mother got out of the car and picked a small posy of the flowers growing there. She took them back to her hotel and pressed them in the pages of her R.A.F. Association souvenir leaflet.

I have them still, also Hugh Lloyd's book, "Briefed to Attack", given to her before the Safi incident and inscribed by him. "Hugh Lloyd. 3rd May 1954. In memory of your boy who did not return after take off from Ta Kali."

MALTA EPILOGUE II

OVER THESE AND
NEIGHBOURING
LANDS AND SEAS
THE AIRMEN
WHOSE NAMES ARE
RECORDED HERE
FELL IN RAID OR
SORTIE AND HAVE
NO KNOWN GRAVE

MALTA
GIBRALTAR
MEDITERRANEAN
ADRIATIC
TUNISIA
SICILY
ITALY
YUGOSLAVIA
AUSTRIA

PROPOSITI INSULA
TENAX TENACES
VIROS
COMMEMORAT

1940
ROYAL AIR FORCE

FLIGHT LIEUTENANT
MacCALLUM B.

SERGEANT
O'DONNELL R.

FLYING OFFICER
BURGESS J. T.
MINCHINTON E. C.

CORPORAL
KEMP V. A.

AIRCRAFTMAN 1ST CL.
WILLANS F. C.

SERGEANT
HUBBARD B. F. R.

ROYAL AUSTRALIAN AIR FORCE

FLIGHT LIEUTENANT
CLARKE G. J. I.

1941
ROYAL AIR FORCE

SQUADRON LEADER
CHARNEY F. R. H. D.F.C.
MOULD P. W. O.
　D.F.C. and BAR
WARREN T. J. S. D.F.C.

FLIGHT LIEUTENANT
BRANDT S.
BURNETT N. W.
FAIRBAIRN G. M.
GAUTREY R. W.
LOWE J. J.
NICHOLLS G. V.
WATSON G.

FLYING OFFICER
AUGER H. E.
BAILEY G. G.
BEBINGTON J. H. S.
CAVAN B. M.
FOXTON J. H. T.
GREENHILL R. A.
HARRIS J. W.
READ A. T.
ROE H. J.
TAYLOR F. F. D.F.C.
WATERFALL J. T.

PILOT OFFICER
BARNWELL D. U. D.F.C.
GARLAND T. B.
HIGGINS P. J.
KEARSEY P. J.
KNIGHT D. F.
LANE P.
LANGDON C. E.
LAW W. F.
LINTERN D. W.
LOWE W. H.
MUNRO R. H. M.
SCOTT R. O. H.
STANDFAST G. H.
STEELE P. J. A.
THOMPSON P. J. A.
VEITCH P. J. B.

WARRANT OFFICER
GULLIVER A. J.

FLIGHT SERGEANT
ADAMSON J. L.
BATCHELOR J. R.
BOXONDALE J. R.
BROWN H. E.
BROWN C.
BROWN W. F. R.

FLIGHT SERGEANT
COUSENS R. A.
CRAMP P.
CROSSLEY H.
EMERY F. R.
GIMSON E. W.
　D.F.M. and BAR
GRIFFITHS W. J.
HANSON B. P.
HAYES B.
HEPPLE R.
JOWETT R. R.
LAWSON R. W.
RICHARDS J.
SAMWAYS S. R.
SIMPSON H. G.
SMITH A. E.
SWAN J.
TYSON H.
VIGNAUX V. R.

SERGEANT
ACKROYD J. T.
AUSTIN R. J.
BAIRD R. E.
BILLETT J. F.
BOLD P. F.
BUCK D. W.
BUTLER W. E.
BUTTERFIELD T. P.
COPE M. H.
DANIELS A. F.
DICK A. C.
FORTH H. M.
GARRICK D. R. A.
GREENHILL C. P.
GUEST M.
HACKSTON J.
HAMBOROUGH J. W.
HARRIS D. R.
HARRISON A. N.
HEALY R. F.
HEWSON R. T.
HILL G. D.
HOARE G. D.
HUNT J. E.
HYSLOP J. S.
　⋮
KING C.
　⋮
XAVIER

I never wanted to go to Malta.

By the time I was able to go, it had become a holiday island.

However, in 1987 a cruise calling at many places that Stuart and I particularly wanted to visit, also called at Malta.

As usual, I bought guide books about the places we were to visit, and searched the pages about Valetta for the location of the R.A.F. memorial. It was nowhere to be found.

I felt unbelievably bitter, especially when, on the ship, I asked the purser and various ship's officers, and not one of them knew. I don't even think they knew that there was a memorial.

So, when we went ashore, it was with a deep feeling of misery and bitterness; among all these jolly holiday-makers who owed so much to those few, not one seemed to know or care.

We climbed the long slope up from the harbour, and I saw the British Consulate, and went in, thinking that once again I would find they neither knew nor cared. It was a Maltese woman behind the desk, and she did know.

So we eventually encountered the tall white needle like monument that reached up toward the blue sky.

We found ourselves at the side with the columns of names of those lost in 1945; and so we walked slowly round until we reached 1941; the side which also bore the inscription "Over these and neighbouring lands and seas the airmen whose names are recorded here fell in air raid or sortie and have no known grave"

I was totally unprepared for the shockwave of intense grief which overwhelmed me when I saw Dennis' name. The tears welled up and just wouldn't stop.

Stuart put his arms round me and comforted me. I think he, too, was weeping - for me, and for Dennis, and his so short life.

I said, "I must leave him some flowers", and looked around, but there was nowhere I could get flowers.

Then I saw the formal flower beds around the Memorial; they were unkempt, but full of little wild flowers.

And so we picked these tiny flowers, and I made them into a posy, tied up with their own stalks, and left them on the plinth, under his name.